Psychotherapy
and Behavior Change
(PGPS-155)

Pergamon Titles of Related Interest

Beutler ECLECTIC PSYCHOTHERAPY: A Systematic Approach

Brenner THE EFFECTIVE PSYCHOTHERAPIST:
Conclusions from Practice and Research

Garfield THE PRACTICE OF BRIEF PSYCHOTHERAPY

Hersen/Kazdin/Bellack THE CLINICAL PSYCHOLOGY HANDBOOK

Kanfer/Goldstein HELPING PEOPLE CHANGE:
A Textbook of Methods, Third Edition

Kazdin CHILD PSYCHOTHERAPY: Developing
and Identifying Effective Treatments

Related Journal*

CLINICAL PSYCHOLOGY REVIEW

*Free sample copies available upon request

PERGAMON GENERAL PSYCHOLOGY SERIES

EDITORS

Arnold P. Goldstein, Syracuse University
Leonard Krasner, Stanford University & SUNY at Stony Brook

Psychotherapy and Behavior Change

Social, Cultural and Methodological Perspectives

H. NICK HIGGINBOTHAM
Newcastle College of Advanced Education
and University of Newcastle, Australia

STEPHEN G. WEST
Arizona State University

DONELSON R. FORSYTH
Virginia Commonwealth University

PERGAMON PRESS

New York • Oxford • Beijing • Frankfurt
São Paulo • Sydney • Tokyo • Toronto

U.S.A.	Pergamon Press Inc., Maxwell House, Fairview Park, Elmsford, New York 10523, U.S.A.
U.K.	Pergamon Press plc, Headington Hill Hall, Oxford OX3 0BW, England
PEOPLE'S REPUBLIC OF CHINA	Pergamon Press, Room 4037, Qianmen Hotel, Beijing, People's Republic of China
FEDERAL REPUBLIC OF GERMANY	Pergamon Press GmbH, Hammerweg 6, D-6242 Kronberg, Federal Republic of Germany
BRAZIL	Pergamon Editora Ltda, Rua Eça de Queiros, 346, CEP 04011, Paraiso, São Paulo, Brazil
AUSTRALIA	Pergamon Press Australia Pty Ltd, P.O. Box 544, Potts Point, N.S.W. 2011, Australia
JAPAN	Pergamon Press, 5th Floor, Matsuoka Central Building, 1-7-1 Nishishinjuku, Shinjuku-ku, Tokyo 160, Japan
CANADA	Pergamon Press Canada Ltd, Suite No. 271, 253 College Street, Toronto, Ontario, Canada M5T 1R5

Copyright © 1988 Pergamon Books, Inc.

First edition 1988

Library of Congress Cataloging-in-Publication Data

Higginbotham, Howard N., 1949–
Psychotherapy and behavior change: social, cultural, and methodological perspectives/H. Nick Higginbotham, Stephen G. West, Donelson R. Forsyth.
p. cm. — (Pergamon general psychology series: 155)
Includes index.
1. Psychotherapy. 2. Behavior Modification.
3. Social psychology. I. West, Stephen G. II. Forsyth, Donelson R., 1953– III. Title. IV. Series.
RC480.5.H5 1988
616.89'14—dc19   87.21648

British Library Cataloguing in Publication Data

Psychotherapy and behavior change: social, cultural and methodological perspectives.
—(Pergamon general psychology series).
1. Psychotherapy
I. Higginbotham, H. Nick II. West, Stephen G.
III. Forsyth, Donelson R.
616.89'14   RC480

ISBN 0-08-028089-7 (Hardcover)
ISBN 0-08-028088-9 (Flexicover)

Printed in Great Britain by A. Wheaton & Co. Ltd, Exeter

Contents

Preface

The present volume is a direct descendent of the pioneering work *Psychotherapy and the psychology of behavior change* by Arnold Goldstein, Kenneth Heller and Lee Sechrest. It is imbued with the spirit and mission of the original volume, and also follows the style and format of the original. We originally began the present work as an updating of the 1966 classic. The original authors recognized the importance of alerting a new generation of clinical researchers to the benefits of generalization across disciplinary lines. Yet their energies were invested elsewhere. So they sought out the present authors with the proposition of undertaking a deep re-examination of social psychology in order to uncover: a) new hypotheses to develop and present, b) new evidence to support some of the 1966 hypotheses, c) new evidence to alter some of the 1966 hypotheses, and d) new evidence to abandon yet other of these hypotheses.

What began as a simple updating, however, subtly evolved into a work that is paradoxically both familiar and original. Part of the explanation for this transformation lies with the fact that it is difficult to trace accurately the waves of influence emanating from the philosophy and specific hypotheses of the 1966 book. This is not because the work's influence has disappeared, but because its ideas have become ingrained in large segments of the empirical clinical enterprise. For example, behavior therapy and modification technologies are extrapolations from operant, respondent, and modeling learning laboratories, and cognitive behavior therapy derives principles from attribution theory studies and research in cognitive psychology. The second impetus for originality is that the social psychology of 1965 bears only a weak resemblance to the dominant perspectives in this field in 1988. Most noticably absent are the motivational constructs, such as cognitive dissonance, and the applications of trait theories to phenomena such as interpersonal attraction. Currently, human cognition, social judgment, self, and information processing models prevail. Third, we have cast our net beyond social psychology to include general-experimental, community, and cross-cultural psychology, along with references to medical anthropology, sociolinguistics, and behavioral medicine. The significant value we derive from broadening the range of research disciplines only further underscores the power of the extrapolation research model originally envisioned by Goldstein, Heller and Sechrest.

In the two decades since the publication of *Psychotherapy and the psychology of behavior change*, other writers have crafted major statements on the linkage of social psychological theory and psychotherapy. Each of explicitly designed her volume for practicing clinicians. She demonstrated how clinicians might utilize cognitive consistency and attribution theories to engineer their own translated strategies for therapeutic change (Brehm, 1976). Weary and Mirels' (1982) volume accomplishes more general aims: It conveys, to practitioner and researcher, the analytic power of the social psychological approach, discussing the development, assessment and treatment of maladaptive behavior patterns. In addition, the Weary and Mirels volume articulates the philosophical assumptions of those drawn to the clinical-social research enterprise.

Our aim, unique to this volume, is to create specific extrapolatory hypotheses that will spark the research efforts of the next generation of clinical scientists. We feel, as do the original authors, that the extrapolatory enterprise produces an essential foundation, one step removed from direct application, for the science of human behavior change. We concur with Goldstein, Heller and Sechrest (1966) that:

> ...the ultimate incorporation or rejection of a given extrapolated research finding... by the researcher into psychotherapeutic theory or by the clinician into psychotherapeutic practice must not be a function of offerings such as this book. Hopefully, such incorporation or rejection will be a function of later formal or clinical research which will attempt the work that this book suggests. (p. 7)

Moreover, we do not wish future researchers to be constrained by the series of hypotheses in this volume, but hope instead to inspire them to their own innovative pursuits. We recognize that although the chapters that follow offer a large number of psychotherapy-relevant hypotheses, we could not be, and have not attempted to be, exhaustive in our coverage.

> The hypotheses presented may be viewed as illustrations of an approach to hypothesis development that we hope will be adopted more widely by others interested in the advance of psychotherapy. Our own philosophy toward psychotherapy research leads us to urge that others becoming involved in such extrapolatory forays attempt to be bold and imaginative in their efforts to develop ideas unfettered by overconventionalized approaches to psychotherapy and the development of associated research proposals. (Goldstein et al, 1966, p. 7).

We owe debts of gratitude to the following individuals who have assisted us with this project by providing us with comments on one or more chapters: Leona Aiken, Manuel Barrera, Jerry Boucher, Laurie Chassin, Linda Connor, Joe Hepworth, David Kenny, Anne Maass, Anthony Marsella, Roger Mitchell, Nancy Murdock, Marc Pilisuk, Irwin Sandler, Stanley Strong, David Thomas, Joseph Tobin, and Geoff White. Our special thanks go to Goldstein and Lee Sechrest for their encouragement and constructive suggestions through many drafts of this project.

1
Introduction

Therapists approach the problem of facilitating therapeutic change from various perspectives. Some operate solely within a specific personality theory, relying on the theory to guide them in their analysis of the client's problems. Others, impressed by the logic of behaviorism, apply this strategy in behavioral treatments that stress overt change rather than covert psychological processes. Still others help their clients through group-level interventions, family systems analysis, drug therapies, or any one of the other numerous forms of psychotherapy.

No matter what approach therapists take, they all face a common problem: How can these techniques be improved? In solving this problem, many rely on their own personal experiences with clients: Experience yields insight into dysfunctional behavior, which can then be tested, verified, and applied to similar cases. Others, by reviewing findings obtained in systematic studies of the therapeutic process, adapt their clinical practices accordingly. However, there is a third source of ideas for both increasing the efficiency of contemporary clinical interventions and the development of new approaches for altering client behavior. This approach does not dispute the value of information obtained through practice or psychotherapy research, but argues that advances in clinical practice can *also* be achieved by drawing extrapolations from theory and findings in basic social research.

THE LOGIC OF EXTRAPOLATION

Extrapolation, whereby basic social science research is mined for its hypotheses and implications for psychotherapeutic and behavior-change, has a long and rich history. As Kopel (1982) notes, one of the most fruitful instances of extrapolation involved using learning theory as a framework for understanding the development, maintenance, and elimination of dysfunctional behavior. From early roots in basic S-R theory, this framework evolved to include social learning theory as well as more recently developed cognitive behavior therapies.

The current volume, however, focuses on the extrapolation of social psychological theory and research to the clinical setting. This approach, which dates back to Lewin's notions concerning "action research," was given additional impetus in the mid-1960s with the publication of Arnold Goldstein, Kenneth Heller and Lee Sechrest's *Psychotherapy and the psy-*

chology of behavior change. By formulating a powerful new orientation toward clinical research, these investigators offered practitioners a method for extrapolating insights from evidence collected by experimental social psychology. The myriad research publications and conceptual papers that followed on the heels of this work attests to its substantial contribution to psychology (e.g, Brehm, 1976; Corrigan, Dell, Lewis & Schmidt, 1980; Goldstein, 1971; Goldstein & Simonson, 1971; Harvey & Weary, 1979; Hill & Weary, 1983; Weary & Mirels, 1982; Strong, 1978, 1982).

The present volume is a direct descendant of the pioneering work by Goldstein, Heller and Sechrest. The contents of the present volume reflect the changes in the field of social psychology that have occurred since the 1960s, but the overarching extrapolatory theme restates the philosophy of its predecessor. It is devoted to imparting to students and professionals an analytic framework, within which to approach any new bit of experimental data or theoretical development. This framework begins with the question: "What are the implications of this finding for increasing an understanding of behavior change among clinical populations?" This "habit of thinking" guides clinicians as they extract from an appealing pool of experimental or field study results, and especially from their theoretical underpinnings, a new array of hypotheses or conditions of therapeutic intervention relevant to client change. This approach follows directly from the Goldstein–Heller–Sechrest tradition:

> It is our basic contention...that increased understanding and efficiency, as well as the development of new techniques for altering patient behavior, may most rapidly and effectively be brought about by having major recourse to research findings from investigations initially oriented toward the psychology of behavior change. (1966, p. 4)

What is involved in extrapolation? Consider the example of so-called paradoxical therapies. This form of therapy is used to reduce highly resistent or hard-to-control behaviors, such as smoking, insomnia, depression, procrastination, overeating, phobias, or drug addiction. In its most basic form, paradoxical therapy involves requiring the client to engage deliberately in the behavior that is to be eliminated. For example, a therapist working with a distressed couple may tell them to schedule sessions each week in which they will argue for one hour. Similarly, an insomniac may be told to lie awake in bed for one hour before trying to go to sleep (Raskin & Klein, 1976; Weeks & L'Abate, 1979).

Surprisingly, when such methods have been applied consistently, the targeted behavior is often eliminated. Solyom, Garza-Perez, Ledwidge and Solyom (1972) report that 50 percent of their clients who were troubled by specific obsessions improved after participating in a paradoxical treatment program. Similarly, Gerz (1966), in a study of phobics, reported that nearly

90 percent of his 51 subjects showed improvement. Yet although therapeutic lore attests to the effectiveness of paradoxical therapy, several significant questions remain unanswered. First, although a number of possible mediating mechanisms have been suggested by therapists and researchers, at present the source of the method's power is unknown. Second, because the psychological factors that mediate behavior change following paradoxical therapy remain unspecified, the differential effectiveness of extant paradoxical techniques has not been established. Issues concerning the timing of the intervention and the rationale given for the paradoxical method have been raised, but remain unsettled.

Social psychological research, however, offers possible answers both these questions. Several well-substantiated theoretical frameworks within social psychology can account for paradoxical effects, including reactance theory (Brehm & Brehm, 1981), attribution theory (Strong, 1982), and impression management theory (Wright & Brehm, 1982). More importantly, these theories can be used to develop explicit suggestions for improving the effectiveness of paradoxical treatment strategies. For example, a reactance approach suggests that paradoxical treatment will be more effective if the therapist is dominant, seems eager to persuade and manipulate the client, demands compliance with the directive, and minimizes the client's choices (Brehm, 1976). Therefore, if we assume reactance is the mediating variable, then increasing the therapists' power should increase the effectiveness of the technique.

Although this analysis is only an example of the extrapolation process, it illustrates how hypotheses relevant to psychotherapeutic variables can be formulated by drawing upon nonclinical research outcomes. In the tradition of "action research" and the earlier Goldstein, Heller and Sechrest volume, the goals of this volume are twofold: a) to enrich basic social psychological research by asking questions that have theoretical implications as well as practical value, and b) to suggest hypotheses that can be tested by psychotherapy researchers in applied settings and clinicians in their daily practice (Goldstein et al, 1966, p. 5).

THE VALUE OF EXTRAPOLATION

Although the unique characteristics of psychotherapeutic settings pose special problems for researchers and therapists alike, the potential contribution of extrapolatory research to the advancement of psychotherapy theory, research, and practice looms as large today as it did twenty years ago. By focusing an expanded body of scientific knowledge on the resolution of human behavioral problems, extrapolatory thinking counteracts what many perceive as an unproductive drift into narrow sub-disciplinary specialization and preoccupation with technique (see Ross, 1985). All too often, empirical findings travel a restricted circuit within the discipline. They fail to impinge upon practicing clinicians and others who deal with human behavior as an integrated, multi-level phenomenon under the influence of diverse variables which are themselves arranged as multiple systems. Hill and Weary (1983) proclaim the value of extrapolation when they state:

> On a general level, an interdisciplinary approach facilitates the development of a new and broader perspective. Different disciplines are likely to focus on different aspects of a problem, identifying particular elements as critical. Combining different perspectives and allowing for cross-fertilization can lead to solutions that could not be achieved by more independent approaches. In fact, the complexity of human behavior problems almost demands the development of links between heretofore disparate lines of inquiry. (p. 11)

Moreover, the benefits of extrapolatory research are not unilateral; social psychology profits from the evaluation of its principles when they are generalized to clinical concerns. The application of social psychological theory to issues of development, maintenance and alteration of problematic behavior is a strong test of the generality and utility of those theories (Strong, 1978, p. 103). It is a strong antidote to the impoverishment of theories that can result when hypotheses are tested only within the confines of a limited number of research paradigms (Saxe & Fine, 1980; West, Reich, Dantchik & McCall, in press).

In addition to disciplinary cross-fertilization, other benefits of linkage research are noteworthy. It is also an antidote to the "atheoretical drift into technology" that characterizes graduate training—both in clinical and counseling psychology in general and in the behaviorally oriented approaches to psychotherapy in particular (Forsyth & Strong, 1986; Hayes, Rincover & Solnick, 1980; Ross, 1985). In his presidential address to the Association for the Advancement of Behavior Therapy in 1985, Alan O. Ross complained that reference to basic research had practically disappeared from the behavior-therapy literature. The field's proponents appeared to be trapped in a closed system, merely seeking new applications for a limited repertoire of well-worn techniques. For behavior therapy to avoid obsolescence and advance anew as the controlled application of the science of human behavior, Ross argues that the field must expand its theoretical base and seek empirically-based formulations from all branches of psychology (Ross, 1985).

Third, the extrapolatory method is the essential tool of those clinical and social psychologists who advocate creating an explicit theory of psychotherapy using social–psychological principles (Brehm, 1976; Hendrick, 1983; Strong, 1982). The efforts to construct a coherent and effective system of therapy arise from two sources: a) a critique of the scientific foundation of dominant treatment practices, and b) the conviction that "psychotherapy can be viewed as a branch of applied social psychology" (Strong, 1978, p. 101).

From a scientific vantage point, the field of psychotherapy is near crisis, with a chaotic proliferation of techniques that are eclectically put into use simply because "they seem intuitively to work" (Wilson & Franks, 1982; Hendrick, 1983). In opposition to standards within social psychology that emphasize precise conceptualization, traditional clinical formulations are often "very tenuously tied to operational descriptions of specific behavior disorders and intervention techniques" (Weary, Mirels & Jordan, 1982, p. 299).

The move to link psychotherapy to social psychology has prompted an interest within the field to develop a new interdisciplinary specialty—clinical social psychology. Proponents claim that because the individual and his or her social context are crucial in the determination of behavior, "systematic consideration of social psychological principles is essential to any understanding of the definition, development, maintenance, and modification of problematic behavior" (Weary, Mirels & Jordan, 1982, p. 288). Hendrick (1983) notes that social psychology is justified in wishing to reclaim its "birthright" of the psychotherapeutic domain, because the generic classes of any human interaction—social cognition about the interaction, social affect, and interpersonal processes—are the mainstream foci of social psychologists. Problems which may arise in these generic classes are necessarily problems of human interaction. "Thus both the purpose and the process of psychotherapy are types of human interactions about other, outside human interactions. Therefore the subject matter of social psychology is the intrinsic basis for the process of psychotherapy and for what it is about (i.e., solving interpersonal problems)" (Hendrick, 1983, pp. 74–75).

A fourth benefit of the extrapolatory perspective is that it offers both method and substance for graduate training and for professionals drawn to the social-clinical interface as their specialty. Harvey and Weary (1979) articulate the need to make explicit the conceptual and programmatic links between graduate programs in clinical and social psychology. Interdisciplinary students would not only profit from acquiring the clinical-social theoretical orientation outlined above, but would secure a grounding in the vital competency of theory construction and verification. To be of maximum value in helping professionals and the public, the clinical-social psychologist masters both the technology of collecting and analyzing data and the application of findings to therapy, especially the vital and creative step of generating transituational propositions from observed relationships (Forsyth & Strong, 1986). Ethical service to the public emanates from, among other things, provision of behavior change strategies drawn from psychological principles that have withstood empirical assault. Similarly, the public is ideally served by graduate training that supplies the clinical or social psychology student with a knowledge base that is "extensive and ever-expanding in light of the development of new findings and techniques in both areas of inquiry" (Harvey & Weary, 1979).

EXTRAPOLATION: PROBLEMS AND CONTROVERSIES

The extrapolatory approach offers a means of answering many questions about the psychotherapy process, but its limitations must be noted along with its advantages. First of all, philosophical and methodological differences between social psychology and psychotherapy have blocked integration of these disciplines for many years. Goldstein (1971) initially reviewed these barriers and noted, for example, that manipulation of situational variables, an essential procedure of the social psychologist, was deemed taboo among traditional therapists. Recent reviews (Brehm, 1980; Hill & Weary, 1983; Weary, Mirels & Jordan, 1982) add to the list of potential barriers which can hinder the production of extrapolatory research and its utilization among clinicians. Least troubling of these is the apprehension that entrenched professional interests will feel threatened by the ascendence of a clinical-social perspective, and will thus seek to exclude the entry of its proponents into treatment settings (Hill & Weary, 1983). Similarly, Hill and Weary (1983) fear that those who adopt an interdisciplinary focus face a potential loss of identity and stunted career development within traditionally organized departments. These problems, short-term difficulties of organizational development and inter-group relations, should diminish as linkage research achieves increased recognition of its value.

Brehm (1980) pinpoints two slightly more serious reasons why we do not see more interest in social psychology among clinicians. First, the advantages of an integrative approach are not effectively communicated to clinicians. Most clinicians do not read scientific articles (Cohen, Sargent & Sechrest, 1986; Morrow-Bradley & Elliott, 1986), let alone social psychological journals. Even studies designed as therapeutic analogues may appear too remote to be seriously considered by clinical journals. Ironically, the *Journal of Abnormal and Social Psychology*, the one journal originally conceived as a union of these two specialties, was dissolved because the pressures of specialization prevented authors from continuing to produce work at the interface of both fields (Hill & Weary, 1983). Brehm's second point is that the continuing fragmentation of social psychology into smaller and smaller "mini" models is an obstacle to application, because the demands of actual clinical work require every therapist to rely on general principles with relevance for the diverse nature of the people and problems encountered. Brehm is frankly pessimistic about the fate of clinical-social integration if, in her words, "applications to clinical practice continue to exist only by implication and theoretical concerns continue to be esoteric if not trivial" (Brehm, 1980, p. 184).

By far, the most serious obstacle to the diffusion of social psychology-inspired innovations within psychotherapy is the basic misunderstanding of science among practitioners and some researchers. The extrapolation approach is grounded in what Forsyth and Strong (1986) term a "unificationist" model of science. This view argues that basic and applied research are needed before the science of psychology can advance, and that all psychologists share the superordinate goal of understanding of human behavior. Some psychotherapists, however, take a more limited view of science and psychotherapy by adopting what can be termed a dualistic approach. Noting their circumscribed interest in a) the psychotherapy process and/or b) problems related to psychological adjustment and functioning, this dualism argues that psychotherapy is so unique that its processes cannot be explained using principles of human behavior derived from other branches of psychology. As one proponent of this view states, "as counseling researchers we are interested in developing principles of human behavior only inasmuch as they tap principles of counseling" (Gelso, 1979, p. 14). According to this perspective, investigators must keep "actual counseling in central focus" with methodologies that closely approximate ongoing psychotherapy.

The unificationist view takes issue with the dualistic approach to science described above. In arguing against dualism, unificationism emphasizes the shared goal of psychological researchers: to develop and test generalizable principles of human behavior. If these "laws" of behavior make reference to specific settings, then inevitable changes in these settings, over time and across situations, undermine the generalizability of the laws themselves. Because researchers should strive to explain clients' actions in terms of general statements that hold across many situations and times, findings obtained in other branches of psychology that bear on these general statements are necessarily relevant in evaluating the adequacy of these propositions. For example, if therapists suggest that paradoxical therapy works by stimulating clients' needs to reassert their freedom, they can buttress this argument by drawing on evidence for reactance theory obtained in experimental research settings. If, however, basic researchers discovered that reactance is mediated more by interpersonal factors (the need to appear free) than by intrapsychic factors (the need to be free), then this finding would warn the therapist that paradoxical therapy may fail unless the behavior is public.

This view argues that evidence concerning the adequacy of a general principle of human behavior should be drawn from all available sources, whether these sources be basic research or applied research within or outside clinical psychology. As Merton (1949) noted long ago, applied researchers cannot afford to adopt a myopic, single-discipline focus, because practical problems often involve variables that do not fall within the scope of any particular subfield of psychology. The extrapolatory approach also suggests that the concern for "generalizability" found among dualists is misguided.

Although several discussants have suggested that laboratory studies that simulate psychotherapy, or those that examine only one particular aspect of the psychotherapeutic setting in detail, are only tangentially relevant to clinical and counseling practices, a unified approach to psychology advocates an empirical eclecticism inconsistent with the wholesale rejection of any research method or theory. As Forsyth and Strong (1986) argue: "The context must be thought of as only one more variable or dimension that must be interpreted within the larger theoretical scheme" (p. 116). Also, results collected in nontherapeutic settings are still "relevant to practical problems if they examine theoretical generalizations that are relevant to these applied problems" (p. 116). They conclude that "psychotherapy will not be better understood by overvaluing generalizability of settings, but by the energetic application of the scientific model to generate a theory of biological, social, interpersonal, and psychological relationships that specifies how the dynamics of therapeutic and nontherapeutic settings differ" (p. 118).

2
Research Methods 1:
Control and Validity

The mid-1960s was an exciting era of new developments in methodology, as evidenced by the publication of such landmark works as Campbell and Stanley's (1966) *Experimental and quasi-experimental designs for research* and Webb, Campbell, Schwartz and Sechrest's (1966) *Unobtrusive measures: Nonreactive research in the social sciences*. The chapter on research methods in the original 1966 volume of *Psychotherapy and the psychology of behavior change* strongly reflected these developments. It brought methodological concepts of the era, including "plausible rival hypotheses," "internal and external validity," "reactivity of measurement," and "alternative design options," to the attention of a generation of clinical treatment researchers. Indeed, it may be argued that the methodological concepts introduced to clinical researchers in the original volume continue to be among the most influential concepts in much of clinical treatment research today.

At the same time, our basic understanding of research methods has continued to advance. Methodologists have moved out of the laboratory; they have tackled the problem of designing evaluations of innovative human service programs, both small and large scale, in the areas of health, criminal justice, social welfare, education, substance abuse, and mental health. This has led to a new recognition of the strength of laboratory experiments for the testing of basic theory; it has also led to a recognition of the limitations of the laboratory experiment as a model for many applied research problems. Field trials of experimental designs in naturalistic settings have also resulted in a new appreciation of both the strengths and the previously undiscovered limitations of these designs. High quality quasi-experimental designs have been developed, designs that are applicable when random assignment is not possible and which permit limited causal inferences to be made—in some cases with a certainty approaching that of a true experiment. Advances in structural equation modeling have aided in the conceptualization of complex causal systems, and permit tests of those systems. A developing post-positivist philosophy of science is helping to

A portion of the writing of chapters 2 and 3 was supported by NIMH grants P50MH39246 and R03MH39235.

PBC—B

9

provide the epistemological underpinnings for the new methodological approaches: this philosophy emphasizes intervention in naturalistic settings and falsification of hypotheses using multiple methods and analyses (Cook, 1985). In short, major methodological advances have occurred over the past 20 years that are not yet fully reflected in much of the current research on the outcomes of psychotherapy.

Dramatic changes have also occurred during this same period in the types of problems being addressed by clinically-trained researchers. Many clinicians now work in hospital or other health care settings, where they have developed psychological interventions to enhance medical compliance, prepare anxious patients for surgery, help patients cope with chronic pain, or help substance abusers to abstain from drugs or alcohol. Other clinicians have focused on preventive interventions; these include changing the behavior of Type A individuals who are at high risk for heart attacks and providing counseling and support for children at high risk of developing serious depression following the death of a parent. Finally, new treatment settings for psychotherapists have begun to emerge, such as Health Maintenance Organizations and national and regional centers specializing in high quality treatment of a specific clinical problem.

These developments in field methodology and in the range of problems addressed by treatment researchers have helped set the general focus for the present chapters on research methods. We address general principles of interventive research with special reference to the issues that arise in the wide range of field settings in which clinical researchers are currently working. For the most part, we do not attempt to identify issues that are unique to the traditional literature on psychotherapy. In this emphasis we have followed in the tradition established by the original authors.

> At the very outset we should like to make it clear that we do not regard research on psychotherapy as being so special or as involving such problems that it is unique as a research field. We believe that sound principles of research design and inference from research findings will lead inexorably to the untangling of the skein of confusion that represents our current level of understanding of the field of psychotherapy. (Goldstein, Heller & Sechrest, 1966, p. 10)

Reflecting the numerous post-Campbell and Stanley (1966) developments, the research methods section of the current volume has been divided into two chapters. The present chapter begins by examining the sources, strengths, and weaknesses of the traditional approaches to control that psychology has imported from other disciplines, and describing the hybrid approaches developed by psychologists in response to these limitations. This is followed by an extensive discussion of Cook and Campbell's (1979) major updating of Campbell and Stanley's (1966) classic analysis of validity issues in research. Special attention is given in this discussion to methods of maximizing each of the four types of validity (statistical conclusion, internal, construct, and external); the tradeoffs that must sometimes be made between validity types; and the different values that are placed on each of the validity types by basic and applied researchers. This final issue presents a particular problem in clinical psychology, since the field hopes to develop both basic theories of psychopathology and applied interventions that are effective in producing positive mental health outcomes.

The second chapter in this section discusses four designs that can be applied to evaluate the effectiveness of clinical interventions. These are social experiments, regression discontinuity designs, time-series designs, and nonequivalent control group designs. The assumptions, strengths, weaknesses, range of applicability, and special problems that arise in implementing the designs in real-world settings are discussed. For each design, methodological and statistical analysis strategies are identified, to aid in addressing validity issues that arise in treatment and prevention research. Finally, some of the general implications of the validity and design issues for the conduct of basic and applied research are discussed, and attention is given to some of the special problems associated with the design of clinical intervention research.

MODELS OF CONTROL

The term "control" is often invoked with near reverence by psychologists as being the key to good research. Indeed, it is. Yet many psychologists have failed to realize that psychology has imported three diverse models of control from other areas of science (see Cook, 1983; Cook & Campbell, 1979). Each of these models has a different history, different assumptions, and has proven useful in the domain of its home science. However, the appropriateness of each of these models for the study of psychological phenomena has rarely been considered. Further, the particular hybrid of these models employed in laboratory experiments in psychology has only rarely received scrutiny (Cook, Dintzer & Mark, 1980).

The first approach comes from the physical sciences, and involves isolation of the phenomena of interest from factors that have been empirically shown to or that may theoretically influence the outcome of the investigation. Test tubes are sterilized to prevent other substances from affecting chemical reactions, lead shielding is employed to prevent external radiation from affecting studies of sensitive materials, and vacuum chambers are utilized to prevent atmospheric influences on particle motion. Such procedures are particularly worthwhile when the specific objects under study are inert, do not spontaneously change over time, and are relatively uniform. These conditions are rarely met in psychology, so that physical isolation in closed systems is normally not a sufficient method of control.

The second approach comes from agriculture, and involves the random assignment of units to treatment conditions. Unlike physical scientists, agricultural researchers have been interested in studying their phenomena of interest under relatively naturalistic, open conditions. They have not been so much interested in showing that a new planting technique would improve crop yields when such variables as rain, wind, soil conditions, and amount of sunshine were precisely controlled. Rather, they were more interested in showing that this treatment had its effect *despite* normal variation of these and other potentially relevant factors. It was the insight of Sir Ronald Fisher (1925)—that randomization would guarantee that the groups would be *initially* equated within known limits of sampling error on all possible extraneous factors—that provides the foundation of modern agricultural research. This approach is most useful when it may be plausibly assumed that the experimental units are relatively passive recipients of treatment, so that they can also be considered to be equated at the *end* of the experiment. With corn plants, this appears to be a relatively safe assumption. However, human subjects in real world settings sometimes agitate to have their treatment changed, migrate to other fields in search of better treatment conditions, or give up or try harder because of their knowledge that other are receiving a different treatment. Thus, in some areas of psychological research randomization alone may not be sufficient to assure the equivalence of treatment and comparison groups at the completion of the experiment, in the absence of any real effects of treatment.

The third approach to control has developed primarily in those social sciences—such as economics, political science, and sociology—where manipulation of treatment conditions often is not possible. Instead, these researchers have taken the tack of attempting to eliminate statistically the influence of important extraneous factors that may causally influence that phenomena of interest. For example, epidemiological studies of the effects of stress on the development of mental illness normally attempt to remove statistically the effects of potential risk factors such as age, gender, and income level. This approach provides exact control for the effects of extraneous variables when it may be assumed that a) all important extraneous variables have been identified, b) they are measured with perfect reliability, c) the functional relationship (e.g., linear or quadratic) between the extraneous and outcome variable is known, and d) all interactions between extraneous variables in producing the outcome variable have been identified. However, these conditions are not normally met in psychology; therefore, this method of control almost always involves some degree of uncertainty as to whether the statistical adjustments have effectively removed the influence of extraneous causal factors on the outcome variable.

Given the problems of each of the methods of control in dealing with psychological phenomena, psychologists have traditionally utilized the laboratory experiment, which is a hybrid of the first two approaches to control. In certain basic research areas (e.g., human learning), the isolation and closed-system model of the physical sciences has been adopted in a very literal sense and combined with the open-system, randomization model of agriculture. Soundproofed cubicles isolate the subject from all extraneous sounds, and nonsense syllables preclude prior experience with the stimulus materials. Randomization insures that the subjects in each group are initially comparable on all potential individual difference factors such as IQ, motivation, and anxiety. Since experiments are typically of relatively short duration and subjects are unaware of the existence of other conditions, problems of subject attrition and contamination from other conditions are minimized. However, this hybrid model reflects a tension between the divergent goals of its closed-system, physical science parent and its open-system, agricultural parent. It assumes that the contextual factors that occur in more naturalistic settings are simply random or systematic errors, so that eliminating such errors would provide the clearest understanding of the phenomenon under investigation. To the extent that these contextual factors alter the effects of the treatment (i.e., a context x treatment interaction occurs), generalization to the applied situation of interest may be problematic.

This hybrid model is sometimes taken one step further in social psychology, personality research, and many areas of basic research in abnormal psychology. Extraneous factors cannot simply be removed by isolation, since the context-based meaning of the situation would be greatly altered. Instead, isolation is utilized in a more metaphorical sense: the experimenter creates a simplified model or analog of the general situation of interest. For example, in early research reported by Lazarus (1966), subjects were exposed to threats of electric shock or movies of painful, primitive circumcision operations, which were assumed to capture the essential features of the stressful situations in people's everyday lives. More interactive variants of this approach have sometimes been described in terms of a dramaturgical metaphor, in which the experimenter "sets the stage" for the treatment and hired accomplices follow a "script" that prescribes their verbal and physical interactions with the subject (Aronson, Brewer & Carlsmith, 1985). In a sense then, subjects become involved in a simple, stylized play with trained actors, in which the responses of the subjects serve as the dependent measures. In each case, it is assumed that the simplified analog contains all of the important causal elements that are present in the applied situation of interest and does *not* contain additional causal elements. Since the plausibility of these assumptions is not typically investigated, the results of this approach to research will be of unknown robustness and generality (Cook, Dintzer & Mark, 1980)[1].

VALIDITY

Cook and Campbell (1976, 1979) have recently revised Campbell and Stanley's (1966) classic analysis of validity issues in research. Perhaps reflecting increased experience with large scale social experiments and quasi-experiments in a variety of research areas, Cook and Campbell have proposed a refinement of the classification of the types of validity, and have identified several new threats to each type of validity. This section reviews Cook and Campbell's current analysis of validity, noting in particular some of the issues arising from the divergent validity priorities of basic and applied clinical researchers.

Statistical Conclusion Validity

The first type of validity, statistical conclusion validity, refers to the ability of the researcher to detect accurately the relationship between variables. Two general threats should normally be examined with regard to statistical conclusion validity: a) violations of the assumptions of the statistical tests, and b) the ability of the design to detect the relationship if, in fact, one does exist.

Violations of assumptions
The issue of violations of the assumptions of statistical tests may arise in two ways. First, each statistical test includes a set of assumptions. For example, analysis of variance assumes normality and equal variances in each treatment group; among the assumptions of traditional structural equation analysis is multivariate normality (Bentler, 1980; Jöreskog & Sörbom, 1979). Violations of the assumptions will have different effects depending on the specific test and the nature of the violation. Simple analysis of variance with no repeated measures and relatively equivalent sample sizes is robust to nearly all violations, meaning that the probability of the type I error remains at .05 or less. Unfortunately, however, violations of the assumptions of analysis of variance may lead to reductions in the ability of the test to detect

---

[1]Another issue concerns the degree to which subjects enact unique roles in the laboratory setting. For example, Orne (1962) has argued that subjects attempt to please the experimenter and Rosenberg (1969) has noted that subjects may act in a socially desirable manner to appear "normal." Such problems can in some cases preclude generalizations to nonlaboratory settings.

true differences among treatment groups, a fact that has often been overlooked by researchers (Levine & Dunlap, 1982, 1983). In the case of traditional structural equation analysis, violations of the multivariate normality assumption can lead to the far more severe consequence of serious misestimation of the relationships among variables (Bentler, 1983). The extent of the violation of each assumption can in many cases be assessed by inspection of appropriate plots of the data or statistical tests, and, if necessary, transformations of the data or alternative statistical procedures involving less stringent assumptions may be used to reduce the effects of this problem.

Second, the researcher needs to consider carefully the possibility that the data are not independent. This problem may arise in longitudinal designs and treatment outcome followup designs in which measures are collected on the same subjects at repeated times. It also arises in designs in which treatment is delivered in a group setting, such as group psychotherapy, group weight-control programs, or alcohol support groups, even if outcome measures are collected from each subject separately. Although the effects of violations of the independence assumption are only beginning to be investigated (Kenny & Judd, 1986), major violations may lead to serious misestimation of the standard errors and biased tests of significance, even in such normally robust procedures as analysis of variance (Winer, 1971). If the nature of the possible violation can be specified, statistical tests that assess the extent of the problem can sometimes be performed. In group treatment research, statistical tests may often be performed that assess whether significant violations of the independence assumption have occurred (e.g., Anderson & Ager, 1978; Kenny & Judd, 1986; Winer, 1971). In designs involving repeated measurement of subjects over time, the statistical models may be respecified to allow for the possibility of correlated errors (Judd, Jessor & Donovan, 1986; Kessler & Greenberg, 1981; O'Brien & Kaiser, 1985; Rogosa, 1980).

Power-related issues
The second class of threats to statistical conclusion validity relate to power, defined as the ability of the design to detect the relationship between variables when, in fact, one does exist. These issues have traditionally been treated by researchers conducting basic research in the laboratory as being, at best, of only minor importance, as the costs of Type II errors in this type of research are normally quite low. Since undergraduate subjects and graduate researchers are normally cheap and plentiful, experiments that are less than optimal can easily be redesigned and additional subjects can be run. In contrast, research in many clinical contexts involves much higher costs. Many populations of interest involve clients or patients with low-prevalence disorders (e.g., schizophrenics; bulimics; severe depressives) or

who have low willingness to be studied (e.g., alcoholics); indeed, one moderate to large sized study may exhaust the population of available subjects in a community or even a metropolitan area. Interventions must be delivered by paid professionals whose availability is often time-limited. Gaining access to the population may be politically difficult, and getting the treatment personnel and client populations together may involve sizeable logistic problems. Subjects may need to be paid to maintain their participation in the study, particularly if there is a substantial measurement burden or they are in a comparison group that does not receive treatment. The higher costs of applied clinical treatment research often mean that investigators may get only one chance to test their hypotheses or newly developed treatment programs, as the continuation or further funding of the project may be contingent on promising initial results. Under these conditions, the costs of Type II errors can become considerable, making it imperative that the investigator implement the strongest possible form of the treatment and utilize the most powerful available design (Sechrest et al., 1979).

How can the investigator maximize the ability of the design to detect treatment effects? Most of the answers involve basic, but often neglected principles of research.

Use reliable measures. Many researchers originally trained in experimental or social psychology have failed to appreciate the importance of reliable measures, often using one-item scales or measures of unknown reliability. Unreliability leads to underestimates of treatment effects. Appropriate aggregation over stimuli, situations, occasions, judges, or measures can often provide another method of enhancing reliability (Epstein, 1983).

Monitor treatment implementation. In basic laboratory research, there is normally little concern that the planned treatment has been delivered. In contrast, concerns about treatment implementation can arise in clinical treatment research at least at two different levels (Sechrest et al., 1979; Yeaton & Sechrest, 1981). At the level of the client, the researcher should monitor the extent of the client's participation in the treatment program. For example, does the client attend sessions, and to what extent does the client participate in the sessions and in recommended other activities (e.g., therapeutic homework activities)? At the level of the therapist, the researcher should assess the extent to which the therapist's background and therapeutic activities match those intended by the treatment program. Does the therapist have the training, experience, and background in the particular treatment modality planned for in the development of the program? To what extent does the therapist follow the planned treatment protocol?

The monitoring of treatment implementation offers advantages to both the researcher and the therapist. It can provide rich descriptive information about the treatment that is useful to other therapists (and researchers) should they wish to implement the treatment in the future. It can also serve to help identify problems in the treatment, so that early corrective action can be taken with a client who is not fully participating in the therapeutic activities or a therapist who is not following the treatment protocol. This serves both to maximize the uniformity of the treatment as it is implemented and to maintain the treatment at its intended strength. Nonetheless, despite the best efforts of the researcher, sometimes there will still be considerable variation in either the extent of client participation or the quality of delivered treatment. In such cases, the researcher may use the treatment implementation data to probe hypotheses about the types of clients (or therapists) and their activities in therapy that are associated with the most positive outcomes (Cook, Leviton & Shadish, 1985; Sechrest, West, Phillips, Redner & Yeaton, 1979).

Maximize subject uniformity. The use of heterogeneous subject populations in research normally tends to increase error variance. Selection of more homogeneous subject samples reduces error variance, although with two potential costs in clinical treatment research. First, using restrictive criteria to identify "pure" subject populations may severely limit the potential population which could participate in the study, in some cases precluding a sufficient sample size for an adequate study. As an illustration, the relatively large number of cocaine abusers who are potentially available to the addiction researcher contrasts sharply with the extremely limited number of cocaine abusers who are not involved with other drugs or alcohol. Second, development of efficacious treatments for these "pure types" may seriously restrict applicability of the treatment in real world settings in which few of the "pure types" exist.

It is useful to note that the measurement and statistical adjustment strategy may sometimes be utilized to reduce error variance due to subject heterogeneity *without* incurring the costs of subject availability and generalization noted above. This simply involves including pretest measures that correlate with the criterion variable in the design and removing the effects of these measures through appropriate statistical analyses.

Increase N. Researchers trained in laboratory research often have woefully optimistic notions about the sizes of effects that can be detected with relatively small samples. All too frequently their tests have at best low to moderate power under the highly controlled conditions that prevail in the laboratory (Cohen, 1962); in less controlled field settings, similar low N tests have little chance of detecting even large effects (Crane, 1976). This is a particular problem in some areas of psychotherapy research where large numbers of appropriate subjects may simply not be available.

Researchers should attempt to estimate the power of their tests (see

Cohen, 1977) when planning their research and make arrangements to obtain a sufficient sample size to provide a fair test of their hypotheses. Sample sizes should normally also be kept as equal as possible across treatment groups to maximize power.[2]

Internal Validity

Once a difference has been established between the treatment and comparison groups on the dependent measure, the issue arises as to how plausibly the effect may be attributed to the treatment. At this point, basic laboratory researchers normally blithely move on to issues of construct validity (see next section), secure in their assumptions that randomization could be successfully maintained throughout the experiment and that no contamination of treatments or subjects by other factors has occurred. In contrast, for the applied clinical treatment researcher, developing procedures that will maximize internal validity is the single most important priority in designing research.

Cook and Campbell (1979) have developed an extensive list of *potential* threats to internal validity. These are factors which may prevent the researcher from unambiguously attributing any observed effects to the treatment. The task of the applied clinical researcher is to identify and enumerate those threats that are plausible given the specific design and area under investigation; not all threats are plausible in all designs. Then the researcher can develop additional procedures that help rule out as many of the plausible threats as possible. A partial list of threats is briefly presented below. Additional threats will be discussed in chapter 3 in the section on social experiments.

Threats arising from the participants' growth and experience
Two threats arise from processes that may occur with the passage of time between the pretest and posttest. These are maturation and history.

---

[2]The primary exception to the rule of equating the sizes of the treatment and control groups occurs when the data are very expensive to collect in one group relative to the other. Here, gains in power can be most economically achieved by increasing the sample size in the lower cost group. Note, however, that the amount of gain in power decreases as the ratio of the number of the subjects in the treatment to the control group moves away from a 1:1 ratio (equal sample size in the two groups). As this ratio reaches 6:1, the standard error approaches its assymptotic minimum value so that continuing to sample additional subjects from the lower cost group will not lead to further detectable increases in power.

Maturation. A number of growth and decay processes occur during the life cycle without any treatment intervention. Children show improvement in a variety of physical and mental abilities as they get older; elderly individuals often show just the opposite pattern. Certain forms of schizophrenia are associated with increasingly severe symptomatology over time. Depression after a major loss event (e.g., death of parent, divorce) typically is most severe during the next 1–2 years, following which it begins to return toward baseline levels.

History. This threat arises when an event that is not part of the treatment occurs between the pretest and posttest, and it is plausible that this event could have caused the observed effect. An investigator studying the possible effects of group therapy with an inpatient population could not be certain as to the effects of this treatment if a change in the patients' medication or conditions occurred at the same time. A wide variety of other events, such as media portrayals of mental illness, changes in economic conditions, or severe winter conditions can also lead to changes in mental health outcomes independent of any treatment, particularly in outpatient populations.

Threats associated with the measurement process
Two threats—testing and instrumentation—arise from the measurement process itself.

Testing. Testing subjects may affect their responses on later measurements. Overweight individuals who are asked about their weight (or actually weighed) may reduce their food consumption, individuals in a divorce adjustment group given a divorce information test may remember which items were correct from a previous testing, and newly diagnosed diabetics given a checklist of diabetic symptoms may monitor those symptoms more carefully in the future.

Instrumentation. Changes in measuring instruments can give the appearance of an effect even when none exists. Problems in this area range from the obvious, such as the difficulties of comparing scores on different instruments used at pretest and posttest, to a variety of issues that can often be more subtle, such as floor and ceiling effects and shifts in the reliability of observers from pretest to posttest.

Threats associated with sampling design
Two threats arise from the method by which subjects are selected to be in the investigation. The first applies in designs with pretests and posttests; the second involves the comparison of a treatment with a control group.

Statistical regression. When subjects are selected on the basis of pretest scores, especially if a less than perfectly reliable measure is used, posttest scores will tend to regress to the mean of the population from which the sample was drawn. A group of students who are selected because they show a high level of depression on the Beck depression inventory will have a lower (i.e., more normal) mean depression score upon retesting. A group of children selected because they have experienced an unusually low number of stressful life events during the past year will, on the average, tend to experience a higher number of stressful life events during the following year. This problem is most severe when groups are selected that are extreme on the initial measure.

Selection. This threat refers to the comparability of the treatment and control groups prior to the delivery of any treatment. Subjects who volunteer for group therapy may be more extroverted, of lower income, and less neurotic than subjects who volunteer to receive individual therapy. To the extent that these or other preexisting group differences are associated with the specific mental health outcomes under investigation, the researcher will be uncertain as to the effects of the treatment.

Interactions with selection
Any of the first five threats can interact with selection to produce possible spurious effects. These threats arise primarily in designs which have nonrandomized treatment and control groups as well as a pretest and posttest. For example, comparisons of the effectiveness of pain control programs in two different hospitals may be compromised if one hospital has greater staff turnover in its pain control unit that the other (selection × history) or if one hospital serves a younger patient population than the other, leading to more complete recoveries in the younger group (selection × maturation).

Reducing threats to internal validity
If one or more of the threats to internal validity discussed above (or the threats that will be discussed in chapter 3) are plausible, then any observed outcomes cannot be confidently attributed to the treatment. In such cases, researchers must, if at all possible, take additional steps to strengthen the internal validity of the design. Such steps normally utilize concepts from either the agricultural, physical sciences, or social sciences approaches to control. Five general strategies for minimizing the above threats to internal validity are presented below, listed in their typical order of preference.

Random assignment to treatment groups. All of the threats discussed above are rendered implausible if subjects can be randomly assigned successfully to treatment and control groups. Because of this strength of the randomized experiment, laboratory researchers have never had to concern themselves with attempting to identify the threats to internal validity that are plausible in their designs. But this strength, so characteristic of the laboratory experiment, has left many researchers ill-prepared to address the difficulties of real-world clinical research. As will be seen in chapter 3, treatment outcome experiments conducted in real-world settings are subject to other threats to internal validity that are *not* ruled out by randomization.

Other design improvements. It is often possible to greatly strengthen a design by making relatively small changes to address a specific, identified threat to internal validity. For example, history can often be minimized as a threat by delivering the treatment and taking the pretest and posttest measures at nonoverlapping times in different replications. Maturation can often be ruled out by including additional pretest measures that establish the nature of any developmental trend.

Measurement and statistical adjustment. Specific threats that can be identified and accurately measured can sometimes be eliminated by statistical adjustment. If it is known that the age of the patients is the primary difference in the populations being treated by two state hospital units, statistical adjustments may be made that reduce the potential effect of this selection threat on the outcome measures. Note that this procedure adjusts only for the specific variable of patient age and not for other unmeasured or unknown threats, such as prior psychiatric history of the patients.

Pattern of current results. Although a threat may be plausible given the specific design that was used, it may not be plausible in the context of the specific pattern of results that were actually obtained. Statistical regression would be implausible if a group of children selected for their high level of anxiety about dental treatment evidenced substantially less dental anxiety than the average child in the community following the intervention. A program focusing exclusively on the reduction of dental anxiety would be substantially stronger in internal validity if participants showed decreased anxiety during dental procedures, but not during other stressful medical procedures (e.g., immunizations) not addressed by the program.

Previous research and theory. In cases where previous research has consistently ruled out specific threats to internal validity, they are less likely to be plausible in the current research. Glass, McGaw and Smith (1981) cite a review of the literature which found that adult stutterers do not change their speech behavior over time in the absence of treatment. This consistent finding helps minimize such threats as maturation and statistical regression as plausible explanations of the successful outcome of a treatment program. However, if a different patient population, such as child stutterers, were used in an investigation, maturation and statistical regression could once again become plausible threats to internal validity. Such observations suggest that the researcher must be extremely cautious when invoking previous research or theory as a means of ruling out threats to internal validity.

Construct Validity

By successfully establishing internal validity, the researcher can conclude that "something" about the treatment caused the observed pattern of effects. But, exactly what that "something" is and exactly what the observed pattern of effects means have not yet been addressed. Herein lies the issue of construct validity.

In discussing construct validity, it is useful to distinguish between two levels of the independent and dependent variables (West & Wicklund, 1980). First is the conceptual level, wherein researchers postulate the general theoretical constructs of interest and hypothesize causal relationships among them. An increase in the amount of perceived control over one's outcomes (independent variable) is expected to cause improvements in health (dependent variable). Strengthening a child's social support network (independent variable) is hypothesized to lead to a decrease in depression (dependent variable) in children suffering parental loss due to divorce or death. Each of these theoretical independent and dependent variables is an abstract construct that must also be specified on a second, operational level. For example, manipulations of perceived control over one's outcomes have included being able to choose the times a visitor will come (Schulz, 1976), being able to make a variety of choices about mundane aspects of one's daily life (Langer & Rodin, 1976), and giving subjects a button which they believe will terminate a noxious noise (Glass & Singer, 1972). In a parallel manner, diverse measures of health have been utilized. Among these are number of doctor visits, number of sick days, nurse ratings of patient health status, and self-reports of physical symptoms. The relationships between the operational and conceptual levels of the independent and dependent variables for this example are depicted in Figure 2.1.

Issues of construct validity arise in that manipulations are potentially fallible operationalizations of the conceptual independent variable, and dependent measures are potentially fallible indicators of the conceptual dependent variable. In each case, researchers must be aware of the possibility that they have manipulated or measured something in addition to, or instead of, the intended theoretical construct. In our example, the manipulation of the patient's ability to make choices about her daily life may not lead to a sense of perceived control, but rather to an increase in her ability to elicit caretaking behavior by the medical staff. Nurse ratings of the

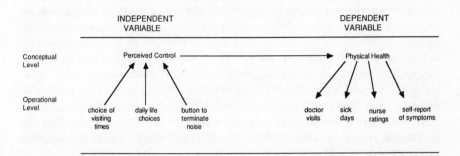

Figure 2.1 Conceptual and operational levels of the independent and dependent variables. Adapted from P. Karoly, *Measurement Strategies in health psychology*. Copyright © John Wiley & Sons, Inc. Reprinted by permission of John Wiley & Sons, Inc.

health of the patient may also reflect other variables such as how much the nurse likes the patient. In such cases, the theoretical interpretation of the results of the investigation is potentially ambiguous. That is, although the researchers may definitely conclude that the manipulation caused the results (internal validity), the conceptual basis for the results may be equivocal, since several plausble alternative explanations of the results may exist.

Strengthening construct validity. A number of alternative methods of strengthening the construct validity of research which focus on different aspects of the problem have been suggested.

1. The construct validity of the conceptual independent variable may often be established through the use of checks on the manipulation and checks for confounding. Asking subjects directly about how much control they feel they have over their outcomes, or assessing the social support network of the children, can provide direct checks on the success of these manipulations. In addition, checking that other potential confounding factors have not changed, such as the amount or quality of care received by the patients, decreases the plausibility of these specific alternative explanations of the results.

2. A conceptually similar process may be used to help establish the construct validity of the conceptual dependent measure. Following the logic outlined by Campbell and Fiske (1959), potential indicators of the same conceptual dependent measure should show substantial correlation (convergent validity), whereas they should be uncorrelated with indicators of other constructs (discriminant validity). Nurse ratings of physical health should correlate with a number of sick days and number of doctor visits, but not with conceptually unrelated measures such as the nurse's liking of the patient.

3. Aronson, Brewer and Carlsmith (1985) have proposed a process which they term *conceptual replication*, in which the same hypothesis is tested in multiple experiments. In each experiment, the operations are changed in an attempt to rule out plausible alternative explanations. To the extent that the pattern of results remain unchanged despite changes in the manipulations and the dependent measures, the construct validity of both the independent and dependent variables is strengthened. This method is particularly useful since other "random irrelevancies" (Campbell, 1968)—such as the particular subjects used, the experimenter, the treatment staff, therapist demeanor, the time when the investigation is conducted, and the setting—are also likely to be altered, ruling out these factors as being potentially critical components of the treatment.

4. Perhaps the most sophisticated method of establishing the construct validity of theoretical variables within a single investigation is through the use of a structural equation approach (Alwin, 1974; Kenny, 1979; see Judd, Jessor & Donovan, 1986, for an illustration). Basically, this approach involves developing a construct model that identifies a) the specific measures that are indicators of each construct and b) the nature of the relationship between each of the conceptual constructs. When multiple indicators of each construct are included, the data may be used to test the adequacy of the construct model (see Wothke, 1984, for a comparative discussion of structural equation approaches).

Emphases of applied and basic clinical researchers

Applied researchers often have more limited goals with respect to construct validity than basic researchers. While basic researchers are interested in pinning down the exact theoretical explanation of their results, applied researchers are often primarily interested in being sure that irrelevant factors associated with the treatment (e.g., the specific staff person who is delivering the treatment, therapist style) are not causing the results. Identifying components of complex treatments that lessen the effectiveness of the treatment package, or those which are costly and have no effect on the outcome, may sometimes also be important to applied researchers. But identifying the *specific* theoretical relationships between each of the components of the treatment and a wide range of potentially relevant outcome variables is likely to be a lower priority goal for the applied than the basic researcher. We will return to this issue again in chapter 3, in our discussion of construct validity in social experiments.

External Validity

Closely linked to the issue of construct validity is external validity. In construct validity, the focus is on the meaning and generality of the theoretical constructs represented by the specific manipulations and measures.

In external validity, the emphasis shifts to the generality of the causal relationship between the conceptual independent and dependent variables. Researchers normally wish to reach causal conclusions that extend beyond the specific group of subjects, the specific setting, and the specific time in history that characterized their investigation. The greater the degree to which the basic findings remain unchanged despite variation in subjects, settings, and times, the greater the external validity of the causal relationship.

There are in reality two different types of external validity questions about which a researcher may be concerned (Cook & Campbell, 1979). The first, which most often but not exclusively characterizes basic research, is the extent to which the causal relationship may be generalized *across* different subject populations, different settings, and different times. From the perspective of the theory being tested, these factors are all irrelevant background characteristics that ideally should not affect the causal relationship. Of course, theories may include specific subject variables, setting variables, or—less characteristically—time variables, as part of the central theoretical constructs. The theory of Type A coronary prone behavior includes Type A and Type B persons and settings with and without deadlines as central constructs (Glass, 1977; Matthews, 1982). Nonetheless, according to the theory, the basic findings should generalize across other subject variables (e.g., college students vs. businessmen), other setting variables (e.g., school vs. work environment) and other time variables (e.g., investigation conducted in 1978 vs. 1988) that are not specified as part of the theory. Whenever a subject, setting, or time variable is identified that alters the nature of the causal relationship, a potential boundary condition that limits the domain of application of the theoretical principle(s) may be established.

Identifying important boundary conditions can contribute to the development of theory by adding to the understanding of the basic processes underlying the observed relationships. Further, boundary conditions often serve to identify necessary conditions; these must be met in the design of treatments if the intervention is to have a positive impact on client outcomes. For example, several early experiments on dissonance theory suggested that perceived choice and foreseeability of the consequences of the choice were important conditions, which had to be met if dissonance effects were to occur. These variables have subsequently been incorporated into revisions of the theory (see West & Wicklund, 1980) and have occupied a central role in the development of dissonance-based psychotherapeutic interventions (Cooper & Axsom, 1982).

The second type of external validity question, which more often characterizes applied research, is the extent to which a causal relationship may be generalized *to* a specific population, a specific setting, and less frequently, a specific time. Researchers who are attempting to investigate the effectiveness of desensitization procedures in alleviating debilitating chronic fears have a specific target population (phobic clients) and therapeutic setting (outpatient treatment clinics) to which they wish to immediately generalize. Schulz (1976) wished to generalize to a specific population (the elderly) and a specific setting (nursing homes) in his studies of perceived control and health. In each case, a more limited and well defined target population of subjects and settings was identified.[3]

The major issue in external validity is the possibility that some unknown population, setting, or time variable may interact with the treatment to modify the results. Consider an intervention program in which hospital patients are given presurgical psychological counseling to reduce their anxiety and assist them in developing more effective coping strategies. At issue is whether the program helps subjects recover more quickly following surgery. Figure 2.2 depicts three sets of hypothetical results of the presurgical counseling program.

Figure 2.2(a) depicts a situation in which highly anxious patients recover more slowly when they receive presurgical counseling, whereas less anxious patients recover more rapidly when they are given the same program. Such a result would indicate that psychological preparation for surgery should be limited to (i.e., not generalized beyond) highly anxious patients. Figure 2.2(b) illustrates a situation in which elderly patients recover more slowly from surgery than young patients; however, both groups benefit equally from the presurgical counseling. This illustrates that *main effects* of population, setting, or time variables do not limit researchers' ability to generalize their findings. Finally, in Figure 2.2(c), subjects who are assigned to receive a new, experimental type of surgery benefit from presurgical counseling. However, subjects who are assigned to receive the traditional surgery for the same medical problem do not benefit from the presurgical counseling program. This illustrates a treatment × setting interaction, in which the benefits of presurgical counseling are limited to the experimental surgery treatment.

In thinking about problems of external validity, it is useful to consider how the specific group of subjects, the specific setting, and the specific time in history that characterize an investigation are typically selected.

---

[3]Schulz's research, in fact, combined applied and theoretical interests. In addition to his interest in developing interventions to improve the lives of the elderly, he has been interested in a variety of theoretical issues associated with responses to loss of control and predictability.

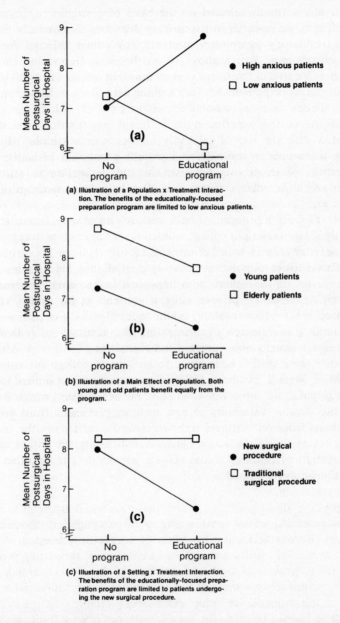

(a) Illustration of a Population x Treatment Interaction. The benefits of the educationally-focused preparation program are limited to low anxious patients.

(b) Illustration of a Main Effect of Population. Both young and old patients benefit equally from the program.

(c) Illustration of a Setting x Treatment Interaction. The benefits of the educationally-focused preparation program are limited to patients undergoing the new surgical procedure.

Figure 2.2 Hypothetical outcomes of an educationally-focused preparation program on speed of recovery from major surgery. From P. Karoly, *Measurement strategies in health psychology*. Copyright © John Wiley & Sons Inc. Reprinted by permission of John Wiley & Sons, Inc.

Subjects

Subjects are normally selected on the basis of convenience. Investigators conducting basic research in psychology departments normally utilize the local introductory psychology students, sometimes selected for certain characteristics (e.g., scores above 10 on the Beck Depression Inventory); researchers located in treatment centers normally utilize the available population of clients or patients who are seeking care. Each of these populations has a specific set of associated characteristics, which may differ. Replications of the experiment by different investigators will often be associated with the use of relatively heterogeneous samples of subjects ranging from college students to inpatient groups. Examination of the effectiveness of treatments both within and across investigations as a function of subject characteristics can often help detect findings of limited generality.

For example, in a program of basic research on obesity, Schachter (1971) primarily used overweight college women from upper-class backgrounds as subjects. Later failures by other investigators to replicate his early findings with other subject populations have suggested that his findings may be limited to dieting individuals who happened to be heavily represented in Schachter's particular private college student population (Woody & Costanzo, 1981). More recently, similar questions have been raised about the generality of research demonstrating the accuracy of judgments by depressed relative to nondepressed individuals (e.g., Alloy & Abramson, 1978) since these studies have relied so heavily on college student samples (Ruehlman, West & Pasahow, 1985). These issues are not limited to college student populations, however. Clinic and medical center populations often show considerable variability in age, income, previous history of mental illness, knowledge of treatment techniques, and a variety of other variables. To the extent that such subject characteristics interact with treatments, generalization of findings across subject populations or to other subject populations may be limited.

Settings

In basic research, an artificial setting is often created in the laboratory (Aronson, Brewer & Carlsmith, 1985) or a specific setting is created or selected in the field (Ellsworth, 1977). In either case, the setting is designed or selected to provide a good representation of the conceptual independent variable, permit measurement of the conceptual dependent variable, and to minimize the influence of other extraneous variables. Seligman's (1975) research on learned helplessness, for example, provided subjects with a large number of trials in which their responses consistently led to failure, and then presented subjects with a new task that clearly reflected any resulting performance deficits. Such a procedure has much to recommend it in terms of construct validity and statistical conclusion validity. However, it may lead to problems of external validity if the treatment interacts with other setting characteristics. A therapist who prescribes therapeutic homework exercises in a highly authoritarian manner may have less compliant clients than a therapist who prescribes the exercises in a less authoritarian manner. If, however, the client's degree of compliance could potentially be monitored at any time—as occurs in some inpatient settings—it is not unlikely that the more authoritarian manner of of prescription would produce the higher degree of compliance. This example illustrates a treatment × setting interaction that would limit generalization of any recommendations concerning the therapist's manner in prescribing therapeutic regimens.

Setting × treatment interactions represent an often overlooked, potentially very severe problem of external validity. Basic researchers often create or select the settings for their investigations on a highly intuitive, creative basis (see Aronson, Brewer & Carlsmith, 1985; Ellsworth, 1977). Their deliberations focus on maximizing the chances of obtaining the predicted outcome of the treatment, while minimizing the likelihood of potential alternative explanations. Only rarely are they concerned with the robustness of the treatment effect across diverse settings, or even across changes in background characteristics within the same setting. When an important treatment effect is found, all background setting characteristics tend to become frozen at their current levels, as the investigator rushes to establish a "research paradigm." Other researchers then adopt the same paradigm to maximize their chances of obtaining statistically significant results and to increase the comparability of their findings with those of the previous literature. This particular tradition of basic research is especially likely to lead to findings of unknown generality. Given the extreme homogeneity of the experimental settings, treatment × setting interactions which limit generalization are unlikely to be detected. Similar problems arise in applied clinical research when previous research has been exclusively conducted in one setting (e.g., clinic-based social skills training programs) and the researcher wishes to generalize to another setting (e.g., a prison-based social skills program for criminal offenders; see Cronbach, 1982).

Time

All research is conducted in the context of a historical background. Normally, historical factors are given little consideration and the research is conducted at whatever time it is possible or convenient. However, factors correlated with time can sometimes have profound effects on treatments. For example, the effectiveness of supportive therapy for AIDS victims relative to no treatment may show an increase from 1983 to 1988 as the possibility of finding a cure improves. The effectiveness of "popular" psychotherapies (e.g., EST) may increase or decrease as a result of favorable or unfavorable attention in the media. In these cases, a treatment × time interaction would limit generalization of the results to a particular point in time. Since time constantly varies, replications of the experiment at different points in time provide a basis for the detection of treatments whose effectiveness is limited to a particular historical period.

Increasing external validity

A number of different approaches may be taken to increase the external validity of an investigation. The specific steps to be taken depend, in part, on whether the investigator wishes to generalize *to* a specific subject population, setting, and time, or whether the investigator wishes to generalize *across* populations of subjects, settings, and times. They also depend on a number of practical issues, notably cost; the extent to which boundary conditions have been identified by the theory; and the variability of characteristics of the subjects and settings available to the researcher, relative to those which may ultimately be of interest.

1. In treatment outcome research, the investigator often wishes to generalize the successful effects of a treatment to a specific target population of subjects and settings. In the Schulz (1976) study on perceived control and health, the researchers wished to generalize the effectiveness of their intervention to enhance predicability and control to a population of elderly individuals (subjects) in nursing homes (settings). In such cases, the researcher should sample as representatively as possible from the target population of subjects and settings. Some degree of statistical conclusion and construct validity that could be achieved in more controlled, laboratory settings *may* have to be sacrificed to maximize the degree of external validity, which is critical in this case.

2. Cook and Campbell (1979) outline three methods of sampling in research to maximize external validity. These are presented in their order of preference.

First, when a population can be defined and resources permit, subjects and settings should be selected randomly from the population. However, most often researchers cannot define the population in a precise manner (e.g., what is the population of all psychotherapy settings?) and, in any event, they do not have sufficient resources to select subjects or settings randomly from the population. Further, except in unusual settings (e.g., prisons, state mental hospitals), clients must volunteer for therapeutic treatment before it can be delivered. Nonetheless, it is often possible to follow the lead of epidemiologists and select potential subjects randomly from a local population base: For example, one might select from the population of all psychiatric emergencies seen in the emergency room of a large urban hospital, or all children in a community whose fathers have died during the previous year.

Second, the investigator can follow a strategy of deliberate sampling for heterogeneity. In this method, the investigator identifies easily discernable variables that could potentially interact with the treatment. A nonrepresentative sample is selected on the basis of convenience, but in such a manner to assure that a wide range of variation is present on each of the variables. A study of the effectiveness of a broad-based therapy for depression might make special attempts to sample various ages, genders, and inpatient and outpatient populations. To the extent that the treatment effects hold *despite* the variation in each of the subject (or setting) variables, the external validity of the finding is enhanced.

Third, using the technique of selecting impressionistic modal instances, the investigator may select one or more convenience samples that seem representative of the typical case. A study of psychological counseling methods to prevent suicide attempts might attempt to select from two of the highest risk groups for suicide, highly depressed elderly and adolescent individuals. The impressionistic modal instances technique is most useful when only very limited generalization is required.

3. As discussed above, replications of the investigation can often enhance external validity. To the degree that heterogeneity of subjects, settings, and times is achieved across the various studies and the basic findings still hold, the investigator's ability to generate the findings on each of these dimensions is enhanced.

4. Within each investigation, more molecular analyses that attempt to detect possible interactions of the treatment with subject variables and with setting variables may be conducted. Those variables that appear to limit generalization may be identified as tentative boundary conditions for the effect. However, conducting a large number of these analyses increases the likelihood that some interactions will be detected by chance, so that replication is needed to avoid unnecessarily limiting the generality of a robust treatment effect. Such analyses can also sometimes be conducted using meta-analytic techniques on the entire set of available investigations (Bangert-Drowns, 1986; Glass, McGaw & Smith, 1981; Light & Pillemer, 1984).

Priorities Among Validity Types

In designing research, difficult tradeoffs must sometimes be made between types of validity. As one example, should the researcher rigidly standardize the treatment protocol, use only one therapist, and limit the study to a homogeneous group of subjects, in order to maximize statistical conclusion validity? Or should the researcher allow some variation in the protocol, use a number of different therapists, and sample a more heterogeneous group of subjects to maximize external validity? The priority that the researcher assigns to each type of validity will determine the necessary tradeoffs.

As has been indicated above, basic and applied researchers often have different goals for their research, which leads to some important differences in the priorities that these groups place on the different validity types. Basic researchers, with their traditional emphasis on theory-testing laboratory experiments, would typically rank internal validity highest, followed by construct validity, statistical conclusion validity, and finally external validity (Cook & Campbell, 1979). Considerably more attention is usually given to the construct validity of the independent than of the dependent variable. It is common to find basic researchers expending enormous effort constructing investigations so that the exact meaning of the conceptual independent variable can be pinned down and possible alternative explanations of the results can be ruled out. It is far less common to see similar efforts being directed at establishing the construct validity of the dependent variable, with researchers sometimes relying on one or two simplistically constructed measures to establish their effect (cf. Aronson, Brewer & Carlsmith, 1985; Leventhal & Nerenz, 1985). Thus, the construct validity of the theoretical dependent variable appears to rank below statistical conclusion validity for many basic researchers.

Applied researchers, with their traditional emphasis on developing interventions to relieve specific mental health problems, have a different set of priorities. These researchers would normally rank internal validity highest, followed by external validity, construct validity of the dependent variable, statistical conclusion validity, and construct validity of the independent variable (Cook & Campbell, 1979). With their focus on generalizing to specific clinical problems, applied researchers are also sometimes willing to give up small amounts of internal validity in order to achieve a large gain in external validity. Basic researchers are normally unwilling to make any compromises in their research design that would at all weaken either internal validity or the construct validity of the independent variable.

Conclusion

Basic and applied researchers need to become more aware of the differences in priorities assigned by each group to the different types of validity, and of the likely effects of these differences on the conclusions reached by each type of research. Basic research, particularly when it follows the approach of investigating a question using a single, nonrepresentative population of subjects (e.g., college students) and a single paradigm, is at risk of being of unknown and possibly very limited generality. Such an approach tends to insulate a research area from real-world concerns and lead to the ignoring of relevant applied work. To provide one illustration of this tendency, citation of applied research by basic researchers in the learned helplessness area is rare and limited to a very small number of studies from a large applied research literature. Such insulation can impoverish a theory, since researchers are more likely to fail to identify important boundary conditions that potentially could lead to revision and improvement of the theory. Further, although the theory may continue to generate predictions that are of interest to its advocates (cf. Mook, 1983), the questions addressed may become too narrow to be of interest or useful to other basic and applied psychologists. Indeed, it may be argued that the rapid shifts in the popularity of topic areas and the "crises" recently experienced in several areas of basic psychology (e.g., social, personality) are associated in part with concerns about the generality of findings produced in laboratory experiments conducted with college students (West, Reich, Dantchik & McCall, in press).

Applied research, in contrast, is at risk of giving too little attention to the construct validity of the independent variable, and hence leading in a different way to an impoverished understanding of why the treatment works. Such an understanding is important when attempts are made to strengthen the treatment, to modify the treatment to make it less costly or less lengthy, or to export the treatment to a new location or a new subject population, or when social conditions associated with the treatment change. Such an understanding or "theory" of the treatment makes it easier to evaluate whether the intended changes are being produced by each component of the intervention and, if necessary, to modify these components. Given the many potential reasons for the failure of therapeutic interventions delivered by humans (Rossi, 1979), a good theoretical understanding of the treatment components and the mechanisms through which they operate is essential in the interpretation of the results of treatment outcome research.

Thus, an interplay between basic research and application is clearly needed. Analyses of "best practice" can provide a fertile hunting ground for ideas about the theoretical principles underlying effective treatments (Cialdini, 1980). Other theoretical principles identified in basic research, in areas such as attitude change and group dynamics, may provide other insights that may be utilized in the development of treatment interventions. These principles can then be tested under highly controlled experimental conditions in the laboratory and the research clinic, assuring high levels of internal and construct validity of the findings, but leaving the question of external validity largely unaddressed. At this point, however, the research needs to move to field trials of actual interventions with real clients and patients, in clinics and medical settings, so that both the practical and theoretical limitations of the treatment can be identified. The results of the initial field trials can provide a basis for modifying and improving the intervention which, in turn, can be tested in further field trials. In addition, the results of the field trials can often raise questions that can serve as a focus for research by laboratory researchers attempting to refine their basic theoretical understanding of the phenomena (Saxe & Fine, 1980; West et al., in press). Coming to recognize the complementary strengths and weaknesses of basic and applied research, and the value of increasing the two-way interplay between them, can enhance the contributions of both the basic and applied sides of clinical psychology.

3
Research Methods 2: Experimental and Quasi-experimental Designs for Field Settings

The training of research psychologists has traditionally emphasized factorial experimental designs, implemented in the laboratory, and analyzed using analysis of variance (Aiken, Sechrest, West & Reno, 1987). These tools are unsurpassed for conducting basic research in the laboratory. As we saw in chapter 2, they maximize internal validity and the construct validity of the independent variable. However, these tools are often not sufficient when clinical psychologists wish to conduct tests of interventions in the field so that they can generalize their results to specific clinical populations and settings. Conducting research directly in the clinic, hospital and community settings and with the client or patient populations of interest frequently gives rise to a host of new problems not addressed by the traditional designs and analyses. Random assignment to treatment groups may be prohibited by senior medical or clinical staff members, or may be impossible for ethical or practical reasons. Even when it can be implemented, randomization may not guarantee that all threats to internal validity have been ruled out. Personnel may fail to deliver treatments or deliver additional medical or psychotherapeutic interventions that are not called for in the treatment protocol. And clients and their families may demand additional or alternative treatments.

Upon being faced with these issues, some researchers have retreated to the safety the laboratory where, at the cost of not being able to address questions of external validity, they could continue to conduct highly controlled experiments. Other researchers have remained in the field, where at the cost of not adequately addressing questions of internal or construct validity–they have utilized weak pre-experimental designs[1] or have conducted "throw it against the wall and see what happens" correlational studies. Between these two extremes, an exciting middle ground has developed during the last 20 years as researchers evaluating a broad range of human service delivery programs have sought to develop experimental and quasi-experimental designs that maximize internal validity within the constraints imposed by real world research settings. Four of these designs, potentially applicable in clinical, community, and health settings, are discussed in this chapter.

SOCIAL EXPERIMENTS

In social experiments, the researcher identifies or develops one or more new treatment programs which can be implemented in the actual field setting. For example, the National Institute of Mental Health (see Elkin, Parloff, Hadley & Autrey, 1985; Weissman, 1984) is currently sponsoring trials as it has in the past of the effectiveness of several commonly used therapeutic interventions for depression. In a current trial (Elkin et al., 1985), the effectiveness of a) Beck's cognitive behavior therapy, b) interpersonal psychotherapy, and c) a regime of antidepressant medication (imipramine) are being compared. To provide a baseline against which to evaluate these treatments, a control condition was established in which patients received only placebo medication. The researchers used a design, termed the social experiment (Riecken et al., 1974), in which patients scheduled for treatment were randomly assigned to one of four treatment conditions to assess the relative effectiveness of each of the treatments.

Social experiments enjoy a well-deserved reputation as the method of choice for maintaining high levels of internal validity. Indeed, *successful* randomization immediately renders implausible all of the standard threats to internal validity that were discussed in the previous chapter. However, like

---

[1]Pre-experimental designs (Campbell & Stanley, 1963) include a) the One Shot Case Study, in which a single group of subjects is measured only after treatment; b) the One-Group Pretest–Posttest Design, in which a single group of subjects is measured prior to treatment and then is remeasured following treatment; and c) the Static Group Comparison Design, in which one of two groups of subjects (which have not been randomly assigned to treatment groups) is given treatment, following which both groups are measured. The results of investigations using such d–Posttest Design is open to the threats of history, maturation, testing, instrumentation, and regression discussed in chapter 2 (see Campbell & Stanley, 1963, pp. 6–13).

all methods, the experiment, with its underlying randomization model of control, is based on several assumptions that must be met to insure maximal interpretability of the results. Among these assumptions are that random assignment to treatment groups and the independence of the experimental units is maintained throughout the experiment. Although these assumptions are normally tenable in agricultural research and within the confines of the laboratory experiment in psychology, violations of these assumptions can and often do occur in experiments investigating important social programs in naturalistic contexts. These violations of assumptions give rise to several new possible threats to internal validity, which are not eliminated by randomization and which must be actively considered in designing research (Cook & Campbell, 1979).

New Threats to Internal Validity

Differential mortality

When research is conducted in real world settings and over extended periods of time, some of the subjects will fail to complete the entire experiment. Subjects may die, move to a distant city, become disillusioned with the treatment program, or be unavailable for the final measures for innumerable other reasons. Whenever subjects are lost, questions may be raised about the success of randomization in equating the groups at the *end* of the experiment in the absence of a treatment effect. Most problematic is differential mortality, in which different proportions of subjects are lost, subjects drop out for different reasons, or different types of subjects drop out in the treatment as compared to the control group. If more severely depressed clients drop out of the cognitive behavior therapy group than the untreated placebo control group (and cannot be remeasured), any beneficial effects of the treatment cannot be unambiguously attributed to the program.

Treatment contamination

In designing experiments, differential treatment of the control and treatment groups is always intended. Such intentions are normally easy to realize in laboratory experiments: treatment and control subjects can be isolated, subjects can be sworn to secrecy regarding the treatments they have just experienced, and subjects do not seek out the "best" possible treatment. However, in social experiments involving therapeutic or prevention programs which may be of real value to the participants, several problems can lead to some "treatment" of untreated control groups. Direct contamination may occur, as in a pain control experiment in which participants in the program may discuss information, relaxation techniques, and medications with control subjects. Control subjects may then adopt versions of some of these treatment procedures, or may agitate to have certain medications included as part of their program. Or treatment diffusion may occur, as when rehabilitation therapists begin including all or part of the experimental therapy in their work with control subjects. Yet another possibility is that of compensation, as when nurses believe that the experimental group is receiving superior treatment and they attempt to restore equity by giving the control group participants an unusually high level of positive attention. In each case, serious misestimation of the effects of treatment may result.

Atypical reactions of control subjects

The knowledge of subjects that they are participating in an experiment sometimes leads to atypical reactions. Control subjects who become aware of the "superior" treatment of the experimental subjects will occasionally work unusually hard in an attempt to outperform their "rivals." More typically, control subjects may simply give up when they learn that another group is receiving a "superior" treatment. One common form of this latter problem occurs in delayed treatment designs in which control group participants are promised treatment at a later time. In this case, subjects will often stop searching for alternative sources of therapeutic help or will cease normal preventive activities, secure in the knowledge that they will later receive treatment. However, such atypical behaviors are likely to lead to more negative outcomes for the control group than would be found in the absence of promised treatment.

Differential reporting biases at pre- and post-test

In designs involving self-report measures collected at pre- and post-test, a number of different reporting biases can occur that lead to misestimates of treatment effects (Aiken & West, 1986). Two illustrations are provided below.

1. If potential subjects believe that clients are being recruited for a limited number of desired treatment slots on the basis of their pretest scores, they may bias their answers on the pretest in a direction that they believe will increase their chances of being selected for treatment. At posttest, treatment subjects no longer have a need to bias their responses, whereas control subjects may still hope that they can gain a desired treatment slot. This differential reporting bias will tend to lead to serious misestimates of the treatment effect, often in a direction that will make the treatment appear to be less effective than it actually is (Aiken, 1986).

2. Treatments that attempt to train individuals to recognize problem behaviors, such as couples communication programs, also may have a built-in bias. Once again, treatment and control subjects would not be expected to

evaluate their abilities or their problems differentially at pretest. However, as treatment subjects learn about "ideal" communication patterns between couples and come to analyze their own behaviors, they may come to evaluate their communication more negatively that at pretest. This bias, which has been well documented in the leadership training area (Howard, 1981), would also be expected to lead to underestimates of treatment effects.

Aiken and West (1986) provide a discussion of the full range of reporting biases that may affect the results of social experiments. They also outline a number of approaches that can help to minimize the impact of this problem such as the use of multiple informants, the utilization of other nonreactive measures, the separation of the pretest from the selection into treatment, and the use of "bogus pipeline" procedures that lead subjects to believe their responses are being validated.

Strengthening Internal Validity

In response to these new threats to internal validity and an increase in the difficulty of detecting treatment effects, a number of methodological strategies have evolved over the past 20 years to help strengthen the internal validity of social experiments. Among the more generally applicable strategies are the following.

Pretest measurement

Although not typically emphasized in standard sources on laboratory experimentation (e.g., Aronson et al., 1985), pretest measurement of subjects is absolutely critical in social experiments for two reasons. First, the power of the statistical tests can often be substantially increased if subject variables that are likely to be correlated with the outcome measures can be measured prior to treatment. A test of a psychotherapeutic intervention for reactive depression should include pretest measures of carefully selected variables known to predict this form of depression, such as pretest level of depression, magnitude of recent stressful life events, amount of social support, and alcohol consumption. Variance associated with these variables can then be removed from the outcome measures through analysis of covariance or other statistical adjustment techniques (see Huitema, 1980), thereby raising the power of the tests. Second, if substantial attrition occurs from the experiment, the pretest measures will be useful in investigating the likely effects of subject mortality. Subjects may be compared on pretest measures to identify variables on which treatment and control group members who do not complete the experiment differ (see section on attrition below). If necessary, statistical adjustments can then be made in outcome analyses to explore possible effects of attrition on the results of the experiment.[2]

Treatment monitoring. In laboratory research it is normally assumed that pilot testing and careful training of the experimenter assure that the treatment is delivered correctly. In psychotherapy research in which the treatment under investigation or ancillary treatments are often delivered by clinical psychologists, psychiatrists, and other mental health care professionals, such an assumption cannot be made. Instead, it is necessary to carefully monitor all treatments that are given. This practice helps enable the researcher to identify and document a number of forms of treatment contamination, when they occur, as well as failures to follow the experimental treatment protocol. Corrective feedback may then be provided to personnel, to minimize treatment contamination and maximize compliance with the treatment protocol. Careful documentation of all treatments received can also provide a basis for process analyses (Cook, Leviton & Shadish, 1985; Posavac & Carey, 1985; Sechrest et al., 1979) that probe the relationship between measures of the amount and quality of treatment and outcomes measures.

Isolating control and treatment groups

As in laboratory research, subject contamination and atypical subject reactions can often be minimized if subjects in the treatment and control groups can be isolated from each other. Large scale tests of substance abuse prevention programs (e.g., Flay, 1985; Johnson, 1980) have often assigned whole schools rather than individual classrooms to treatment and control conditions in an attempt to minimize this problem. Temporal isolation may also be used as when all patients admitted for each of a series of nonoverlapping treatment cycles are randomly assigned to treatment or control groups. Although these procedures are normally effective in minimizing problems of internal validity, this may come at some cost in

---

[2]When the number of experimental units (e.g., groups, communities, subjects) is small, a better strategy is to initially rank the subjects from lowest to highest on the pretest measures and then randomly assign one member of each matched pair (triplet, etc.) to the treatment group and one to the control group. As an illustration, imagine conducting a six-city study of the effects of an information campaign to inform the public about the symptoms of depression and the availability of effective treatments. If cities of diverse size have been chosen for study and size of media market is known to be an important variable in the success of media campaigns, a) New York and Los Angeles, b) Dayton and Syracuse, and c) Athens, OH and Springfield, MO could initially form the matched pairs; one member of each pair could be randomly assigned to the treatment group and the other to the control group. Randomization is most effective in equating treatment groups when there are a large number of experimental units or when the units are very homogeneous.

statistical conclusion validity since the larger group (e.g., school, clinic, treatment cycle) may be the appropriate unit of analysis (see Judd & Kenny, 1981a; Kenny & Judd, 1986) and geographically or temporally distant groups may be less similar than more proximal groups, thus leading to greater error variance.

Addressing attrition

Attrition can often be minimized by pre-experimental planning and careful attention to this issue throughout the experiment. Securing the addresses and telephone numbers of subjects, their employer or school, and their close friends and relatives at the beginning of the experiment will greatly assist tracking dropouts. Keeping in touch with both control and treatment subjects and providing incentives for continued participation also helps minimize subject loss. A number of specialized techniques now exist for tracing subjects, such as the periodic mailing of address-verification postcards which result in notification by the U.S. Postal Service if a change of address card has been filed.

Even given the most careful procedures, attrition still typically does occur. Consequently, a multi-step statistical procedure has been developed that can help detect possible biases introduced by differential mortality (Cook & Campbell, 1979).

1. The first step is to test the percentage of subjects who drop out in the treatment and control groups to see if these values differ. If they do, subject mortality may be interpreted as a treatment effect, as when one therapeutic treatment is more attractive or more effective than the other so that the former group of subjects are more likely to remain in treatment. However, the interpretation of all other outcome variables becomes more problematic (e.g., Sackett & Gent, 1979).

2. The second step is to compare subjects on pretest measures. Following a procedure originally developed by Jurs and Glass (1971), subjects' scores on each of the pretest measures are entered into a series of 2×2 analyses of variance. One factor in this analysis is whether the subject was originally assigned to the treatment or control group. The second is whether the subject completed or did not complete the experiment. Of most concern in this analysis are treatment group $\times$ mortality interactions, which suggest that different types of subjects are dropping out of the treatment and control groups.

3. When data are available—for example from exit interviews—on subjects' reasons for dropping out of the experiment, these reasons should be compared for treatment and control subjects. If subjects drop out of the first treatment group because they are disturbed by unpleasant thoughts and

PBC—D

memories that arise during therapy, whereas subjects drop out of the second treatment group because they fail to see a logical rationale for the therapeutic procedures, the interpretation of the outcome of the experiment is likely to be biased.

The use of this multi-step procedure permits the researcher to detect a wide range of types of differential mortality which may occur in social experiments. The researchers may then investigate the influence on their results of statistical adjustments that correct for the detected types of differential mortality (Madow, 1983).

Strengthening Construct Validity

In basic research, investigating the construct validity of the independent variable is easy. Investigators simply develop multiple methods of manipulating the conceptual independent variable, either within a single experiment or across multiple experiments. Then the extent of convergence of the results across the multiple operations of a single construct establishes the degree of construct validity (Aronson, Brewer & Carlsmith, 1985).

However, there are two notable differences between basic research and applied treatment research that preclude the application of this strategy in the latter case. First, although it is not difficult to develop different manipulations of simple constructs, e.g., frustration or effort that would be expected to have an effect for a few minutes in the laboratory, it is far more difficult to develop a variety of *distinctly* different treatments that would be expected to have long-term effects on complex constructs, e.g., the level of social competence displayed by subjects across various settings. Further, although each of the treatments developed to address the same clinical problem would likely be complex and of extended duration, they would each need to be implemented with equal fidelity as a precondition for establishing the degree of convergence of the results. Finally, the number of actual clinical cases available for inclusion in such a study is likely to be low, seriously compromising the ability of a study with several different treatment groups to detect any effects of treatment if they do in fact exist.

Second, even more serious difficulties with the basic research approach to construct validity develop because of the complex nature of applied treatments. In contrast to basic research, where the focus is typically on a single construct, applied treatment programs often represent a package comprised of several constructs. For example, smoking prevention programs attempt to manipulate such diverse components as a) commitment to not smoke, b) exposure to nonsmoking models, c) knowledge of short-term health consequences of smoking, and d) social skills (Flay, 1985). Although there are theoretical and empirical bases for the inclusion of each of these components in the program, the interest of the program developer is in the effectiveness of the overall program. With a program that included eight components, a total of 256 different conditions would be needed to provide a full factorial examination of the contribution of the simple presence or absence of each of the treatment components. Needless to say, the difficulties in mounting so many different treatment variations and in recruiting the necessary number of appropriate subjects preclude such a strategy.

Consequently, applied researchers have developed other methods of providing some examination of the construct validity of their treatments. Although these methods often do not provide the microscopic examination of construct validity associated with basic research, all probe construct validity on the more molar level that is of most interest to applied clinical researchers. Three potential strategies are outlined below. Kazdin (1980, chapter 12) and Shapiro and Morris (1978) present more complete discussions of the first two strategies as well as other traditional design solutions that address nonspecific treatment effects.

Subtraction design
In the design of treatment programs, the basis for the inclusion of certain components may be less certain than for other components. For example, some researchers may believe that the inclusion of a component on the long-term health consequences of smoking would enhance the effectiveness of a smoking prevention program for preteenagers, whereas others may believe that the inclusion of this component could actually weaken the effectiveness of the overall program. In such cases in which the inclusion of one (or more) of the components is a) theoretically equivocable or b) involves substantially higher costs than for the other components in the package, the developers of the treatment may wish to evaluate the contribution of the questioned component to the overall effectiveness of the treatment package. To do this, the *subtraction design* may be used. In this design, subjects are randomly assigned to one of three treatment conditions: no treatment control, full treatment program, and a version of the full treatment in which the treatment component under question has been removed. This design permits the treatment developer to evaluate whether the critical treatment component contributes to the overall effectiveness of the treatment over and above the remainder of the treatment components, or whether it can be removed without reducing or possibly even increasing the effectiveness of the treatment program.

Attention placebo
Most interventions can be conceptualized as having components that are designed to achieve specific therapeutic goals. For example, children are at greatly increased risk of developing depression or conduct problems following

the divorce of their parents (Heatherington, Cox & Cox, 1981). Divorce-education and support groups attempt to prevent the development of these problems in children whose parents have recently divorced by a) providing children with knowledge about divorce that may lead to greater understanding of their parents' divorce, b) helping children develop support groups, and c) helping children express their own feelings about their parents' divorce to reduce anger and hostility. Pedro-Carroll and Cowen (1985) have demonstrated in a randomized experiment that members of such divorce education and support groups display lower symptomatology than an untreated control group.

Even given the observed positive results, the question may be raised as to whether *any* of the theoretically important components of treatment actually produced the observed positive benefits. For example, the divorce education and support groups could be beneficial not because of any of the three listed therapeutic components, but because *any* kind of group interaction with other children (e.g., playground activities) would produce similar positive results. A behavior modification program for hospitalized schizophrenics may be effective not because of the specific treatments that are delivered, but because this is the first attention of any type that these patients have received in several years. In short, any "treatment" delivered by a human service provider *may* lead to nonspecific positive effects that make it difficult to establish that the theoretically important treatment components were in fact responsible for the observed outcome (cf. Frank, 1973; Goldstein, 1962; Kazdin & Wilcoxon, 1976). These nonspecific effects are most problematic in cases where general dependent measures such as mood or global symptomatology are assessed; in such cases theoretically plausible rationales for expecting a relationship between nonspecific aspects of the dependent measure can plausibly be constructed. In cases in which specific, complex, or uncommon behavioral outcomes are predicted, it is often far more difficult to construct a viable theoretical rationale for nonspecific treatment effects. In such cases, additional controls for nonspecific treatment effects are typically not needed.

In cases in which it is necessary to rule out the possibility of nonspecific treatment effects, an additional control group must be added to the design. In such *attention placebo* groups, attempts are made to equate the amount and the nature of the "nontherapeutic" human contact received by the subjects with that received by subjects in the treatment group. Thus, attention placebo control groups for individual treatments require similar individual contact; attention placebo control groups for group-based treatments require similar group-based contact. In the design of an attention placebo group, carefully addressing the question of the *type* of nonspecific "treatment" for which the attention placebo group should control can greatly enhance the investigator's ability to confidently attribute the obtained results to one or more theoretically important components of the treatment.

Process analysis

A final strategy for establishing the construct validity of the independent variable may be undertaken when the treatment can be linked to a theory. The optimal use of this method occurs when the development of the treatment program is theoretically driven. For example, Reynolds, West and Aiken (1988) have recently developed a medical compliance program that is specifically designed to influence each of the components of the health belief model—e.g., perceived susceptibility to the illness; perceived barriers to action (Becker & Maiman, 1975; see Figure 3.1). The processes through which each of the measurable components are expected to influence the other constructs are specified by the theory upon which the treatment is based. However, even when treatments are not based upon explicit theory, "theories of treatment" can sometimes be developed through carefully interviewing the developers and practitioners of the treatment. These interviews focus on developing a model of the therapeutic processes in which treatment components are linked to specific, measurable intervening variables—which, in turn, are linked to the ultimate outcome variables of interest. That is, a model or "theory of treatment" is developed which serves as a basis from which to begin to probe the construct validity of the treatment components.

Once each of the constructs identified by the theory has been assessed and the theoretical causal links between constructs have been specified, a multi-step procedure is followed to establish that the treatment components are producing changes in the mediating variables, which, in turn, produce changes in the ultimate outcome variables of interest (Judd & Kenny, 1981a; 1981b).

1. The treatment group must be shown to have a more positive level than the control group on the ultimate outcome variables of interest. In the medical compliance example above, a test would be performed to determine whether a higher percentage of the subjects complied with recommended medical procedures in the treatment than in the control group.

2. The treatment group must be shown to have a more positive level than the control group on each of the variables hypothesized by the theory to be directly affected by the treatment. In the medical compliance example above, tests would be performed to determine whether the treatment group had higher scores on the measures of perceived severity, perceived consequences, and perceived benefits and lower scores on the measures of perceived barriers to action than the control group.

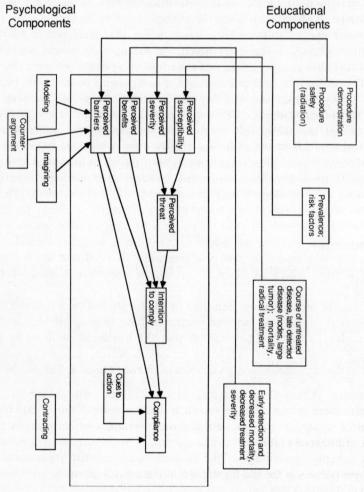

Figure 3.1 Process Analysis: Health Belief Model

Note: Health Belief Model variables (e.g., Perceived Susceptibility, Perceived Threat) are contained within the large box. An arrow between the variables indicates a causal relation predicted by the theory. Indicated outside the large box are the Educational and Psychological Components of a program designed to increase the use of screening mammograms by eligible women. Each program component should theoretically influence a Health Belief Model variable in the manner indicated. Measurement of each of the Health Belief Model variables allows a test of the theory.

3. Finally, using structural equation modeling techniques, two final sets of tests must be performed (Baron & Kenny, 1986; Kenny, 1979; Reis, 1980). First, the structural (path) coefficients must be examined to see if the relationships between constructs predicted by the theory are in fact significant and in the predicted direction. To illustrate, in the medical compliance example the relationship between the magnitude of perceived consequences of the illness and intentions to take preventive action should be positive and differ significantly from 0. Second, the adequacy of the theory in accounting for the obtained data must be examined using an overall test of goodness of fit. If the data fit the model, then the processes proposed by the theory continue to be plausible. In cases in which the theoretical model does not adequately account for the results, places where the model appears to have failed may be identified and the original model may be revised or new alternative models may be developed (Heise, 1975). The revised or alternative models then serve as a new theory of the treatment process which can be investigated in further research.

Conclusion

Conducting social experiments in naturalistic settings gives rise to a number of problems not normally faced by the laboratory experimenter. However, reasonable solutions to these problems exist that help the researcher maintain relatively high levels of internal and statistical conclusion validity. At the same time, conducting research with the clinical population and in the therapeutic setting of ultimate interest leads to an enormous increase in the external validity of the results. Finally, strategies are available that permit some examination of the construct validity of the treatment components. Although quasi-experimental designs exist which permit reasonable causal inferences in some circumstances, the randomized experiment is the design of choice and should be used whenever possible. As Cook and Fitzgerald (1985, p. 320) note:

> *The principal reason for choosing to conduct randomized experiments over other types of research is that they are less imperfect for making causal inference in as far as they usually rule out rival explanations better than other methods. (italics in original)*

A second important reason for conducting randomized experiments also exists. As will be seen as we examine the major quasi-experimental alternatives to the social experiment, the randomized experiment is also statistically the most powerful design for detecting treatment effects when in fact they do exist. This is often a very important consideration given the relatively small sample sizes that frequently characterize clinical prevention and treatment outcome research.

REGRESSION DISCONTINUITY DESIGN

Researchers often confront situations in which they cannot conduct social experiments. One common case in which this occurs is when legal or administrative prohibitions exist against randomization. The rationale for this position is that treatment should be given on the basis of need or merit and should not be given on a chance basis. According to this position, denying the best possible treatment to especially needy or meritorious individuals is unethical. Although strong logical (Cook & Campbell, 1979; Imber et al., 1986; Tukey, 1977) and empirical (Boruch, 1975; Gilbert, McPeek & Mosteller, 1977) arguments can and often should be raised against this position[3], the rarely utilized regression discontinuity design exists as an important fall back option if persuasive arguments for experimentation fail. The primary issue that the researcher must address is whether a sufficient sample size exists to assure that this design has adequate power to detect treatment effects if, in fact, they do exist.

The regression discontinuity design takes seriously administrative pronouncements about the necessity of assigning subjects to treatment on the basis of need or merit. In this design, subjects are assigned to treatment specifically on the basis of a *quantitative* measure of need or merit. Subjects who do not meet the quantitative criterion are typically assigned to the no treatment control condition. For example, clients could be assigned to cognitive behavior therapy for depression on the basis of having a Beck Depression Inventory score of 16. College students are assigned to receive special commendation (Dean's List) on the basis of achieving at least a 3.5 grade point average during the previous semester (Seaver & Quarton, 1976). Prisoners in California who worked a minimum of 652 hours during the year before their release were assigned to receive unemployment payments for up to 6 months following their release from prison (Berk & Rauma, 1983). In each case, subjects are assigned to treatment conditions using a

---

[3]For example, Gilbert et al. (1977) show that in controlled clinical trials of promising new surgical and anesthetic treatments, the new treatment was superior to the standard treatment in 31 percent of the cases, there was no difference between the two treatments in 36 percent of the cases, and the standard treatment was superior to the new treatment in 22 percent of the cases. And, as Gilbert et al. note, "Since innovations brought to the stage of randomized trials are usually expected by the innovators to be sure winners, we ee that in the surgery and anesthesia area the evidence is strong that the value of the innovation needs empirical checking" (p.685) Another empirical example is described by Miao (1977), who documents how a medical treatment for ulcers known as gastric freezing was widely adopted on the basis of the results of case studies and nonequivalent control group designs that did not adequately address standard threats to internal validity. Later randomized clinical trials showed that the procedure was a totally ineffective treatment, which—like other major medical procedures—involved some risk of negative side effects to patients.

known rule based *solely* on their pretest scores. Measures taken following treatment constitute the dependent variables.

Let us consider the depression treatment example in more detail to illustrate this design. Suppose several clinics test 200 clients for possible inclusion in a cognitive therapy program for depressives. The clinics make an a priori decision to assign patients to the treatment on the basis of need, which is defined as a Beck Depression Inventory (BDI) score of at least 16[4]. All 110 clients with scores of 16 or higher are assigned to the cognitive therapy program; the remaining 90 patients are not given any treatment, since they are classified as only being mildly depressed and treatment slots are limited. Beck Depression Inventory scores are obtained from all 200 clients (both treatment and control) six months later after the planned treatment program is completed. Data from this hypothetical investigation are plotted in Figure 3.2.

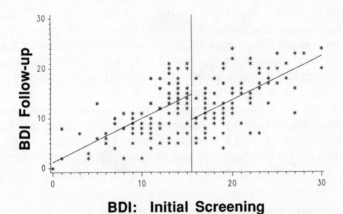

BDI: Initial Screening

Figure 3.2 Illustration of regression discontinuity design:
Evaluation of a cognitive therapy program

Note: Clients having scores of 16 or greater on the Beck Depression Inventory at initial screening receive cognitive therapy. Clients with scores below 16 receive no treatment. The points plotted indicate each client's score at initial screening and three month follow-up.

[4]The Beck Depression Inventory is a well known measure of depression that is used here for illustrative purposes. Other measures or even weighted combinations of inventories and clinical ratings might serve as preferred quantitative indices, given criticisms of the BDI in the literature (e.g., Hesselbrock, Hesselbrock, Tennen, Meyer & Workman, 1983). The critical point in the regression discontinuity design is that assignment to treatment and control groups be made on the basis of a quantitative measure. Even if the quantitative measure used for assignment is totally unreliable, the results are still interpretable assuming that the outcome measure is reliable. In this case, the design would simply approximate a randomized experiment.

Figure 3.2 indicates that there is a moderate correlation between the Beck Depression Inventory scores taken at the initial screening and the three month followup. However, in these hypothetical results a sizable discontinuity occurs at the cutting point for treatment assignment. Approximately a 7 point drop in the score on the Beck Depression measure at followup occurs at the point of the initial score of 16, corresponding to assignment to cognitive behavior therapy. This discontinuity in the regression line is potentially interpretable as a treatment effect in this design.

Statistically, this effect would be evaluated through tests of the terms in the following regression equation:

$$Y = b_0 + b_1X + b_2Z + e \qquad \text{(Equation 1)}$$

In this equation, Y is the outcome variable, the score on the BDI at followup, and X is the pretest variable, the BDI score at the initial screening, Z is a dummy variable which has a value of 0 if no cognitive therapy is received and 1 if cognitive therapy is received. Each of the b's is a coefficient estimated by regression programs available in any of the standard statistical packages. Of most importance, the test of b_2 reveals whether the cognitive therapy program had a significant effect on the BDI score at followup. The coefficients b_0 and b_1 provide estimates of the intercept and slope, respectively, of the regression line.[5] Readers desiring a more detailed presentation of the statistical procedures should consult Cohen and Cohen (1983) or Pedhazur (1982) for a general discussion of regression analysis and Judd and Kenny (1981a, chapter 5) and Trochim (1984) for more thorough discussions of the analysis of the regression discontinuity design.

Two Important Statistical Assumptions

Underlying the use of the regression discontinuity design are two important statistical assumptions (Rubin, 1977; Trochim, 1984). First is that the functional form of the relationship between the pretest and outcome variables is correctly specified. Second is that parallel regression lines may be fit to both the treatment and no treatment groups (i.e., no treatment × pretest interaction). Both assumptions should always be carefully examined and, if necessary, the regression model should be respecified.

---

[5]Normally, in the analysis of the regression discontinuity design, the value of X is rescaled so that it has a value of 0 at the cutpoint. In this case, b_0 is the estimate of the value of the outcome variable at the cutpoint in the absence of treatment rather than an arbitrary value. Similar rescaling procedures are utilized in time series analysis for the same reason.

Functional form

Normally, in psychology, researchers do not have a strong a priori theoretical or empirical basis for specifying the exact form of the relationship between two variables. Consequently, researchers typically follow the dictates of simplicity and assume that a linear model provides an adequate description of the functional form of the relationship between the two variables. Unfortunately, it is less typical for researchers to then examine the adequacy of the fit between the assumed linear model and the actual data. In the analysis of the regression discontinuity design, this often neglected step in statistical analysis is critical in order to avoid serious misestimation of treatment effects and to minimize some threats to validity.

Two simple probes of the functional form of the relationship are normally undertaken. First, a scatter plot of the relationship between the pretest and the outcome measure is carefully inspected for any systematic pattern of outliers that might indicate that the form of the relationship was misspecified. Of most importance is any systematic pattern of deviation of data points from the regression line in the vicinity of the cutpoint. Such a pattern would suggest that the treatment effect had been incorrectly estimated. Second, higher degree polynomial terms (e.g., X^2) can be added to the regression equation and tested for significance. Only those terms that attain statistical significance would then be retained in the final model. Both probes of functional form are most effective with large samples. Cohen and Cohen (1983), Daniel and Wood (1980), and Mosteller and Tukey (1977) discuss strategies for probing functional form and methods of transforming variables to achieve linear form in greater detail.

Parallel regression lines

Researchers normally make the initial assumption that the regression lines will be parallel in the no-treatment and treatment groups. Once again, this assumption should be checked through the careful examination of scatterplots of the relationship between the pretest and outcome measures. Researchers may also test this assumption by including a treatment × pretest measure interaction variable in the regression equation. In the depression example discussed above, an XZ term could be added to the regression equation, to probe possible changes in the slope of the regression lines in the two treatment conditions. These checks are most effective in detecting deviations from parallel slopes when large sample sizes are used and the cutpoint is not too extreme.

When significant changes in slope are detected, researchers need to be cautious in their interpretation of the results. Indeed, in the absence of a discontinuity between the two regression lines (a treatment main effect), differences in slope are not usually interpretable as an effect of treatment. In such cases, the most parsimonious interpretation is typically that the relationship between the pretest and outcome measures is nonlinear when their full range of variation is considered. In cases where there is a substantial discontunuity at the cutpoint where the treatment is implemented, however, such an alternative interpretation becomes considerably less plausible.

Validity Issues

Internal validity. Like the randomized experiment, the regression discontinuity design utilizes a known rule for assigning subjects to treatment conditions. Thus, this design is very strong in terms of ruling out the standard threats to internal validity presented in chapter 2. The primary threat to be considered in this design is that of a selection × maturation interaction.[6]

In this threat, subjects above the cut point would be maturing at a faster (or slower) rate than subjects below the cut point. For example, students who are placed on the Dean's List may be growing faster academically than students with lower GPAs so that they would have shown the same subsequent gains in their GPAs whether or not they were given the special recognition associated with this honor. The existence of a strong treatment effect combined with careful examination of the statistical assumptions of the design helps make this threat less plausible. More definitive evidence regarding this threat can be provided by a replication of the study using a different set of cutpoints (e.g., subjects are assigned to cognitive behavior therapy if they have an initial BDI score of at least 20 rather than 16).

Statistical conclusion validity. The regression discontinuity design will typically be of substantially lower power than a randomized experiment. The degree to which power is reduced depends on the pretest–posttest correlation and the extremity of the cut points. The higher the pretest–posttest correlation, the lower the ability of the design to detect actual treatment effects. The more extreme the cut points and hence the less equal the size of the treatment and control groups, the lower the power of the test.

Little work to date has directly investigated the ability of the regression discontinuity design to detect treatment effects when in fact they do exist. Goldberger (1972) compared the regression discontinuity design with the

---

[6]Attrition can also be a major problem in regression discontinuity designs, if subjects opt out of either the treatment or control groups. For example, Meier (1972) reports that the Salk polio vaccine was tested in some states using a randomized experimental design and in other states using a simple version of the regression discontinuity design. Gilbert, Light and Mosteller (1975) document how refusals receive treatment in the vaccination group in the regression discontinuity design led to a large bias in the estimates of the effectiveness of the vaccine.

randomized experiment under conditions in which a) the exact functional form of the relationship between the pretest and posttest is known and b) both pretest and posttest are bivariate normal. He found that 2.75 times as many subjects would be required using the regression discontinuity design to achieve the same level of statistical power as in the randomized experiment.

Following the procedures outlined by Cohen (1977), we can illustrate the sample sizes needed to reject the null hypothesis with 0.80 probability, given true differences of varying known size between the treatment and control groups. First, as a baseline, if we assume there is no pretest (or alternatively that the pretest is uncorrelated with the dependent variable) and there are an equal number of subjects in the treatment and control groups, 52 subjects would be needed to detect a large effect, 128 subjects would be needed to detect a moderate effect, and 786 subjects would be needed to detect a small effect in a randomized social experiment. Recall that Cohen defined large, moderate, and small effects as corresponding to a difference between the treatment and control means of 0.8, 0.5, and 0.2 standard deviations, respectively. If a pretest measure with a 0.5 correlation with the dependent variable is included in the social experiment, the number of subjects needed to detect a large, moderate and small effect size is reduced to 19, 61, and 584, respectively. Finally, applying the 2.75 multiplier from Goldberger (1972) to the second example, 40, 153, and 1460 subjects would be needed to detect large, moderate, and small effects, respectively, with 0.8 power in the regression discontinuity design.

The lessons of this illustration are clear: Researchers must plan large N studies using the regression discontinuity design to allow for reasonable tests of the statistical assumptions underlying the analysis and to provide a fair test of the effectiveness of the treatments. Further, it will typically be difficult to demonstrate small effects with any degree of certainty using this design unless large sample sizes are employed. Finally, researchers should attempt to include other covariates that ideally correlate highly with the outcome variable, but minimally with the premeasure (assignment variable) in the analysis to further enhance the ability of the design to detect treatment effects when in fact they do exist.[7]

---

[7]Regression discontinuity designs have been strongly recommended as a method of evaluating Title I compensatory education programs. The Users Guide for Title I Evaluation recommends that a minimum of 60 subjects be available before implementing a regression discontinuity design. Part of the basis for this recommendation was the understanding that several different schools would be evaluating the same program, so that comparisons of the results would be possible across replications. In clinical and prevention outcome studies, replication cannot be routinely expected, and therefore a larger minimum number of subjects would be necessary.

External validity

Regression discontinuity designs are high in external validity, in the sense that they are almost always utilized with the populations and in the settings of ultimate interest. However, the confounding of the pretest score and the rule for assigning subjects to treatments in this design can limit generalization. No subject having an initial BDI score of less than 16 was assigned to treatment, limiting generalization of the positive effects of treatment to subjects having initial scores around this value. However, note that practitioners would be primarily interested in knowing the effects of the treatment on patients with elevated BDI scores, so that this limitation is less likely to be a serious practical concern.

Fuzzy Assignment Rules

A major issue that may arise in the use of regression discontinuity design is that individuals having scores just below the cutpoints may be assigned by practitioners to treatment. For example, some clients having initial BDI scores of only 14 or 15 may be assigned to the cognitive therapy program, because the clinician believes either that they will benefit especially from this treatment or that these clients are particularly in need of treatment. Such procedures violate the fundamental assumption upon which the regression discontinuity design is based, namely that the premeasure is the sole basis upon which subjects are assigned to treatment and control groups.

To minimize this problem, assignment to treatment groups should be carefully monitored by the researchers; subjects who are incorrectly assigned should typically be dropped from the analysis. Examination of the frequency distribution of initial scores can also provide a check on whether subjects are being given systematically high (or low) scores near the cut point so that they receive the more desirable treatment. Delaying announcement of the cut points until after the initial testing can also help prevent this problem from developing. Finally, when fuzzy assignment to treatment does occur, alternative econometric approaches to the analysis of the design are available, with statistical adjustments that attempt to correct for this problem (Trochim, 1984).

Note that this problem of "cheating" in assignment of subjects to treatment groups is not unique to the regression discontinuity design. Similar care must be exercised in social experiments, to make sure that treatment or administrative personnel do not tamper with the random assignment of subjects to treatment groups or that random assignment does not break down (See Boruch, McSweeny & Soderstrom, 1978; Connor, 1977). Indeed, careful monitoring and checking of the assigment of subjects to treatments is one of the more important aspects of field research.

Conclusion

The regression discontinuity design provides an excellent approach when subjects are assigned to conditions on the basis of a quantitative measure of need or merit. It is very high in internal validity, has reasonable external validity for many applications, but is normally considerably lower in power than the randomized experiment. The above discussion provides only an introduction to the basic design. More complex versions with multiple pretest measures, additional covariates, multiple treatment groups, multiple outcome measures, and nonidentical pretest and outcome measures can also be implemented (see Trochim, 1984; Judd & Kenny, 1981a).

INTERRUPTED TIME SERIES

Interrupted time series designs related to clinical treatment programs can arise in two ways. The first application of this design occurs when an overall change in policy related to clinical treatment is introduced at a specific point in time. For example, a hospital may introduce presurgical psychological counseling for all major surgery patients. Or large insurance carriers may substantially reduce the number of therapy sessions for which they will reimburse the client, thereby decreasing the average length of therapy. In such cases, assignment to treatment conditions (e.g., no presurgical counseling vs. presurgical counseling; extended vs. brief therapy) is based on the time at which the client enters treatment. If relevant outcome measures have been collected, researchers may employ an interrupted time series design to investigate the effects of such changes in policy.

The second and more traditional application of this design in clinical treatment research is in single-subject research. In the simplest form of this application, repeated behavioral observations are made on a subject throughout the investigation, typically on a daily basis. The subject is initially observed under normal (no treatment) conditions to establish a baseline level of the behavior. After a specified number of observations have been collected, the experimenter implements the treatment, and periodic observations then continue for an extended period of time after the treatment is introduced. Once again, treatment in this design has been assigned on the basis of time (actually, number of observations) and possible treatment effects may be inferred if a change in the level of the observed behavior has occurred between the baseline and treatment periods.

Like the regression discontinuity design, the interrupted time series design provides a strong quasi-experimental alternative when randomized experiments are infeasible, particularly if additional design features can be added to help rule out threats to internal validity. Distinct literatures associated with the two applications of time series designs have developed. Since the single-subject time series literature is likely to be more familiar to most clinical psychologists (e.g., Barlow & Hersen, 1984; Kazdin, 1982; Kratochwill, 1978), we will focus on time series designs oriented toward changes in policy. However, many of the principles and analyses that we will discuss apply equally well to both of the applications of this design (cf. Horne, Yang & Ware, 1982; Kazdin, 1984).

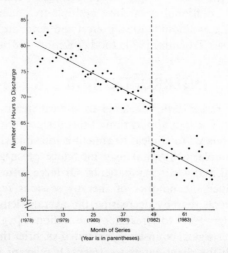

Figure 3.3 Illustration of an interrupted time series design:
Evaluation of a pre-surgical psychological counseling program. From P. Karoly, *Measurement strategies in health psychology.* Copyright © 1985 John Wiley & Sons, Inc. Reprinted by permission of John Wiley & Sons Inc.

Figure 3.3 illustrates the basic interrupted time series design, using the hypothetical example of an evaluation of a presurgical psychological counseling program. Imagine that complete data for the years 1978–1983 are available from a large university hospital on the number of hours between the completion of major surgery and discharge from the hospital. These data are aggregated and are presented as mean values for each month. At the beginning of January 1982, this hospital introduced a treatment program in which trained nurses provided presurgical psychological counseling for all major surgery patients. As can be detected in the data presented in Figure 3.3, the time to discharge has shown a slow decline over the years and there is a tendency for the time to discharge to be higher during the summer months. Of most importance, following the introduction of the psychological counseling program (January, 1982), there is approximately an 8-hour decrease in the time to discharge for major surgery patients. Given appropriate statistical analyses and attention to threats to internal validity, this result is potentially interpretable as an effect of the treatment program.

The reader may have detected a strong similarity between the interrupted time series design and the regression discontinuity design presented in the previous section. Note, however, there is one major difference: In the interrupted time series analysis design, subjects are assigned to treatment groups on the basis of the time at which they enter treatment rather than on the basis of their pretest scores. As will be seen, this change leads to a number of complications in statistical analysis and to a different set of potential threats to internal validity.

Statistical Analyses: A Brief Overview

At first glance, the analysis of an interrupted time series would seem to parallel exactly the analysis in the regression discontinuity design. To test the effect of the psychological counseling program on time to discharge from the hospital, the following regression equation would be used:

$$Y = b_0 + b_1 T + b_2 Z + e \qquad \text{(Equation 2)}$$

In this equation, Y is the average time from the completion of surgery to discharge, T is the month of the series in which January, 1978 represents month 1 and December, 1983 represents month 72, and Z is a dummy variable that has a value of 0 prior to implementation and 1 following implementation of the psychological counseling program. Once again, the bs are regression coefficients, with b_0 estimating the intercept of the regression line, b_1 estimating the slope of the regression line, and b_2 estimating the treatment effect. This equation duplicates equation 1 (p. 50) for the regression discontinuity design, except that month of the series (T) has been substituted for pretest score (X). This latter change introduces a major complication: Whenever measurements are made over time, there is a strong possibility of serial dependency in the data (Kenny & Judd, 1986). Data from adjacent months may be more similar than data from months that are more removed in time; similarly, data collected during the first summer may be more highly related to data collected during other summers than to data collected during the other seasons. In such cases, the normal assumption of uncorrelated error terms in multiple regression is violated, resulting in potential misestimation of treatment effect (Hibbs, 1974).

The problem of time series analysis is, first, to identify the nature of the serial dependency, and then to transform the data to remove the dependency, so that unbiased tests of treatment effects can be performed. This is accomplished by first identifying any trends or seasonal patterns in the data and removing them. In our example, there is a linear decrease in the time to discharge over the period of the study and a pattern in which values are high during the summer months. The data must be transformed to remove such trend and seasonal components before the analysis can proceed. Then the correlation between adjacent data points (autocorrelation) is examined to identify the nature of the remaining serial dependency. When the type of the remaining serial dependency has been identified, a transformation can be applied that will remove this problem from the data. Since the error terms in the data will now be uncorrelated, the effects of treatment can at last be correctly estimated.

The primary task in the statistical analysis of time series data is to identify the nature of the serial dependency. Several techniques that rely heavily on graphical displays of specialized statistics have been developed to assist the analyst in this task. Good introductions to two of the more commonly used techniques are provided by McCleary and Hay (1980) for the Box-Jenkins ARIMA approach, Gottman (1981) for spectral analysis, and Hepworth, West and Woodfield (1987) for a comparative treatment.

Threats to Internal Validity

The strength of the basic time series design lies in its ability to rule out most threats associated with maturation, regression, and with influences of a cyclical nature. Typically more problematic are the three threats to internal validity illustrated below:

History. New surgical or anesthetic techniques may also be implemented in the hospital, or insurance carriers may decrease the amount of reimbursement for postsurgical hospital stays, thus possibly accounting for the decrease in recovery time.

Selection. The patient population of the hospital may shift, so that a larger proportion of younger and healthier patients or less anxious patients are being served. These patients would be expected to recover more quickly from surgery.

Instrumentation. The hospital may change its record-keeping procedures, reclassifying the surgical procedures that are considered to be "major." Less severe cases who could be expected to recover more quickly from surgery would now be included in the data.

In evaluating the plausibility of each of these threats, an important point must be kept in mind: Only changes that occur at about the same point in time as the implementation of the treatment can lead to effects that could be spuriously attributed to the treatment. If a change in anesthetic techniques occurred during month 6 of the series, it is extremely unlikely that this change would cause an abrupt decrease in postsurgical hospital stays beginning in month 49 of the series when presurgical psychological counseling was implemented. Therefore, researchers using simple time series designs should focus on identifying other changes that coincide with treatment implementation, evaluating the plausibility with which such changes may have caused the observed outcome.

Design Improvements: Strengthening Internal Validity

Certain threats to internal validity can often be ruled out by the addition of one or more of the following design features to the simple time series design.

No treatment control series

Comparable time series data for the same period may be available from another unit that did not implement the treatment. Data on the length of hospital stays following major surgery may be available from another university hospital that did not implement a presurgical counseling program during the 1978–1983 period. If the analysis of the control series did not reveal a comparable decrease in postsurgical hospital stays in early 1981, the observed decrease in the treatment series could be more confidently attributed to the psychological counseling program. The addition of the control series rules out the threat of history, through the threat of selection × history (local history) may still be problematic, depending on the degree of comparability of the two hospitals.

Other control series

Sometimes other dependent measures or other breakdowns of the data may be identified which help serve as a control for the interrupted series. Towards this end, the present data could be broken down into scheduled surgery cases who receive psychological counseling and emergency cases who are unconscious and hence cannot receive counseling prior to surgery. Demonstrating that the effects differed in the control and treatment series at the point of intervention would further strengthen the internal validity of the design.

Switching replications

Perhaps the most elegant design addition is to identify a comparable series in which the same treatment is implemented at a different point in time. Cook (1983) investigated the effects of price reductions on participation rates in school lunch programs in New York State. In his examination of the monthly data for a multi-year period, he discovered that some schools lowered their prices during one month whereas other schools lowered their prices during another month of the same school year. Similar increases in participation rates occurred at the point of the implementation of price reductions in each set of schools. Based on the strong time series design and clearcut results, Cook was able to attribute the observed effects in participation rates to the treatment with a degree of confidence approaching that obtained through the use of a randomized experiment.

Formal and Informal Publicity

Special problems can arise in time series designs because of the effects of both formal and informal, word of mouth publicity regarding the treatment program. Publication of a laudatory newspaper article on the psychological counseling program may lead to a marked shift in the patient population being served. Such problems are particularly likely to be troublesome when the program offered is very attractive and few restrictions are placed on program participation. Thus, a private hospital that introduced a popular new psychological counseling program would very likely experience an influx of new patients; however, a school district that lowered the price of its lunches would be unlikely to experience an inmigration of new students. This special problem of publicity-induced selection will often be a potential threat in clinical research, since clients are normally free to select among treatment programs. This means that careful monitoring of program-related publicity, new clients' reasons for selecting the program, and client characteristics likely to be related to outcome measures will be necessary to evaluate the plausibility of this threat. In some cases, statistical adjustments may also be undertaken to probe the effects of bias introduced by publicity-induced selection.

Publicity may also impact the effectiveness of some programs in a second way. With certain programs, subjects' perceptions of the policy may be more important than the actual policy in determining the behavioral outcome. Publicity about the future plans of insurance carriers to increase benefits for outpatient psychotherapy clients can lead to an increase in clients seeking treatment prior to implementation of the new policy. Later, as publicity about the change in benefits decreases over time, the number of clients seeking care may decrease as people's awareness of the available benefits diminishes. In such cases, monitoring program publicity and periodically surveying the population's awareness of the program can be useful in interpreting program effects (Hepworth & West, 1987; Legge & Webb, 1982).

Statistical Conclusion Validity

Problems of statistical conclusion validity in time series analysis arise primarily from two sources. First is the issue of whether the underlying model of serial dependency has been correctly identified. Correct identification of the model is facilitated by a) the use of multiple diagnostic tools that assist in the identification of the nature of the serial dependency and b) checking the transformed data to be sure this problem has been eliminated (Hepworth et al., 1987). If more than one acceptable model of serial dependency can be identified, tests of the intervention effects should be performed with each model to provide assurance that significant treatment effects are not dependent on the fortuitous selection of a specific model of serial dependency. The degree of success of the various techniques for diagnosing the underlying model is also dependent on the length of the series. Most authors (e.g., Glass, Willson & Gottman, 1975) recommend a minimum of 50 observations to provide stable estimates of the parameter values in models of serial dependency.

A second issue in time series analysis is power. Researchers are often asked to analyze time series data shortly after a treatment has been implemented. As in the regression discontinuity design, the ability of the analysis to detect treatment effects is greatest when the intervention occurs in the middle rather than at the end of the series. The power of time series designs may sometimes be increased, if multiple, highly comparable series are available, by adjusting each point in the intervention series by the corresponding point in the control series (e.g., Cook, 1983).

Interpretation of Treatment Effects

Time series analyses normally attempt to detect changes in the level of the series and in the slope of the series following each intervention. Indeed, the effects of several interventions may be examined in the same extended series if they are sufficiently separated in time. Both changes in level and changes in slope are potentially interpretable as treatment effects if they occur immediately following the intervention point. Changes that occur at a later point in the series are more equivocal, unless strong a priori theoretical or empirical arguments can be made for a delayed treatment effect. A decrease in birth rates beginning 9 months following the implementation of a large-scale family planning program could justifiably be interpreted as a treatment effect, if the normal threats to internal validity in time series designs could be ruled out. In contrast, a similar interpretation following an abrupt decrease in family arguments 9 months after the implementation of a family counseling program would be equivocal in light of present theory. The use of empirical evidence concerning the actual course of implementation of the treatment program can also lead to more precise models for testing the effects of the treatment. A presurgical psychological counseling program would more likely be phased in over a period of months, as the treatment staff is training in psychological counseling techniques, rather than abruptly instituted as was implied in the example. Correct specification of treatment implementation can substantially increase the power of time series analysis to detect treatment effects.

Conclusion

Time series designs present an excellent alternative to randomized experiments when new programs are implemented. The basic time series design can often achieve reasonable levels of internal validity; the inclusion of additional design features further strengthens the internal validity of the design. The major practical difficulty with the design is that either high-quality archival data or data collected by the experimenter must be available for a large number of time periods, both pre- and post-intervention, to provide optimal estimates of treatment effects. This difficulty can often be overcome in health care settings, because patient health status must be frequently or continuously monitored and high-quality records may already exist. In mental health settings it may be possible to collect periodic ratings from multiple sources including therapists, clients, and other knowledgeable informants such as family members. Periodic behavioral observations may also be collected.

Although the discussion has focused on the application of the design to the detection of the effects of changes in policy and the analysis of aggregate data, these same basic techniques are also useful in the evaluation of experimental treatments delivered to single subjects (Barlow & Hersen, 1984; Kazdin, 1982; Kratochwill, 1978). Indeed, single subject time-series designs have important advantages over policy-oriented time series designs, because of the greater control that can be exerted over the situation by the experimenter. In terms of internal validity, selection is ruled out since the same subject is measured at each time point, and many forms of the instrumentation threat are less plausible since changes in record-keeping practices are less likely to occur during the investigation. The experimenter can also introduce and remove the treatment at different points in time for different subjects, further strengthening the design by ruling out history threats. Behavioral researchers have recognized the power of this class of designs and have utilized them frequently; other treatment researchers have less frequently used these designs, possibly because of the measurement burden that is involved. At the same time, behavioral researchers have rarely utilized nonbehavioral sources of data, such as the reports of multiple informants including the client. Nor have they always attended to the remaining problems of internal validity that may not always be ruled out by these designs and the problems of statistical analysis that stem from serial dependency in the data. Finally, the problems of construct validity that arise when treatments are tailored to individual subjects and problems of external validity associated with the nonrandom sampling of a very small number of subjects have been rarely addressed in this literature.

Thus, time series designs which investigate changes in policy having treatment-related implications represent an important and overlooked source of information about the effectiveness of clinical treatments. In addition, the literature from this first application of time series designs holds a number of valuable insights, which may be useful in further strengthening the ability of single-subject applications to address a wide range of validity concerns. Finally, expansion of the types of measures   collected and the types of treatment investigated will encourage broader use of this important design by nonbehavioral researchers.

NONEQUIVALENT CONTROL GROUP DESIGN

The most intuitively obvious—and hence most utilized—alternative to the randomized experiment is the nonequivalent control group design. Here, a group is identified or recruited and is given a treatment. A school system institutes a divorce information and support group for children whose parents have recently divorced. A medical center clinic provides cognitive therapy and antidepressant medication for all of its clients who suffer from depression. A hospital solicits presurgical patients to participate in a psychological counseling program. Then an appropriate control group, which ideally is similar to the treatment group, is identified or constructed. Another school system that does not have a divorce education and support group is found; another clinic, whose depressed patients receive only antidepressant medication is located; or presurgical patients who choose not to have counseling, or who are in another hospital without access to a counseling program, are identified. Measures of important outcome-related variables are taken prior to and following treatment so that the degree of improvement in the treatment group may be easily compared with the degree of improvement in the control group. Or so it seems. Unfortunately, despite their apparent simplicity and ease of implementation, nonequivalent control group designs raise a variety of difficult statistical and interpretational issues. Indeed, many of the major methodological battles in the applied literature over the past several years have been fought over the "true" effectiveness of treatments evaluated using just this type of design, as in the debate over Head Start (see Barnow, 1973; Bentler & Woodward, 1978), Cicarelli et al., 1969; Magidson, 1977.

At issue in the design are the often forgotten assumptions that the treatment and control groups must a) be equivalent in terms of important background characteristics and b) be growing at the same rate prior to treatment. Although these assumptions will frequently be plausible when subjects have been randomly assigned to treatment groups, this is not the case in the nonequivalent control group design. Instead, subjects are assigned to treatment and control groups on the basis of rules that are unknown to the researcher and often can only be guessed at. Ruling out the possibility that the groups may differ in these important ways prior to treatment is the central task faced by the researcher who employs this design. And even given extraordinary efforts, the researcher may in some cases still be left with considerable uncertainty as to whether the treatment is effective or not.

General Strategies for Statistically Equating Groups

Since subjects are not assigned to treatment groups in the nonequivalent control group according to any known rule, researchers must use whatever information and intuition that they have available in their attempts to statistically equate the groups. Two different general strategies may be used in this quest (Reichardt, Minton & Schellenger, 1986).

Causal model of the posttest. Researchers may attempt to identify variables related to the primary outcome variables and measure them during the pretest. If posttreatment level of depression were the primary dependent variable, researchers following the first strategy would measure variables such as alcohol intake, magnitude of recent stressful events, social support, and level of depression prior to treatment.

Causal model of the pretest. Alternatively, researchers may attempt to model the factors that determine treatment group assignment. Following this strategy, researchers would identify and measure factors that were likely to be associated with selection of the control clinic or treatment clinic. Such factors might include income, area of residence, and patient perceptions of the quality of psychotherapy at each clinic.

Both strategies will lead to accurate estimates of treatment effects when the stringent assumptions of the adjustment procedure are met. These include identification of all important variables; perfect reliability of each of the pretest measures; correct specification of the functional form of the relationship between pretest and outcome measures; and no group × pretest interactions. The plausibility of the last three assumptions can be probed through examination of reliability estimates for the pretest measures and through plots depicting the relationship between pretest and outcome measures. The detection of omitted variables depends primarily on knowledge of the rules or process(es) through which subjects were assigned to treatment and control groups.[8] In the usual case where the assignment rule

---

[8]When pretest measurements are taken on two or more occasions, an econometric procedure developed by Dwyer (1984) may be used; the technique estimates the effects of the omitted variables, provided that strong statistical assumptions can be met.

is unknown, all methods of estimating treatment effects are associated with a high degree of uncertainty. Normally, uncertainty will be lowest when operationally identical pretests and outcome measures are employed, time intervals are relatively short, and the measures are assessing relatively stable dispositions or behaviors (Reichardt et al., 1986).

Traditional Statistical Adjustment Procedures

When identical pretest and outcome measures are available, the first three statistical analyses described below are normally performed. Each of these analyses has a somewhat different bias. The hope is that the results of the three analyses will converge, giving the researcher a high degree of confidence, though not certainty (Bryk & Weisberg, 1977), that the treatment effect has been correctly estimated.

Analysis of covariance
Simple analysis of covariance adjusts the estimate of the treatment effect for the *measured* pretest scores. No adjustment, of course, is made for variables that are not included in the analysis. Pretest scores will almost certainly be less than perfectly reliable, resulting in some bias in the estimate of the treatment effect. When one covariate is used, too little adjustment is made for initial differences between the treatment groups; with multiple covariates, underadjustment is also the most likely outcome, although overadjustment may also occur in some cases (Reichardt, 1979).

"True score" analysis of covariance
In this procedure, an attempt is made to adjust the treatment effect based on an estimate of what the pretest scores would have been if they were measured without error (true scores). With a single covariate, a relatively simple procedure, Porter's true score analysis of covariance (see Huitema, 1980, chapter 14), can be used to make the appropriate adjustments. The major issue in the use of this procedure is the choice of an appropriate estimate of reliability with which the correct pretest scores. The test–retest correlation for a relatively brief time interval will often provide a good estimate of this value, but other measures may be preferred in some situations (Campbell & Boruch, 1975; Linn & Werts, 1973). Hence, following the recommendations of Cook and Reichardt (1976) and Judd and Kenny (1981a), it is useful to perform these analyses using a range of reliability values so as to bracket the true effect of treatment.

Standardized gain score analysis
Kenny (1975) has developed an approach to the analysis of nonequivalent control group designs that is applicable when the unknown rules for assignment to treatment and control groups may be presumed to be stable over

time. In this approach, pretest and posttest scores are first standardized, so that the within-group pretest and posttest variances are equated. Then the mean gain in the treatment group is compared with the mean gain in the control group to provide an estimate of the treatment effect (see Kenny, 1975; Huitema, 1980, chapter 15). This approach can provide particularly good estimates of treatment effects when it may be assumed that the treatment and control groups are growing at the same rate, or at rates proportional to their respective levels on the pretest measure.

More complex statistical adjustment procedures

A variety of new, highly sophisticated approaches to the analysis of the nonequivalent control group design have been developed during the past several years. Each of these approaches can provide excellent estimates of treatment effects when the assumptions underlying its use are met. However, the success with which violations of assumptions can be identified in practice and the effect of such violations on the treatment estimates is not fully known at present.

Structural equation modeling

The structural equation approach attempts to develop a causal model of the selection process using multiple indicators of each construct (Magidson, 1977; Magidson & Sörbom, 1980; Sörbom, 1978). This approach has the important advantage of potentially providing error-free estimates of each of the theoretical constructs postulated to be involved in the selection process. Unfortunately, the procedure requires relatively large sample sizes. The success of the adjustment procedure in producing accurate estimates of the "true" treatment effect will depend on the extent to which a) the hypothesized selection model is correct and b) the statistical assumptions underlying the procedure are correct (see Bentler and Woodward's [1978] critique of Magidson [1977] for an example). Recent advances in statistical theory (Bentler, 1983, 1985) now permit accurate estimation of effects even when the distributional assumptions of the procedure (i.e., multivariate normality) are not met, provided that a very large N is used.

Short time series

When repeated pretests and repeated posttests are available in the nonequivalent control group design, short time series analyses can rule out nearly all possible forms of the selection × maturation threat. Two general approaches have been developed.

Simonton (1977; see also Kmenta, 1986) has developed an econometric procedure that provides accurate and powerful tests of treatment effects, when its assumption of an autoregressive error structure that is identical for all subjects is met; however, its assumptions cannot be probed in the context of short series. It permits estimation of treatment effects in both small N (e.g., single subject designs) and large N studies.

Algina and Swaminathan (1979; Swaminathan & Algina, 1977) have developed a complex sequential testing strategy based on a series of multivariate profile analyses. This procedure compares the maturational patterns of the treatment and control groups during a) the pretest and b) the posttest series. Only when the sequence of tests show that differential maturational patterns in the two groups cannot provide a plausible alternative explanation (a relatively small set of outcomes) can a significant treatment effect be interpreted. Since its statistical assumptions are far less stringent than the Simonton procedure, the Algina–Swaminathan procedure will be preferred under most circumstances in which there are substantially more subjects than repeated measurements over time.

Other Approaches

Econometric approaches attempt to correct for selection differences between groups by estimating the probability of treatment group assignment as a function of pretest scores (Barnow, Cain & Goldberger, 1980; Berk, 1983; Heckman, 1979; Murname, Newstead & Olson, 1985; Muthén & Joreskög, 1983). These procedures require the use of large sample sizes; highly reliable measures of all variables related to the selection process; and that strong statistical assumptions be met, before accurate estimates of treatment effects can be made.

Value-added analysis (Bryk & Weisberg, 1977) is particularly useful in studies of children, where patterns of development are strongly related to age. This procedure can be extended to include other measured variables that may modify the growth rate (Bryk, Strenio & Weisberg, 1980). The procedure estimates the expected growth between the pretest and posttest from the cross-sectional data; a treatment effect is inferred if significant gain occurs over and above the expected amount of growth. For the procedure to be useful, the same measure must be used at pretest and posttest.

Conclusion

Each of the statistical adjustment procedures outlined above will produce unbiased estimates of treatment effects when its assumptions are met. Unfortunately, the assumptions will often not be fully met in practice and the extent of the violations cannot always be estimated. Hence, the strategy has evolved of conducting several different analyses that make different assumptions about underlying selection and growth processes in the hope that they will converge on the same result, providing some degree of confidence that the treatment effect has been correctly estimated. The newer, more complex analyses also hold considerable promise for better estimates of treatment effects in some applications. Unfortunately, when a set of analyses yield contradictory or equivocable results, researchers cannot reach any conclusion about the effects of treatment. As Huitema (1980, p. 350) notes: "The consequence of not being able to specify the selection model is not being able to state which, if any, of the analyses yield the appropriate solution."

Threats to Internal Validity

The nonequivalent control group design rules out many of the standard threats to internal validity such as history and maturation. This design does not rule out, however, threats arising from interactions with selection, of which four are the most problematic. These are illustrated using the example of a multi-week treatment program to reduce cigarette smoking.

Selection × maturation

Suppose a group of smokers succeeds in reducing their cigarette consumption five cigarettes per week for each of 3 weeks prior to treatment, whereas a second group continues to smoke a constant number of cigarettes each week. If the first group were then recruited to participate in a smoking reduction program (with the second group serving as a control group), considerably ambiguity would surround the interpretation of any further decreases in cigarette consumption in the treatment group.

Selection × history

Subjects may inadvertently be selected for the treatment group whose family and friends have recently become intolerant of their smoking and have put them under considerable pressure to stop smoking. In contrast, subjects in the control group have associates who are much more tolerant of their smoking.

Selection × regression

Subjects may be selected for the treatment group who have been temporarily smoking an unusually large number of cigarettes, whereas control subjects may have been smoking their normal number of cigarettes each week. With the passage of time, the treatment group may be expected to reduce to their usual level of smoking even without treatment.

Selection × instrumentation

Following the beginning of treatment, smokers in the treatment group may begin smoking a smaller number of cigarettes clear down to the filter, so that their actual tar and nicotine intake does not change. Control subjects may not show a similar change in their smoking habits. Note that this threat may arise in a wide variety of different forms in this design. The factor structure and the reliability of the scale may differ between treatment and control groups. Or the interval properties of the scale itself may differ between groups, as when one of the group means is near the end of the scale, making further change hard to detect (ceiling or floor effect).

Strengthening the Nonequivalent Control Group Design

Multiple control groups
Since it is virtually impossible to identify a control group that is comparable to the treatment group on all factors that could affect the outcome of the study, it is often useful to identify several "imperfect" control groups to allow multiple tests of the treatment effect. Although this strategy has rarely been utilized in nonequivalent control group designs in the clinical treatment literature, numerous illustrations can be found in the health literature. For example, Roos, Roos and Henteleff (1978) compared the pre-and post-operation health of tonsillectomy patients with a) a nonoperated control group matched on age and medical diagnosis (respiratory illness with tonsillar tissue involvement) and b) a control group of siblings who in each case were within five years of the tonsillectomy patient's age. Each control group has its strengths and weaknesses; however, obtaining similar estimates of the effects of treatment across each of the comparisons helps minimize the plausibility of a number of alternative explanations of the results.

One rarely used type of control group that can be useful when the population can be enumerated is the random comparison group (Mohr, 1982). In this design, the control group is selected randomly from the population of ultimate interest. The data from the control group only may then be used to estimate the regression coefficients in the statistical analyses of the treatment effects. As documented by Mohr, such a comparison group will typically yield less biased estimates of the treatment effect than a nonrandomly selected comparison group. An even more accurate estimate of the treatment effect can sometimes be achieved by selecting control group subjects randomly, subject to the following constraints: that they match the treatment subjects on variables known to be associated with selection into treatment, and that the reliability of each of the measures is very high.

Nonequivalent dependent variables
Adding additional dependent variables, conceptually related to the primary dependent measures but which should theoretically be unaffected by the treatment, can also help strengthen the interpretation of nonequivalent control group studies. Roos et al. (1978) examined both the number of

health insurance claims made by their subjects for respiratory illness which would be expected to decrease following tonsillectomy and those claims made for other, nonrespiratory illnesses which would be expected to decrease following tonsillectomy. To the extent that this pattern is obtained, the interpretation of the results as a treatment effect is strengthened.

Multiple pretests

The nonequivalent control group design can also be improved by including several pretest measurements prior to treatment. The short time series design discussed above is employed to examine the possibility that differential regression or differential growth rates in the treatment and control groups could be responsible for the observed results. As we saw in our discussion of statistical adjustments, the threat of selection × maturation or differential growth can often be a major problem in the interpretation of the results of studies using the nonequivalent control group design. To the extent that an empirical basis is available upon which to estimate growth rates, in both the treatment and control groups, the statistical adjustment techniques discussed above can be utilized to minimize the plausibility of the selection × maturation threat.

Plausibility of Threats to Internal Validity: Outcome Patterns

Cook and Campbell (1979) have noted that the four major threats to internal validity in the nonequivalent control groups design may be more or less plausible depending on the specific area of research and the pattern of results that are obtained. For example, they note that the threat of selection × maturation normally involves different rates of growth in the treatment and control groups; cases in which one group is growing and the other is not, or in which the two groups are growing in opposite directions, are far less common. Applying this reasoning to Figure 3.4, we can see that selection × maturation is likely to be a threat to internal validity in Outcomes B and E, but is less likely to be a threat in Outcomes A, C, and D.

Figure 3.4 provides an excellent guideline for identifying the likely threats to internal validity that are associated with each outcome pattern. The crossover interaction pattern depicted in Outcome D, for example, makes three of the four threats to validity unlikely, so that selection × history is the primary threat that must be examined. If examination of careful documentation of other possible influences on the treatment and control groups throughout the study failed to identify plausible historical influences that differed in the two groups, the researcher could tentatively conclude that a treatment effect had been demonstrated.

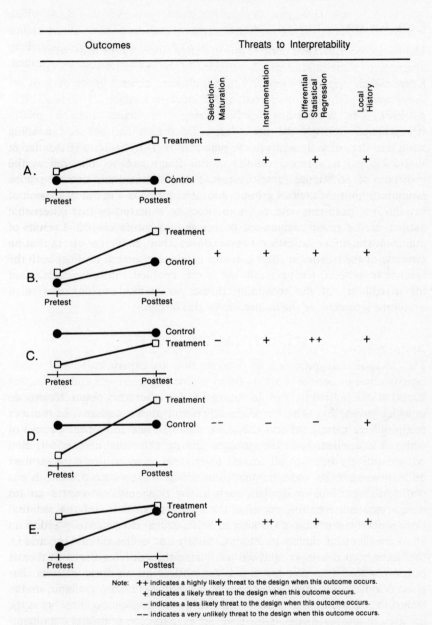

Note: ++ indicates a highly likely threat to the design when this outcome occurs.
        + indicates a likely threat to the design when this outcome occurs.
        − indicates a less likely threat to the design when this outcome occurs.
        −− indicates a very unlikely threat to the design when this outcome occurs.

Figure 3.4 Interpretable outcomes associated with the nonequivalent control group design with pretest and posttest. From P. Karoly, *Measurement strategies in health psychology.* **Copyright © 1985 John Wiley & Sons, Inc. Reprinted by permission of John Wiley & Sons, Inc.**

Conclusion

The basic nonequivalent control group design provides the least satisfactory alternative to the randomized experiment of the designs we have examined. Despite their apparent simplicity, nonequivalent control group designs are "very weak, easily misinterpreted, and difficult to analyze" (Huitema, 1980, p. 352). The conclusions reached using this design can be greatly strengthened through the use of specific design features and analysis strategies that directly address the plausible rival hypotheses (Reynolds & West, 1987). The internal validity of the design can be enhanced by the inclusion of additional pretest measures (so that growth trends may be estimated) multiple control groups, and nonequivalent dependent measures. In addition, pertinent data can sometimes be collected so that reasonable models of the group assignment processes may be developed. The use of multiple statistical adjustment procedures that converge on the same estimate of the treatment effect can also produce increased confidence in the results. In general, strong treatment effects coupled with consideration of the plausibility of the remaining threats to internal validity can often overcome a number of the limitations of this design.

SOME FINAL THOUGHTS

This chapter has provided an introduction to experimental and quasi-experimental designs that are useful in evaluating treatment and prevention interventions in field settings. In contrast to the laboratory research methods in which psychologists have traditionally been trained, modern field research methodology clearly reflects the more complex and less certain world in which it is applied. Even the strongest design, the social experiment, may not definitively rule out all threats to internal validity; problems such as differential mortality and treatment contamination are always possible in real world settings. Weaker designs, such as the nonequivalent control group design, may not even rule out all of the standard threats to internal validity. Consequently, researchers working in field settings must carefully articulate all of the plausible threats to internal validity and utilize specific procedures that have been developed and refined during the past 20 years to probe the possibility that a specific threat was responsible for an observed treatment effect (Cook, 1983). Among the general procedures that are available are the inclusion of additional design features (e.g., multiple control groups), additional measurements (e.g., time series data), and multiple statistical analyses with different assumptions to rule out identified threats to internal validity. The use of these procedures can, in some cases, produce designs that closely approach the internal validity of the laboratory experiment; in other cases, threats to internal validity may remain even after the investigator's best efforts have been undertaken.

Because of the complexity and uncertainty associated with applied research conducted in the field, it is important for researchers to acknowledge publicly the known limitations of their findings, and to make both the data and detailed accounts of the design and procedures available for analysis by others (Cook, 1983, 1985; Sechrest et al., 1979). Public criticism of research provides an important mechanism through which possible threats to internal validity and their probable effects on the findings can be articulated. Additional studies, with different strengths and weaknesses, can then be conducted to help triangulate the true effect. While considerable uncertainty may be associated with the findings of any one study, a consistent finding in a research literature can provide greater confidence in the robustness of the effect.

The focus in this chapter was primarily on internal validity; however, investigators must carefully address the full range of validity issues discussed in chapter 2 in designing their research. Opportunities to enhance external validity through careful sampling of subjects, or to study issues of generality by careful probing of potential moderator variables, have often been missed. Some attention has been given in the clinical treatment literature to the issue of the construct validity of the independent variable, through the use of attention placebo groups and subtraction designs. Substantial gains in construct validity can be achieved through the development of theoretical models of treatment which are then tested through structural equation modeling techniques; these advances are yet to be realized. The problems of statistical conclusion validity generated by the nonindependence of observations in group treatment and prevention research, and those which result when repeated observations are taken over time, have been only rarely considered. Finally, suprisingly little effort has been directed to assure that research designs have adequate statistical power to detect treatment effects. The statistical power of the design needs to be estimated in advance, and in cases in which it is inadequate, procedures need to be taken to raise statistical power to assure that the intervention receives a fair test.[9] Only when attention is given to the full range of validity issues will the results of

---

[9]Some important clinical diagnoses are so rare that, despite utilizing the strategies discussed in chapters 2 and 3 to enhance statistical power, the number of subjects that can be recruited for the study will still be too low to assure an adequate test of the intervention. In such cases the preferred strategy is to organize a multi-site collaborative research program. Such colloborate efforts can be organized around large grants, in the NIMH Collaborative Treatment of Depression Study, or even through a multi-university project in which dissertion students at several universities evaluate a common treatment protocol using common measures. A less satisfactory but still useful approach is to meta-analytically combine the results of several small-scale interventions on the same problem conducted at different sites (cf. Smith, Glass & Miller, 1980).

our research on treatment interventions come to be valued both by academic clinicians, who will evaluate the contribution of the research to the development of basic theory, and professional clinicians, who will evaluate the contribution of the research to the development of effective treatments.

4
Relationship Building, Part One. The Negotiation of Client–Therapist Communication Strategies

RELATIONSHIP BUILDING IN PSYCHOTHERAPY: THE ASSUMED PROMISE

The "Quality" Relationship in Clinical Folklore

The point of departure for chapters 4 and 5 is the long-standing professional quest for positive interpersonal relationships in psychotherapy. Clinicians of all persuasions adhere to the common sense belief that the quality of the client–therapist relationship is an essential, if not sufficient, ingredient in effective treatment. Widespread agreement among divergent theorists on the centrality of the therapeutic relationship was evident in Goldstein, Heller and Sechrest (1966). It is no less prominent today, both in expressions of clinical intuition and in the literature evaluating clinical process and outcome (see Garfield & Bergin, 1978; Gurman & Razin, 1977; Harvey & Parks, 1982).

Simply stated, this collective wisdom maintains that the quality of the therapeutic relationship inspires and constrains client change. An interpersonal bond comprised of mutual trust, liking, and respect evokes client willingness to disclose thoughts and feelings, listen carefully to therapist suggestions, and enact treatment strategies. Clinicians in the humanistic and psychodynamic mold look upon the evolving interpersonal experience with the client as a rich source of diagnostic and prognostic indicators. The relationship becomes the context in which mature self-perceptions and constructions of the social environment can emerge. Behaviorists, of course, deemphasize relationship development as an ultimate target. They regard it more as a vehicle for prompting and reinforcing changes in client cognition or situational behavior.

The corollary to this assumed promise is that a quality relationship will circumvent client resistance as a byproduct of the cooperation it engenders. Failure to comply with therapist instructions, or even with the health-pertinent prescriptions of medical specialists, is now a deeply troubling issue in the helping professions (e.g., DiMatteo & DiNicola, 1982). A harmonious bond between the participants, and the sense of cohesiveness that it implies, is expected to produce a more intense investment of energy in the work of therapy by both client and helpter (Orlinsky & Howard, 1978). As client fondness for the therapist grows, so does his or her commitment to the treatment rationale. Diminished is the possibility that the client will experience reactance, and initiate countercontrol or abandon treatment altogether. Difficulty with client compliance promises to become an unavoidable dilemma for clinicians, as middle-class and working-class Americans become ever more imbued with a consumer advocacy ideology and question the efficacy of professional techniques. The exponential increase in malpractice lawsuits in medicine and now psychology attests to this point.

A second—and equally compelling—circumstance underscores the need to develop satisfying relationships. This occurs when the help-seeker differs from the professional along such significant dimensions of social experience as race, ethnicity, class, gender, and personal status. Proponents of cross-cultural counseling convincingly argue that intervention steps should not and typically *can* not be taken unless the helper demonstrates a comprehensive grounding in the client's linguistic environment and understands the social organization in which the client is embedded (e.g., Acosta, Yamamoto & Evans, 1982; Marsella & Pedersen, 1981). In addition, the cross-cultural therapist must be able to tap into the client's phenomenological construction of self and social reality, which arise from his or her social position and exposure to cultural expectations. Obviously, such competencies and prerequisites define both the process and the consequences of a positive interpersonal alliance between client and service provider.

Redefining "Quality Relationship": a Negotiated Working Alliance Between Persons of Unequal Status

In 1966, Goldstein, Heller and Sechrest saw the tremendous promise in striving to clarify and specify the relationship construct. Until that time, relationship had suffered from definitional diversity and lack of agreement concerning its specific nature and implications for therapeutic outcomes (Goldstein et al., 1966, p. 75). The powerful strategy they chose for accomplishing this task entailed a reconception of relationship in terms of interpersonal attraction—a variable with a long history of research in social psychology. These authors reasoned that heightened patient attraction to the therapist would increase patient receptivity to therapist influence attempts, and thus would yield a more efficient psychotherapeutic exchange. From cognitive dissonance theory, they extrapolated a series of explicit procedures for increasing patient attraction to the therapist, by eliciting dissonance arousal and carefully channeling dissonance reduction (see Goldstein et al., 1966, pp. 97–135).

A testimony to the heuristic power of this mode of reasoning is the accumulation of analogue research—and indeed clinical techniques—predicated on the definition of therapeutic relationship as attraction (Goldstein, 1971). For example, therapist attraction has been studied as a product of physical attractiveness; expressions of value similarity; client need to be liked and accepted; and therapist self-disclosure. Experimenters have successfully encouraged therapist attraction through presentation of positive information about the therapist (structuring), imitation, and conformity pressure. (For reviews see Goldstein, 1971, 1980; and Strong, 1978.) In addition, other authors have pursued the Goldstein, Heller and Sechrest extrapolation paradigm and redefined relationship formation in terms of reactance motivation (Brehm, 1976), congruent role expectancies (see Berzins, 1977), reciprocal self-disclosure (see Doster & Nesbitt, 1979) and social power (Ruppel & Kaul, 1982; Strong & Matross, 1973).

In this and the next chapter, we select research examples from three types of unequal status relations, including psychotherapist–client, doctor–patient, and teacher–pupil, to provide insights into the dynamics of clinical negotiation. We also examine how status relations are further complicated when there are linguistic, ethnic, and cultural differences separating helper and client. The overall position we attempt to demonstrate is that negotiation is most profitably directed toward two objectives: a) establishment of a mutually comprehensible rhythm of verbal and nonverbal communication, and b) evolution of a common conceptual framework for discussing the target problem. To focus our argument, we draw upon findings from sociolinguistics and nonverbal communication to show how conversational synchrony requires negotiation of both discourse strategies and unspoken emotional reactions. In chapter 5, we explore theoretical contributions from medical anthropology and from the social psychology of medicine, to clarify the question of how clinical reality (including symptom meaning) is constructed out of the negotiations taking place between participants in the healing enterprise.

Succinctly stated, our premise is that the face-to-face clinical encounter can never again be seen as a context in which the professional's grasp of reality, whether it be defined as discourse strategy, idiom and explanation of illness, or curative formula, can be considered an unwavering constant around which client perceptions are thought to deviate. Instead, it seems more fruitful to proceed as if the meaning of the clinical experience is the product of a contractual agreement hewn through negotiation. Furthermore, the style of speech participants' adopt as the medium for reaching negotiated understanding is itself the first point open for self-reflection and consensual agreement.

NEGOTIATING CONVERSATIONAL COOPERATION IN CLIENT-THERAPIST COMMUNICATION

Negotiation Dynamics and the Quest for Communication

When client–therapist exchange is conceptualized as negotiation, we can apply a broad range of social-psychological principles and findings to the therapeutic endeavor. Most social psychologists view negotiation as an interactive process, involving at least two parties who voluntarily agree to discuss disputed issues. Although some researchers use the terms negotiation and bargaining interchangeably (Raven & Rubin, 1976), others note that bargaining tends to involve parties with disparate goals, while negotiation implies potentially compatible goals that must be defined through cooperative communication. A similar distinction is drawn between distributive and integrative relationships. While in some instances one party will benefit if the other party agrees to make a concession (distributive negotiation), the therapeutic relationship can be likened to integrative negotiation: both the client and the therapist are working together to seek a solution that will help both parties.

Like psychotherapy, effective negotiation is based on a continuous two-way flow of information. Each party formulates a set of expectations and preferences relative to conceivable outcomes of the dispute, and then expresses his or her position to the other party. This communication demands that both sides accurately express their goals or preferences, and thereby reduces vagueness and uncertainty concerning areas of agreement or disagreement. This explicit statement of preferences also prompts reciprocal disclosure from the other party, and a cyclical process evolves as each party learns about the other's expectations and demands. At minimum, it permits each side to gain a better appreciation of what is probable, possible, and impossible, and what the opportunity costs might be (Gullivar, 1979, p. 89).

Like psychotherapy, the process of negotiation can be efficient and productive, or inefficient and counterproductive. In describing several "errors" that individuals make in negotiations, Bazerman (1983) notes that too often the two parties adopt adversarial roles that virtually ensure a poor solution to the problem. Furthermore, they sometimes assume that whenever one "side" gains, the other side is losing, and that maintaining one's position in a disagreement is a sign of power and independence. Similarly, Pruitt (1983) notes that negotiators sometimes abandon problem-solving strategies in favor of less effective methods, such as contending (forcing your will onto another), yielding (giving in but remaining dissatisfied), inaction (doing as little as possible during negotiation), and withdrawal (leaving the situation). Negotiators sometimes engage in positional bargaining—each side states his or her position, defends that position, and then makes small concessions until a middle range is reached—despite the possibility of integrative, mutually satisfying solutions (Fisher and Ury, 1981).

Negotiators also tend to display particular "styles" of bargaining (Fisher & Ury, 1981; Gilliver, 1979). Some adopt a "hard" negotiation style based on winning; the goal is to "get" as much as possible from the other person, while giving as little as possible. In contrast, the "soft" negotiator strives to maintain the relationship linking the parties, and so minimizes the risk to the *relationship* rather than maximizing personal gain. Yet between these two extremes is the "principled" negotiator (Fisher, 1983), who seeks to increase the benefit for both sides while protecting the relationship from harm. According to Fisher, the principled negotiator avoids arguing over positions by focusing on shared and compatible interests, inventing options for mutual gain, and insisting on objective and fair criteria.

Evidence also indicates that negotiation tends to be more effective when each party is expected to change and the power differences between bargainers are minimized. Gulliver (1979) suggests that change occurs through a cyclic (and developmental) process of information exchange, whereby each party's position is subtly shaped by learning about and adjusting to the other party's expectations, preferences, and outcome requirements. Rubin and Brown (1975, pp. 213–233) propose that equal power among bargainers results in more effective bargaining than unequal power. It also diminishes both exploitative behavior by the high power party and, reciprocally, the need for submissive behavior from the less powerful party. Yet, what does the professional gain by declining the lofty, detached status that earmarks traditional psychotherapy, and pursuing a more equal and humanistic relationship characterized by negotiated decisions? The latter approach, we believe, affords both the greatest opportunity for a mutually satisfying and productive therapeutic bond, and the highest possible assurance of the legitimacy for those behavior changes that accrue over the course of the relationship.

The "psychotherapy as negotiation" analogy illuminates why individual differences assume a major role in relationship formation and offers procedures for how such differences can be ethically resolved. Although clients may be willing to change many areas of their ideas and values to improve their adjustment, they may not be willing to proceed in therapy unless deeply felt preferences are honored. Some preferences may be unpalatable to the therapist, such as achieving emotional intimacy with the therapist; physical touching; mutual self-disclosure; or discussion of non-psychological issues. From the clinician's perspective, there are professional standards to uphold, and it is necessary to preserve one's status, dignity and objectivity on the client's life situation. Certain issues are therefore not open for negotiation on either side. However, to the extent that therapeutic efficacy can profit from breadth of experience, it seems essential for the clinician to openly negotiate even his or her most cherished preferences and come to fully comprehend the client's perspective.

Once issues central to the therapeutic relationship are identified and subjected to negotiation, both participants experience an intensified awareness of their own fundamental assumptions about the helping exchange, and of the assumptions of their "opponent." The outcome of these encounters is the recognition that therapy is, in many respects, an interpersonal reality constructed through mutual agreement. In essence, it is a contract making explicit those events which will and will not transpire between the two speakers. Moreover, Goldberg (1977) advises that stringent ethical conditions be fulfilled when a contractual arrangement guides client–therapist encounters. The client is active in making goal choices, knows his or her obligations and those of the care provider, and is thus able to review and evaluate the progress achieved and renegotiate when dissatisfactions occur. Therapy is divested of its mystique when its specific purposes and procedures are held accountable, through contractual agreement achieved by negotiation.

Finally, a negotiation paradigm could be a challenge to apply with certain clients—particularly those who are less willing to shift their interpersonal perspective and "take the role of the other" in the give and take of bargaining (see Rubin & Brown, 1975, pp. 191–194, for a discussion of bargaining capacities of schizophrenic and paranoid patients). Yet even such "difficult cases" are likely to seek to cooperate, once they observe that the therapist is sincerely interested in their preferences and wishes to fully consider the client's views in all aspects of treatment.

Counseling Strategies and the Negotiation of Conversational Cooperation

Counseling transpires through the medium of effective, face-to-face communication. Two fundamental components of effective communication are mutually understood conversation and accurately interpreted nonverbal signals. This section explains how cooperative conversation is created and sustained when speakers are of unequal status and culturally dissimilar. Conversationalists must negotiate access to culture-specific knowledge if they are to accurately interpret and respond to the literal and social meaning of intentional spoken information. The next section notes the urgency of negotiating the meaning of client nonverbal communication, given that such channels reveal a great deal about client feelings toward the treatment relationship.

When client and therapist face one another at their first session, each brings to the encounter linguistic abilities finely tuned to the unique conventions of their respective speech communities. Mutually understood conversation becomes possible only when the speakers are able to successfully negotiate a common interpretation of the linguistic signals used in their verbal and nonverbal exchanges. When both speakers have the same interpretation of these cues, they can coordinate exchanges and produce the primary requirement of conversation: "being seen to hear and see what your interlocutor hears and sees" (Robillard, White & Maretzski, 1983, p. 111).

Sociolinguists have observed that persons socialized in divergent speech communities will signal the intended meaning of what is said by following utterly different unspoken ground rules (Gumprez, 1982). To sustain conversation, speakers must share enough linguistic and cultural knowledge about these implicit ground rules to be able to detect their occurrence and draw accurate inferences from them. Cues to signal the meaning of speech include eye contact; gesticulation; posture shifts; changes in voice tone, loudness, and phrasing; how questions are posed; and other subtleties. In our highly mobile and urbanized society, intensive communication with speakers of differing sociocultural backgrounds is the rule rather than the exception (Gumprez, 1982). Clinicians must accurately identify breakdowns in conversational coordination, and deftly negotiate with speech partners more compatible interpretations of speech signals to reestablish fluent conversation.

Consider the following hypothetical interview situation, as a context for our discussion of key findings and analytic tools from sociolinguistics:

At a state-run community mental health center in urban Honolulu, Hawaii, a 27-year-old clinical psychology intern is about to have his first session with a male high school student who is 17 years old. The intern is white and comes from a Protestant, upper-middle-class family. Although he was raised in Honolulu and attended a prestiguous private high school there, the intern spent 5 years doing undergraduate work at an East Coast university before returning to Hawaii for Ph.D studies. The client, in contrast, is a "streetwise" youth who grew up in a tough, lower income neighborhood. He is of mixed Asian ancestry; his grandparents originally moved to Hawaii to work as laborers on the sugarcane plantations. Like many others with this history, the student now considers himself to be a "local," and most comfortably speak Hawaiian creole English (pidgin), a language with origins in plantation life. Recently he was arrested for selling stolen automobile parts. During the hearings before the juvenile court judge, it was found that the youth had undertaken the thefts to support a newly acquired—and expensive—cocaine habit. This was the student's first arrest, and the judge was willing to permit him to remain outside of the youth correctional facility if the student successfully completed a drug counseling program and returned to high school. At this point, the youth was referred to the psychologist for screening, to determine his suitability as a counselee in the clinic-run program.

How is it possible for the clinician and client to attract and sustain one another's attention? This question is especially pertinent given their readily distinguishable differences in educational, economic, and sociocultural status and the commensurate difference in their speech communities determined by these status variables. Even if both were highly motivated to establish conversational cooperation—to enlist each other's active participation in a dialogue, and effectively pass information back and forth—how could it come about? Is it not more likely that a lack of semantic fit will mar their efforts and throw off the rhythmic regularity that coordinates the timing of their exchanges? Sociolinguists would predict the occurrence of unnatural pauses; interruptions; or complete silence, to show the speakers that misunderstanding abounds and lead them to blame one another for the frustration they both feel. More importantly, the failure to create conversational cooperation may cause the clinician to misattribute this outcome to resistance and insincerity on the student's part. Assessment data produced through an unsatisfying exchange will lead to an inference that the client is unmotivated to change and is a poor risk for drug counseling. In fact, the outcome only represents a failure by the speakers to negotiate a common interpretation of what is being focused on and where the discourse is going at any one time (Gumprez, 1982, p. 132).

Let us review a plausible transcript of the initial exchanges between the intern (*I*) and his client (*C*).

1.   *I:*   Eh, Howzit! You must be Ross, I'm Nathan.

2.   *C:*   Howzit. (pause)

3.   *I:*   You mind, I talk story wit chu?

4.   *C:*   What fo'? [spoken with a tone of defiance]

5.   *I:*   I hea' you go Oahu High School?

6.   *C:*   Yeah.

7.   *I:*   You know dat guy, Eddie DeSilva?

8.   *C:*   Da football player? Sure!

9.   *I:*   Oh yeah? Dat guy wen marry my cousin, you know. Eh,
10.   you remember the game against Kauái? Da buggah was
11.   hot. Yeah?

12. *C:* Eh, was radical to da max, man. I played too, you
13.   know. Wen was sophmore.

14. *I:* Fah-out, bruddah! I never made da team at Diamond
15.   Head, cuz was too skinny. All da time coach used to call
16.   me "chopstick legs."

17. *C:* (laughs)...Ey, brah, what year you was at dat place?

18. *I:* Was pau [finished] der in '75.

19. *C:* No kidding, then you was one shrink or what?

20. *I:* Well, first I went to college on the mainland, then I
21.   returned to Hawai'i and studied to become a
22.   counselor. I'm almost pau with the university and
23.   this will be my first job.

24. *C:* Oh, I thought you was one shrink already. I'm not
25.   pupule [crazy] or mental, like dat, you know!

26. *I:* No, no brah. I like explain to you...my job is to
27.   talk story with the guys, you know, about what we do
28.   here. You can check 'em out that way. If it looks
29.   OK, try come, yeah? It's up to you brah.

30. *C:* I know! I know!

Within this brief and seemingly trivial conversation has transpired a remarkably complex negotiation and conveyance of information. To illuminate what has occurred, sociolinguists will videotape a transaction such as this then play it back to a panel of listeners, including those who participated in the original encounter. John Gumprez's speaker-oriented approach analyzes an instance of recorded verbal interaction by a) observing whether or not actors understand one another; b) eliciting participants' interpretations of what goes on, then c) deducing the social assumptions that speakers must have made in order to act as they do, and d) showing empirically how linguistic signs communicate in the interpretation process (Gumprez, 1982, pp. 35–36). Gumprez uses this method to pull from a conversation each speaker's discourse strategy of communication and persuasion, and to evaluate its effectiveness.

Erickson and Shultz (1982) use a similar speaker-oriented analysis. They videotape junior college counselors during regular student interview sessions, and then show the tape to each counselor separately, with instructions to stop the action and comment wherever they wish. This technique enables each person to indicate their perception of the sequential structure of the interview and also to identify those points in the continuous stream of behavior which are especially salient.

Let us proceed with out transcript analysis from the perspective of the two actors. The first order of business is to agree upon a "participation structure." They seek to identify the activity of mutual involvement and its ground rules that govern speaking, listening and turn-taking (Au, 1980; Erickson & Shultz, 1982). The intern in line 1 offers a colloquial greeting, and introduces himself using a first name basis. This signals his desire to have an informal meeting and minimize the obvious social distance between them. By the use of "Howzit?", a pidgin expression meaning "How is it going?," the intern employs a contextualization cue (Gumprez, 1982, chapter 6) informing the listener that he encourages "local" speech and is not restricting his own utterrances to standard English. The risk of choosing this discourse strategy is that it will appear condescending to the student. And, of course, the intern is required to comprehend the basic conventions of intonation, syntax, inflection and word play that pidgin demands, lest he make a fool of himself. The potential gains are twofold. First, the intern elicits the student's attention. Secondly, he acknowledges that he will abide by local verbal etiquette and social values—such as not causing the loss of face—that are reassuring to a youngster facing an adult authority. We gain perspective on this process by recognizing that the interview is an occasion where status differences that predominate society at large are reenacted in counseling conversations; each speaker has assigned to the other a more or less inescapable role (Erickson & Shultz, 1982).

In line 2, the student returns the pidgin greeting, thereby acknowledging the intern's use of local dialect and his own preference to avoid standard English as the participation structure. However, the student says nothing more because he is uncertain about what is expected of him. He does feel that being sent to a mental health clinic is a "put down," and expects that the doctor-types will say that he is a mental case. Perhaps by not saying anything and "playing it cool," he can prevent their unwelcome intrusion into his own identity.

What this youth shares with other minority Americans who enter treatment is a justified disinclination toward self-disclosures that increase one's vulnerability to an agent of the dominant society's institutions—in this instance, a white, middle class therapist. The black male client in particular is often characterized by his caution and distrust of the white therapist, his reluctance to disclose his innermost thoughts and feelings to such professionals, and his skill at preventing penetration of his intrapsychic world by displaying a "cool" and unperturbable image of himself (see Ridley, 1984 and Vontress, 1971, 1976 for reviews). The black client's suspicion and style of "playing it cool" can be construed as "healthy cultural paranoia" when viewed in the context of growing up in a discriminatory society, where "every white man is viewed as a potential enemy, and every social system is an opponent" (Grier & Cobbs, 1968, cited by Ridley, 1984). To some extent, this description also represents the wider social order that the two speakers in our dialogue are reenacting. The interviewer confronts the weighty burden both of selecting a participation structure *and* demonstrating an interpersonal sensitivity that will allow the student to feel comfortable about, and see the value in, exposing some of his innermost concerns and intentions.

The intern has thus chosen his second statement carefully. Spoken in a pidgin intonation, phrasing, and grammar, the statement provides a contextualization cue, informing the student that their activity is "talk story." This conversation convention, common on the island, allows for animated, colorful and relaxed story-telling where each is allowed a turn without restriction of content. The intern presumes that this activity is the best forum for the student to fully express, in his own practiced eloquence, what he thinks and feels about his situation. Significantly, this is phrased as a question, allowing the student the option of either declining an interaction altogether or verbally committing himself to "talk story."

In his reply, "What fo'?", the student issues a challenge and reveals his discomfort at having to visit a mental health clinic. But he has *not* rejected the invitation to talk story, just offered the intern an opportunity to explain why he thinks he is here and what will happen. This is a critical moment. If the intern gives an explanation that in any way comments on the student's sanity, the student will dismiss the whole program and opt for jail to avoid being called a mental case.

With the incongruent question about high school attendance in line 5, the intern avoids giving a direct answer to the above question. He knows that without rapport, a comment about the drug counseling could be interpreted as a put-down, or as hassling from an adult. Still, this abrupt shift in content is a sure sign of discomfort and a breakdown in coversational coordination. In their study of college counselors, Erickson and Shultz (1982) found a higher frequency of interruptions in the flow of conversation between speakers who did not share the same ethnic background. When these "arrhythmic," uncomfortable moments did arise, they indicated a mismatch in cultural communication style. Greater arrhythmia covaried with lower overall friendliness of the encounter, and decreased the chances that the counselor would offer "special help" to the student. The lack of synchrony in line 5 points to the dissimilarity of interactional experience between the student and counselor, which makes it difficult for them to evolve a predictable and routinized session together. It is vitally important for a clinician to detect asynchronous and uncomfortable moments as they arise, and to pause at some point to follow up their source.

A second feature of the intern's question about high school attendance is that it begins a search for some point of common experience with the student. The questions and answers which follow are again synchronous, while the animation and humor of pidgin "talk story" come into play when it is found that they have a friend in common and share a background in football. Importantly, the intern was able to produce a "formulaic phrase" in line 10—"Da buggah was hot" or "He performed well." In Gumprez terms, these phrases "reflect indirect conversational strategies that make conditions favorable to establishing personal contact and negotiating shared interpretations...their use signals both expectations about what is to be accomplished and about the form that replies must take" (Gumprez, 1982, pp. 133–134). The student replies with a formulaic phrase of his own; he agrees enthusiastically with the intern's judgment of Eddie's performance. Then the student shows he is more relaxed, by disclosing that he also used to play football.

Lines 5 through 18 contain the deliberate effort by the speakers to identify elements of perceived similarity in their personal backgrounds to bridge the sociocultural gap separating them. Erickson and Schultz (1982) found that those speakers who were able to successfully locate a shared interest during their face-to-face encounter could override cultural differences and enjoy more satisfying and productive outcomes. When the speakers successfully identified their similarities (i.e., established high group comembership) the counselor acted as an advocate rather than as a judge of the student. The researchers recommend that interview time initially be devoted to small talk and the quest for common experience. Vontress (1971) cautions, however, that not all small talk builds rapport with black clients. Trite or inappropriate conversational gambits may be interpreted as disrespect for the black client and the urgency of his or her problem, and be falsely understood as an attempt to delay the unpleasant (Vontress, 1971, p. 7).

With the situation firmly defined now as "talk story," the student is able to phrase a more pertinent question (line 19) indicating that he interprets the intern as a "head shrinker" or "shrink" (psychiatrist)—a category of helper that he feels uncomfortable with.

The intern seizes this opportunity to disclose his professional background, defining himself as a locally trained "counselor" rather than a "shrink." Therapist self-disclosure can be a useful prompt for further intimacy in the relationship when it is consistent with the client's expectations in terms of timing and level of information revealed (Doster & Nesbitt, 1979; Ridley, 1984). However, at this point the student would reject the intern if he offered any disclosure of affect, unless it were very indirectly expressed through some humorous pidgin word play.

The student reacts to the intern's description of himself as a counselor in-training by disclosing that he has mistaken the intern for a psychiatrist (line 24). Having said that, the student then forcefully disclaims being a psychiatric case. He does so using a Hawaiian word for crazy (pupule) and a similar pidgin term ("mental") that have obvious emotional significance for him. But, by using the formulaic phrase at the end of his sentence, "like dat [that], you know, "the student implies that he knows that the intern too could not have thought that about him. Thus the intern is given the benefit of the doubt.

Unfortunately, at line 26 we find that the intern's comprehension of pidgin's subtlety is inadequate and he doesn't pick up this last point. Hence the intern thinks he must convince the student that he doesn't regard him as "mental" and so provides an explanation of the intern's clinical function. In his eagerness to make everything explicit, the intern explains that his job is to describe the clinic and reassures the student explicitly that the choice is his own.

In line 30, the student reveals his annoyance with the overly long explanation he has just received. Of course he knows that he is checking the clinic out, and that it is his own decision whether or not to participate! This comment on his freedom to operate need not and should not be overtly made, because to do so implies that the opportunity to choose is being granted by the organization. If the intern were truly sensitive to the student's language and value system, the student reasons, he would have been much more subtle on the question of choice, especially since a verbal commitment to the program is not something one acknowledges. From the student's position, the lengthy reply is a kind of "conversational hyperactivity" and he aims to diminish it through his follow-up comment ("I know! I know!"). This inveighs "Stop carrying on like that." Erickson and Shultz (1982) note a similar phenomenon, "hyperexplanation," that occurs when the speaker is unable to detect cues from the listener that he or she actively follows what is being said. They postulate that listening style regulates speaking style, and that a cultural mismatch can lead the speaker to lengthy elaboration when positive feedback cues from the listener follow a unique cultural style and remain undetected.

The Negotiation of Conversational Cooperation as a Clinical Procedure

Sociolinguistics is a new research domain; however it already offers analytic concepts and methods of conversational description that can be profitably extended into the clinical interview situation. The seminal work of Gumprez (1982) and Erickson and Shultz (1982), among others, renders a general formula that clinicians can apply in their encounter with new clients, in order to negotiate conversational cooperation and the common interpretation of linguistic signals. The formula contains three procedural phases.

First, the clinician is primed to carefully monitor initial verbal exchanges with the client, and to listen for an uneven flow of talk, hesitant pauses, or abrupt changes in sentence rhythm, pitch level and intonation contour. The listener can also identify an instance of miscommunication and asynchrony by the momentary discomfort it produces. The uncomfortable moment draws the listener's attention to the breakdown in rhythmic interchange of signals, verbal and nonverbal, between self and speech partner. The participants cannot assume that they have successfully negotiated shared interpretations of speech without conversational rhythm and the clear match between speech content and its accompanying linguistic signals. When partners miss each other's cues regarding how what is said is to be understood, it is clear that they have not yet agreed on what activity is being enacted and the ground rules by which it is carried out.

The detection of uncomfortable moments prompts the clinician to institute a procedure whereby he or she reins in any tendency to allocate blame for the poor communication, either to oneself or to the client. Instead it is understood that troublesome or troublefree interactions are both jointly produced by the speech partners, and neither is solely responsible for an outcome. This critical awareness permits the clinician to "bracket" his or her inferences about the client's motivation or competencies. This means the listener consciously refrains from assessing the speaker as uncooperative, hostile, or of low intelligence. The aware clinician holds in abeyance judgmental attributions until other hypotheses can be explored.

Alternative hypotheses of the communication gap include cultural differences in speech conventions and lack of mutual understanding of the conversation at hand. Another plausible explanation, discussed below, is that the client perceives the counseling relationship as accelerating too quickly. The interviewer's questions are felt to require an unacceptable level of self-disclosure and intimacy; the client acts to avoid these probes, while expressing discomfort through hesitant speech and anxious gestures. However, even when the participants do share a language network and have the ability and desire to readily coordinate their interaction, the interview may end in mutual frustration. Despite genuine efforts, both speakers may fail to "negotiate a common frame in terms of which to decide on what is being focused on and where the argument is going at any one time" (Gumprez, 1982, p. 185). Thus, the clinician needs to be prepared with each client to undertake a momentary diagnosis of the interactional process—in the midst of an uncomfortable moment *as it happens.*

The clinician then enters a phase of active reflection, where inferences regarding the client's speech patterns are consciously bracketed and treated as hypotheses. It is through this intermediate step of active reflection that the clinician can determine how best to negotiate a common meaning of speech cues. In the transcript above, the intern actively searched for personal similarities with the client (i.e., situational comembership) and used small talk to identify mutual interests or experiences. High comembership enhances synchronous verbal exchange, even when the speakers differ in their ethnic and linguistic communities. Self-disclosure appropriate to the partner's expectations is the vehicle for identifying background commonalities. Erickson and Shultz (1982) make the point that active listening and self-disclosure, which enhance comembership feelings and help coordinate interactions, are not discrete skills. Rather, they are part of a general, flexible insight or formula that can enhance the clinician's contribution to the interactive partnership. These authors rightly point out that clinical training which approaches cross-cultural communication as simply skills training—i.e., how to talk with Blacks, Asians, Chicanos, and other minorities—will probably only reinforce or reinvent racial, ethnic, and social class stereotypes.

A critical danger, however, is that instead of appropriate self-disclosure and small talk, the interviewer moves too rapidly with personal disclosure and intimate questions that overstep the client's limits of acceptable intimacy for that stage of the relationship (Derlega & Chaikin, 1975). The "intimacy equilibrium" hypothesis of Argyle and Dean (1965) (amended by Argyle & Cook, 1976) proposes that individuals arrive at an equilibrium level of intimacy in their interactions. This baseline of intimacy is reflected in their mutual expressions of affiliation, such as interpersonal distance, gaze, smiling, body orientation and intimacy of topic of conversation. When this comfortable level of intimacy is disturbed, as through an increase by one partner in physical proximity, then the other affiliation components (e.g., gaze, smiling, intimacy of conversation) will compensate and diminish (in frequency, intensity or duration) in order to maintain the equilibrium. The compensation process predicted by equilibrium theory is well documented under many conditions, although increases in affiliation behaviors sometimes produce reciprocity or matching intimacy inputs (see Cappella, 1981; Patterson, 1973, 1976, 1977, 1982).

In essence, studies support the proposition that if clinicians attempt too quickly to elicit personal dialogue from clients, by offering self revealing statements or probing them with high-intimacy questions, then clients are apt to feel threatened and anxious, and to compensate for the intimacy disequilibrium by decreasing various affiliative responses (Cappella, 1981; Derlega & Chaikin, 1975; Simonson & Bahr, 1974). In addition, with certain psychiatric patients, therapist openness, steady gaze, forward body lean and other nonverbal gestures to increase contact may actually prompt reactions of extreme avoidance and withdrawal. Such therapist approaches were found to increase delusional activity and negative self-disclosures, avoidance of eye contact, postural rigidity, and nonfunctional nervous movements among psychiatric inpatients (Doster, Surratt & Webster, 1975; Fairbanks, McGuire & Harris, 1982; Shimkunas, 1972).

The preceding argument is condensed in a hypothesis with implications for both clinical research and education.

Hypothesis 4.1

A mutually satisfying therapeutic alliance depends upon conversational cooperation that is negotiated within initial clinical encounters through a three-phase formula: a) detection of uncomfortable moments; b) conscious restraint by the listener from making judgmental inferences; and, c) a search for background commonality or comembership through small talk and appropriate self-disclosure, while avoiding self-statements and probes which violate the intimacy equilibrium.

Clinical Conversation Without Negotiated Cooperation

Indirect support for our hypothesis is contained within literature which documents communication difficulties both between doctors and patients and between teachers and minority pupils. Researchers using a direct-observation method have described how hospital consultations that lack conversational cooperation result in dissatisfying outcomes of various types. Important examples include: the loss of significant information regarding patient affect and patient self-description of the medical problem (White & Robillard, 1982); misdiagnosis and inappropriate care (Paget, 1983; Fisher & Todd, 1983); confusion concerning the physician's diagnosis (Korsch & Negrete, 1972); exacerbation of patient tension, fear and helplessness (Korsch & Negrete, 1972); noncompliance (Davis, 1968); and detached collaboration with the medical interviewer, providing only vague and imprecise answers (Plaja, Cohen & Samora, 1968; see also Fisher and Todd's [1983] review of these issues).

Two studies in separate institutional settings that contain part-Hawaiian participants clarify these general findings. White and Robillard (1982) videotaped a medical consultation in an outpatient clinic in a Honolulu hospital. It involved a white male physician in his third year of residency training and an older female part-Hawaiian who visits the clinic regularly for treatment of diabetes. From the transcript of this encounter, White and Robillard draw a major conclusion in line with out hypothesis: "...Ultimately, the lack of complementarity between [doctor and patient] styles of speaking limits the patient's ability to participate in the conversation and influence the "seen-heard" course of interaction" (White & Robillard, 1982, p. 1).

The part-Hawaiian patient labored to introduce information she considered relevant to her health status using a "talk-story" format—brief first-person narrative accounts of everyday events, qualified by references to her own thoughts and perceptions. Unfortunately, these personalized accounts, which are appropriate in the Hawaiian speech community when talking about personal concerns, fail to conform with the medical model interview format. Physician discourse is dominated by "instrumentally specific and direct questions," which comprise the ritual of the routine service encounter. As he guides her through a staccato "review of systems," the physician fails to acknowledge his patient's bids to introduce new topics. Consequently, "significant medical information embedded within narrative forms is either truncated or does not surfaces at all in the course of the conversation" (White & Robillard, 1982, p. 18).

Complementary evidence was gathered by Au in her analyses of how Hawaiian children participate in classroom speech and reading activities (Au, 1980; Au & Jordan, 1981; Au & Mason, 1983). One study exposed a group of six second-grade pupils to two reading lessons taught by different teachers. The first teacher presented a conventionally structured reading lesson. It was not congruent with the Hawaiian children's customary "participation structures"—preferred rules of speaking, listening and turn-taking behavior. Instead, the teacher sought to strictly enforce an "exclusive rights" interaction, where she selected both the topic of discussion and a single child who was supposed to answer her questions. The second teacher sought a balance of interactional rights between herself and the pupils by enacting an "open turn" activity (similar to "talk story") where she controlled the topic but not the role and number of student speakers. Outcome data revealed that the first teacher was frequently sidetracked, as the pupils struggled to redress the felt imbalance by assuming control over the topic of discussion. In contrast, the second teacher spent much less time in teacher-dominated participation structures, and could achieve high levels of student cooperation on the task of learning to read.

Gumprez (1982) contributes a third example of communication disparities between teachers and minority students. In two instances, white teachers failed to recognize the meaning of rising intonation in black pupils' answers to their questions. In the first instance, the teacher told a student to read. "The student responded, 'I don't wanna read.' The teacher got annoyed and said, 'All right, then, sit down'" (Gumprez, 1982, p. 147). Black informants listening to the tape pointed out that the rising intonation at the end of the child's statement actually indicated that he meant, "Push me a little and I'll read. I can do it, but I need to know that you really want me." Another classroom interchange demonstrates the same use of rising intonation.

T: James, what does this word say?
J: I don't know.
T: Well, if you don't want to try someone else will. Freddy?
F: Is that a p or a b?
T: (encouragingly) It's a p.
F: Pen.

James (J) gave his reply to the teacher's question with rising intonation and thus implied he needed some encouragement. Unaware of this meaning, the teacher assumed James was refusing to try and so moved on to Freddy (F).

Freddy's hesitant question also used rising intonation but was conveyed in terms the teacher expected. With her encouragement then Freddy gave his answer. Unfortunately, James seeing this exchange concluded that the teacher was willing to encourage Freddy but not him, and was thus "prejudiced against him" (Gumprez, 1982, p. 148).

Brudner (1977) alerts us to a second level of difficulty, which unfolds when clinical conversation proceeds outside the frame of negotiated cooperation. Psychotherapy is a subtle yet persuasive form of language enculturation. Language learning in therapy is predicated on the individual subordinating his or her expressive behavior to a linguistic code that the language coach (therapist) deems is more broadly communicative and less autistic. Two hazards persist, though, unless it is made explicit to the client that his or her enculturation into a new linguistic perception pattern is a *process*, one that invites mutual decision-making.

First, Brudner notes, therapeutic conversation does not unfold as a true dialogue but is a highly structured activity, consisting of a number of covertly directive messages from the clinician and a series of monologues by the patient. She compares a transcript of an initial session with one made after a dozen therapy sessions, and describes how much of what the patient says is discarded in the first session by the therapist and how the attention of the patient is channeled toward affective topics (Brudner, 1977, p. 279). After only a handful of contacts, the patient has already learned to channel his own verbal behavior toward a limited set of topics, and to express his emotions and conscious states using the technical language of the therapist. Language enculturation is shaped by therapist methods such as restricting the topic of discussion, modeling the use of selected words and phrases and repeating them often, and refocusing client attention through specific questions and rephrasing of verbal content.

The net result, Brudner asserts, is a bold alteration of the patient's language habits at the lexical level; he or she is more oriented to the verbal channel of expression and labors to transform information from other channels into verbal messages. If so, it would represent for some persons a dramatic departure from their current speech communities. It may be desirable for clients "in general" to be able to move fluidly across speech networks, but those from minority backgrounds may find that the enculturation experience has alienated them from available speech networks and that alternative mainstream groups are now inaccessible to them as well. This possibility is diminished when the clients' definitions of their own speech communities are given prominence in negotiations concerned with the goals of therapeutic discourse.

The second hazard, which requires alleviation through open negotiation, is due to the high degree of structure imposed upon the psychotherapy relationship by professional ritual, the regulatory mechanisms of treatment institutions, and general social custom (Scheflen, 1963). Clinicians naturally manipulate the highly structured interview situation, to transmit their therapeutic lesson plan and signify the new language pattern to be learned. The implicit danger is that the complementary client role is one of passive recipient of the clinical messages. Goldberg (1977) cautions that this structure reinforces subordination and dependency. It undermines the client's ability to collaborate in defining and actively working toward an agreed outcome. Such circumstances can be overcome, by creation of a contract holding each party accountable for the explicit process of change as it unfolds.

NEGOTIATING THE INTERPRETATION OF DISCREPANT NONVERBAL CUES AND UNSPOKEN FEELINGS IN CLIENT–THERAPIST COMMUNICATION

The previous hypothesis states that the negotiation of conversational cooperation enhances the therapeutic alliance. This proposition is further refined by considering the contribution of nonverbal cues to the evolution of synchronous communication between client and clinician. Conversationalists are not only listeners who strain to accurately interpret the intention of their partner's discourse. They are also observers, scanning the speaker's face and body for nonverbal clues that reveal the affect, intensity, and sincerity of the accompanying words.

In this section, we argue that the working alliance is extended when the clinician assumes the role of "lie detector" and becomes particularly sensitive to discrepancies between nonverbal and verbal communication channels, as well as to inconsistencies among the various nonverbal channels. Just as uncomfortable moments of conversation alert the therapist that mutual understanding is deteriorating, so too discrepant nonverbal cues discriminate moments when clients' unspoken emotional reactions more accurately describe their experience of the therapeutic relationship than does the verbal content of their speech. When these inconsistencies remain obscured, asynchronous and unsatisfying patterns of communication result. Therefore, the therapeutic task is to pinpoint these moments, and then to negotiate with the client (via verbal and nonverbal channels) his or her definition of the situational and affective meaning associated with those unspoken reactions. A therapist sensitive to nonverbal communication will penetrate the client's masked and unspoken emotions, and will strive to coordinate his or her rhythm of therapeutic communication with the system of cues sent by the client.

Nonverbal Synchrony Between Client and Therapist

The structuralist approach to human communication advanced by Birdwhistell (1970) and his followers seeks to describe the verbal and nonverbal components of communication as inseparable parts of the total system (Harper, Wiens & Matarazzo, 1978). Within this approach, the most common method involves filming natural segments of social interaction. Filmed sequences are reviewed in detail, to relate discrete body movements with their recurring contexts and to reveal the function of the movement within the total communication situation (see Scherer & Ekman, 1982, for reviews of nonverbal research methods). Harper et al. (1978) relate Kendon's (1972) example of the man with a raised fist. "Unless the whole communicational context were known, we could not decide whether that action represented a greeting, a sign of anger, accompanied a verbal description of another person as 'tightfisted', or represented a political symbol of 'power'" (Harper et al., 1978, p. 122).

Film analyses of clinical interviews by structuralist researchers such as Condon and Ogston (1966, 1967) have led to the discovery that conversational coordination between speaker and listener is accompanied by a distinct pattern of nonverbal synchrony. After a painstaking scrutiny of filmed interviews frame by frame, Condon and Ogston found "harmonious or synchronous organizations of change between body motion and speech in *both* intra-individual and interactional behavior. Thus, the body of the speaker dances in time with his speech. Further, the body of the listener dances in rhythm with that of the speaker!" (Condon & Ogston, 1966, p. 338). (See Cappella, 1981, for a critical review of the movement–synchrony hypothesis.)

The significance of this finding is underscored by subsequent research that has identified the diverse functions of nonverbal synchrony (see Harper et al, 1978). First, it is an index of therapeutic "rapport." Charny (1966) studies upper-body "mirror congruent" postures of client and therapist. He found that when each interactant's posture behavior was the mirror image of the other, the coincident content of their speech reflected mutual involvement in topics related to therapeutic gain. "In contrast, the content themes of the noncongruent periods were highly self-oriented, self-contradictory, and frequently negational or non-specific" (Charny, 1966, p. 314). Second, nonverbal synchrony tells the speaker that his or her speech phrases are being properly "tracked" and decoded (Kendon, 1970). That listener body movements are so precisely synchronized in response to the stream of speech probably reflects anticipation of what the speaker is going to say (Kendon, 1970, p. 164).

Similarly, a high degree of self-synchrony, where the speaker's kinesic activity (head, hand and body movements) is coordinated with the primary vocal stress points within phonemic clauses, has been shown by Woodall and

Burgoon (1981) to enhance the recall and persuasiveness of the speaker's message. In their experiment, the authors defined a phonemic clause as a discernable "chunk" of spontaneous speech, characterized by rising intonation and loudness patterns and a primary stress point at the end of the clause. Subjects exposed to a message in which kinesic activities converged at the primary stress points were better able to remember the message arguments, in comparison with other subjects who were exposed to dysynchronous messages or messages that lacked kinesic-primary stress coordination altogether. These researchers reasoned that kinesic synchrony, in addition to helping the receiver organize the information to be processed, aids comprehension and recall of material by accenting high-information words in the clause and reinforcing the overall rhythm through visual punctuation of the stress point (Woodall & Burgoon, 1981).

In addition, Scheflen (1963) observed that nonverbal synchrony helps regulate the nature of the relationship, pace of communication, and the expression of deviant individual behaviors during the psychotherapeutic encounter. One of his filmed examples involved a psychiatrist and a young Italian-American girl diagnosed as schizophrenic.

> The doctor sat at each interview on the sofa next to the patient with his left arm over the back of the sofa. In this position he could press the patient's left shoulder with his index finger...[and could monitor] any deviation on her part from his instructions. By grasping her right hand, he monitored her tendency to become incoherent and to speak too quickly.
>
> The following sequence appeared over and over. When the patient appeared remote or inattentive, the doctor demanded that she recall her original psychotic symptomatology. He would then regulate the speed and appropriateness of her speaking by the use of physical contact...On reexamination of the sequences, it was noticed that the girl's inattentiveness to the doctor followed periods in which he had been inattentive to her. Her withdrawal had the effect of prompting him to attend to her in the form of forcing her to be attentive. This mutual behavior regulated remoteness between them. Yet the doctor's remoteness, in turn, followed periods in which she was overly flirtatious with him or when she sat close to him. Remoteness then regulated overcloseness...There was a mutual regulation of oscillations from closeness to remoteness which kept them within fixed limits (Scheflen, 1963, pp. 129–130).

In review, we propose that:

Hypothesis 4.2
Nonverbal synchrony amplifies conversational cooperation within the therapeutic dyad because it a) enables the participants "to be seen to hear and to see what the other hears and sees", b) increases the saliency of significant spoken information, and c) allows mutual regulation of discourse tempo and content.

Clinician Sensitivity to Nonverbal Cues

When the rhythm of discourse between clinician and client prompts a *pas de deux* of their body movements, the conversationalists are likely to experience a sense of rapport. They note a feeling that the other is actively processing and comprehending one's message, and perhaps evolve an awareness that the pace and nature of the encounter is locked in a cycle of mutual regulation. How do interactants achieve this level of nonverbal coordination? Obviously it must be related to the partners' ability to comprehend (decode) each other's nonverbal language and to express (encode) reactions using body channels and movement codes that one's partner can easily interpret. Robert Rosenthal, M. Robin DiMatteo and their colleagues address this issue, as part of a comprehensive experimental program to explain the relationship between sensitivity to nonverbal cues and such variables as individual differences, therapeutic relationship, and training.

Rosenthal et al. (1979) reasoned that people differ in their sensitivity to nonverbal communication expressed in different body systems or channels (e.g., face, hands, voice). Such differences may account for the well documented "expectancy effect" in education. Pupils, sensitive to their teacher's unintended paralanguage, are apparently influenced to change their performance in the direction of the teacher's expectation (Rosenthal, 1974). They further reasoned that the most effective dyad is one in which the partners' best encoding channels corresponded with each other's best decoding channels. To test these hypotheses, Rosenthal et al. (1979) devised the Profile of Nonverbal Sensitivity (PONS) test. It measures an individual's ability to accurately decode 220 two-second segments of nonverbal expression of affect by an encoder. The PONS test uses eleven nonverbal channels to present each segment. It includes three "pure" visual channels (face, body from the neck to the knees, entire figure), two auditory channels that convey tone of voice, pitch and affect but distort the actual words, and six other channels that represent paired combinations of a single visual channel with a single auditory channel.

For over a decade, researchers have employed the PONS test with scores of groups in the United States and abroad. This work has yielded findings with important implications for our argument that relationship formation profits through the negotiation of unspoken affect. First, the eight groups of American clinicians sampled were not outstanding decoders of emotion. They ranked fourth behind samples of actors, students of nonverbal communication, and students of the visual arts, and were comparable to the overall sample of college students. Moreover, those with higher academic status did more poorly on the PONS. This indicates "either that clinicians 'lose' some of their sensitivity to nonverbal cues as they advance academically and professionally and/or that those who achieve greater advancement are those who are less sensitive to begin with" (Rosenthal et al.,

1979, p. 298). If high PONS skill is associated with positive relational development, it supports our general proposition that negotiation strategies which pinpoint and make use of client interpretations of the therapeutic encounter deserve greater consideration as core components of professional socialization and practice.

Several studies do suggest that clinicians with greater nonverbal sensitivity are evaluated more positively by their supervisors and patients. Rosenthal et al. (1979) found median correlations between PONS total scores and supervisors' ratings of clinical effectiveness to be 0.20 for 13 groups of clinicians. Subsequently, DiMatteo, Taranta, Friedman, and Prince (1980) interviewed patients of 64 doctors receiving training in internal medicine at an urban hospital. They noted significant positive correlations between patient's ratings of satisfaction and the physicians' accuracy on the PONS test in *decoding* the emotion expressed through body posture and movement. In this same setting, physicians who demonstrated skill at *encoding* emotions through facial expressions and voice tone were also able to produce patient ratings of satisfaction (DiMatteo et al., 1980).

Similarly, a third study revealed that some physicians were perceived by their patients as caring, concerned and warm. Patients with these positive perceptions of their physician also expressed an intention to return to the same physician (DiMatteo, Prince & Taranta, 1979). After reviewing these and similar findings, DiMatteo and DiNicola (1982) conclude that "...the art of medicine, and rapport in the practitioner–patient relationship, depends partly upon the practitioner's ability to understand the patient's nonverbal cues of affect, and to communicate that understanding by means of his or her nonverbal expressiveness" (p. 101).

One caveat regarding highly interpersonally sensitive physicians should be noted. Among a group of allergy subspecialists in training, the most sensitive trainees appeared to deviate from their accurate appraisal of their patient' pulmonary pathology, prescribing medicine based in large part on the patients' psychological distress (level of Panic–Fear). In contrast, their more moderately sensitive colleagues were minimally influenced by patient personality variables, and prescribed oral corticosteroids based solely on objective indices of pulmonary illness (Dirks, Horton, Kinsman, Fross & Jones, 1978).

Display Rules and Client Expression of Nonverbal Emotion

One major impediment to conversational and nonverbal coordination between client and therapist is the manner in which psychotherapy, as with all professional services, is culturally structured. Most often, the therapist is perceived as an authority figure and a person with high social status. However, even when status and cultural differences are small, it is unlikely that during the early stages of relationship formation (if ever) the client will comment directly on the quality or comfort level of intimacy of his or her interaction with the help provider. Changes in the quality of an ongoing interpersonal relationship and in the intimacy equilibrium (Argyle & Dean, 1965) are too direct or too embarrassing to be easily stated. Therefore, Ekman and Friesen (1968) argue, nonverbal behavior becomes the "language" of the relationship.

Similarly, Friedman (1979) argues that medical patients are frequently reluctant to communicate their feelings regarding such difficult matters as death; fear of treatment procedures; and desire for additional services. Hence, emotions are communicated in channels that are not deliberate. At the same time, the patient is especially observant of, and sensitive to, nonverbal messages from the health practitioner that reveal his or her attitude toward the patient and concern with the patient's illness. Friedman (1979) further observes that patients, like other classes of stigmatized people, are quite vigilant for clues as to how they will really be treated (Goffman, 1962). They watch for signs of "whether they are liked, respected and expected to improve or are repugnant, worthless or untreatable" (Friedman, 1979, p. 87). Because of this, DiMatteo (1979) warns physicians to learn to read the facial and body movement cues associated with patient dissatisfaction so that they can deal with the patient's distress before the relationship is terminated, treatment effects decrease through lack of cooperation, or the patient sues. It is especially important, as Fairbanks et al. (1982) observed in psychotherapeutic dyads, for therapists to be more acutely aware of how their own nonverbal approaches to conversational intimacy may actually be accompanied, among certain patients, by increases in nonverbal aversion to such intimacy.

Ekman (1972) explains the influence of cultural context on affect display in his neurocultural model of facial expressions of emotion. His work demonstrates that particular emotions such as happiness, anger, sadness, and fear are universally recognizable because the same, innate set of facial muscle movements is triggered when a given emotion is elicited. However, "Cultural differences in facial expression occur a) because most of the events which through learning become established as the elicitors of particular emotions will vary across cultures, b) because the rules for controlling facial expressions in particular social settings will also vary across cultures, and c) because some of the consequences of emotional arousal will also vary with culture" (Ekman, 1972, p. 212).

This proposition—that culture-specific rules govern the display of facial emotions—deepens our understanding of how the clinical context functions as a culturally constructed situation, above and beyond the intentions of the therapist. Boucher (1974) defines display rules as socially learned instructions that specify, for the persons in an interaction, which management technique is applied to which facial behavior and in which context. If the clinician were able to assess the display rule meaning of the interview situation for each client, he or she would then know the probable handling of a felt emotion. The client's options, according to Ekman (1972), are to intensify or exaggerate the feeling; deintensify and understate the felt emotion; neutralize the emotion, as is the custom among white American males in reaction to grief; or mask the feeling with a different and more socially acceptable display.

Factors that appear to diminish nonverbal synchrony are distilled in hypothesis 4.3.

Hypothesis 4.3
Non-synchronous nonverbal coordination weakens the therapeutic alliance and occurs when cultural display rules distort the expression of nonverbal affect and prevent the therapist from a) accurately decoding the client's emotional response to the therapeutic relationship and b) encoding nonverbal cues responsive to those unspoken relational feelings.

Clinician as Lie Detector

How can a therapist, even with finely tuned nonverbal sensitivity, decipher the affective meaning of an interview conversation? This question is particularly troublesome given that clients are not likely to readily verbalize their evaluation of the quality of therapeutic relationship *or* their discomfort with deviations from the intimacy equilibrium, and that display rules mediate their nonverbal expression of certain emotions elicited by the clinical encounter. Fortunately, a body of research begun by Ekman and Friesen (1969, 1974) and vigorously pursued by DePaulo, Zuckerman and Rosenthal (1980) has analyzed deception in nonverbal communication and the strategies humans use to penetrate deliberate dissimulation of unspoken feelings.

Ekman and Friesen (1969) convincingly argue that the face, with its superior visibility and capacity to transmit affect, is the most closely monitored and controlled nonverbal channel. Social feedback on facial displays and subsequent internal monitoring cause the individual to take more responsibility for what is shown on the face. The lack of this intense scrutiny to other body channels—hands, feet, and legs—means that people are less aware of the information conveyed by these channels and, consequently, the affect sent is less disguised or controlled. Therefore, Ekman and Friesen (1969) hypothesize, the sender's true feelings are more often "leaked" via the body (and possibly voice tone) rather than the face.

When people wish to conceal their affect, the face becomes the source of deception, with its well-practiced dissimulation or suppression of facial displays.

Over a decade of research concerning the leakage hypothesis generally supports the notion that "feelings of ambivalence, attempts at lying, and grudging adherence to norms of etiquette [display rules] all may lead to the communication of different messages in different channels" (DePaulo, Rosenthal, Eisenstat, Rogers & Finkelstein, 1978, p. 313; see also Zuckerman, DePaulo & Rosenthal's [1980] comprehensive review of this research). Clinicians can take advantage of leakage hypothesis research to penetrate the interviewee's system of unspoken responses and initiate the negotiation cycle.

First, people are more gifted at detection accuracy—the ability to recognize a deception—than leakage accuracy, which is the ability to see through to the underlying affect that the deceiver is trying to hide (DePaulo & Rosenthal, 1979). For example, when DePaulo and Rosenthal (1979) had subjects who feigned liking or dislike toward someone whom they actually held an opposite feeling, observers accurately sensed deception but read the speaker's intended affect rather than their actual feeling. In fact, the majority of studies examining human lie detection show that, while not infallible, people can diagnose deception at levels substantially better than chance (DePaulo, Zuckerman & Rosenthal, 1980).

Second, the lie detection strategy commonly used is one predicted by Ekman and Friesen's (1969) theory. When DePaulo et al. (1978) confronted observers with increasingly discrepant messages, sent via multiple channel visual cues (face or body) and audio cues (taken from the PONS test), the observers began to show a stronger reliance upon the "leakier" audio cues for decoding the messages. A second set of observers, who were told to suspect that the stimulus person in the test may be lying, discounted the readily faked face more than the leakier voice and body (Zuckerman, Spiegel, DePaulo & Rosenthal, 1980). In brief, observers become suspicious when the nonverbal channels convey conflicting messages, and trust the face less than the body or voice when seeking to decide what the true feeling might be.

Third, what specific clues predict deception? Interestingly, writers discount the utility of searching for the single set of irrefutible indices that indicate dissimulation. Kraut (1980) expresses a strong view that natural selection would not have favored clear and unambiguous signs of deception. Others argue that deception is probably less related to the identification of constant signals than to the interpretation of behavioral cues according to the context in which it is perceived (Zuckerman, DePaulo & Rosenthal, 1981). Thus, as Zuckerman et al. (1981) suggest, "a smiling sender may cause a suspicious perceiver to become more suspicious and a trusting perceiver to become more trusting" (p. 23).

Nevertheless, 21 empirical studies of lying summarized by Kraut (1980) do report at least four vocal and nonverbal behaviors that are significantly associated with deception across studies (see Kraut, 1980, Table 1, pp. 212–213). When subjects were experimentally induced to lie, they blinked at a higher rate, hesitated longer before answering, groomed and touched themselves more frequently, and had more frequent errors and hesitations in speech. These findings, as well as a comparable list of cues compiled by Zuckerman et al. (1981; see Table 1, p. 12), support the view that deception is itself emotionally arousing, appears controlled or rehearsed, and is associated with negative affect.

In their consideration of negative affect and lying, Ekman and Friesen (1972, 1974) predicted that during deceptive interviews, an uncomfortable and anxious person would increase face play "self-adaptors." By definition, self-adaptors are habits carried over from early childhood that developed in the context of problem management and need satisfaction. Anxiety about the conversation, or the affect that is being vocalized, may trigger such self-adaptors as nose picking and head scratching. Yet adaptors have no intrinsic relationship to speech content, nor are they deliberately performed as a communication act (Ekman & Friesen, 1972). These authors give specific instructions of what to look for when deceit is suspected: the person "may scratch or pick at himself to punish himself for deceiving, or he may tend to hide his face with his hands, an adaptor for concealing embarrassment, or he may engage in abortive flight movements with his legs/feet" (Ekman & Friesen, 1969, p. 98). Therefore, assessment of a client's unique array of self-adaptors gives the clinician three types of information: a) knowledge of when discomfort is felt; b) knowledge of what types of discomfort result in efforts to mask emotion; and c) the person's characteristic style of handling unpleasant events (e.g., self punishment, avoidance, prevention of input).

Fourth, a finding from Ekman and Friesen's (1974) laboratory can help the clinical observer penetrate deceptive displays. These experimenters had nurses view both a pleasant and an unpleasant film. Then they were asked to offer a frank description of the pleasant film to an interviewer and a deceptive description of the stressful film. In the second case, the nurses attempted to withhold negative affect and cover it with simulated pleasant feelings. When observers were familiar with a subject's idiosyncratic body movement—they were shown a sample of their repertoire during the honest interview—they could more accurately identify deception than when they had only a single sample of nurses' nonverbal behavior. However, this finding was only true for comparisons involving body movement. The nurses were apparently quite able to match their facial expressions during deception with the natural displays they had provided for the pleasant film.

Clinician Education for Nonverbal Sensitivity

This outcome is one of several that can guide clinical education efforts to enhance nonverbal sensitivity. It suggests an idiographic method of assessment in which the clinician records baseline observations of an individual's nonverbal repertoire under pleasant conditions—e.g., recalling a happy event. The baseline data could be compared with subsequent expressions and gestures displayed when potentially distressful topics are brought into the conversation. A more subtle point is that training efforts are more profitably directed at teaching observers to decode body rather than facial leakage. There are two reasons for this. First, "micro" facial expressions that send leaked affect last less than half a second, and are beyond the threshold of recognition for observers without extensive training (Ekman & Friesen, 1969, 1974). Second, most people already have a wealth of experience reading facial expressions—in contrast with body cues—and have little room for improvement. The experience of Rosenthal et al. (1979) with the PONS test supports this point. Eight samples of subjects tested twice showed large performance increases, especially on the 60 scenes in which only the body was shown. Similarly, these researchers examined the effects of direct training on the nonverbal sensitivity of a subset of 14 mental health practitioners. The 90 minute educational exposure appeared to increase decoding accuracy more for stimuli involving any body cues than for stimuli employing only facial cues (Rosenthal et al., 1979, p. 336).

Another component of training involves increased awareness of the factors that cause observers to misdiagnose deception. DePaulo and Rosenthal (1979) noted that liars who "ham it up" are less likely to get caught than those who lack histrionic tactics. Observers readily believed those senders who exaggerated sentiments of liking which they did not really feel and similarly failed to suspect people who exaggerated feigned feelings of dislike. Conversely, cues that people claim to use to detect lies may not overlap with the cues they actually use, while cues that do distinguish deception may not enter conscious judgments of lying (Krauss, Geller & Olson, 1976, cited in DePaulo, Zuckerman & Rosenthal 1980). Ekman & Friesen (1972) did find, however, that subjects accurately associated deception with frequent use of self-adaptors. Generally, the qualities that socially mark a deceiver involve nervous fidgeting and gesturing, responses that appear implausible or uncertain, and replies that are a little too long or short, a little too quick or slow (DePaulo et al., 1980). It appears from this rather narrow set of clues that when people judge deception, they follow the same reasoning used to rate speaker credibility. Therefore, speech fluency—errors and hesitations—is overemphasized (see Zuckerman et al., 1981).

Finally, a clinician's penetration of deceit is tied to his or her willingness to look for and interpret the available evidence. An observer may have the perceptual competence to recognize masked emotion but either selectively ignore the indices or choose to interpret them according to the sender's desire. This "politeness" strategy is chosen because of the social costs associated with eavesdropping on others' leaky nonverbal channels (Rosenthal & DePaulo, 1979). Moreover, women lose their superior decoding skill when the least controllable channels are considered. Apparently, it is women who pay the higher social cost for lie detection, and thus "retreat to the face," where their sensitivity at decoding intended affect translates into more satisfactory interpersonal relationships (DePaulo & Rosenthal, 1979; Rosenthal & DePaulo, 1979). In short, some individuals may tend to discount their own suspicion of other's underlying affect and fail to accurately interpret clearly evident indices of deceit. This strategy would weaken the evolution of a therapeutic alliance based upon the negotiation processes we have proposed in this chapter. It denies clinicians access to the very information that they require to synchronize their discourse and nonverbal signaling system with that of the client.

Therefore, we infer a corollary to our previous hypothesis:

Hypothesis 4.3(a)
To increase nonverbal synchrony in the therapeutic dyad, the therapist: a) interprets discrepant communications among the nonverbal channels as deception; b) identifies the presence (if not the nature) of underlying affect through careful scrutiny of those unintended cues sent via the leakier body and voice channels; and c) coordinates the therapeutic discourse and nonverbal expressions to synchronize with the client's true feelings toward the dyadic encounter.

5
Relationship Building, Part Two
Negotiation of Symptom Meaning

Chapter 4 described how the client–therapist negotiation cycle can give meaningful form to the ambiguous linguistic and paralinguistic events which punctuate the dyadic encounter. We hypothesized that negotiations within this sphere would insure a more effective working alliance. We also noted how accurate interpretation of linguistic and paralinguistic events permit the interactants to "be seen to hear and see what the other hears and sees," and thus to surpass a threshold of communication, enabling partners to grasp the other's intentions and perceptions. The present chapter considers the second important sphere of interpersonal exchange that is drawn into the negotiation cycle: namely, the conceptualization or cognitive representation of the presenting problem, as formulated by the central actors—clinician, client, and significant others. After a brief description of cognitive therapists' advocacy of a common client–therapist conception of treatment, we will review theories of how the central actors construct personal (implicit) theories of illness and problem behavior. Based on this review, the final section presents four clinical steps, which can facilitate the negotiation of mutually validated and interpretable illness realities and interventions.

A CONCEPTION OF THE PROBLEM:
THE COGNITIVE THERAPIST'S VIEW

The cognitive–semantic therapists, in the tradition of George Kelly and Jerome Frank, have long endorsed as a universal condition of healing the sufferer's and therapist's willingness to share a conceptual framework (see Frank, 1961; Torrey, 1972). Healing transpires when the therapist helps sufferers draw upon this conceptual framework, to translate the cognitive expressions of their demoralization into verbal referents and assumptions that are more meaningful and therefore more manageable. Meichenbaum (1977) draws upon this tradition as a cornerstone of his cognitive approach to behavior modification, but reformulates the proposition to emphasize the client's *active* contribution to the evolution of a common conceptualization of his or her problem and of a treatment rationale. He states:

> The manner in which the therapist queries the client about his presenting problem, the type of assessment procedures the therapist employs, the kinds of homework assignments he gives, the type of therapy rationale he offers, all influence the conceptualization process. Thus, the therapist tries to understand the client's description and definition of his problem but does not merely accept uncritically the client's view. Instead the therapist and client attempt to redefine the problem in terms that are meaningful to both of them... With skill, the therapist has the client come to view his problem from a different perspective, to fabricate a new meaning or explanation for the etiology and maintenance of his maladaptive behavior. (Meichenbaum, 1977, pp. 222–223)

Meichenbaum feels that the client accepts a particular conceptualization *implicitly*, as a byproduct of therapeutic interaction. We propose, however, that it be made an *explicit* aim of the negotiation cycle. In order to adopt a mutual conception, client and clinician must first decode each other's theories of the problem behavior. The participants then translate to each other their respective images of the target concern, which may be strikingly divergent. The construction of clinical reality, therefore, derives from the mutual elicitation of theories of behavioral dysfunction, and from the negotiation of which component of whose theory—whether it be that of the clinician, patient, or significant other(s)—constitutes the agreed representation of what is wrong. Our basic hypothesis is:

Hypothesis 5.1
The therapeutic alliance can not proceed until client and therapist expressly negotiate a mutually interpretable explanation (i.e., explanatory model) of the presenting problem or symptom events.

Recent advances in ethnomedicine, as well as cognitive models of stress and illness, permit us to examine how patient and practitioner construct personal models of problem behavior or illness; how these cognitions change; and how they regulate health care decisions. While much of this literature deals with physical symptoms and lay versus professional models of disease, the methods and findings have direct application to behavioral and psychosocial complaints.

THE INTERPRETATIVE HYPOTHESIS AND MEANING CENTERED ANALYSIS

Recent ethnomedical accounts of how people produce common sense theories of somatic and psychological dysfunction are part of an emerging social science paradigm. The new perspective emphasizes the semantic structure of illness discourse and processes, whereby both patient and practitioner construct illness realities through their interpretations of medical models (Good & Good, 1982, p. 147). This "meaning centered" approach (see Good & Good, 1980, 1981) contrasts with what Harrison (1972) terms the "empiricist theory of medical language." The latter assumes a direct correspondence between symptom complaints, underlying processes, and universal disease entities which are considered realities that lie outside of language and are thereby independent of social and cultural context. Good and Good call for an alternative view, to correct the "context-independent" bias of empiricist language theory and establish the *social* construction of medical knowledge and practice its central focus of study. The Goods advance a core set of assumptions, which comprise their meaning-centered theory of medical discourse.

The primary assumption is that language—i.e., semantics—attaches fundamental and irreducible meaning to disease and psychiatric symptoms. Whatever may be the underlying phsyiological and psychological processes affecting disease and psychiatric syndromes, they enter into human experience and become objects of human action only as they are made meaningful. Through the mediation of language and networks of words and images, pain and other symptoms enter into the experience of the sufferer. Symptom events are imbued with meaning as they are perceived, thought about, labeled, reacted to, set off as objects of experience, ritualized and articulated in social discourse (Good & Good, 1981, p. 187).

Secondly, illness is constructed from the discourse of popular medical subcultures, as the sufferer draws upon available theories and networks of meaning to interpret and communicate a particular symptom event. Medical subcultures, whether lay or professional, each provide distinctive "explanatory models" of illness. Explanatory models link together a set of reasons explaining why the dysfunction is happening at this point in time, what it is called, how long it will last, and what are appropriate healing alternatives (see Kleinman, 1980). Subcultures also construct models of human physiology and personality and forms of therapies. Each model is based upon a particular world view, epistemology, and set of values. Each illness category is a cultural product and brings together a specific set of words and images. These "semantic illness networks" are made up of socially produced meanings and powerful personal (affective) experiences. An illness reality, therefore, is "a 'syndrome' of typical experiences, a set of words, experiences, and feelings which typically 'run together' for members of a society," a "set of experiences associated through networks of meaning and social interaction" (Good, 1977, p. 27).

From the individual's standpoint, "illness" represents a configuration of personal trauma; life stresses; fears and expectations about the illness; social reactions of friends and authorities; and therapeutic experiences. In turn, this configuration is based upon the network of meanings an illness possesses in the broader subculture: the metaphors associated with a disease, the popular disease theories, the basic values, and the care patterns that shape the experience of illness and social reactions to the sufferer (Good & Good, 1980, p. 176).

In order to understand a particular semantic network, the cultural experience of "units of meaning" associated with the illness category are explored. This involves observing how key themes are used in specified medical contexts, by investigating the stressful experiences linked to the illness and by eliciting the explanatory models and affect-laden images associated with the illness category. These units of meaning will be linked to the illness category and to each other through various associational relationships, including metaphorical, spatial, causal and symbolic relationships (Good & Good, 1982, pp. 148–149).

A case study reported by Nichter provides one example of a psychiatric patient's semantic network.

A semantic network analysis proved of value in deciphering the behavior of a middle class American college educated woman admitted to the ward for depression associated with chronic multiple sclerosis. The woman became psychotic after being hospitalized for a week and her psychosis was found to be linked to hypoatremia associated with excessive water drinking. [My interview] revealed that the patient felt her body was being clogged with impurities leading to inertia and fatigue. The patient's behavior took on a different meaning and was deemed less bizarre when it was placed within a semantic network. It was found to be related to a hydraulic model of body physiology and pathology as well as a core concept of purity which the patient had incorporated from an alternative health care system. Belief in this health care system had psychologically sustained the patient through years of chronic illness and provided her an entry into a social support network within an alternative health culture. (Nichter & Trockman, 1983, p. 16).

Finally, the Goods assume that since human illness is essentially semantic or meaningful, that all clinical practice is fundamentally interpretive. In every encounter the clinician employs a set of interpretive models—whether they be biochemical, genetic, psychodynamic, or cognitive–behavioral—to interpret the patient's condition and his or her subjective and meaningful expression of illness symptoms. The interpretive model enables the clinician to identify certain data as relevant, to abstract from the complex totality of the distressed patient, to interpret the abstracted data, and to construct a clincial reality that then becomes the object of therapeutic endeavor (Good & Good, 1980, p. 177). Significantly, the clinician is constantly engaged in translating across systems of meaning. Most often, this entails translating between professional interpretive models and popular or folk models of illness and psychological dysfunction.

This final assumption provides a rationale for redefining *healing*, as an outcome of the mutual interpretation or translation across systems of meaning—across medical models and idioms, across perspectives and pholosphies of human nature, and across medical subcultures. The therapist interprets the intentions of the patient's discourse in order to identify and construct a clinical dysfunction; the patient then interprets the therapist's discourse in order to construct new understandings of the dysfunction. This negotiation of a common understanding of the cause of suffering allows the healer to bring to understanding hidden aspects of illness reality. Patients are led to reinterpret basic assumptions about their suffering, to define therapeutic goals, and ultimately to transform the illness reality (see Good & Good, 1980, p. 178; 1981, p. 193). In fact, researchers have long recognized that a powerful healing force rests with the therapist's ability to transform the patient's sense of ill health as a basic reality, and to thereby alleviate demoralization (Frank, 1961; Kleinman & Sung, 1979). In sum, "clinical [interpretive] models are 'models of' reality, mirroring or making sense of observed phenomena; at the same time they are 'models for' reality, influencing perception and behavior, shaping the course of illness and the evaluation of medical outcomes, and producing the realities they posit" (Good & Good, 1981, p. 178).

LEVENTHAL'S COGNITIVE REPRESENTATION OF ILLNESS DANGER

Although not grounded within the same perspective, case study findings of hypertension and cancer patients by medical psychologist Howard Leventhal and his associates complement and extend the Goods' assumptions. Leventhal, Meyer and Nerenz (1980) completed an extensive investigation of hypertensives, including those who were newly discovered, newly treated, continuing in treatment, and reentry patients. They also interviewed patients undergoing chemotherapy for malignant lymphoma and breast cancer. From the case study data and earlier experimental work, Leventhal has devised a model of how patients construct their own "representations" (i.e., interpretive models) of health danger. His model explains how these representations, based largely on concrete symptoms, serve as part of a self-regulatory system to guide coping efforts and set goals through which coping efforts are evaluated (Leventhal et al., 1980, p. 26).

Specifically, Leventhal's studies found that symptom sensations play two critical roles: they prompt information-seeking to label body states, and they are sought out to serve as concrete representations of an illness label. For example, although there was no empirical evidence that any symptom is a valid indicator of high blood pressure, the longer hypertensive patients received treatment, the more likely they were to search for—and find—a symptom to represent their disorder (Leventhal et al., 1980, p. 16). Leventhal et al. (1980) speculate that sufferers eagerly seize upon concrete symptoms because they are instantly available cues giving feedback about the progress of one's illness. More importantly, these symptoms enable the sufferer to determine, within the realm of their own private experience, the cause of a dysfunction and to evaluate its remediation.

Also observed was how patients formulate a "theory of illness" from the configuration of their symptoms, beliefs about symptom etiology, and beliefs about treatment. The description of Leventhal et al. (1980) of these implicit, commonsense theories is comparable to what Kleinman (1980) and Good (1977) define as "explanatory models" of illness. For instance, almost one-third of the hypertensives interpreted their condition in terms of an acute episode model, distinct from cyclic and chronic illness models. They pinpointed recent situational events and a specific time and place for the onset of their high blood pressure, and typically associated the symptomatology with stressful home or work circumstances. Many cancer patients devised a similar acute episode model to evaluate the cause and course of their illness. They perceived causal connections between life stress events and tumor recurrence. Pennebaker (1982) has also generalized these findings to insulin-dependent diabetics. As with the hypertensives, diabetics hold firm beliefs about the symptoms that they assume covary with fluctuations in blood glucose levels (Pennebaker, 1983, p. 471).

What is important to note in this material is the finding that the implicit theories patients use to interpret experience are resistant to change. While hypertensives agree with the professionals' proclamations that *other* patients can't tell the onset of high blood pressure, they segregate their own realities from such contradictory information, and deftly avoid confronting their discrepant beliefs with those of the biomedical subculture. Of course, some of these patients are probably correct. An idiographic analysis could potentially reveal that certain individuals have evolved implicit theories of psychophysiology that greatly overlap with their actual physiological states (Pennebaker, 1983). Moreover, the "accuracy" of encoding symptom fluctuation depends upon the ambiguity of the physiological cues on which symptoms are based (e.g., heart rate change versus skin temperature). Pennebaker (1983, p. 489) showed that the more subtle or ambiguous the information, the more subjects must rely on commonsense beliefs about what they think their bodies are doing. Hence Leventhal and Pennebaker's research underscores a key meaning-centered assumption: the desirability of bringing to light the unique attributions that comprise the patient's coherent theory of illness. Equally important is the need to pinpoint the sources which elaborate these theories: patient bodily experiences, the settings in which they are felt, information from the popular and professional medical subcultures, and information based on past experience with illness.

Leventhal's writings offer two additional points that broaden our comprehension of how patient interpretive models operate. First, illness representations—consisting of concrete symptoms and their environmental contingencies—can direct specific coping behaviors and are used to appraise the effectiveness of planned action. Features of the representation are directly reflected in the elaboration of action goals. For instance, the content of the illness label influences *where* and *with whom* care is sought. The waxing and waning of symptoms influences utilization practices, as well as evaluation of treatment and disease progress. Those hypertensives who attend to felt symptoms use them as cues to reenter treatment or take their medication (Leventhal et al., 1980). Moreover, patients who showed slow but constant tumor regression with chemotherapy reported the lowest level of distress. The steady diminution of symptoms reinforced the rationale for continuing the uncomfortable and distressing treatment (Leventhal et al., 1980, pp. 20–21).

Furthermore, attributions of disease etiology lead to construction of coping procedures that can be additional means for fighting the disease or subtracting components of treatment recommended by physicians. Leventhal and Nerenz state:

> Patients in our studies who believed their cancer was due to stress often cut back on work commitments and sought assistance with work from friends and family. They also became indifferent to minor life annoyances, more sharply differentiated between important and trivial events, and refused to become involved in those they regarded as trivial. Patients who defined the illness in mechanical terms, as bad cells and tumors, often engaged in intensive exercise, adopted health and food diets, and made other changes to strengthen their bodily resources. (Leventhal & Nerenz, 1983, p. 18).

The second important point is that Leventhal and Nerenz (1982) posit a subsystem which processes emotional reactions to illness threats within their model of self-regulatory coping. This "parallel systems" hypothesis—that two relatively separate regulatory systems are involved in creating conscious awareness and associated feelings about an illness—counterbalances the meaning-centered perspective's heavier emphasis upon conceptual level or semantic level processing in the construction of illness representations. Leventhal and Nerenz (1983) describe how illness pain stimulation is processed both by an information or objective system and by a distress or emotion system. Both systems function at stimulus reception, and both continue to act and interact in interpretation, coping and monitoring of the dysfunction episode.

However, differences in interpretation and thus coping reactions are noted depending upon the regulatory system involved. The emotion system makes use of perceptual memories, involving visual, auditory, and tactile features of past episodes, that are repositories of emotional experience. The objective system draws more upon conceptual or language memory codes, containing abstractions and verbal representations derived from specific experiences.

Interpretations of symptom events based on abstract, conceptual memory appear to require conscious intervention prior to action (Leventhal & Nerenz, 1983). In other words, the sufferer's sensation (leg pain) is combined with language codes (it could be muscle strain or possible bone metastases of breast cancer), and leads to volitional, planned responses (*I'll observe the pain awhile longer, ask friends' opinions, take an aspirin, call the doctor if it persists*).

In contrast, interpretation of stimulation based on perceptual memory codes leads to "automatic" responding that is outside the focal awareness of the person and difficult to bring under volitional control. For instance, emotional memory schemata (Leventhal, 1980) are the coalescence of specific events with emotional feelings and experiences and automatic response patterns. Activation of these schemata, as when one encounters an associate who has chronic cancer, may arouse feelings of depression intertwined with the images of pain and death. Individuals who respond emotionally are unlikely to be aware of their expressive reactions, or of the various defensive or instrumental actions taken to control their emotional memory schemata. Therefore, according to Leventhal and Nerenz (1983), verbal persuasion is clearly insufficient to change these concrete memory structures.

In sum, the theoretical and empirical contributions of Good and Good, Leventhal and Pennebaker demonstrate that symptoms are irreducibly meaningful both to practitioner and patient, and show how each strives to formulate interpretive models for explaining and handling distressful health episodes. This body of thought and its preliminary findings suggest an extension to our previous hypothesis.

Hypothesis 5.2
The resiliency and effectiveness of the therapeutic alliance depends upon the degree of overlap in the interpretive models evoked by therapist and client to explain the presenting problem and select a treatment rationale.

CLINICAL STEPS TOWARD A NEGOTIATED REALITY

Assumptions drawn from the meaning-centered perspective, as well as from Leventhal's insights on interpretive processes, inform a series of four clinical steps which therapists and help-seekers can pursue in the negotiation of mutually validated, interpretable illness realities and interventions. First, initial conversations aim to draw out the patient's explanatory model of the problematic behavior and decode its associated semantic illness network. Second, the therapist discloses the explanatory model he or she evokes to interpret the problem; third, the clinician then compares the two frameworks for communalities and discrepancies. Fourth, and last, the two parties negotiate a translation of one explanatory model into the other. They jointly establish the therapeutic content and outcome criteria as a shared "clincial reality," and thereby fully actualize their therapeutic alliance. Our final hypothesis postulates that these steps are necessary, in order to achieve the desired unity of conceptual thought between the two negotiators that ultimately decides this dyadic alliance.

Hypothesis 5.2(b)
The successful negotiation of clinical reality is constituted by maximum overlap in client–therapist interpretive models, and requires completion of four negotiation stages: a) elicitation of the clients's explanatory model and semantic illness network; b) therapist disclosure of his or her interpretive model; c) comparison across the two parties' interpretations to identify discrepancies; and d) negotiation and conceptual translation of one interpretive model into the other.

Kleinman (1980), Good and Good (1980), and Nichter (Nichter & Trockman, 1983) report a series of psychiatric and medical cases successfully managed through the consideration of these steps. Their work forms the basis for advocating the following clinical algorithm.

Step One: Eliciting the Client's Explanatory Model and Semantic Illness Network

The first step requires bringing into sharp conversational focus the personal and interpersonal meaning associated with the distressful symptom or problem behavior. To pursue this, the therapist probes for elements of the client's explanatory model. These comprise sets of specific propositions about the dysfunction episode that simultaneously explain why it is happening and evoke plans for "reasonable" action (Nichter, Trockman & Grippen, 1985). Explanatory models typically address five questions regarding the dysfunction: a) its cause; b) why the symptom emerged when it did, and why it assumed a particular form; c) how the dysfunction works socially, psychologically, and/or physiologically to produce its effects; d) the severity of the dysfunction and how long it will last (acute versus chronic sick role); and e) the most suitable treatment and the expected treatment outcome (see Kleinman, 1980, pp. 105–106).

Explanatory models assist patients and their families and friends in thinking about the cause of the dysfunction and in efforts to locate a remedy. This reasoning process is frequently a salient feature of the client's conversations with family and friends, and is readily obtainable through direct interview questioning. In addition, a dysfunction category, such as "depression" or "nervous breakdown", condenses for the client a whole interlinked network of emotional experiences, as well as social and semantic meanings. For the client, this semantic illness network is the felt reality that is evoked through the perception of her or his symptoms. No single set of questions or interview protocol is suitable for decoding the semantic illness network of either an individual or group, because the experiences and social meanings associated with dysfunction can be quite variable across persons as well as cultural subgroups. The clinician may in fact be rather surprised at the range of unpredictable associations that do surface, unless he or she is intimately familiar with the spectrum of kinship, peer, medical, economic, educational, and political institutions that have shaped the client's past experiences and interpretations of disability.

Although decoding semantic illness networks is seldom straightforward, the Goods suggest that they can be interpreted from responses that clients and their subgroups provide to a series of questions. These consider such experience domains as personal trauma; culture-specific life stresses; fears and expectations about the dysfunction and its economic impact; social reactions of friends and authorities; and intervention experiences. Useful probes include the following:

1. When this problem began, what other things were happening in your life?

2. How do you think those are related to your problem?

3. What previous experiences have you had with this problem?

4. What difficulties in your life have been caused by this problem?

5. What have you had to give up because of it?

6. Do you know others who have had this condition? What difficulties did it cause for them?

7. How serious do you think your problem will become in the future? In what ways will it affect your economic position?

8. What are the most difficult, fearful, or important experiences that you associate with this problem?

9. Are such experiences especially important for your, for your family (church, work mates, social group, ethnic group)?

The interviewer can continue with additional queries.

1. What do other people think about your having this problem?

2. How do they react to you? How do you feel about their reactions?

3. What is the most suitable treatment to relieve this problem?

4. What personal qualities and therapeutic skills should the healer possess to resolve this problem?

5. What role should you and your social group play in the treatment procedure? (See Good & Good, 1980, p. 180.)

The Goods draw upon case studies presented at their Family Practice resident seminars to demonstrate how the semantic network approach can help clarify and suggest ways to address case management difficulties arising from patient–practitioner differences in explanatory models.

Mr. A., a 28 year old black male ex-convict employed in the maintenance department of a large firm, came to the clinic for treatment several times for treatment of a lower back injury sustained at work. He was given the standard treatment for lumbar muscle spasm/strain, including recommend-ation of hot baths and stretching exercises, but subsequently reinjured his back at work. When Mr. A. returned to the clinic, blaming his foreman for treating him as a malingerer and not assigning him lighter work until his back healed, the resident feared Mr. A.'s problem would become chronic and asked the Goods to do a consultation.

Mr. A. revealed a very clear explanatory model of his back problem during the interview. The injury happened because a muscle in his lower back had been stretched—"like a rubber band that is stretched too far and loses its elasticity." Healing would occur, he believed, when the muscle was allowed to rest and regain its former strength and elasticity. Hence he had not done the physician's prescribed stretching exercises, because stretching had caused the problem and that was what he was trying to avoid. When asked about other underlying causes, Mr. A. felt the condition could be related to worries about finances, his mother's ill health, and difficulties with his girlfriend. These had caused his back pain indirectly by preventing him from eating and sleeping well, and by generally weakening or "zupping" his physical condition.

In a subsequent consultation with the medical resident, Mr. A. revealed his explanatory model which stated why stretching should be avoided. The physician countered with a clear model of a muscle spasm. "It is like a charlie horse. You slowly stretch out the cramped muscle." Before leaving, Mr. A. brought up the other life difficulties that he had just rehearsed with the Goods, and asked if they could be related. After exploring each one carefully, the resident agreed that these difficulties could be prolonging the back pains, suggesting: "Your body may be trying to tell you something." He encouraged Mr. A. to quickly resolve the difficult relationship with his girlfriend. An informal follow-up assessment suggested that he had improved.

This case study illustrates that Mr. A.'s illness reality, of a stretched muscle causing back pain, prompted his desire to avoid certain work tasks (causing conflict with his foreman) and caused him to reject the physician's recommended treatment. The resident was treating a quite different reality—muscle spasm. Unaware of the differences between the two explanatory models, he had suspected Mr. A. of offering resistance to treatment.

In addition, the case illuminates how illness meaning is derived from the network of associated stressful experiences and is embedded in a broader set of meanings associated with back pain in American medicine. The researchers represent this configuration of associated meanings in figure 5.1.

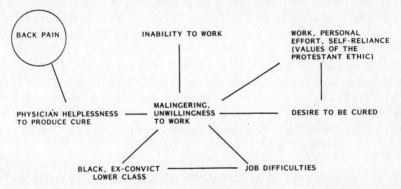

Figure 5.1 Partial semantic network of back pain in American medicine. From "The Meaning of Symptoms: A Cultural Hermeneutic Model for Clinical Practice," by B. Good and M. J. Good, in *The relevance of social science for medicine*, L. Eisenberg and A. Kleinman, Eds. Boston: Reidel

They note:

For patients and physicians alike, lower back pain is often frustrating and difficult to manage. The patient is often partially incapacitated and unable to work; and because the cause of the pain is often difficult to document and the physician helpless to produce a cure, the back pain patient is often suspected of malingering and hypochondriasis. In a society in which work, self-reliance, will power and personal effort are central values associated with the Protestant ethic (Hsu, 1972), an inability to work because of pain, especially pain of undocumented origin, evokes mistrust, anger and negative sanctions. This is even more likely if the patient is lower class, black, or an ex-convict. This semantic network, specific to back pain in American society, provided the context for social responses to Mr. A. and invaded the clinician transactions between him and the therapists. (Good & Good, 1980, p. 184)

In a pioneering effort, Mark Nichter applied semantic network analysis as a framework for negotiating mutual understanding between multi-ethnic patients on a Honolulu psychiatric ward and the psychiatric team handling care management. (See Nichter & Trockman [1983] for a summary of two year's psychiatric experience with semantic network analysis.) The uniformly positive evaluation of this approach, through informal reactions of the patients and formal responses from attending psychiatrists, residents, medical students, psychiatric nurses and others, is encouraging (Nichter, Trockman & Grippen, 1985).

Based on ward experience, Nichter advocated two complementary procedures for elaborating semantic networks. The first of these is an assessment of the patient's "idiom of distress." The clinician examines both the tacit and overt ways in which patients communicate distress. An accurate judgment of the client's behavior, as either dysfunctional or adaptive, cannot be performed without considering several factors: a) an individual's sociocultural constraints against, and opportunities for, expression of particular idioms; b) the alternative modes of expression available; c) personal and cultural meaning and social ramifications of employing such modes; and d) a person's past experience and familiarity with alternative modes. He concludes that "involvement with an idiom which may well be a sign or symptom of maladaptive behavior for one individual may be the only option or a last resort for another. It may indeed be an adaptive response or attempt to resolve a pathological situation in a culturally meaningful way" (Nichter, 1981, p. 402).

A second technique for grasping the meaning of dysfunction is through elicitation of the key metaphors patients rely upon to convey their image of the problem. Speech metaphor or analogy has been described as "complete" communication, given that it conveys an image comprised of words, images, and emotions (Lakoff & Johnson, 1980; Ricoeur, 1979). It is thus highly instructive to have the client share his or her metaphoric perception of the dysfunction. Is it construed as an "enemy" or a "challenge," that must be "met head on" and "defeated"? Does the problem make the person feel as though he or she is "out of tune with the rest of the world" or "playing the game with the cards stacked against you"? Patients may report that "my feelings are frozen," "my thoughts have come unglued," "my body is like lead." Earlier we reported Leventhal and Nerenz's (1983) observation that many cancer patients employed a mechanical metaphor (e.g., bad cells) to describe their condition. Similarly, Nichter's psychiatric ward conversations yielded common cultural metaphors for the patient's problem in terms of its physiology (hydraulic, mechanical, electrical) and its pathology (illness as a battle, deterioration, blockage). Patient conversation also contained metaphors for health (being in balance, tune, shape, control) and psychotropic medication ("just like" vitamins for deficiences; a "filter" for clarity; "crazy glue" to keep the mind together) (Nichter & Trockman, 1983, p. 45).

In sum, the clinician listens for patterns of metaphoric speech, observes the social contexts in which they occur, and can then explore with the patient how such metaphors are used in relation to other elements within his or her explanatory model. This investigation is guided by the Goods' hypothesis that cultural experiences or units of meaning associated with the dysfunction category may in fact be linked with it, through the use of metaphoric relationships.

Figure 5.2 schematically represents our discussion of this first clinical step toward the negotiation of a mutual conception of the problem. At the core of the diagram is the client's explanatory model. The units of meaning associated with the explanatory model's core elements comprise the semantic illness network. Dysfunction reality is constructed and communicated through these interassociated meaning units. The semantic units and dysfunction experiences shown in Figure 5.2 are suggestive, rather than exhaustive or even representative, of the universe of possible associations. Familiarity with the client and his or her cultural subgroup will suggest which elements can be deleted and which meaning units are highly salient.

Step Two: Disclosure of the Therapist's Explanatory Model

The second clinical step in negotiating illness realities involves therapist self-disclosure of the explanatory model with which he or she interprets the client's presenting problem or symptoms. Observers have noted that while clients seldom spontaneously disclose their own explanatory models, they may elicit those of the practitioner (Kleinman, 1980, p. 113). However, these models are not presented as a whole at one point in time, but rather in a piecemeal fashion, as the need for interpretation of the dysfunction experience arises (Blumhagen, 1980, p. 215). Thus, Kleinman, Eisenberg and Good (1978) advise that the professional's model should be conveyed in nontechnical and direct terms for each of the five clinical questions addressed by explanatory models.

Nichter found that if a patient embraced a particular metaphor as the frame of reference for voicing his or her subjective experience, the interviewer could then enhance communication and rapport by adopting the same metaphor with which to share his or her professional model. Not all patients express health metaphors that can absorb a professional's explanation, but Nichter demonstrated the technique by working within the metaphor of a patient diagnosed as manic-depressive. With the daughter of an electrical contractor, Nichter used electrical system imagery as a referential framework to explain to her the bipolar illness model and why she should take lithium carbonate after her manic state subsided.

Lithium carbonate was redescribed as "like a fuse" in the patient's nervous electrical system. Her "system" was described as prone to "overload" and

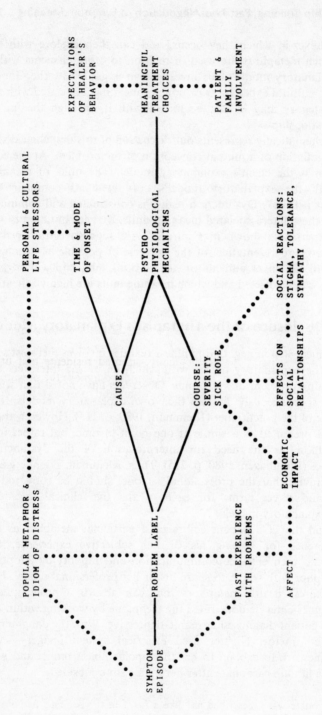

Figure 5.2 Relationship between client explanatory model and semantic illness network

"burnout" due to the patient's perceived "sensitive nature" and her tendency to "plug in" large numbers of inputs into her life system at one time. Just as a fuse need be kept in the system to absorb overload and to prevent burnout, so it was necessary for the patient to maintain a lithium level so as to absorb 'bioemotional overload' (the patient's term). (Nichter & Trockman, 1983, p. 48)

In a unique ethnographic probe, Gaines has found attributes of practitioners' explanatory models that may affect the negotiation process. Gaines elicited etiological models of mental disorder from psychiatric residents in the emergency rooms of two teaching hospitals (Gaines, 1979; 1982). He found, coexisting within one psychoanalytically-oriented residency program, four different definitional and diagnostic orientations among the four residents studied. These orientations showed no sign of shifting during the course of the residency training, based on a content analysis of the doctors' case management records. Moreover, the theory of etiology not only determined diagnostic style (multi-axial versus uni-axial) but governed the residents' ways of relating to their patients. Those who were seen as distant and uninvolved with their patients (and who saw themselves as "objective" and "efficient") held a biological or organic view of the etiology of symptoms (Gaines, 1979, p. 406). The reverse was true for those who included psychosocial factors in their assumptions of etiology.

Gaines (1982) discovered that biologically oriented residents had little need to "understand" the patient, and would rapidly diagnose the presumed underlying condition after a few brief questions and observations. One physician generally spent less than ten minutes with each patient. In contrast, his colleague in the emergency room could spend up to $2\frac{1}{2}$ hours in an interview, trying to get to know the patient (gain insight) and obtain enough information from the sufferer to formulate an opinion about the precipitating causes of the episode, the dynamics of the individual, and, ultimately, some understanding of the person's crisis (Gaines, 1982, p. 175). Gaines explains these discrepancies by arguing that each orientation, though different, fulfills cultural commandments which are meaningful and understandable at the folk level. Since practitioners' explanations are ultimately rooted in broadly shared cultural traditions, they cannot help but grasp the patient's illness experience in *both* professional and lay terms. He adds: "The meaningfulness of professional healers' actions in psychiatry and medicine, as well as the healing traditions of other areas, may not derive from 'professional' evaluations of conduct, but from cultural criteria which are used to make sense of and evaluate their behavior, such as those of elegance [efficiency] and insight" (Gaines, 1982, p. 176).

The research of social psychologist Wrightsman complements Gaines' explanations, with evidence that each of us, including psychiatrists, carries around a fundamental philosophy of human nature that we use to judge the actions and characteristics of others (see Wrightsman, 1977, pages 79–92). Our basic beliefs about human nature are formed at an early age and are unlikely to shift significantly through later education, as Gaines found with the psychiatric residents' notions of etiology. Wrightsman proposes that philosophies of human nature are represented by six dimensions; four of a substantive nature (trustworthiness versus untrustworthiness; strength of will and rationality versis lack of will power and irrationality; altruism versus selfishness; independence versus conformity to group pressure), and two reflecting the complexity of human nature (variability versus similarity, complexity versus simplicity). Application of Wrightsman's (1964) scale measuring Philosophy of Human Nature to Gaines' subjects could further explain the diagnostic style of the two residents cited above. Presumably, the rapid diagnostician would express more negative beliefs regarding strength of will, trustworthiness or responsibility, and independence, and view others as generally more similar and less complex, than the resident who followed the lengthy "insight oriented" assessment style.

Step Three: Comparing Across Client and Therapist Explanatory Models

In the third step, client and therapist examine the discrepancies and "fit" between their respective explanatory models. The purpose of this examination is to bring into sharp focus tacit conflicts in problem conception which will require either clarification and further explanation or frank negotiation to resolve (Kleinman et al., 1978). Kleinman proposes measuring the "cognitive distance" or disparity between patient and practitioner explanatory models by judging (scaling) the discrepancies in their responses to the five major questions (See Kleinman, 1980, p. 113, for scoring criteria). This measurement permits an evaluation of the effectiveness of subsequent communication aimed at formulating a common interpretation of the problem. Kleinman predicts that decreasing the disparity between cognitive models (through negotiation procedures or use of pre-existing familiarity with each other's sociocultural background) will have a positive influence on such health care variables as satisfaction, dropout rate, compliance, and self-disclosure of treatment progress.

Similarly, Wrightsman's (1977) work suggests critical dimensions along which fundamental explanations of human nature and of the source of behavioral problems could differ between therapist and patient. For example, an orthodox psychoanalyst or radical behaviorist, who would view behavior as lacking rationality and self-determination, may show a much greater conflict in mutual problem conception with clients tacitly holding existentialist beliefs of free will and self-understanding. Rogerians may well experience less conflict in negotiating common problem conceptions with clients whose philosophies of human nature include trustworthiness and strength of will and rationality.

Harwood (1981) warns clinicians that conceptual differences with their patients can assume several forms, and that each possibility should be kept in mind. First, the speakers may use the same term but define its meaning differently. This occurs most often when lay persons "misuse" (from the professional's perspective) biomedical and psychological terminology. However, even when client and therapist share a common definition of a term, they may infer that the problem has different causes, and therefore endorse conflicting treatment regimens. For example, the low back pain patient saw his pain as originating from an over-stretched muscle, and hence refused to comply with the physician's recommended stretching exercises. Third, the emotional and social stigma experiences associated with a term may be so aversive to a patient, and to his or her social group, that the patient will reject its application to the problem situation by the therapist. Those interviewed may distort or withhold information about the client or family history that they think will contribute to a stigmatizing label such as "mental illness" or "psychotic." Finally, client and therapist may not share the same basic lexicon. This occurs when the speakers occupy different sub-cultures within the same society, one of them speaks a foreign language, or when the professional uses technical jargon (see section beginning on p. 105 of this book). Involvement of translators may help to clarify conceptual differences of this nature. But distortions will continue to arise unless the translator has a firm grasp of both the client's semantic illness network and the subtle meanings associated with the explanatory model evoked by the practitioner (see Katon & Kleinman, 1981, pp. 268–269).

Blumhagen (1980) and Leventhal et al. (1980) raise an additional caveat. In independent investigations, they found that hypertension patients consciously (and sometimes without awareness) avoided a confrontation between their implicit theories of the illness and the physician's biomedical model. Blumhagen interviewed a group fo 34 patients who held a "stress" theory of hypertension, in opposition to the contents of an educational pamphlet from their clinic which they had all read. Sixty-eight percent stated they have never found anything in the pamphlet that did not agree with their conception of their illness. The remaining 32 percent claimed awareness of the differences and *consciously* rejected the information, feeling that while a particular thing may be true in general, it didn't apply specifically to them (Blumhagen, 1980, p. 217).

Similarly, Leventhal et al. observed that patients would invent "little white lies" to explain why medication was not taken according to instructions in order to avoid confessing the real reason—their private illness beliefs. These investigators believe that clients avoid confrontation "because they feel awkward about arguing, are concerned about looking foolish, fear losing the support and help of the doctor by challenging his authority, and do not wish to express fears which may be associated with their underlying interpretations of their illness" (Leventhal et al., 1980, p. 18). The potential for lack of candor and conceptual differences, even when partners communicate honestly, gives added impetus for a thorough translation process which is the next step.

Step Four: Negotiation and Conceptual Translation From One Explanatory Model Into Another

The fourth step requires the two parties to confront their conceptual discrepancies and mismatched treatment expectancies, and either move towards convergence or break off the quest for a therapeutic alliance. The negotiation of meaning begins by further circular exchange of information, to determine if differences between the two explanatory models are more apparent than real. The simple clarification of terms and concepts may yield hidden similarities between the models. However, "conceptual translation" may be required, where one speaker explains the meaning of his or her concepts and experiences through the use of metaphors, images or idioms which the listener is known to understand (see Nichter & Trockman, 1983, pp. 46–49). In the earlier example of the "manic" patient, Nichter used the woman's knowledge of electrical systems to carry out a conceptual translation of what lithium does as a psychoactive medication. Valins and Nisbett (1972, pp. 138–139) report a second clinical example in which a therapist transformed the meaning of the client's upsetting behavior by providing a "normal" explanation for the behavior (poor sexual relations, worry about penis size) that the client presumed proved he was "abnormal."

If neither of the above procedures reduces conceptual disparity, then either or both partners need to change their position so that a mutually desired treatment can be agreed upon. While some authors emphasize the need for negotiation when problems are anticipated with treatment compliance (e.g., Kleinman et al., 1978), discrepancies in explanatory models can also affect the patient's evaluation of therapeutic change and their efforts to generalize and maintain treatment gains (see chapter 7). Therefore, the client's explanatory model should be analyzed in terms of its implications for organizing his or her post-treatment behavior as well.

When a clear disparity between positions persists, it may be wise for the therapist to offer a compromise or agree to a position conceptually closer to that of the client. After all, if the clinician has fulfilled the professional role to communicate clearly one's expert advice and rationale for treatment recommendations, then it is the client and significant others who have exercised their prerogative as final arbiters to reject elements of that advice (see Katon & Kleinman, 1981). The therapist's choice to enter into a compromise agreement will be influenced, among other things, by personal and professional ethics, perceptions of possible harm to the client, reaction of colleagues, and concerns regarding liability. Similarly, it would be difficult for a client to endorse a conception of the problem and treatment which ran counter to fundamental values, conceptions of self, and the common sense interpretations of one's family and cultural subgroup (e.g., Leventhal & Nerenz, 1983).

Nevertheless, the negotiation partners can expect that the transaction between their explanatory models will yield one of four possible outcomes: a) the client adopts the therapist's explanatory model *in addition to* his or her original model; b) elements of the therapist's model are incorporated into the original client model; c) the client adopts only his or her original model *or* the therapist's model without alterations; or d) a totally new model is reported by the client, usually based on a new source of information (Kleinman, 1975, cited in Kleinman, 1980, p. 111).

At this juncture in the negotiation, the partners must decide whether they have achieved a workable (i.e., mutually validated) conception of the dysfunction and can thereby establish a therapeutic alliance. If so, Kleinman argues, the therapist has accomplished the single most important task in "engaging the patient's trust, preventing major discrepancies in the evaluation of therapeutic outcome, promoting compliance, and reducing patient dissatisfaction" (Kleinman et al., 1978, p. 257). If not, they may choose to begin anew the negotiation cycle, perhaps seeking additional input into the deliberations from other "translators" as well as members of the client's social support network. However, if the negotiations have produced a stalemate, and the client's decision remains unacceptable on therapeutic and ethical grounds (Katon & Kleinman, 1981), then the evolution of a satisfying working relationship is dubious. Familiarity with the individual's semantic illness network will enable the practitioner to make an accurate referral to another care provider, whether it be to a psychologist with a specific orientation, a health specialist, a minister, or a self-help organization.

Finally, preliminary studies of hypertension (Blumhagen, 1980) and cancer (Leventhal & Nerenz, 1983) suggest that explanatory models are not unchanging entities, but represent concise statements of illness beliefs that are salient in an individual's experience at a particular point in time. As the focus of concern about the disorder shifts, perhaps from a physical to a psychosocial or spiritual contemplation of it, the person's explanatory model will change, sometimes with amazing rapidity (Blumhagen, 1980, p. 199).

Patients' tandem use of divergent healing traditions is based on their maintenance of parallel explanatory models. On the other hand, Blumhagen noted that what did remain constant were the units of meaning—the factors which were included in explanations of etiology, pathophysiology, and outcome—that the individuals could draw upon to construct the models. The causal relationships, used to link the various units of meaning together to form such models, were amenable to change in response to different lines of questioning from Blumhagen's interviewers (Blumhagen, 1980, p. 207). Similarly, Leventhal's data show that the way cancer patients represent their illness will undergo major transitions as the illness experience unfolds, although disconfirming experiences probably lead the patient to substitute an alternative model and to store, rather than discard, the old one (Leventhal & Nerenz, 1983). These authors explain:

> A breast cancer patient with advanced metastatic disease may experience substantial joy if chemotherapy produces a reduction in pain and allows her to do simple household chores (Ringler, 1981). To the healthy person or to the person receiving preventive chemotherapy treatment, such minimal gains may seem no gain at all. But the metastatic patient does not compare her current condition to pre-illness conditions. Her underlying model is no longer that of acute illness; it is of terminal chronic disease, and she no longer expects to be cured. Within her new "chronic" regulatory framework, gains and losses are measured in terms of change in daily function; small reductions in pain and small gains in mobility and gains in quality time represent positive outcomes." (Leventhal & Nerenz, 1983, p. 24).

CONCLUSIONS REGARDING CLIENT–THERAPIST NEGOTIATION

The reader may question whether the subtle and complicated negotiations of discourse meaning, nonverbal synchrony, and illness realities advocated in chapters 4 and 5 are actually required with every case. Are such considerations not best left to clinical encounters of obvious cross-cultural significance, lest there be inefficient use of precious (and expensive) professional time? Is it not sensible, the reader may suggest, to use the negotiation cycle selectively, only when difficulties of interpersonal rapport and noncompliance persist?

In brief, we respond "no" to both questions. First of all, the meaning-centered analysis perspective argues for recognition of idiosyncratic experiences that link together to form an individual's semantic illness network. And it is from this semantic network that the client constructs his or her unique disability reality, and communicates those perceptions to others. We therefore anticipate critical differences across individuals' interpretive models, although variation in these models is partially accounted for by identifiable social contexts with which the help provider may become familiar. Influential contexts for shaping dysfunction experience include social class, education, occupation, religion and ethnicity. Obvious sociocultural similarities shared by the speakers may augur well for commonality of discourse strategies, but tells the professional little about the client's commonsense representation of psychopathology or its emotive connotations.

Second, we see merit in Kleinman's (1975) premise that all clinician–patient interactions, regardless of ethnicity, are cross-cultural by the very nature of the divergent professional and lay interpretations of the same health events (see also, Nichter & Trockman, 1983). Even though both partners may share a common ethnicity or social class stratum, the professional's technical education and role socialization draws him or her into a conceptual sphere distinct from that of the help seeker's. The latter's interpretive model, derives from a mixture of popular culture conceptions, explanatory models familiar to the family, and prior experience with the dysfunction and professional care.

We argue, finally, that it is the most efficient use of therapeutic time to work towards the successful negotiation of a common clinical reality. Unless identified and negotiated, divergent images of the presenting problem and subsequent misconceptions of the treatment rationale will jeopardize later interactions. Therapist influence will be diminished, during both the behavior change and treatment generalization phases of intervention. Patient dissatisfaction, noncompliance, and, eventually, premature termination of treatment and litigation, are all logical consequences of a failure to negotiate a mutually satisfying interpretation of clinical reality. It is no coincidence, we believe, that such issues are paramount in both the popular media and the professional literature of the helping professions, given the relatively little effort to date on the part of most clinicians to develop and apply an explicitly negotiation-based therapy perspective.

6
The Influence of Client Expectancies upon the Therapeutic Alliance: Promise, Problems, and Possibilities

Over the past thirty years the construct "client expectancy" has been cited as a potent determinant of treatment process and gain. Since its "discovery" in the early 1950s (Rosenthal & Frank, 1956), this variable has been assigned numerous roles across an assortment of theoretical and empirical publications. Some writers have touted expectancy as an active change-producing ingredient in psychotherapy (e.g., Chance, 1959; Berren & Gillis, 1976; Bootzin & Lick, 1979; Coe, 1980; Fish, 1973; Frank, 1961 Goldstein, 1962; Lick & Bootzin, 1975). Others delegate expectancy to the domain of "nonspecific" treatment effects and seek to control for it (e.g., Bednar, 1970; Kazdin, 1979; Paul, 1966; Wilkins, 1979). Clinicians conducting outcome studies find it a nuisance variable (confound) in assessing specific procedures (see Thoresen & Mahoney, 1974) or use expectancy as a rival hypothesis to demolish evidence supporting specific techniques (Critelli & Neumann, 1984; Kazdin & Wilcoxon, 1976; Russell, 1974).

While it has served many masters, the concept of expectancy maintains wide acceptance among clinicians of all persuasions as well as medical providers (e.g., DiMatteo & DiNicola, 1982; Turk, Meichenabum & Genest, 1983.) Expectancy thrives because it appears to be a powerful vehicle for describing key dynamics in the evolving client–therapist relationship, explaining how in-therapy processes relate to outcome phenomena and linking the therapeutic encounter with facets of the sociocultural milieu. Nevertheless, recent quantitative reviews of the client expectancy literature (Berman, 1979; Duckro, Beal & George, 1979) have added substantial weight to Wilkins' (1973, 1977) long-term skepticism regarding expectancy, and have effectively challenged the basic assumption that this variable is a predictor or determinant of therapeutic gain. This chapter describes the original promise of client expectancy as an explanatory construct, reviews the recent critique opposing it, examines theoretical and methodological rationales for the conflicting findings, and discusses the merits of further empirical probing if the concept is to be rehabilitated.

THE "DEMONSTRATED" EFFECTS OF CLIENT EXPECTANCY ON TREATMENT COURSE AND OUTCOME

A. P. Goldstein, whose early work sparked empirical attention to the expectancy phenomena (see Goldstein, 1960, 1962; Goldstein & Shipman, 1961), has recorded his perceptions of the field's progress (Goldstein, 1981). His evaluations of expectancy effects, taken together with comprehensive reviews by other authors (Duckro, Beal & George, 1979; Coe, 1980; Higginbotham, 1977; Lorion, 1974; Wilkins, 1973), yields a concise enumeration of the positive findings of several dozen studies. The experimental designs that produced these findings most often conform to Goldstein's distinction between prognostic expectancies and role expectancies. Prognostic expectancies are defined as "anticipations of client gain as a function of counseling, held by the client himself and by the counselor. Role expectancies relate more to anticipated in-therapy behaviors, and are expectations held by client and counselor regarding their own and each other's responsibilities, rights, and obligations regarding desired and desirable, as well as undesired and undesirable future in-therapy behavior" (Goldstein, 1981, pp. 85–86). The following five points distill the major empirical conclusions drawn by Goldstein (1981, pp. 86–87) and others.

1. Oftentimes, clients entering psychotherapy express well-defined anticipations and preferences for therapist role behaviors and in turn expect to assume a specified client role. As organized beliefs, role expectancies are strongly influenced by the client's position in society—social class, gender, education and cultural background—as well as previous contact with health and mental health professionals. Early questionnaires identified a triad of role behaviors expected of the helper, including nurturant (protective), model (personally well adjusted), and critic (probing) (see Apfelbaum, 1958). Added to this list are dimensions found through factor analytic studies that mixed *a priori* items with those suggested by clients themselves, including personally committed or cooperative, facilitative, expert, and friendly (e.g., Duffin, 1981; Tinsley, Workman & Kass, 1980).

2. Mutuality or congruence of client and counselor role expectations significantly influences the content, duration and outcome of counseling. Conversely, failure to confirm client expectations of the therapist's personal qualities, tactics, pronouncements and prescriptions results in negative consequences to the therapeutic relationship and potential behavior change.

3. Role induction or anticipatory socialization procedures offered clients during precounseling interviews effectively convey congruent expectations about later in-therapy behaviors. Actively shaping client expectations toward those of the clinician reduces the risk of premature client termination and enhances outcome results.

4. Client prognostic expectancy consistently correlates positively and sig-

nificantly with duration of therapy and with client improvement. Goldstein cautions, however, that "whether the client expectancy–client change relationship is also directional (causal) seems likely but still somewhat equivocal" (Goldstein, 1981, p. 86).

5. Client prognostic expectancy is amenable to direct manipulation through various relationship enhancement methods that aim to increase therapist attractiveness (see Goldstein, 1980). For example, "structuring" clients so that they will like or be attracted to their therapist involves giving explicit information describing positive characteristics of the helper—how attractive he or she is as a person, how the helper will be liked by the client— or emphasizing the therapist's status, skill and similarity in personal background and life style. A second procedure involves identifying relevant dimensions on which clients and counselor relate, then following a matching process to devise optimal participant pairs. The selective assignment of clients to professionals based on preferences, anticipations, cognitive styles, background similarity, and so forth capitalizes on existing individual differences to arouse prognostic expectancies (see Berzins, 1977).

Commensurate with these findings, Higginbotham (1977), proposed a model of the expectancy process that draws together client pretherapy beliefs and confirmation of role expectancies with the subsequent cognitive, emotional, and behavioral responses on the part of the client. The model first points out that an applicant enters the treatment setting with his or her unique set of beliefs about what will (and should) happen, as well as with a conceptualization of what constitutes the problem (see chapter 5). Secondly, he or she encounters an established pattern of behavior that represents the interviewing style, discourse strategy, treatment orientation, and system of personal attributes of the therapist. These behavioral elements are embedded in the identifiable microculture of the professional's clinic, hospital, or private office. At this moment, the client–therapist interaction makes salient one of two divergent and critical perceptions: a) there is an essential congruity between expectations and what is encountered; or b) incongruity and discord is felt between those expectations and the situation at hand. Both sets of perceptions have profound implications for subsequent client performance in and out of therapy.

Congruent role expectations mobilize the client's affective arousal in a positive vein, facilitating certain adaptive cognitions and hope-engendering self-statements. That is, the client recognizes that he or she is receiving the necessary and correct help that was sought. It is coming from a recognizable expert possessing the required skill to ameliorate suffering, solve personal problems, and help make lasting changes. Under these conditions, positive prognostic expectations are evoked. The client has hope, confidence, and faith in improvement; demoralization and hopelessness are counteracted. He or she is motivated to stay in treatment for the length of time required. The behavioral effect is to open the client to further social influence and induce a rigorous attending to therapist instructions. Compliance in carrying out treatment procedures may increase. The client more willingly tests reality by performing previously fearful behaviors. Successful performance reduces fear and prompts self-reinforcement of behavior gains. Further, the expectation of ultimate success serves to bridge the gap between the immediate, taxing tasks required by the therapist and the eventual improvement.

When role expectations are met, it quickens the evolution of a common client–therapist conceptualization of the problem. Attainment of an agreement on how to view the client's problem is a major therapeutic event, given that a particular conceptualization leads to specific behavioral procedures and subsequent behavioral change that can be transferred to real-life situations (see chapter 5; also Meichenbaum, 1975, 1977). Moreover, to the extent that a reconceptualization provides the client with a new perspective, meaning, and grasp of his or her problem, it engenders a sense of control and hope, which will facilitate change as well. Client improvement associated with the mere naming and explanation of a problem is termed "assessment therapy" (Davison, 1969; Meichenbaum, 1977; Schachter, 1966; Wilson & Evans, 1976. See also "Rumpelstiltskin effect", Torrey, 1972).

Sharply contrasting with this scenario is the one arising from unmet expectations or incongruity between preconceived ideas and the actual clinical encounter. It is likely that a negative patient reaction (i.e., psychological reactance, noncompliance, countercontrol) will ensue when it is found that the necessary help-giving conditions are not provided. Unless the initial contact is devoted to the skillful application of a role induction procedure (e.g., Orne & Wender, 1968), aimed at offsetting this felt discrepancy, the likelihood of forming a satisfying relationship is low and the probability of a "premature" termination is high.

The logic of this prediction is straightforward. Unfulfilled expectations are sparked by a treatment rationale with low credibility (Borkovec & Nau, 1972; Kazdin & Wilcoxon, 1976; Wollersheim et al., 1982), the absence of face validity in naming and explaining the problem (Meichenbaum, 1977), and a perceived lack of relevance in the content of the therapist's responses (Epperson, Bushway & Warman, 1983; Rosen, 1972; Rosen & Wish, 1980). Low expectations also follow from a therapist style, attitude, and manner which are unfavorably evaluated (e.g., Dunbar, 1980). Since these are associated with incompetent help, they do not arouse faith, hope, trust or positive prognostic expectancies. The client thinks to him or herself, "This therapist is a dud. She doesn't understand me or the distress I feel and can't be of any use." Compliance with therapeutic instructions is minimal, as the client fails to understand how meeting therapist demands will be profitable in reaching her or his own personal goals for change and relief (Heitler, 1976).

In short, discrepant expectations foster a failure in mutual collaboration. The patient–professional alliance does not materialize, social influence cannot be exercised, and further treatment contact is deemed useless and a waste of time. The client discontinues therapy either overtly, by dropping out, or covertly, through a failure to "work" at behavior change. Presumably, these negative expectations are communicated to the counselor, and factor into his or her judgments of the client's prospects for improvement. As Ullmann and Krasner (1975) point out, a therapist evaluating the client as a poor risk is less likely to establish rapport with him or her, thus providing the conditions for a self-fulfilling prophecy.

In summary, Higginbotham's model presumes that the process of expectancy can be analyzed into three components. It initiates with a cognitive event: A set of self-statements, organized as a belief system, is activated by the treatment encounter. These cognitions are particular anticipations of, and assumptions about, future events. They are probability statements held by the individual that certain desired or undesired outcomes will occur as a function of specific therapist behaviors. The belief is triggered, for example, when a client realizes that the counselor is open and friendly, yet probing, just as was anticipated, and thus views the counselor as a credible expert who can help relieve distress.

The second component is the emotional arousal tied to the belief system. Therapy congruent with role expectations invokes positive prognostic expectancies—the client's faith and confidence in a positive outcome. This belief in eventual treatment efficacy arouses hopefulness and associated feelings of optimism, energy, and well-being; these feelings in themselves may actually promote symptom reduction, especially in affective disorders (Frank, 1961). The release of positive emotion and commensurate tonic effects on physical health comprises the placebo effect that emerges during the early stages of therapy (Rosenthal & Frank, 1956).

The third component is behavioral in nature. It involves selective attention and response utilization on the part of the client (Mahoney, 1974). Once established, credibility and faith motivate the client to rigorously pay attention to and comply with therapeutic instructions (Lick & Bootzin, 1975). The professional's personal influence is maximized; he or she gains potential as a model, educator, and reinforcer while introducing procedures that may result in permanent behavior change. Lick and Bootzin (1975) argue that this component of expectancy mediates change during systematic desensitization. With high expectancy, there is an increased tendency for clients to test the hypothesis that they are cured by exposing themselves more extensively to phobic stimuli in the natural environment. This exposure may result in fear extinction and self-reinforcement for behavioral improvement (Bootzin & Lick, 1979).

CHALLENGES TO THE ASSUMED "DEMONSTRATED" EFFECTS OF EXPECTANCY

The validity of the above "facts" and model of expectancy processes have been disputed recently by several reviewers. Wilkins (1973a, b; 1977a, b; 1979) was an early and persistent opponent of client prognostic expectancy as a deterministic construct, and considers the notions of therapist prognostic expectancy and self-fulfilling prophecy to be of equally dubious merit. First of all, Wilkins (1973a) seriously doubts the existence of rigorous empirical support to justify employing expectancy to account for gain in psychotherapy. He cites 11 studies, all of which attempted to manipulate expectancy (high versus low) through differential instructions to clients (Bednar & Parker, 1969; Grosz, 1968; Imber et al., 1970; Krause, 1968; Krause et al., 1969; Marcia et al., 1969; McGlynn et al., 1969, 1971; McGlynn & Mapp, 1970; McGlynn & Williams, 1970; Sloane et al., 1970). Nonsignificant results were reported for the eight studies in which the therapist was experimentally "blind" to the instructions. Positive expectancy effects were reported for the remaining three studies, in which therapists had knowledge of the instructional content.

Secondly, Wilkins points to the methodological confounds that flaw many of the earlier studies. Some failed to include measures of improvement independent of the client's own self-rating (i.e., nonindependent source bias), or lacked an assessment of the client's induced state of expectancy independent of the treatment outcome which the expectancy was supposed to produce. Other designs procedurally confounded instructed expectancy with the delivery of praise or feedback of improvement, thus precluding the latter variable from being ruled out as a cause for treatment effectiveness. Moreover, discovery of a reliable correlation between client expectancies and clinical outcomes merely demonstrates that clients are accurate predictors of future events. Correlational evidence does not allow the conclusion that such predictions actually cause expected outcomes to occur.

Finally, Wilkins' sharpest critique of the expectancy concept is that it is an inappropriate reification of the medical placebo effect. Early psychotherapy researchers employing correlational designs to appraise treatment efficacy could legitimately consider expectancy as an "interpretive contaminant," because the effects of therapy were yet to be shown superior to and independent of expectancy factors. Yet it was empirically premature, and logically incorrect, for workers to assume that expectancy manipulations—the psychological equivalent to a medical placebo—actually *caused* client change to occur. In addition, Wilkins (1973, 1979) invokes a behaviorist analysis to deny the necessity of the expectancy construct. If behavior change follows the introduction of observable therapy procedures, such as a placebo manipulation or expectancy of success instructions, it is more appropriate to account for such change in terms of observable events rather than a presumed (covert) expectancy state that these manupulations are intended to evoke. In brief, Wilkins asserts that client prognostic expectancy is a superfluous construct as a causal explanation for outcome events, and can be abandoned on empirical, conceptual, and intellectual grounds.

While Wilkins evaluated the client prognostic expectancy literature, Duckro, Beal and George (1979) carefully reviewed 32 empirical efforts since 1962, all of which explore the effects of disconfirmed client role expectations upon a) client satisfaction; b) premature termination, c) changes in client expectations, d) therapeutic process and e) outcome. For each of these five dependent variables, they calculated the percentage of studies supporting and opposing the hypothesis that disconfirmed role expectations result in negative consequences. Across the five categories, the percentage of studies supporting the hypothesis fluctuated between 33 to 62 per cent. Duckro et al. conclude that the empirical foundation for this previously "proven" hypothesis is imbued with ambiguity. Only those experimental designs which contain role induction strategies, devised for shaping role expectations, give a "hint" of a consistent positive relationship with favorable outcomes.

Since Duckro et al.'s publication, at least 12 studies addressing the disconfirmed role expectancy hypothesis have been reported in Dissertation Abstracts (the source for 16 of the 32 research reports they cited). Of the ten reports examining the effects of role expectancy congruence on premature client termination, 80 percent found no relationship between dropout rate and low congruence (negative outcomes: Haspel, 1982; Hoffman, 1982; Hoyt, 1980; Kriesberg, 1977; Malzer, 1980; Silverberg, 1982; Smith, 1977; Timothy, 1981; positive outcomes: Lambert, 1982; Talbot, 1983). The six studies that include measures of client improvement yielded only two findings in support of the prediction (negative outcomes: Brisbin, 1981; Hoyt, 1980; Kriesberg, 1977; Silverberg, 1982; positive outcomes: Lambert, 1982; Wynne, 1982). In contrast, three of the four designs in which congruence was manipulated through role induction preparations did show some favorable results. The outcomes include the reduction of attrition rates (Lambert, 1982; Talbot, 1983) and enhancement of treatment gains (Hoyt, 1980; Lambert, 1982). Two of the four efforts, however, found no association between dropout rate and exposure to the role preparation interview. In brief, these more recent investigations, although consistent with Duckro et al.'s findings that pretherapy socialization techniques may influence persistence and outcome in therapy, are, if anything, more pessimistic about associations between level of client–therapist role expectations congruence and premature termination or actual behavioral improvements.

If the negative box scores tallied by Wilkins and Duckro et al. do not completely undermine the client expectancy construct, the *coup de grace* may come from Berman's (1979) quantitative review of 15 studies relating client prognostic expectancy to a measure of outcome. With this subset of well-designed studies of actual clinical populations, Berman performed a "meta-analysis" in which the findings of the original 15 investigations were treated as raw observations and their reported effect sizes and probability estimates were combined in a common metric (a weighted correlation coefficient [Berman, 1979, p. 2]). The results strengthen and clarify the negative findings previously reviewed. First, although the overall expectancy effect size of 0.13 was statistically significant, it accounted for only 2 percent of the variance in treatment outcome, and is due to the large number of degrees of freedom. Second, the reported correlation between client expectancy and outcome fluctuates markedly according to the type of study under consideration. When inpatient studies are isolated, the average effect size virtually disappears, while outpatient studies report the strongest effect ($r = 0.25$).

However, isolation of the most "sophisticated studies" produces the most damaging results. Those 6 reports in which a) the client was not the source for the outcome measure and b) expectancy was not confounded with knowledge of gain (i.e., assessed prior to measurement of outcome), revealed a non-significant correlation (0.08) between prognostic expectancy and gain. Thus, Berman garners quantitative support for Wilkins' argument that significant correlations between client expectancy and outcome only arise in designs where the outcome ratings are derived from client self-report. Nevertheless, client subjective judgment of improvement is a necessary source of information about the effects of intervention, and deserves more weight in these outcome designs than these authors appear to suggest.

POSSIBLE EXPLANATIONS
FOR THE LACK OF CLIENT EXPECTANCY EFFECTS
AND DIRECTIONS FOR FURTHER RESEARCH

The previous reviews, taken together with our own survey of recent literature (all appearing in Dissertation Abstracts), leads us to consider two conclusions:

1. Client expectancies have an insignificant influence on therapeutic process and outcome. Original positive results are attributable to methodological and procedural artifacts that disappear with the introduction

of design rigor, such as independent measures of treatment gain and the disentanglement of knowledge of results or "predictions" from expectancies (see Higginbotham, 1977).

2. Client expectancies influence only a selected set of process and outcome events. Furthermore, expectancy effects occur under a more restricted range of conditions and in a more complicated (interactive) fashion than originally assumed.

Acceptance of the first conclusion leads us to abandon client expectancy as a meaningful consideration for clinic practice and for psychotherapy research: to do so at this point may be premature. In contrast, attention to the second conclusion leads to speculation regarding those events, conditions, and complex interactions that might be associated with the occurrence of client expectancy effects. We initiate our speculation with a general proposition:

Conceptual and theoretical refinement of the expectancy construct—by attending to its multidimensional attributes and phenomenological meaning to individual clients—will increase expectancies' predictive validity of specific in-therapy events as well as client improvement.

Problems in Defining Expectancies

The cognitive structure of expectancies

Reviewers critical of current expectancy studies point to the conceptual confusion that shrouds the term. Researchers have been accused of using imprecisely defined or globally assessed expectancies in their work (Klepac & Page, 1974), and terms so ambiguously referenced that they were open to several interpretations by respondents (Duckro et al., 1979). Other definitions are limited in the range of expectancy elements assessed (Tinsley et al., 1980) or else are broad and indiscriminate (Wilkins, 1979). The most compelling conceptual difficulty, though, is whether expectancy, as a cognition, refers to anticipation or to preference, or whether it encompasses both meanings in some hierarchical fashion (Duckro et al., 1979).

Reference to the term's usage in experimental social psychology helps clarify its distinctive characteristics, shows how the notion is measured, and gives a list of the various kinds of expectancies that have been postulated. The Expectancy × Value model tradition (see Feather, 1982, for summary) generally defines expectancies as specific beliefs that individuals maintain about the likelihood that particular outcomes will follow certain other events, including actions, situations, and/or other outcomes. Knowledge of expectancy processes is important for theoretical and practical reasons. These processes are assumed to determine goal-directed action, in association with the individual's perceived attraction toward or avoidance of those anticipated outcomes. Translated into clinical relationship terms, the

Expectancy × Value model suggests that the client's initial response to the therapeutic interview (e.g., drop out or continued compliance) bears some relation to the expectations that he or she holds regarding the therapist's action and the subjective value of the consequences that might occur following the action (e.g., desire for behavior change) (see Feather, 1982, p. 1).

The Expectancy × Value model indicates that in order for a clinical research design to begin to account for clients' actions in terms of their expectancies, the researcher needs to: a) elicit a precise itemization from subjects of those treatment event(s) about which they actually maintain an expectancy; b) obtain a reliable subjective judgment regarding the probability that such treatment events lead to particular outcomes; and c) ask the individuals to evaluate the desirability of those anticipated outcomes. The research procedure must be sufficiently sensitive to illuminate not simply that client A, a middle-aged woman with marital problems, has preferences about being seen by a woman therapist. The design must reveal the other elements in this client's expectancy structure. These include her belief that a woman therapist will very likely have a sympathetic understanding of her unhappy life situation, and that such an accurate understanding is a necessary condition to enable the client to fully express her unspoken emotions regarding the unsatisfying marriage and openly consider what are her future options (a highly desired outcome).

Few, if any, studies have used such a comprehensive measurement of expectancy. However, Higginbotham, Yamamoto and Takemoto-Chock (1978) have made a preliminary step in this direction. These workers constructed an expectancy inventory for cross-cultural surveys that asked subjects in New Zealand, Japan, and Hawaii to evaluate a list of 125 treatment characteristics, according to how much each one is expected to contribute to a successful outcome for a hypothetical psychiatric case. Six categories of treatment event-outcome expectancies were rated, including situation (type of clinic), therapist characteristics (gender, training, etc.), therapist actions (style, techniques, causal explanation), goals and goal setting, and client actions (dependency, loyalty, self-initiation, etc.). In addition, each of the general expectancy categories was rated in terms of its importance in determining the successful treatment of the client. This permitted discrimination of which class of treatment events are indeed expected to be the most powerful in bringing about the assumed desired consequence (i.e., successfully curing the client) and which events subjects either have not formed expectations about or perceive as irrelevant.

The instrument devised by Higginbotham et al. attempts to measure the *magnitude* of an individual's subjective probability for each expectancy—the level of likelihood that a particular action by the therapist will lead to a desired goal. Feather (1982) suggests that when expectancies are measured, consideration should be given to several additional parameters along which expectancies may vary. For instance, some clients hold strongly to their expectancies, while others change them rapidly. Certain expectancies may be widely shared within a social group, while other beliefs are more idiosyncratic. In sum, investigating the contribution of a particular expectancy to planful behavior requires measuring the expectancy at the same level of generality as the outcome behavior under consideration. If the clinician is seeking to predict treatment outcome using fine-grained measures of cognitive, affective and behavioral functioning, so too must the measures of expectancy yield fine-grained scores that can be correlated with the outcome data.

Kinds of treatment expectancies

A second reason for the conceptual confusion in the literature is the failure of investigators to realize that several different kinds of expectancies operate in therapy and each kind may comprise numerous referents that change from person to person. In order to establish greater clarity across experiments and to identify the relationships among the *kinds* of expectancies measured within the same design, we need to refine Goldstein's original distinction between role and prognostic expectancies. This can be done by synthesizing into a common framework (seen in figure 6.1) those expectancies identified by cognitive social psychologists as strongly associated with self-regulated behavior change and motivation (see Bandura, 1977; Carver & Scheier, 1981; Feather, 1982; Heckhausen, 1977; Mischel, 1973).

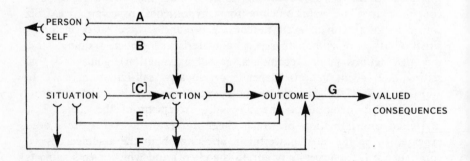

Figure 6.1 Kinds of expectancies theoretically linked to choice behavior and self-regulation

Figure 6.1 is derived from Heckhausen's (1977) model where expectancies are related to a four-stage sequence of events: first, the initial situation as perceived, and then the person's own action, the outcome of the action (or the situation), and the consequences of the outcome. Heckhausen (1977) posits that the anticipated outcome, with its associated incentive value, is the critical reference people use in formulating expectancies. He defines four different kinds of expectancies in terms of how the outcome relates to the other three stages in the sequence:

1. *Situation–Outcome Expectancies* refer to the degree to which the present situation will lead toward a desired outcome apart from any contribution of the person (relationship E in figure 6.1).

2. In contrast, *Action–Outcome Expectancies* concern the probability that the current situation is modifiable through one's own actions to produce a desired outcome (relationship A).

3. When situational constraints and resources impinge upon the person's actions while striving for a valued outcome, it is termed an *Action-by-Situation Expectancy* (relatonship F).

4. Relationship G denotes *Outcome–Consequence Expectancies*, those expectancies concerning the degree to which outcomes produced by oneself or by others are instrumental to bring about consequences having particular incentive values (Heckhausen, 1977, pp. 288–289).

Like other Expectancy × Value theorists, Heckhausen considers behavior as predictable and interpretable in motivational terms only when we have knowledge of an outcome's particular incentive value, and of its particular probability of occurrence, from the perspective of the individual.

Heckhausen's Action–Outcome Expectancy differs from Bandura's (1977a) definition of *outcome expectancy* in that Bandura does not assume that it is the person's own efforts which are instrumental for a particular outcome. Relationship D depicts the client's estimate that a given action will lead to certain outcomes. Consequently, a person who does not know the typical outcomes of a given action cannot have an outcome expectancy regarding that action (Carver & Scheier, 1981). Bandura's definition of action–outcome expectancies purposely excludes the actor's sense of personal instrumentality, because it is this latter process that he has chosen to isolate and elaborate within his theory of self-efficacy. Bandura states that "an efficacy expectation is the conviction that one can successfully execute the behavior required to produce the outcomes [action]" (Bandura, 1977a, p. 193). His theory posits that such expectancies determine people's choice of behavioral settings and activities, the amount of effort individuals will expend, and how long they will persist in the face of obstacles (see Goldfried & Robins, 1982).

Such assertions have been generally supported (Bandura, 1982). Yet under

certain conditions (e.g., pain patients), self-efficacy and outcome expectancies
are highly intercorrelated (Manning & Wright, 1983); at other times,
outcome expectancy alone determines increased intentions to perform
(Maddux, Sherer & Rogers, 1982). We map efficacy expectancy onto Figure
6.1 as relationship B, the expectancy linking the person with the action
events.

Finally, Carver and Scheier (1981), in the context of developing a control
theory model of self-regulation, postulate the existence of an *outcome
expectancy assessment* process. Their outcome expectancy concept constitutes
a more broadly derived estimate of the likelihood of occurrence of a desired
outcome, because it is based upon an integration of the person's other
expectancy perceptions. Hence, there is a weighing up of the accumulated
physical, time, and social constraints upon one's behavior (i.e., Heckhausen's
Situation–Outcome, Action–Outcome, and Situation–Action–Outcome expectancies), as well as the breadth and depth of one's available resources
(efficacy expectancies) to evaluate the probability of goal attainment. Within
Carver and Scheier's (1981) theory, the result of the outcome expectancy
assessment is highly critical. It leads to a decision of whether or not to try
and reduce the perceived discrepancy between a behavioral performance and
the standard of performance toward which one strives. Expectancy
assessments are pivotal in control-theory terms, since they signal the system
(Person) to either continue to try (Operate) or withdraw from the attempt
(Exit).

Kinds of treatment expectancies in the clinical literature
At this juncture it may prove illuminating to compare operational
definitions of expectancy in the clinical literature with the kinds of
expectancies, shown in Figure 6.1, that cognitive scientists deem significant
for behavior change and self-regulation. A startling discovery is made when
one carefully examines the wordings used on questionnaires and interviews
to measure role and prognostic expectancies. Much of what has been studied
as expectancy bears little, if any, resemblance to the constructs that the
Expectancy × Value theorists investigate in relation to behavior motivation
and prediction. Of the dozens of reports examined, not one considered
outcomes in terms of the incentive values of the probable consequences of
those outcomes (relationship G). Moreover, only studies by Rosen (e.g.,
Rosen & Wish, 1980) include measures of what behaviors are anticipated
(from the therapist) and how important those behaviors are to the client.
Rosen proposes that therapist behaviors that are both highly anticipated and
viewed as important will possess reinforcement value for the client and
signal the likelihood of goal achievement (i.e., a value-laden outcome).

The majority of those studies that seek to assess "role expectancies" are
actually concerned with only a sub-component of the expectancy structure,

identified as relationship C in Figure 6.1. In essence, role expectations constitute the client's anticipation that exposure to a certain treatment situation (or therapist) will lead to contact with a set of specific social demands and responsibilities, with personal and behavioral qualities from other actors, and with those interpersonal and technological actions that comprise the "technique" of therapy. Some studies simply compile a list of what "actions" are anticipated (e.g., Begley & Lieberman, 1970; Hartlage & Sperr, 1980; Heine & Trosman, 1960; Overall & Aronson, 1963; Tracey, Heck & Lichtenberg, 1981). Others include some measure of the probability or strength of belief that certain actions will occur within the treatment situation (e.g., Bernstein, 1964; Berzins, Friedman & Seidman, 1969; Boulware & Holmes, 1970; Goldstein & Heller, 1960; Rosen & Wish, 1980; Schonfield, Stone, Hoehn-Saric, Imber & Pande, 1969; Tinsley et al., 1980). It is apparent that role expectancy studies fail to consider how the client conceptually relates this list of anticipated actions with subjective probabilities of subsequent outcomes. In so doing, they also fail to gauge any incentive values attached to outcomes. Thus, according to expectancy theory, these studies omit the key knowledge that motivates clients to become concerned with action events in the first place.

In fact, investigators concerned with the negative effects of discrepant expectancies have assumed that a highly anticipated action is a preferred event (see Duckro et al., 1979), which implies the possibility of desired outcomes following from those action conditions. But without knowledge of the action–outcome component of the client's expectancy and associated incentives, measures of the discrepancy between client and counselor anticipations cannot be meaningfully interpreted as a potent stimulus for dissatisfaction, resistance, or either physical or psychological drop out from counseling (see Bolles, 1972). The client may not prefer his or her anticipations, may have beliefs that are only vaguely formulated, or may see little connection between a satisfactory problem solution and what may transpire during the clinical interview. Researchers' omission of these components of the expectancy equation may help account for the present listing of confused and poor results (Duckro et al., 1979; Berman, 1979). In essence, we suggest that most role expectancy studies to date have not dealt with expectancy. Rather, they have elicited client anticipations of situational events and demand characteristics—beliefs which are less related theoretically to motivation and behavior choice.

A comparable critique may be applied to the conceptualizations found within reports of client prognostic expectancies. Such studies aim to determine the strength of the client's belief that treatment will produce symptom improvement. Martin's frequently cited studies with the Patient Prognostic Expectancy Inventory is characteristic of this genre of work

(Martin & Sterne, 1975; Martin, Sterne, Claveaux & Acree, 1976; Martin, Sterne, Moore & Friedmeyer, 1976). The inventory lists 15 symptoms reflecting serious disturbance and asks the patient how much improvement he or she anticipates in each area as a result of hospital treatment. Like many of the interviews designed to assess prognostic expectancies, Martin and Sterne's procedure actually measures situation–outcome expectancies, depicted as relationship E in Figure 6.1 (e.g., Goldstein, 1960; Goldstein & Shipman, 1961; Greer, 1980; Gulas, 1974; Kemmerling, 1973; cf. Bloch et al., 1976). The patient is asked to rate anticipated improvement for each of 15 possible outcome behaviors in the context of a situation that is only globally defined as "hospital treatment." No effort is made to determine which symptoms (if any) the patient acknowledges experiencing, or how desirable it is for the patient to secure "improvement" for each assumed problem area. Certain anticipated change areas, such as the client's tendency to be overexcited, depend on other people, or have difficulty in keeping a job, may be completely irrelevant to the interviewee's actual belief about which behavior changes are most desirable through one's stay in the hospital.

In brief, these studies fail to clarify which dimensions of the situation the client views as associated with personally relevant outcomes. More importantly, inattention to Situation–Action–Outcome expectancies results in an abbreviated understanding of the client's sense of personal contribution to treatment success (cf. Tinsley et al, 1980). The meaning of an outcome as a motivating stimulus, as well as its implications for self-esteem, can only be understood when there is knowledge of the client's confidence in his or her ability to assume an active role, and to produce events in treatment that are expected to yield desirable changes (i.e., assessment of relationships A, B, and F).

Problems in Measuring Expectancies Through Self-Report Methods

The internal validity of expectancy research can also be challenged on methodological grounds, especially in terms of the instrumentation used to measure type and strength of client expectancies. The numerous self-report instruments which have been constructed presume to map, accurately, those relevant subjective judgments and values maintained by the client. However, people do not always have well-articulated anticipations and preferences about treatment, and their values of desired outcomes may be incoherent, fluid, or not thought through (Brisbin, 1981; Fischoff, Goiten & Shapira, 1982; Heppner & Heesacker, 1983). When expectations are not well formulated or nonexistent, direct self-report procedures may become major forces in shaping those judgments that *are* elicited (see Fischoff et al., 1982).

For those subjects who *have* formulated relevant expectations, the use of questionnaires which restrict their responses to a fixed format and preselected vocabulary could hinder the accurate portrayal of those beliefs, by omitting categories these subjects deem most meaningful (Jones, 1977). Tinsley et al. (1980) note that prominent client expectancy inventories—for example, those developed by Apfelbaum (1958), Begley & Lieberman (1970), and Lorr (1965)—restrict the range of focus to client expectancies of counselor's behaviors and attitudes. They ignore expectancies of both treatment success and the behaviors to be displayed by the client.

Moreover, inventory items frequently reflect the biases of prevailing counseling theories and professional viewpoints. For example, the Expectations About Counseling questionnaire was constructed by Tinsley et al. (1980) to measure *all* of the theoretically important expectations a prospective client might have about counseling. Yet this scale is itself heavily flavored with items derived from Rogerian thought. Scales that make up the questionnaire include openness, genuineness, empathy, self-disclosure, concreteness, tolerance, and nurturance. Rather than eliciting items from clients preparing to enter their first therapy session or from other lay groups, researchers have relied almost exclusively on the judgments of practicing therapists, or on dimensions from published inventories, as the sources for new scale development (cf. Duffin, 1981).

In order to more fully gather data on expectations from the client's perspective, Goldstein (1981) urges the use of free response approaches, open-minded interviews, and more phenomenological participant observer techniques. The presence of phenomenological probes for each subject also permits the investigator to verify how the individual is interpreting the expectancy questions. Some may interpret the task as an inquiry as to what outcomes they *want* to attain, as opposed to those outcomes they think will actually occur given the situation and their own ability (Carver & Scheier, 1981). The present literature is especially vulnerable to this threat to internal validity, given the lack of definitional certainty and conceptual clarity among workers.

In their discussion of the relationship between self-report and behavior, Carver and Scheier (1981), point to two sources of error, both of which weaken the predictive link between people's statements and their overt actions. Their observation illuminates the difficulties with expectancy instruments. One prominent error source concerns the veridicality of self-reports: whether or not one pursues a thorough search of one's memory for information about one's behavior, in response to items of the instrument. If the client's memory is sampled too superficially and he or she is distracted by atypical recollections, the report will not be representative of the encoded information that may later be used to guide actions in the treatment context

(Carver & Scheier, 1981).

Taylor and Fiske (1978) label such recall bias "top of the head" phenomena. Oftentimes people attend largely to the salient stimuli in their environment and such information, although perhaps trivial and atypical, becomes overrepresented in their causal explanations, beliefs and opinions. Taylor and Fiske (1978) offer two reasons why engulfment of a person's attention produces this effect. First, attention may increase the *amount* of encoded information about a salient stimulus, and lead the person to overrate its importance in later recall. Second, information about salient aspects of the environment is stored in a more *easily retrieved* form in memory, i.e. "at the top of the mental heap." Some evidence suggests that salient information is more available and easily brought to mind because it has been doubly encoded, both in words and images. Therefore, when an individual is asked to make a causal judgment or statement of probability (i.e., state an expectancy), he or she is likely to retrieve a colorful, immediate, and vivid piece of case history information, rather than produce an inference based upon a statistical summary of past events. Case history information is more imageable (and doubly encoded) than statistical information, but it prompts a more biased interview response than a more reflective consideration of nonsalient past experiences.

Another source of error is introduced when the expectancy researcher ignores the general finding that "attitudes formed on the basis of one's previous personal involvement with an attitude object appear to be better predictors of subsequent behavior than are attitudes formed on the basis of nonbehavioral information" (Carver & Scheier, 1981, p. 277). Clients with prior therapeutic experience may have better defined and more sharply focused expectancies, and be more confident of these expectancies, than first-time clients. This latter group can only draw upon the stated experiences and value positions of their social network members when responding to questionnaire probes. In short, the client's own past experience in counseling is a much stronger determinant of his or her subjective probability estimate of successful outcome than is information regarding the performance of significant others and associates who have received counseling.

Outcome Expectancy and Time of Assessment

A third explanation for the lack of reliable client expectancy effects is that outcome expectancy fluctuates during the course of treatment. Since most designs fail to include multiple probes, these trends are not adequately accounted for in efforts to correlate expectancies with subsequent behavioral measures. The results produced are low or insignificant correlations between predictor and predicted variables. The timing of the probe is critical to the expectancy image produced, and must be reiterated at each significant phase of therapy in order to gauge fairly the predictive power of those expectancies elicited during these critical periods.

This reasoning follows from Expectancy × Value theorists' notion of the person as a dynamic, self-regulating actor, who continually constructs and reconstructs psychological reality. Perceptions of reality draw from the immediate situation, legacies from the past, and anticipations about the short- and long-term future (Feather, 1982). Client responses during therapy are more than a succession of discrete episodic reactions. They comprise an extended and ongoing stream of that client's behavior. Hence, Feather urges us to discover how such action can be understood, in a framework that includes, past, present, and future as represented in the immediate or momentary determinants. The point to be made here is that as these determinants change at various critical points, clients' perceptions are altered, and with them their expectations of various outcomes. This assumption conforms well with a growing number of empirical studies indicating that precounseling and initial treatment expectations are not highly durable and, in fact, are readily modified during the middle and closing moments of therapeutic contact (e.g., Heppner & Heesacker, 1983).

Precontact phase expectancies
What are the determinants and characteristics of client outcome expectancies at various time frames in the therapy cycle? Prior to the initial counseling session, client expectation of improvement is obviously influenced by various nontherapeutic factors. These could include the person's image of how intransigent the problem is; previous experience in controlling the condition; and prognostic information, conveyed by the client's social support system, about the general efficacy of professional help for such difficulties. A consistent research finding is that initial expectations are strongly influenced by past performance at comparable tasks (Feather, 1982). However, in the absence of prior experience, people evaluate their chances of success by comparing themselves with others like them who have faced comparable circumstances (Jones, 1977).

The majority of studies that employ expectancy measurements include only single probes, are administered either prior to or just after the initial treatment session (e.g., Bloch et al., 1976; Borin, 1974). Client assessments at this time tap prognostic beliefs that may be heavily influenced by the client's intimate associates. Also reflected are memories of earlier efforts to control the problem, and perhaps general feelings of hopefulness. Yet these outcome ratings may bear little resemblance to those judgments the client will make following an actual exposure to the clinician, treatment rationale, and therapeutic environment. For example, Greer (1980) found that a subset of clients seen at an outpatient community mental health center actually lowered their prognostic expectancies from the time of intake to after the first visit. Those who did so evidenced better adjustment than clients who maintained high expectations.

Moreover, precontact probes may be particularly unreliable given that some persons will not have formulated sharply defined expectancies by this stage (see section beginning on p. 140). The effort to develop specific treatment expectancies for the first time may only bring out "top of the head" answers (Taylor & Fiske, 1978). These judgments are brought into temporary consciousness and saliency, and are subsequently lost as the expectancy becomes progressively more integrated and refined. Probes that only occur at a later stage would not produce the same level of conscious reflection about expectancies as would assessments during the formative phases of expectancy development. In contrast, a "pretest effect" may operate, whereby initial client assessment encourages a tendency towards self-consistency (i.e., for the client to report an outcome consistent with stated expectancy [Frank, 1973; Friedman, 1963]) or sensitivity to later procedures and thus makes the client more critical and suspicious of therapist offered conditions.

Expectancies after initial sessions
The client's outcome expectancy after exposure to one or two therapy sessions may differ sharply in either direction from precontact judgments. Once familiar with the clinician's personal qualities, style of discourse, explanation of the problem, and therapy rationale, the doubtful client may increase his or her subjective perception of the probability of success. For example, a series of studies by Wollersheim (Wollersheim et al., 1982; Wollersheim & Bugge, 1977) pinpointed the considerable influence exerted by different therapy rationales upon perceptions of prognosis, length of time needed for improvement, and perceptions of the credibility and effectiveness of treatment.

Other subjects may associate different treatment components with positive outcomes, including therapist gender, ethnicity, social class background, or capacity to convey personal warmth. Takemoto-Chock and Higginbotham (1982) found that New Zealand University students considered treatment technique to be associated with outcome for a severe psychological disturbance, while a comparable sample of Japanese-American students in Hawaii considered outcome to be more related to the therapist's description of the cause of the disorder. With the Hawaiian sample, treatment technique itself was not correlated with outcome. Also, Ford (1978) noticed that during the early sessions clients' ratings of the therapeutic relationship depended on how well the therapist fulfilled their "good versus bad" expectancy. Clients saw the relationship as optimal at that point when the therapist communicated verbal and/or nonverbal encouragement, involvement, and respect, and chose to focus upon the client rather than her or his significant other.

These findings suggest that during the initial contact phase, the client actively evaluates helper qualities and treatment events for their change-producing potential. This appraisal yields a *Situation–Outcome Expectancy*— a belief concerning the degree to which the situation contains the conditions sufficient to bring about improvement apart from the client's own contribution (Heckhausen, 1977). In control theory terms, the client compares the actual treatment events with those events that are hypothesized to facilitate behavior change. When conditions offered by the therapist meet the "standard" regarded by the client as necessary for improvement, then a strongly positive Situation–Outcome expectancy is generated. However, this expectancy by itself only partially determines the client's estimate of the chances for improvement (Carver & Scheier's Outcome Expectancy Assessment). The latter is also determined by the level of self-efficacy expectancy that the client brings with him or her into therapy (see Figure 6.1). In this instance, personal efficacy is the conviction that one is capable of competently performing those behaviors which are the desired fruits of therapy (Bandura, 1977a; Goldfried and Robins, 1982). This argument is summarized in the hypothesis below:

Hypothesis 6.1
The client's initial estimate of the likelihood of success (i.e., outcome expectancy assessment) is a function of the interaction between level of self-efficacy for behavior change and degree of Situation–Outcome Expectancy.

Table 6.1 explains the nature of this interaction. Clients who enter treatment with high self-efficacy and discover a good match after comparing the actual treatment with their hypothesized standard for adequate care (and thus generate a high Situation–Outcome Expectancy) will report a high subjective probability of success. This Outcome Expectancy Assessment (OEA) will probably remain fairly constant across the treatment experience. However, if those same high self-efficacy clients perceive a poor match between actual and standard treatments, and thus form a low Situation–Outcome Expectancy, they will have an initially low subjective probability of success. This estimate may move upward rather quickly, though, if the therapist can construct a convincing argument for the merits of his or her techniques, style, experience, and so forth. It may be that high self-efficacy individuals do not often seek therapy. Yet "Type A" individuals—those who express a high need for achievement, in combination with a great sense of time urgency, need for control, and hostility when thwarted—may indeed seek help. Negative effects of this high expectancy life style include heart disease, interpersonal conflict, and maladaptive persistence in hopeless situations (see Janoff-Bulman & Brickman, 1982).

Table 6.1 Predicted value and fluctuation in Outcome Expectancy
Assessment (O.E.A.) under different conditions of client self-efficacy and situation
× outcome expectancy

CLIENT SELF-EFFICACY

High   Low

		High	Low
INITIAL		High Outcome Expectancy Assessment (Stable)	Low O.E.A. Moderate O.E.A.
SITUATION	High		
X			
OUTCOME		Low O.E.A.	Low Outcome Expectancy Assessment (Stable)
EXPECTANCY	Low	High O.E.A.	

   Low self-efficacy subjects present a different scenario. Even if there is a good match with what the client believes to be the best possible therapeutic situation, he or she may never experience more than a middle range probability of improvement. Even with the best imaginable help, the client simply cannot imagine a strong possibility that he or she is capable of solving this problem or reducing the current level of distress. Low self-efficacy clients who formulate a low Situation–Outcome Expectancy regarding the therapeutic conditions will report the lowest level of outcome expectancy. This estimate is not likely to fluctuate significantly, and the person will probably leave treatment if they can and drop out psychologically if they are unable to phsyically leave.
   In brief, our argument is twofold: First, a differential prediction of outcome expectancy assessment can be made based upon level of self-efficacy and Situation–Outcome Expectancy. Secondly, under specified circumstances the client's estimate is likely to fluctuate over time. Both high self-efficacy clients finding a poor match with their standard of treatment and low self-efficacy clients finding a good match with their standard are likely to raise their estimates of success. This prediction may help explain why expectancy probes during initial treatment stages do not always reliably correlate with subsequent estimates, nor with other in-therapy and outcome variables.

Expectancies during middle and closing sessions
Finally, client outcome expectancies during the middle portion of therapy (i.e., sessions 4, 5, and 6 of a 10 week cycle) and at the closing moments of the relationship (i.e., final two or three contacts) are influenced by self-evaluations of actual behavior change as well as the client's sense of confidence that such gains can be maintained in the absence of therapist support. A series of studies by Feather (1961, 1963, 1965) demonstrated that subjects' initial expectations—cued by knowledge of other's performance and the task structure—were subsequently altered to conform with their own actual task performance. Later experiments by this researcher (Feather, 1966; Feather & Saville, 1967) on the effects of prior success and failure at a task confirmed the notion that task performance assumes a dominant role in influencing the subjects' estimates of their chances of success (see Feather, 1982, and Jones, 1977).

This finding is echoed in Ford's interpretations of his data of client perceptions of the therapy relationship obtained during the mid to late portion of the treatment cycle. Perceptions of the relationship by this group of female clients seemed to be largely a function of the gains that these women saw themselves making toward personal objectives, such as becoming more assertive and less anxious in extra-therapy social situations. Ford observed that "the therapists seemed to enhance, and perhaps elicit these positive self-perceptions by encouraging the client to discuss her successful attempts at assertion from the past week and the cognitions that accompanied such occurrences" (Ford, 1978, p. 1312). Furthermore, the clients' feelings about ending treatment guided their ratings of the therapeutic relationship at the final session. The women who lacked confidence to proceed on their own without the supportive relationship expressed this apprehension through a low relationship evaluation, while those who felt "finished" and confident enough to move forward on their own gave high ratings (Ford, 1978).

In general, the timing of the expectancy probe is critical. Subject estimates are likely to vary across the several phases in the intervention cycle. Precontact estimates of outcome may be particularly unreliable and reflect combinations of generalized feelings of hopefulness or despair regarding the problem and the prognostications of family and friends. Initial contact expectancies are a function of how well the treatment environment matches the person's standard for what is deemed essential to produce a cure *along with* the sense of self-efficacy carried into the clinic. Once treatment has begun in earnest, or upon client termination, the expectancy report is influenced by actual or perceived treatment gains. Those who have changed report higher expectancies of success; those who feel doubtful about maintaining improvement once therapy discontinues offer lower estimates.

Given these multiple determinants operating at different times, it becomes imperative to make repeated probes of outcome expectancy over the course of contact. Research designs with repeated measurements afford the best opportunity to determine rigorously whether any relationship exists between clients' outcome expectancy assessments and the degree to which they contribute to and profit from their professional contact.

Therapist Expectancy as a Mediating Variable

Therapist enhancement of client expectancy effects
A fourth explanation for the failure to substantiate a connection between client expectancy and treatment effects involves the role of therapist expectancy as an intervening variable. Previous research has not adequately considered the possibility that an interaction often occurs between client and therapist levels of outcome expectancy, canceling the influence that an initial client estimate would have upon subsequent performance. We hypothesize that:

Hypothesis 6.2
The effect of client level of outcome expectancy upon subsequent treatment gain is determined by the level of therapist outcome expectancy. A high correspondence between client and therapist expectancies strengthens the relationship between client estimate of success and actual outcome; a low correspondence between interactant's expectancies reduces or nullifies the relationship.

The interaction between client and therapist expectancies is presented in Table 6.2. The predictions associated with conditions 1 and 4 of Table 6.2 are straightforward and can be explained in the general terms of the Expectancy × Value model.

In condition 1, the client with a high success expectancy (based upon Situation–Outcome Expectancy and self-efficacy) is motivated to persist in his or her efforts to achieve symptom reduction or personal competency within the context of this specific therapy relationship. The client's judgment that she or he is able to reduce the discrepancy between present behavior and the target or standard behavior has positive affective consequences—hope and elation—proportional to the subjective importance of reducing that discrepancy. Whether such positive feelings take the form of gratitude toward the helper or an increase in client self-efficacy depends on the extent to which the client attributes potential improvements to his or her own abilities or to the helpfulness of the therapist (Carver & Scheier, 1982). Client tendencies toward persistence at therapy tasks and positive affect are reinforced, amplified, and maintained through the nonverbal and verbal communications of those therapists who hold a corresponding high expectation of the client's chances for improvement.

Table 6.2 Predicted client expectancy effects upon treatment outcome as a function of therapist outcome expectancy assessment

| | | THERAPIST OUTCOME EXPECTANCY ASSESSMENT | |
		High	Low
CLIENT OUTCOME EXPECTANCY ASSESSMENT	High	Strong Client Expectancy Effect [1]	Weak/No Client Expectancy Effect [2]
	Low	Weak/No Effect [3]	Strong Effect [4]

Conversely, condition 4 in Table 6.2 predicts that the person who expects to do poorly under present treatment conditions will persist less to solve the target problem, even if it only takes minimal effort to resolve (Janoff-Bulman & Brickman, 1982; Jones, 1977). Unfavorable expectancies lead to negative affect and withdrawal of one's effort to attain the target behavior. If withdrawal from the treatment environment is constrained physically, as when an individual is pressured to continue treatment by family or authorities, then he or she is likely to withdraw psychologically from the task and not comply with therapeutic instructions. The therapist who implicitly agrees that there is little hope for improvement or maintenance of behavior change has minimal incentive to persist in efforts to convince the client that meaningful change is possible. In fact, if the therapist does not soon refer the client elsewhere, it is likely that the content and style of therapist communication (echoing the hopelessness belief) will encourage the client to disengage from the relationship and seek premature termination.

In brief, conditions 1 and 4 are associated with scenarios in which clients' estimates of success are most strongly predictive of two types of patient participation in the activities of behavior change, as well as the levels of outcome which accrue through each type of participation. Clients' outcome expectancies should therefore correlate highly with process variables measuring persistence and hopefulness (e.g., commitment to therapy; involvement; attendance; cooperation; and completion of homework assignments). Initial client predictions will correlate with ratings of improvement to the extent that persistence- and hopefulness-related process variables contribute to the level of change on target behaviors.

Therapist cancellation of client expectancy effect

The general assumption associated with conditions 2 and 3 of Table 6.2 is that the therapist's expectancies are more powerful determinants of counseling events and outcomes than are those of the client. When the two interactants' beliefs are discrepant, therapist expectancies will overwhelm and cancel the effects of the initial expectancies of those clients who remain in therapy.

Therapist outcome expectancies cause client change

Empirical support for our general prediction comes from several sources. First, a small number of researchers have examined whether therapist expectancies are causative or merely predictive of client change (e.g., Berman & Wenzlaff, 1983; Brucato, 1980; Martin, Moore, Sterne & McNairy, 1977). Goldstein (1981) holds that counselor prognostic expectancy for client change does causally influence such change through a chaining process. He states that "counselor prognostic expectancy directly influences such other counselor states and behaviors as commitment, interest and involvement, effort put forth, the amount of counselor talk, and the amount of actual treatment, all of which in turn appear to bear upon client change" (Goldstein, 1981, p. 86). Martin et al. (1977) tested the hypothesis using a group of 19 psychiatric residents working with some 84 adult patients diagnosed as schizophrenic. The pattern of correlations between the residents' prognostic expectancies and patient adjustment (both at the time of intake and at discharge from the hospital) suggested to these authors that therapist judgments predicted rather than caused patient outcomes. See Berman (in press) for a critique of data analysis techniques used by Martin's research group.

In contrast with Martin et al.'s negative results, Berman's studies provide firm evidence that therapist expectancies do help determine the results of intervention. In his quantitative analysis of 12 therapist expectancy studies, Berman (1979) found that therapist judgments achieved a reliable relationship with the success of therapy (weighted mean correlation of .25 over all studies). Even the most rigorously designed studies, including both an over-time analysis and a separate source of outcome, reflected this significant relationship. Encouraged by this trend, Berman performed two studies of his own that established the therapist expectancy–client outcome association. The first quasi-experimental design ruled out two rival hypotheses: a) the significant relationship can be attributed to general prognostic accuracy of the therapist (as Martin et al. [1977] claimed), and b) the relationship reflects a stable ability of the therapists involved. These two rival hypotheses were disclaimed for two reasons. First, therapists' prognostic expectations about clients they interviewed *but did not treat* were unrelated to those patients' outcomes (i.e., revealing low prognostic accuracy). Second, the therapists' prognostic expectations about the clients they did not treat were also unrelated to the patients they did treat (i.e., showing that therapists' expectancies are not based on their own ability) (Berman, in press).

A second investigation by Berman and Wenzlaff (1983) provided a true experimental test of the hypothesis that therapist expectancy has a direct impact on the outcome. Seventeen therapists at the University of Texas at Austin counseling center were given contrived prognostic information that led them to expect that one of their incoming clients would exhibit rapid improvement during the early treatment session. No such expectancy was induced concerning a second control client that each therapist also treated as part of the study. Probes after the first, second, fourth, and sixth therapy sessions indicated that expectations for the experimental clients were reliably greater than controls at each assessment point. Moreover, positive therapist expectations had an effect on both client and therapist ratings of improvement. Experimental clients reported reliably lower levels of anxiety after the fourth and sixth sessions of therapy and they also reported reliably lower levels of depression after the sixth session of treatment. Berman asserts that these findings "provide firm experimental evidence that the expectations of a psychotherapist are not just predictive of therapy outcome but they can have a direct *and substantial* influence on the amount of improvement that occurs" (Berman & Wenzlaff, 1983, p. 6).

High therapist expectancy versus low client expectancy

Other sources of evidence about the therapist's dominant perspective are specific to condition 3—when high therapist outcome expectancy nullifies the client's low subjective probability of success. How can we explain treatment gain (a strong therapist expectancy effect) when the client perceives poor chances for problem solving, and is assumed to have withdrawn from any change effort? A configuration of three influences associated with condition 3 appear to undermine the client's prediction of failure.

Therapist status and influence on client conformity. First, the therapist is generally accorded dominant social status in the counseling dyad. An experienced therapist can transform his or her ascribed credibility, expertise, and authority into sufficient interpersonal influence to persuade the lower-status client to adopt the professional's positive prognostic outlook. Berman (in press), underscores this point in his application of Rosenthal's (1969, 1976) concept of self-fulfilling prophecy to explain therapist expectancy effects. He describes therapy as an ideal milieu for the effective communication of expectancies, given that the individual holding the expectations is perceived as having higher status (e.g., Rosenthal, 1976), and that the target of the expectancies is in a state of evaluation apprehension— i.e., feeling high concern about being judged by an expert or authority figure (Rosenberg, 1969).

Evidence from two distinct types of research designs converge to support the assumption that exposure to the therapist's perceptions transforms client beliefs. Longitudinal studies of client role expectancies indicate that as treatment progresses, some individuals revise their beliefs to more closely approximate those of the therapist (Cundick, 1963; Gulas, 1974; Hoffman, 1982; Klepac, 1970). Clients who eventually drop out often exhibit a lesser tendency to change their expectations (Sandler, 1975). In fact, unsatisfactory results with low congruence clients prompted clinicians to devise role induction procedures. Such pretherapy socialization interviews explicitly shape client conceptions and anticipations to conform with the therapeutic regimen which they are about to receive (see reviews by Duckro et al., 1979; Heitler, 1976; Higginbotham, 1977).

Similarly, Berman's (1979) quantitative analysis of 12 therapist expectancy studies yields indirect, although compelling, evidence that therapist rather than client perceptions come in time to dominate the clinical interaction. In line with our general prediction, he found that correlations between therapist expectancies and outcome were more robust in studies involving longer periods of treatment ($r[10] = 0.55$, $p = 0.06$). In contrast, the correlations between client expectancies and outcome were unrelated to length of treatment ($r[13] = -.11$, ns). Berman concludes that treatment duration increases the impact of therapist expectancies but has no significant effect on the relationship between client expectations and outcome.

More direct information is available from Brucato's (1980) study, which produced evidence for the hypothesized interaction between levels of therapist and client expectancies. Her findings were twofold. First, therapists' expectancies clearly affected outcome; high therapist expectancies were more consistently associated with better outcome than low therapist expectancies. Second, the combination of low client expectancies and high therapist expectancies was associated with the best outcome from psychotherapy. Brucato speculated that the superiority of the Low Client Expectancy/High Therapist Expectancy group could have been due to the predominance of the therapist expectancy effect—a result, she notes, which builds support for the causative rather than the predictive model of expectancy effects. However, those subjects labeled as "low" really had more moderate expectancy levels. Thus, it remains to be determined whether low expectancy persons actually give up their perceptions in the face of an authority's strong opposite prediction.

Immediate treatment experience override client expectations. Other events that immediately confront the client can also undermine his or her initial estimate of imminent failure. Recall that low initial expectations are thought to be determined either by low self-efficacy, low Situation–Outcome Expectancy or these two variables in combination (see Table 6.1). Client Situation–Outcome predictions are most amenable to immediate intervention, while alterations to self–efficacy beliefs are more time consuming. This is because the actual performance accomplishments that generally occur in later sessions, such as *in vivo* desensitization and participant modeling, are the most dependable and heavily weighted sources of efficacy information. Increments in self-efficacy expectancies often take time to develop, even after behavior changes have been enacted (Bandura, 1977a; Goldfried & Robins, 1982). In contrast, clinicians have an armamentarium of procedures at their ready disposal with which to elevate Situation–Outcome predictions. First, therapist-offered conditions do not necessarily violate all of the client's preferences regarding essential therapeutic events. Gladstein's (1969) research suggests that disconfirmation of role expectations results in reduced client satisfaction only when *none* of the multiple dimensions of expectation are confirmed. Outcome estimates can be increased by pinpointing and emphasizing the preferred events both participants hold in common.

A second procedure is to elicit and actively discuss discrepant Situation–Outcome expectancies (e.g., Wollersheim, 1980). This tactic is used by helpers either to accommodate their responses to client expectations or to initiate the negotiation of alternative client expectancies aligned more with the professional's perspective. Therapists routinely encounter idiosyncratic problem conceptualizations, as well as treatment goals held by clients with which they disagree (see chapter 5). In these circumstances therapists face the prospect of trying to convince the individual to give up their "inaccurate" or "maladaptive" beliefs and adopt the professional's own idiom of interpretation. Clients more willingly abandon lay conceptions, and the poor prognoses associated with them, when the professional offers a highly plausible alternative interpretation of the problem, and describes a logical connection between the symptom explanation and the intervention techniques about to be offered.

More specifically, client assimilation of the helper's positive expectancy is enhanced by presentation of a therapy rationale that is believable, convincing, and couched in metaphors familiar to the client. Beliefs are more likely to shift when the client receives hopeful assurances of change, clear homework instructions, and an immediate experience during therapy implying improvement (e.g., movement up a desensitization hierarchy, proprioceptive feedback from muscle relaxation) (Bootzin & Lick, 1979; Kazdin, 1979). However, therapy rationales are not uniformly convincing. At least among college subjects, behavior therapy engenders more confidence in treatment, and is related to greater perceptions of therapist competence and experience, than psychoanalytic and rational emotive therapy (Wollersheim et al, 1982). In brief, as we argued with our sociolinguistic analyses of doctor–patient communication (see chapter 4), therapeutic communications aggressively shape the client's lexicon and belief structure regarding the problem and appropriate content of therapy. It is not surprising that an initially low level of agreement between patient and therapist on goals of treatment does not predict poor outcome or reduced duration of treatment (Kreisberg, 1977).

In addition to offering a plausible problem interpretation tied to a potent sounding intervention, the helper can manipulate subtle nonverbal and linguistic cues to promote the credibility of the treatment and raise Situation–Outcome expectancies. One way to accomplish this is through manipulation of affiliative nonverbal behaviors. The therapist who, in the opening sessions, demonstrates smiling, positive head nods, animated hand movements, high eye contact, a direct angle of shoulder orientation, a 20 degree forward body lean, and who is otherwise an active interactant, will be seen as both more attractive and persuasive than counselors who do not manifest these responses (LaCrosse, 1975). Similarly, Smith-Hanen (1977) found that judged levels of counselor warmth and empathy can actually be reduced by certain body postures, such as sitting with the arms crossed, with one leg up on a chair and one leg with the foot on the floor, and with no movement.

Closely corresponding to these findings is Ford's (1978) analysis of what therapists do to establish rapport during the third session and obtain a positive client perception of the therapeutic relationship. An optimal perception was associated with a warm, relaxed, and energetic nonverbal style, plus a focus on the client and not on his or her significant others. Toward the end of the session, positive perceptions were cued by therapist stress on a collegial client–therapist relationship (i.e., "We" statements) plus either encouragement to take action or a positive nonverbal style (Ford, 1978). It may be that counselors who are able to encode subtle messages of affiliation, encouragement, involvement and concern simultaneously through several nonverbal channels (i.e., redundant communication) will elicit higher ratings of credibility and be able to more dependably raise Situation–Outcome expectancies (Berman, personal communication).

Influence of prior client expectancies restricted to initial sessions. A third factor curtails the influence of a client's initially low subjective probability of success on treatment outcome. We reason that sooner or later, perhaps by the third or fourth counseling session, clients either give in to their growing doubts and terminate the relationship, or give up their pessimistic perceptions and become more fully involved in the therapy. Indirect support for our assumption is marshalled from divergent sources. In the course of developing the Vanderbilt Psychotherapy Process Scale, Strupp and his colleagues observed that critical aspects of the therapeutic relationship emerged in the first few sessions (O'Malley, Suh & Strupp, 1983). They reported that the association between outcome measures and three process variables (Exploratory Processes, Patient Involvement and Therapist-Offered Relationship) became stronger across the three sessions studied. First session ratings by trained observers were virtually unrelated to outcome, while their third-session ratings consistently predicted the different outcome measures.

A pertinent insight into what may be occurring during this critical phase is indicated by the finding that Patient Involvement showed the most consistent relationship with outcome. This result is in line with Gomez-Schwartz's (1978) earlier experience with the same scale, and her speculation that "the patient's capacity and willingness to participate in the therapy interaction are among the most important determinants of improvement in short-term therapy" (p. 1032). Strupp's group infers from this pattern of results that the course of therapy is, to a certain extent, set in this early phase of therapy. Their statements converge with our own belief that low expectations are probably abandoned at some early point in treatment in order for the patient to fully engage the therapeutic resources offered.

A second explanation for why initial counseling encounters follow our predicted pattern derives from Feather's description of the circumstances under which Expectancy × Value models are most appropriately applied (1982, pp. 397–401). An individual's subjective reality of expectations and values achieves greatest potency for determining behavior under conditions where foresight and thoughtful planning are possible. Conditions such as these include, first of all, situations where the person is encouraged to seek information about alternative courses of action, to evaluate action consequences, and to reflect upon competencies and obstructions in relation to possible behaviors. Second, behaviors under volitional control where the individual perceives freedom of choice and movement are more amenable to expectancy influence. Third, expectancy thrives when the situation allows vigilance—where there is time to search and deliberate about a better solution, and where the stress is neither too high nor too low.

From Feather's account, we conclude that client precontact expectancies have a rather short life span. Precontact expectations produce behavioral effects only during that time when the help seeker remains aloof from the clinician's persuasive communications and from the role socialization pressure that most immediate treatment experiences are designed to produce. As shown above, the clinician has an armamentarium of conceptual, interpersonal, and nonverbal tactics, with which to interrupt the clients' prior reflections upon the nature of their distress and to constrict client interpretations to pathways in line with professional perspectives. Hence, the heat of the therapeutic encounter is intended to prevent prior thoughtful planning from being actualized. This permits client and therapist to negotiate and commit themselves to a substitute set of treatment-generated plans. Several studies of clients who terminate therapy prematurely support this extrapolation. It appears that terminators are more likely to be persons who do not give up initial low estimates of success (Smith, 1977), who retain high dissimilarity of role expectancies with their therapists (Borghi, 1968; Sandler, 1975), and who have more negative perceptions of the therapeutic relationship and therapist-offered conditions (Ford, 1978; Malzer, 1980).

Finally, a somewhat different explanation of why certain low Situation–Outcome or low self-efficacy clients desire to leave therapy derives from Carver and Scheier's control theory. These authors provide evidence that under conditions of self-focused attention, the presence of a behavioral standard will normally lead to an active comparison between that standard and one's present behavior or state (Carver & Scheier, 1981). However, there is one set of circumstances in which self-focus becomes aversive and reduces rather than increases this comparison process. This occurs when the individual holds the expectation that the "discrepancy between the standard and one's behavior is not reducible. Continued focusing on the discrepancy creates negative affect, and the person will attempt to withdraw from further comparisons with that standard" (Carver & Scheier, 1981, p. 151). Hence, clients with low outcome expectancies who do not perceive the possibility of attaining desired improvements may be at risk of leaving therapy during the assessment phase, particularly when interview questions call for detailed consideration of the clients' "ideal self", or for a profile of behavioral competencies that the clients would like to be able to perform as a result of counseling.

Low therapist expectancy versus high client expectancy. Hypothesis 6.2 also predicts that a client's initial favorable prediction will not contribute to later treatment gains when the therapist holds an opposing low Outcome–Expectancy evaluation (i.e., Condition 2). Our final discussion of therapist expectancy as a moderating variable considers the possibility that therapists themselves sometimes adopt negative expectations. We argue that these low estimates promote a reverse "Pygmalion Effect"—a negative self-fulfilling prophecy—and that clients have but two options: either terminate what promises to be a fruitless relationship, or attempt to "pull" from the therapist a more favorable prognostic judgment.

Person perception biases among counselors
First, therapists are as vulnerable to person perception biases as other social groups. Apart from observable symptomatology, clinical judgments can be affected by the client's gender, class, and racial characteristics (see Murray & Abramson's [1983] review of bias in psychotherapy). It is well documented that in contrast with those from the middle class, working class members of society are considered by mental health professionals to be more severely impaired (Lee & Temerlin, 1970); poor candidates for insight-oriented therapies (Garfield, 1971); less competent (Settin & Bramel, 1981); and motivationally impaired (Kleiner & Parker, 1963). Members of lower socioeconomic groups are less likely to be accepted for treatment, to enter treatment when accepted, and to remain in treatment once initiated (Jones, 1982). In a similar fashion, black patients are judged to suffer from more serious disorders than their white counterparts, although this diagnostic bias is associated more with white than black counselors (Baskin, Bluestone & Nelson, 1981; Jones, 1982).

Additionally, concern is expressed that sex-role stereotyping may carry a subtle yet persistent influence in determining prognostic or diagnostic judgments of helping professionals (Broverman et al., 1972; Chesler, 1971), although studies have not upheld the gender discrimination hypothesis (Abramowitz & Dokecki, 1977; Bernstein & Lecomte, 1982). In addition, a meta-analysis of sex bias in psychotherapy concluded that studies that demonstrate a bias of counselors against women or against nonstereotyped roles for women are balanced by an equal number of studies that showed the opposite condition—that therapists express empathy and acceptance perhaps even in greater amounts for women than men (Smith, 1980).

The failure of recent literature to find bias is explained by Lopez (1983) in terms of the failure of researchers to look for an interaciton between the type of presenting problem and the specific client background characteristic under study. Bias does not occur *as a main effect* across all presenting problems, but rather it is most likely to occur in the diagnoses of those presenting problems that clinicians perceive to be related to gender, race, age, or social class. When clinicians have preconceived ideas about the appropriateness of a presenting problem to the person's age, sex, race, or social class, it increases the likelihood that clinicians will either overlook behavioral disturbance (termed "minimizing bias") or will overlook normative behavior and emphasize the pathological behavior (termed "pathologizing bias") (Lopez, 1983). Through similar reasoning, Settin and Bramel (1981) raise the possibility that when it does occur, gender discrimination may be linked to social class prejudice. Their study noted that among male clients, the higher the social class, the more favorable the attitude of therapists, while for female clients an opposite trend was observed. Settin and Bramel believe that their results support Zedlow's (1978) contention that "patient sex must be considered in combination with other variables in order for sex-related treatment and assessment differences to emerge" (p. 93).

The danger exists that person perception biases become expressed in low expectancy of treatment outcome for certain clients, independent of other indicators of their probable gains. Ethnicity-linked distortions in expectancy surfaced in a study of accuracy of clinician's predictions for psychiatric rehospitalization. Stack, Lannon and Miley (1983) asked primary therapists at a newly opened community mental health center to state their expectations for readmission of 269 patients at the time of their discharge. Multiple regression analyses found that the most significant influence on therapists' expectations was severity of illness, followed by previous hospitalization, age (younger patients were more likely to return), cooperativeness, and patient ethnicity (approximately 81 percent of the black patients were expected back). In fact, only number of previous hospitalizations, age, and neighborhood mobility predicted actual readmissions recorded during a 2 year follow-up. Therapists over-predicted the number of returnees (66 percent expected versus 45 percent actual readmissions) and erroneously relied upon behavior within the institution (severity of illness and cooperation) to predict behavior within the community. Moreover, because ethnicity is the one variable in which expectations were clearly the opposite of actuality, it can be considered a source of bias. Therapists expected twice the number of minority patients to return that eventually did get rehospitalized. They also expected erroneously that white patients would return less often than their black counterparts.

Therapist person perception biases which derogate outcome potentials for certain patients may constitute reflections of a broader professional ideology that constrains the therapist's fundamental beliefs about the person. Today's dominant mode of professional socialization is predisposed toward an individualistic construction of the person. The standard of professional competency is accurate identification of defects within hypothesized personality structures, enduring traits, or faulty motivational systems. Unraveling the complexities of person–environment interaction and the situational/ecological determinants of behavior is clearly secondary (Novaco & Monahan, 1980). As a consequence, clinicians' judgments of their clientele tend to be more negative than positive (Wills, 1978). Wills relates this tendency among helpers toward negative perceptions—which may work against the therapist's desire to help clients—to several processes. Among them are: a) the personalistic tendency in attributions, in which clients are viewed as manipulative rather than acting in logical response to situational factors; b) the perceptual consequences of clients' resistance to influence (uncooperative patients seen as ungrateful, unmotivated, and refractory), and c) the tendency to sample negative aspects of clients' behavior, either due to time pressures or to the temptation to focus on salient negative aspects in formulating causal hypotheses (cited in Stack et al., 1983).

Interestingly, Bernstein and Lecomte (1982) found that professional experience is associated with less positive anticipations of client outcomes. In their survey of the diagnostic, prognostic and process expectancies held by 893 clinicians, it was professional therapists, in contrast with beginning and ending master students, who were most pessimistic regarding a hypothetical client's chances for improvement. Such a finding may reflect, as Bernstein and Lecomte suggest, the complaint of many professionals that graduate training programs ill prepare practitioners, and allow students to attribute greater efficacy to psychotherapeutic intervention than warranted. On the other hand, it may reflect the more deeply ingrained ideological bias of experienced professionals which prompts them to interpret minimal cues presented in the case study as indices of deeper underlying pathology.

Negative self-fulfilling prophecy

Second, we suspect that therapists' evaluations of low probability of success are translated into interpersonal cues, reactions, and roles which diminish the clients' inspiration for behavior change, and eventually lead to discontinuance of treatment or poor results. Like other people, counselors who expect to do poorly will persist less in their efforts to solve a problem, especially when their prior experience or professional wisdom informs them that no amount of therapeutic input will alter the patient's condition or circumstances. If required to continue to see such a client, the counselor is likely to act in a passive manner rather than actively attempt to find a solution, to discount the suitability of intervention techniques known to work with other patients, and perhaps have a hard time keeping attention focused on the consultation process even while carrying it out (see Janoff-Bulman & Brickman, 1982).

Current research is unable to specify the precise configuration of verbal and nonverbal cues used by therapists to communicate low expectancy of success. Earlier we cited studies of body posture by LaCrosse (1975) and Smith-Hanen (1977) suggesting that onlookers rated therapists as coldest, least empathic and least attractive when they displayed crossed arms, held one leg crossed over the other such that the ankle of the crossed leg rested on the knee of the other leg, established minimal eye contact, and oriented their shoulder away from the listener. Undoubtedly, such cues—in combination with a lack of animation in hands and voice—are decoded by the client as lack of interest, concern, empathy and understanding. This is especially likely given that the help seeker, sensitized by the stressful circumstances that have brought them to treatment, will scan the professional's demeanor for information about how he or she evaluates the problem.

The client's subsequent emotional reactions will involve either giving voice to the negative affect aroused by such rejection or a display of apathy equal to that of the therapist. What may add further to the client's sense of confusion and helplessness is her or his own inability to pinpoint as the source of her or his negative affect the therapist's subtle rejection or absence of expected encouragement. Ross (1977) points out that when people are forming inferences about the intentions of someone else, they often overlook the informational value of a nonincident or nonoccurrence. Thus, a client will find it difficult to actively label as "rejection" the fact that the therapist did *not* deliberately prolong the session, and did *not* show other responses that signal liking, interest or involvement. Ross concludes that such "nonoccurrences are rarely as salient or as cognitively 'available' to the potential attributer as are occurrences. As a consequence, recognition, storage, retrieval, and interpretation all become less likely" (Ross, 1977, p. 197).

Unfortunately, whichever way the client manifests his or her negative feelings about the unsatisfying encounter, it is interpreted as evidence confirming the professional's initial estimate that this person is unsuitable for counseling. Thus, a cycle of interaction constituting a negative self-fulfilling prophecy is completed. This negative cycle is comparable to interpersonal interactions noted in studies of stereotyping and stigmatization. For example, a laboratory study by Farina, Allen and Saul (1968) found that when people believe they are stigmatized, they apparently give off interpersonal cues that lead others to talk less to them and to initiate fewer conversations with them (cited by Jones, 1977). Jones further states that not only may one's expectations about another influence one's own behavior, they may actually lead the other to behave differently simply because the other is aware that such expectations exist (Jones, 1977; see also Feldman & Theiss, 1982).

Similarly, Snyder, Tanke and Berscheid (1977) present a dramatic example of how a stereotypic perception can guide interaction in a dyad and produce one partner's *behavioral confirmation* of the other's initial impression (stereotype) of her. In their study, male students spoke on the telephone with female students they believed (from having been shown a snapshot) were either physically attractive or unattractive. Tape recordings of the women's comments during the conversation revealed that the women who were presumed attractive did indeed speak in a more friendly, likeable, and sociable manner than the women the perceivers believed to be unattractive. Thus, the men's erroneous beliefs about the women had become real, leading them to act in a fashion that prompted the women to fulfill their stereotype that beautiful people are more desirable (Snyder et al. 1977; Myers, 1983).

The presence of this negative cycle within psychotherapy practice is noted in a discussion of four case studies by Friedmann, Procci and Fenn (1980). Their report underscores Ziemelis' (1974) contention that preventing clients from establishing negative expectations about counseling, or "innoculating" them against the occurrence of harmful expectancies, may be more important than arousing positive expectations. Friedmann et al. (1980) described how four patients diagnosed as schizophrenic were conveyed the expectation of a poor prognosis and treated as if they had no hope for recovery. Three of the four cases were later found to be misdiagnosed—their symptom picture suggested manic-depression—yet the impact of the negative therapeutic expectation appeared to outweigh the usually benign course noted for this affective disorder. Subsequent diagnostic and therapeutic reorientation for these patients, involving an alternative classification and expression of increased hope, resulted in improvement for all four cases. One case, however, illustrated the potential for permanent and perhaps irreversible iatrogenic damage caused by declaring an individual "permanently disabled" (Friedmann et al., 1980, p. 193). Outcomes such as these highlight the continuing significance of educating all helping professionals about the harmful consequences of negative expectations.

Client options: Discontinue treatment or change therapist expectancies
Our third point concerns the client's ability to maneuver within the counseling relationship when the therapist holds an opposing low estimate of improvement. Basically, the help seeker has two options when he or she recognizes signs of doubt in the helper's manner and conversation. If able, the client can either discontinue the relationship or strive to convince the therapist that indeed there is a good chance of success. When the client accurately perceives the helper's low expectancy, his or her decision to terminate the relationship is rational and correct. In control theory terms, the person is acutely aware that with this set of therapeutic resources it is futile to further attempt to reduce the felt discrepancy between one's performance and the behavioral standard aspired towards. This analysis provides a possible reinterpretation of the drop out phenomenon in psychotherapy research as a judicious withdrawal from insufficient helping conditions. Some decisions to discontinue, far from indicating failure for

either or both participants, may be seen as reflecting highly motivated "health" seeking behavior and as positively related to later behavior change.

Some support for this extrapolation comes from Epperson et al.'s (1983) analysis of counseling records for 145 clients who self-terminated and 388 who remained for three or more sessions at the Iowa State University Student Counseling Service. A checklist procedure permitted raters to determine whether clients' primary problems or concerns expressed before the first counseling contact were accurately recognized by the professionals during that initial session. The authors found a strong relationship between problem recognition and continuation in counseling. Overall, 55 percent of clients whose counselor did not recognize their specific problem definition self-terminated after the first contact, compared with 19 percent who left although counselors did recognize their concerns.

Apparently, counselors who do not accurately "hear" the help seeker's request or move too quickly toward reconceptualizing the problem are evaluated as unhelpful. Moreover, the finding that significantly fewer clients terminate with male counselors, and that counselor recognition of clients' problem definitions did not underlie this gender difference, suggests that dissatisfied clients find it easier (less intimidating?) to leave female therapists. (The effect of client gender was not analyzed.) It may be that counselor gender differences—males expecting to be more directive and anticipating greater client need than female therapists (Bernstein & Lecomte, 1982)—differentially influence continuance when clients are uncertain about treatment efficacy. Additional research to clarify this possibility is certainly warranted, given that for such clients immediate referral to a professional or other helper with positive outcome expectancies is desirable.

The second client option is to somehow redirect therapist perceptions such that a low expectancy gives way to a more positive estimate of probable outcome. Berman's (in press) research suggests one avenue by which therapists' beliefs may be changed. While measures of therapist's attraction toward the patient were not linked to the professional's rating of improvement, he did find that the therapists' initial perceptions of how much their patients liked them is predictive of the therapists' later judgments of improvement. Berman's interpretation is that therapists' clinical assessments of improvement are colored not so much by how much they like a patient but rather by how much they think the patient likes them (Berman, in press). Hence, a client may trap his or her therapist's interest and motivation by displays of positive regard and appreciation of the therapist as a person.

A second possibility, suggested by the Vanderbilt studies (O'Malley et al., 1983; Gomez-Schwartz, 1978), is that high levels of patient involvement in therapy will spark enhanced expectancy. This could be accomplished by the client who manages to show some spontaneity and actively participates in the interaction, who is not too passive, inhibited, or withdrawn, and who does not appear too hostile, impatient, frustrated, defensive or upset with the counselor's comments. Of course, the client who is obviously competent at portraying this range and versatility of qualities may never be judged as a poor risk in the first place. Nevertheless, Janoff-Bulman and Brickman (1982) argue that persons with high expectations for success often work harder and do better after failures. The danger for high expectancy people is that they will persist in a fruitless treatment relationship, attribute the lack of progress to their own lack of effort, and not immediately recognize that they need to relieve themselves from the pursuit of help in relation to this particular professional.

Client self-focus and therapist suggestibility
A final hypothesis dealing with the interaction of client and therapist expectancies derives from summaries by Carver and Scheier and Gibbons of their laboratory investigations, which examined the impact of self-focus upon placebo and other suggestibility effects (see Carver & Scheier, 1982, and Gibbons, 1983). A consistent finding across several studies was that the effects of placebo manipulations and other experimenter-induced antici-pations (involving emotional arousal and taste perception) could be minimized by increasing the subject's self focus or by selecting subjects who are high in dispositional private self-consciousness. People high on the self-consciousness trait typically behave as if they are self-aware and appear to be more aware of their internal states as well as their values and attitudes (see Fenigstein, Scheier & Buss, 1975). One study (Scheier et al., 1979) demonstrated that subjects who were high in private self-consciousness were misled less by the experimenter's remarks about how strong a taste stimulus would be (when those remarks were incorrect) than were subjects lower in self-consciousness.

Comparable findings were found in two subsequent experiments by Gibbons and Gaeddert (unpublished studies cited in Gibbons, 1983). Subjects made self-aware (through the presence of a mirror) reported that they were not affected by a bogus "arousing pill" they had ingested, which was the opposite report of those who were relying on false external information about their somatic states—the nonself-focused subjects. A second experiment included manipulation of the subjects' arousal by requesting they complete an intelligence test. Low self-awareness subjects reported that the bogus pill either inhibited or did not facilitate greatly their performance (depending on what they had been led to believe about the pill's effects). Again, high self-awareness subjects did not respond differentially to the drugs in light of the external information provided. This latter group attributed some arousal to both drugs: an accurate assessment of the arousal they were experiencing in anticipation of the impending intelligence test. Even more remarkable, it appears that self-focused persons will attempt to report accurately about themselves even when accuracy goes against making a good impression. In brief, the desire not to misrepresent one's internal states seems to outweigh the desire to self-aggrandize (Gibbons, 1983).

To extrapolate from this information, we hypothesize that clients who are high in private self-consciousness, or who are induced into high self-focus during treatment, are more apt to rely upon their own perceptions in judging whether or not they are actually improving over the course of therapy. These persons are less drawn to and influenced by therapist expressions of hopefulness or doubt regarding outcome. In contrast, we assume that low self-consciousness clients look for, amplify, and rely upon therapist perceptions of therapy progress and therapist prognostic expectancies. Furthermore, we suspect that low expectancy of success clients—those whose low estimate is derived from low self-efficacy—tend to avoid high self-focus and private self-consciousness, because of the pain and frustration associated with dwelling upon one's perceived inability to accomplish goals and attain desired competencies (see Gibbons' (1983) data suggesting that self-awareness exacerbated negative mood states of depressed VA patients). Low expectancy clients are therefore more open and vulnerable to therapist cues, given that they are vigilant for situational information that will enable them to avoid exposure to the pain of possible failure. Unlike these persons, high expectancy of success clients (with moderate to high self-efficacy) do not fear failure because they can attribute it to external factors (bad luck) or unstable internal factors (lack of effort) (Janoff-Bulman & Brickman, 1982). Hence they can more easily engage in self-focus and high private self-consciousness, and thereby avoid the therapist's suggestibility effects. In sum, high expectancy clients can afford the luxury of dwelling on the performance situation, persist at it, and not be distracted by subtle encouragement or cues as to its difficulty conveyed by the counselor.

Hypothesis 6.3 predicts that the degree to which the therapist's positive or negative expectancies will influence the client is determined by an interaction between client outcome expectancies (arising from self-efficacy) and their level of self-awareness. High outcome expectancy clients produce high self-focus which diminishes their suggestibility. Low self-efficacy clients find self-focus aversive and are more dependent upon external information sources for their evaluations.

Hypothesis 6.3

In comparison with high outcome expectancy/high self-efficacy clients, those expressing low outcome expectancy/low self-efficacy perform more poorly in situations requiring self-focus and private self-consciousness, and are therefore significantly more influenced by therapist communication of hopefulness or doubt regarding therapy outcome.

Limitation of Expectancy Effects to Specific Clinical Problems

A fifth and final explanation for the ambiguous findings pertaining to expectancy effects is given by Hypothesis 6.4.

Hypothesis 6.4

Client and therapist outcome expectancies positively influence improvement scores only for presenting problems that can be directly alleviated through arousal of positive affect, and/or the elicitation of previously acquired cognitive and behavioral responses (e.g., depression, fear, anxiety). Conversely, outcome expectancy has little or no positive effect upon improvement scores for presenting complaints that require the long-term acquisition of extensive novel responses for their alleviation (e.g., interpersonal skills, obsessive-compulsive habits).

The inspiration for this hypothesis comes from Berman's collection of studies described earlier (Berman, 1979, in press; Berman & Wenzlaff, 1983). First, his quantitative review paper of 15 client expectancy studies found a significant expectancy effect for studies involving outpatient populations, but no such effect for inpatient subjects. Berman (1979) reasoned that expectancies may have less of an impact on the more serious complaints of a hospitalized population. Second, the quasi-experimental study of therapists' initial expectancies and actual client change noted that therapists' initial estimates correlated with follow-up status for somatic complaints and depression, but were not associated with the "more difficult areas involving obsessive-compulsive or interpersonal problems" (p. 193). This appeared to conform with the Johns Hopkins researchers' suggestion that expectancies may influence general feelings of symptom distress but have less of an impact on more enduring issues of social effectiveness (Frank, Gliedman, Imber, Stone & Nash, 1959). Third, Berman's true experimental design effort, in which counselors received positive prognostic information about one of two clients, demonstrated almost identical results. Analyses of covariance performed for each symptom factor for the Hopkins Symptom Checklist indicated that therapist expectancies exerted their primary influence on the symptoms of anxiety and depression (Berman & Wenzlaff, 1983). The positive expectancy manipulation had no such effect on symptoms relating to interpersonal problems, obsessive-compulsive concerns, or somatic complaints.

Studies previously cited provide further encouragement, especially for the proposition that outcome expectancies directly impinge upon symptoms that arise from negative affect. For example, Bootzin and Lick (1979) have argued that expectancy mechanisms, operating within attention-placebo conditions, are as effective as systematic desensitization in producing durable reduction of maladaptive fear. High expectancy of success clients are motivated to expose themselves more extensively to phobic stimuli (a response that they are fully capable of doing). Anxious persons thereby benefit through both fear extinction and self-reinforcement for obvious mastery. Similarly, Rosen and Wish (1980) noted that male veterans at a VA outpatient clinic were judged less dejected and less apprehensive when their expectations were met regarding the content of treatment sessions. Finally, among the group psychotherapy outpatients studied by Bloch et al. (1976), problems with affect were commonly cited as the targets for therapy (e.g., depression, tension, inability to express feelings). Other concerns voiced included symptoms that are also likely to be remediated through arousal of positive affect or elicitation of previously learned behavior, such as inability to achieve intimacy, a specific problem in a marital relationship, and low self-esteem.

In conclusion, this chapter has brought to the surface five hidden sources underlying the ambiguous connection between client expectancy and treatment effects. Our painstaking effort to sort out these sources of confusion has, we believe, paid off. It validates our initial feeling that the expectancy construct merits rehabilitation. Moreover, we have confirmed our general proposition that conceptual and theoretical refinement of expectancy will yield a novel series of empirical predictions regarding in-therapy events (i.e., Hypotheses 6.1 and 6.3) and the relationship between in-therapy events and client improvement (i.e., Hypotheses 6.2 and 6.4).

The next generation of clinical researchers to take up client and therapist expectancy as an explanatory tool will have five advantages in designing their studies. First, they will recognize that definitions of expectancy are best couched within an established Expectancy × Value model that accounts for the client's evaluation of the desirability of anticipated outcomes. Second, researchers will know how to circumvent problems in self-report measures of expectancies, such as biased and restricted response formats and superficial sampling of the client's memory. Third, expectancy researchers will initiate multiple probes, one at each significant phase of therapy, in order to track the fluctuating levels of client outcome expectancy across the course of treatment. Fourth, their studies will measure or control for the complex interaction between client and therapist levels of outcome expectancy that cancels the influence of the client's initial estimate upon subsequent performance. Finally, the next generation of expectancy researchers will narrow their focus to those specific presenting problems which are postulated either to yield under the arousal of positive affect or to be alleviated through performance of already acquired cognitions and behaviors.

7
Generalization of Treatment Gains: A Network Analysis

DEFINITION OF THE ISSUE
Overview

Under the rubric "Transfer of therapeutic learning" the 1966 volume heralded examination of what has recently become the most compelling question to stimulate clinical outcome research. Namely, do treatment-attributed changes transfer to extratherapy settings and persist beyond the immediacy of active clinical intervention? This chapter reexamines the issue of treatment persistence and generalization which the 1966 volume analyzed exclusively from a learning laboratory data base. However, while the earlier analysis focused on conditions of learning during clinical consultation which, if present, would enhance transfer of training beyond the clinic, the present analysis takes as its point of departure the client's posttreatment environment. Social network analysis is examined as a potential clinical tool for illuminating the social structure of natural settings. The power of social network analysis, and its contribution toward resolving the vexing dilemma of nontransferable therapeutic gains, rests with its capacity to predict which type of posttreatment network environment covaries with either increased personal stress, deviance maintenance or the enhancement of behavior change. Furthermore, the essential processes underlying the formation of change-enhancing networks—social cognition, interpersonal exchange, and social ecology—are identified as novel intervention priorities, displacing the short-sighted goals used currently, which lack an interactionist perspective.

In brief, the chapter begins by discussing the implications of the generalization question, and then traces its conceptual development in the behavioral literature. Next we describe the pattern of treatment generalization failure emerging from follow-up studies and the consequent development of a generalization technology, including self-monitoring, to reduce these failures. The pervasive lack of generalization, which continues despite recent technological advances, is interpreted as a paradigm crisis for current micro-level conceptions of behavioral intervention. The crux of our argument is that the treatment transfer issue will remain unresolved until behavior change procedures are derived from a more complex conception of person–environment transactions. A conceptual and methodological strategy must arise which simultaneously accounts for the behavior change influences operating through the interpersonal structure of social settings and for those arising from the personal attributes of clients which allow them to become active determinants of their own interpersonal environments. The remainder of the chapter is devoted to elaborating social network analysis as a promising clinical tool for assessing posttreatment environments according to their behavior change potential. We specify competencies—encompassing both interpersonal and environmental evaluation—which clients could employ in the formation of their own change-enhancing social networks. We term these *Person-Environment Fit* meta-skills. Because behavior therapists developed generalization techniques, our examples are drawn from this literature. Conventional "talk" therapies experience the same difficulties, however, so the chapter's findings apply equally to these orientations.

Why This Issue Is So Compelling

In mining general learning theory for laws governing the transfer of training, Goldstein, Heller and Sechrest were searching for procedures which would correspond closely with what they felt should be the therapist's central motive—to institute conditions under which changes that take place in therapy will be carried over into extratherapy situations (Goldstein, Heller & Sechrest, 1966). Remarkably, these authors foreshadowed numerous procedures which have recently been integrated into an "explicit technology of generalization" (Stokes & Baer, 1977). Even more noteworthy, it was nearly fifteen years *after* they boldly underscored this critical focus that the subject achieved wide recognition as the most compelling clinical research problem. The reasons why treatment generalization research took so long to mature remain obscure. It now appears obvious why the carryover and persistence of clinic-based gains ought to secure a prominent position within psychotherapy research, training and practice.

Current reasoning evidences concern with generalization through criteria of efficacy, cost and ethics. It is now widely accepted that generalization is part and parcel of any definition of psychotherapeutic efficacy. Thus, psychotherapy is judged valuable if and only if therapeutic gains endure and are available to clients when needed in real life situations and with significant others (Goldstein, Lopez & Greenleaf, 1979; Marholin & Siegel, 1978). Given the costs associated with the clinical enterprise and the ascendance of consumer accountability, psychotherapy is only found to be a successful and worthy resource expenditure when behavioral improvements persist and transfer to contexts beyond the consulting room (Goldstein et al., 1979). Similarly, there is a call to make explicit in the therapy contract some guarantee of the lasting usefulness offered by our professional service, or, at minimum, adequate outcome information to permit clients to evaluate the quality of services offered (Steffen & Karoly, 1980). This position implies that generalization is more than simply a practical matter for clients—it is the clinician's ethical and moral responsibility (Wolpe, 1981). Thus, it is inappropriate to solicit client trust and confidence unless there is some assurance that the effects will not disappear once treatment is terminated. Nor can we expect parents or others to consider using our techniques unless the demonstrated effects carry over to other interventions (Drabman, Hammer & Rosenbaum, 1979; Marholin, Siegel & Phillips, 1976). In the same vein, without the support of generalization data, trainers cannot imbue mental health providers with confidence in specific treatments nor advocate their use among diverse sociocultural populations (Higginbotham & Tanaka-Matsumi, 1981).

Conceptual Evolution of Generalization

Having established the dominant rationales for concern with generalization among outcome researchers, its conceptual evolution can now be traced. Interestingly, generalization has evolved from a diffuse, passive and "theoretically expected" phenomenon to an empirically differentiated, active, and testable set of conditions. Historically the term was used among psychotherapists with little real precision simply to describe what was expected to follow automatically from in-therapy processes (Goldstein et al., 1979; Steffen & Karoly, 1980). Traditional insight-oriented therapies assumed that client change (i.e., personality restructuring) was irreversible, if not dramatic, precluding a "return to baseline." This pervasive assumption directed clinicians to examine only those processes intrinsic to the therapeutic encounter, such as strength of emotional "transference" and verbal expressions of change in the patient's self-evaluation. The ideology of psychoanalysis in particular made no provision for empirical scrutiny of treatment outcome (Prochaska, 1979), let alone generalization processes. This is cogently reflected in Garfield's critique of the much publicized Menninger study, an intensive eighteen-year appraisal of psychoanalysis and psychoanalytic-oriented psychotherapy applied to forty-two patients (Kernberg et al., 1972): "From the point of view of not reporting data on outcome, the report is a masterpiece" (Garfield, 1981, p. 180). Traditional psychotherapists, it appears, take responsibility for structuring their office encounters with patients according to an ideology which specifies those conditions precipitating intra-psychic change. The patients, on the other hand, are expected to take responsibility for their own self-evolution—i.e., not offer "resistance"—and for integrating those changes into their other life spheres, if they so choose.

Treatment transfer and maintenance remained dormant as a research question until theoretically distinct therapies, especially behavior therapy, gained ascendance. However, despite the exhortations of behavior analysis pioneer Don Baer that generalization should be deliberately programed, "rather than expected or lamented" (Baer, Wolf & Risley, 1968), it lagged well behind other advances in behavior therapy (Franks & Wilson, 1978). Stokes and Baer (1977) attribute this developmental lag to the behaviorists' understanding of generalization as a "passive" by-product of failure to practice discrimination training adequately. As a "descriptive" rather than an "explanatory" concept (Sanders, 1981) behavior therapists were willing to allow the concept to remain devoid of a technology (Stokes & Baer, 1977). They continued to be preoccupied with single subject reversal design experiments and with the technical trappings for establishing the experimental control of behavior through various reinforcement and stimulus discrimination procedures (Hayes, Rincover & Solnick, 1980). This preoccupation ended with the recognition that desired behavior change, brought about through experimental contingencies in one setting, "was often seen in only transitory forms in other places at other times" (Stokes & Baer, 1977, p. 350). Henceforth, active programing of generalization and maintenance procedures gained momentum.

Three distinct generations mark the conceptual evolution of generalization. Preliminary descriptions broadly differentiated two classes of generalization. *Transfer of training* is the term Goldstein, Heller and Sechrest used generically to denote "all the various effects that the acquisition of one response may have on responses that must be acquired and/or emitted later" (p. 215). Subsequently, Goldstein et al. (1979) restricted the definition of training transfer to two descriptive processes—stimulus and response generalization—involving whether behavior changes permeate beyond the original learning setting. Once a desired response has transferred to a new environment, *response maintenance* refers to its durability in the absence of reward contingencies deliberately placed into the real life situation by the therapist.

Behavior analysts, dissatisfied with these broad definitions, created a second generation of thought. They sought to describe response durability with more specificity in relation to either naturally occurring or deliberately programed reinforcement sources. Stokes and Baer's (1977) review of 270 applied behavioral analysis studies illustrated a taxonomy of generalization enhancing procedures. The more recent accumulation of studies aimed at follow-up assessment and the deliberate programing of generalization (e.g., Koegel, Glahn & Niemann, 1978; Robinson & Swanton, 1980; Sanders & Glynn, 1981) received initial momentum from Stokes and Baer's (1977) operational definition: Generalization is viewed as "the occurrence of relevant behavior under different, nontraining conditions (i.e., across subjects, settings, people, behaviors and/or time) without the scheduling of the same events in those conditions as had been scheduled in training conditions" (p. 350). They further assert that generalization may be claimed when additional training manipulations are required to produce change in extra-therapy settings, providing the cost or extent is clearly less than that of the initial intervention (Sanders & James, 1983).

Drabman and Sanders are progenitors of the latest and most highly differentiated conceptual analysis of the phenomena—the "generalization map." According to Drabman, Hammer and Rosenbaum (1979), the four primary categories describing generalization effects—generalization across settings, behaviors, individuals, and time (maintenance)—can be paired together in all possible combinations to form 16 discrete classes. The resulting generalization map permits researchers to anticipate which classes of generalization are likely to occur, and to design studies verifying those expectations (Drabman et al., 1979). The generalization map was first applied by Sanders (Sanders & James, 1983) as a template for reviewing the behavioral parent training literature, and he achieved the fullest articulation to date of the 16 distinct classifications. Sanders' careful review procedure brought to light the further need to distinguish between *time generalization*— referring to change in the client's target behavior in a training setting which endures in the absence of therapist controlled posttraining contingencies— and *maintenance of generalization*. This second concept involves the same endurance of desired behavior change, but the therapist continues to provide treatment on an intermittent basis during the posttraining period. This clarification is essential, given the rise of techniques for maximizing treatment gains that involve continued therapist monitoring of events during the posttraining phase (e.g., arranging direct reinforcement of generalized responding). Calculating the implications of these extra-therapy arranged contingencies, Sanders concludes that observed maintenance can be described as *maintenance of generalization* for either setting, behavior, subject or various combinations of these three categories.

Our understanding of the meanings ascribed to generalization provides a critical perspective for observing the pattern of treatment generalization failure and those techniques derived for offsetting the crisis. Assessment of the occurrence of the 16 generalization and maintenance classes requires unobtrusive, longitudinal observations of individuals—and those with whom their lives are bound—across significant life settings of home, work and recreation. Our real task is to establish a correspondence between desired behavior which is therapeutically engendered, and the survival of that behavior at a socially valid (and appropriate) level at other times, in other places, with different people, perhaps in a slightly different form, or even when adopted by someone close to the client.

Having pinpointed the subset of life arenas into which newly acquired responses are expected to generalize, two questions logically follow: a) What evidence is there for training transfer and durability? for which clinical problems? using what intervention modes? and b) What constitutes a valid generalization technology, given that success is equated with treatment gains being absorbed into not only the client's lifestyle but also into the enduring structure of the client's multifarious social settings? For our purposes, it would be unproductive to undertake a complete survey of clinical reports presenting long-term followup and generalization failure data. Rather, we have selected for review a single domain, behavioral parent training, because it has recently received rigorous experimental attention focused on the generalization issue and because the empirical findings support our vigorous contention that contemporary methods of behavioral intervention often produce weak or transitory generalization effects. Moreover, we see that remedial measures to maximize treatment gain, coupled with extant therapies, add little to long-term positive outcome. The inadequacy of existing generalization technology compels us to search for alternative concepts with which to understand and influence behavioral systems in extra-therapy contexts. However, before we explore the social networks literature for promising hypotheses, the crisis enveloping generalization research will be examined.

PATTERN OF TREATMENT GENERALIZATION FAILURE AND CONSEQUENT DEVELOPMENT OF A GENERALIZATION TECHNOLOGY

Given the stature of critical inquiry within behavior therapy, why has it taken so long to acknowledge that the follow-up interval commonly used in evlauating behavioral programs is wholly inadequate for valid appraisal of the durability of desired behavior change? Unquestionably, practitioners in the 1970s were preoccupied with producing studies to demonstrate the efficacy of behavioral approaches with diverse client populations in varied institutional and community settings (Garfield & Bergin, 1978; Ullmann & Krasner, 1975). Initial behavioral ideology focused on too narrow an idea of treatment efficacy verification, although the conceptual distinction between initial treatment-produced changes and long-term response maintenance had long been understood (Franks & Wilson, 1978).

In the early stages of conditioning therapy's development, researchers confined their attention to identifying elements present in the training program that accounted for extinction, reconditioning, and new response acquisition. Kanfer (1979) recalled that generalization effects were of little concern—something that just happened, perhaps through unprogramed fluctuations during the reconditioning process, both in the client and in the environment, and were viewed as distant consequences of the change program. Single subject experimental procedures, using reversal and multiple baseline designs, only focus on behavior change nuances during the client's exposure to the treatment conditions. In fact, the simple reversal design (ABAB) assumes the reversibility of responses (i.e., the problem behavior will reemerge) in order to gauge the strength of the functional relationship between experimental phase stimulus conditions and target responses. Ironically, the much sought after "return to baseline" level of behavior during the reversal phase of these designs is exactly the opposite effect desired under clinical circumstances. Viewed differently, reversal designs can serve the generalization researcher by probing for evidence of response maintenance during the reversal phase and helping to isolate those variables that actually enhance generalization. Obviously, the most beneficial therapeutic technique is one that produces persistent effects, even after treatment is stopped (Kanfer, 1979). Yet those chronicling the progress of behavior modification lamented the absence of follow-up as one of the field's major limitations (Franks & Wilson, 1978).

The era of mounting confidence regarding behavioral methods was followed by a disturbing accumulation of equally compelling evidence from the initially tiny percentage of studies bothering to report follow-up data. This evidence revealed that treatment-related behavior changes, dramatic though they were during intervention, were often transitory and reversible during follow-up (Forehand & Atkeson, 1977; Franks & Wilson, 1978; Goldstein & Stein, 1976; Nay, 1979; O'Donnell, 1977). One highly alarming review (Keeley, Shemberg & Carbonell, 1976) found that of 146 operant clinical interventions appearing in three key journals during 1972 and 1973, only 11.6%, 10.3%, and 8.9% considered temporal, setting, and behavior generalization data respectively. Guided by their evidence that operant research was confined to prostheses, Keeley et al. (1976) made a plea for a moratorium on trivial studies further demonstrating the power of reversal designs, urging more work establishing the boundary conditions of each technique and on complex problems in complex settings.

Research evidence subsequently began to accumulate across a variety of social and clinical problems bearing on behavioral technology's success in fostering generalization. Investigators concerned with such wide ranging issues as environmental pollution (Cone & Hayes, 1980), social skills training (Shepherd, 1977, 1980), delinquency prevention (Davidson & Seidman, 1974; Davidson & Wolfred, 1977; O'Donnell, Lydgate & Fo, 1979), training the parents of oppositional children (Forehand & Atkeson, 1971; Nay, 1979; Wahler, Leske & Rogers, 1979), drug abuse (Hall, 1980), and effectiveness training of cub scout den leaders (Conter, Hatch & D'Augelli, 1980) all report a paucity of empirical documentation to show their procedure's capacity to induce generalization. These data have forced the discipline to realign its priorities, to confront the limitation of situation specific techniques, and to search for methods of programing transfer effects, as taken up first by Kazdin (1975) and later by Stokes and Baer (1977).

Behavioral parent training researchers, concerned with evaluating the continued effects of their programs, have moved swiftly to initiate research on the generalization question. Thus, this body of experiments can credibly illuminate the problems in resolving this issue. Parent training typically entails therapist-provided instruction in the application of behavioral procedures (prompting, fading, contingent reinforcement and punishment, etc.) and often accompanies a social learning theory rationale—for example, the "coercion trap" explanation of why undesirable parent–child interaction is maintained. Trainers hope that child management skills, effectively developed through a combination of instructions, modeling, rehearsal, and verbal or video feedback (Sanders & James, 1982), will be skillfully applied when the therapist withdraws to untreated child behavior problems, other siblings, and in new settings. Careful consideration of available studies, however, casts doubt on the realization of this hope; indicating rather that parents don't always use target procedures when conditions vary significantly from initial training settings. Moreover, it should not be surprising that mapping the results of the parent behavior modification literature against our latest understanding of generalization reveals that conceptual refinement of the phenomenon outpaces empirical advances. Sanders and James' (1983) review located active experimental interest in only five of Drabman et al.'s (1979) generalization categories, leaving eleven classes without exemplars.

The majority of studies Sanders and James (1983) located reported time generalization and maintenance data. That is, measures were presented assessing the continuation of parent and/or child behavior change during follow-up, some with and some without the withdrawal of training contingencies. Typically, parents (usually mothers) of oppositional children are tutored in the use of contingent attention for compliance, instruction giving, and time-out administration, until some level of mastery is reached and diminution of a targeted undesirable child behavior is noted. Follow-up assessment can be a phone call, questionnaire, or home observation within six months or a year's time and, for those experiencing difficulty, could result in retraining or "booster" sessions. Although a number of researchers found parents continuing to employ certain procedures acquired under instruction and/or the maintenance of desirable behavior change among their children, the unqualified acceptance of these findings withers under rigorous methodological critique. Sanders and James (1983), Nay (1979), O'Donnell (1977), and Forehand and Atkeson (1977) enumerate a litany of flaws, clouding our ability to identify which aspects of the training procedures were responsible for observed generalization effects. These critics question whether transfer effects occur in more than one narrow class of generalization conditions. Also, can gains be attributed to prior training, or to covarying historical and maturational processes both inside and outside the family, such as starting school or improvement in spouse relationship?

Other authors add weight to the evidence that training skills haphazardly generalize across time or fail altogether (Bernal, Klinnert & Schultz, 1980; Ferber, Keeley & Shemberg, 1974; Johnson & Christensen, 1975; Wahler, 1980a; Wahler, Leske & Rogers, 1979). Robert Wahler's sustained line of inquiry into the constellation of family and demographic characteristics predicting lack of maintenance offers the most inclusive commentary on why some parents discontinue training strategems. Early on, Wahler and colleagues discovered that large behavioral gains made by oppositional youngsters attending a highly regarded residential-community program, including academic and social skill building for children and re-education experiences for their parents, were time limited (Wahler, Berland & Leske, 1975). Disappointingly, 82 percent of the 30 Riverbend adolescents and pre-adolescents regressed back to their initial presenting problems within one year of follow-up. Subsequently, a similar group of nine "high risk" families—experiencing poverty, poor education, single parent households, and living in crowded, high crime neighborhoods—completed treatment through the federally funded Child Behavior Institute (Wahler, Leske & Rogers, 1979). Parents received social learning-based didactic instruction, and help in implementing contingency contracts with their children to reduce oppositional behavior (complaints, non-compliance, rule violations) and enhance time spent with school work and household chores. Direct observation of family interactions at home during critical times using Wahler, House and Stambaugh's (1976) standardized observation code (SOC) afforded the strongest evidence that targeted problems underwent little or no change from baseline through treatment. By the end of the first year of treatment, all eight families had dropped out of the Child Behavior Institute Program, offering further dismal proof of its inadequacies for the high risk sample.

Wahler next obtained a third high-risk sample of 18 mother–child pairs. He taught them to view the evolution of their child's oppositional behavior as a "coercion trap", and to use a point reward system and "time out" as means of escaping coercive interations. During the training phase, the eight SOC recordings detected a replacement of problem exchanges with largely non-aversive interactions: the number of child opposition responses dropped substantially, along with pronounced reductions in mother's aversive behaviors (yelling, screaming, etc.). Seven home visits by SOC observers, during the following eight months to one year follow-up phase found, unfortunately, that these behavior reductions gained during the treatment sessions were clearly not durable. The mothers increased their child-directed aversive acts to a level almost identical to baseline, while their children's opposition and complaints increased sharply from treatment to follow up

(Wahler, 1980a). Contrasting favorable maintenance results associated with a sample of "low-risk" mother-child dyads—those socially advantaged—led Wahler to posit a functional relationship between the quality of the parent's extra-family relationships and the continuation of family changes prompted by outside intervention. His "mother insularity hypothesis" reasons that those having limited social ties, dominated by aversive contacts with kinfolk and with helping agency representatives as opposed to frequent rewarding social exchanges with friends, would receive little reinforcement to sustain newly recommended child management procedures. Instead, the insular mother would terminate compliance with these instructions, once the outside party was no longer around to pressure her and such compliance was not needed to satisfy the outside party's demands. Wahler's hypothesis is a fine precursor to the perspective elaborated below describing more precisely how social network resources determine behavior change outcomes.

In a second research vein, Sanders overcame key methodological flaws by tracking both time generalization and gains transferred to various home and community settings. His research series examined the differential effects of two training components (instruction plus feedback and self-management training) on both parent and child behavior, pinpointing self-management as a potentially robust means of programing generalization. Sanders and Glynn (1981) and Sanders (1982b) used a time sampling instrument to monitor six deviant child behaviors and the parent's accuracy of implementing behavior modification procedures, including social attention, clear instructions, ignoring, and contingent consequences. Observers sampled behavior in the home training situation and in generalization settings in the community (play center, shopping trips, travelling by car) and in the household (breakfast time, friend's arrival). Instructions regarding accurate implementation of the behavioral child management program, plus feedback from observers' family interaction data, resulted in significant improvement for both parent and child, but only in the home training and breakfast settings. Generalization to community settings required introduction of a multiple component self-management training package, comprised of: a) teaching parents goal selection, program design, and self-monitoring; b) planning or arranging their own stimulus environment; and, c) specific focus on parent's behavior during hectic times when accurate program implementation was "at risk" (Sanders, 1982b). Adding the self-management component effectively taught parents to modify problem behavior in nontraining settings and to consolidate gains achieved during home treatment, which were maintained up to a four month follow-up recording. But these results leave future researchers to disentangle the effects of naturally occurring contingencies within the family, such as spouse change and improved child behaviour.

Sanders endorses self-regulatory procedures as a promising technology for enhancing generalization and maintenance effects. Significantly, the primary impetus for involving self-management training was to effectively grapple with competing environmental constraints which inhibit accurate implementation of proven behavioral strategies. Essentially, self-management steps prompted already facile use of training skills to manage misbehavior at critical times without therapist guidance. Sanders examined the social ecology of parenting settings and discovered distinct occasions where dominant contingencies and demands on parents' time were incompatible with stimuli sustaining parent behavior during training, and thus were "high risk" occasions for inaccurate program implementation. High risk settings included, for example, where parents are under pressure due to time constraints (getting the children off to school) and where there are competing demands on the parent's time (e.g. driving the car, talking with a friend on the telephone, or meeting other adults) (Sanders, 1982).

In a similar fashion, Wahler's insular mothers were at high risk of regressing to aversive management tactics and "giving in" to oppositional actions—coercion trap hallmarks—when outsider pressure was withdrawn or in the absence of friends' reinforcement. This description is consonant with the belief of drug addiction researchers that critical periods arise when the former substance abuse patient is at high risk of relapse (Hall, 1980; Marlatt, 1978). Each critical period confronts the abstainer with a decision point: either the individual activates coping responses to maintain abstinence, or he or she engages in the forbidden behavior and relapses. Unfortunately, client interpretation of relapse may include "catastrophyzing" and negative self-attributions—termed the "abstinence violation effect" by Marlatt (1978; Marlatt & Gordon, 1985)—which confirms one's inability to exercise control. Consequently, generalization processes terminate as the client "gives up," disregards previous treatment success, and fails to persist in implementing the self-control strategies that earlier enabled him or her to resist temptation and withstand pressure to drink (Franks & Wilson, 1978).

Clearly, the most pressing research need is to establish cognitive and setting-specific tactics, permitting generalization effects to survive the threat of high-risk relapse situations, and to circumvent the onset following relapse of negative self-attributions which completely dissolve self-control initiatives. The cognitive mediation perspective (Bandura, 1977; Franks & Wilson, 1978; Kanfer, 1979; Shepherd, 1980) posits the necessity for a core perceptual organizing process, to bridge the identification of relapse risk situations with the accurate implementation of freshly learned behavior change principles. In essence, referrring again to parent behavior training, the client acquires a *"meta-skill"* tying together three basic processes. First, relapse situations are *anticipated*; the parent is primed to look for future settings or times where identifiable pressures conspire against correct use of child management procedures. Second, *self-monitoring* or *self-awareness* of parent–child interaction occurs during critical periods. The parent uses critical occasions as a cue for observing whether their responses are consistent with standards for accurate program deployment, and magnifies feedback of incorrect implementation (e.g., "catching oneself" giving aversive social attention or failing to ignore a targeted oppositional behavior). Third, any discrepancies observed between parent–child interaction and specified performance standards are targeted for *self-correction*. This final process involves choosing steps or measures to be taken for maintaining accurate program implementation, such as rearranging physical settings, initiating discussion of rules with the child before entering the setting again, or seeking out friends who will support one's child management efforts.

Self-monitoring and self-awareness processes are recognized as critical in the formula of cognitively mediated generalization—they activate and guide information processing related to high risk situations, parent–child interaction, and matching self-performance with standards. Self-monitoring cues decision-making and self-regulated action. It also prompts the cycle of self-correction; self-criticism, rehearsal of an alternative way of handling the child's behavior, setting performance goals, self-evaluations of whether the goal was achieved, and self-reinforcement for achieving the goal (Sanders & James, 1982). Specifically, Sanders (1982b) identified self-monitoring as a key component of his successful self-management regimen for maximizing parent training generalization. He prompted parents to use a formal self-monitoring checklist, cueing them to engage in advance planning, directing their discussion of rules for outings, and priming parents to respond to misbehavior in community settings, in a manner consistent with training suggestions. In this fashion, parent application of their training was guided by the anticipatory checklist and the monitoring of child actions in various parenting settings. Similar studies, employing parents' self-observation and self-recording of their own behavior against some specified standard (Caspo, 1979; Doleys, Dorster, & Cartelli, 1976; Sanders, 1980; Wells, Griest & Forehand, 1980) turn up evidence suggesting that self-monitoring and self-awareness are vitally useful, both at the initial skill acquisition phase and during later training phases as a supplementary procedure to facilitate change maintenance (Sanders & James, 1982; see Wicklund's [1975, 1979] review of self-awareness theory). Thus we arrive at out first treatment transfer hypothesis.

Hypothesis 7.1
Generalization programing which develops client "meta-skill" competencies—
i.e., the ability to anticipate relapse situations, obtain self-awareness of one's
performance, and self-correct discrepancies—will increase generalization

across time and settings for accurate use of self-management techniques learned during therapy.

BEHAVIORAL CONCEPTIONS OF NATURAL SETTINGS

While the cognitive behavior modification literature contains information about cognitively mediated processes which strengthen generalization, an even more innovative approach entails shifting away from micro-level processes to examine the social structure of natural settings. Behavioral clinicians posited interference in posttraining settings as a possible cause of generalization failure. The rationale is that new responses engendered by therapy will naturally extinguish when a) controlling stimuli dominant during training are not present in the real world; b) non-training settings fail to oblige with reinforcing consequences for generalized responses—or punish the new actions; and c) the transfer environment provokes behavior incompatible with those achieved during therapy or provides powerful incentives for maintenance of counter-therapeutic behavior (Marholin, Siegel & Phillips, 1976; Marholin & Touchette, 1979; Steffen & Karoly, 1980). Suspecting that environmental forces in the clients' life outside of therapy can easily overwhelm even the best designed program (Steffen & Karoly, 1980), these clinicians requested refined methods for illuminating milieu forces. Identifying contextual variables would conceivably enable practitioners to specify sources of obstruction in advance and to anticipate them therapeutically, to select transfer settings which do not compete with positive treatment outcome, or to design prosthetic social environments promoting a salutory level of client functioning (Shepherd, 1977). In general, it would encourage promoting those client changes which are expected and rewarded by key persons in the client's home and work subculture (Davidson & Wolfred, 1977; Goldstein, Lopez & Greenleaf, 1979; Marholin & Touchette, 1979).

Unfortunately, the behaviorally-inspired concepts used in formulating ecologically relevant clinical case descriptions appear coarse and inadequate; such analyses rely on terms usually reserved for describing micro-level processes in the environment, in order to describe events which are organized at more macro levels. Typically, the client's surroundings are construed as *nothing more than* a collection of salient stimuli (hopefully somewhat overlapping with training conditions) or contingencies of natural community reinforcement. Some of these can be trusted to "trap" or strengthen the client's new skill, while other contingencies undermine treatment gains (Marholin et al., 1976; Marholin & Touchette, 1979; Stokes & Baer, 1977). Elsewhere, the transfer context is understood as sets of significant others and dyads within families, analyzed in terms of coercive interchanges or as reciprocal sources of stimulus control where aversive behavior is the common mode of social exchange (Patterson, 1976; Patterson & Moore, 1979; Patterson & Reid, 1970; Tharp & Wetzel, 1969). Slightly more comprehensive behavioral approaches consider the entire family unit as the extra-therapy environment. The family constellation—its composition, demography, cohesion, support capacity, and quality of relationship with kinfolk and friends—is to be observed and described as a prelude to constructing treatment plans (Nay, 1979; Wahler, 1980b). Moos and his associates' extensive series of alcohol treatment follow-up studies amply demonstrates the viability of this approach, by finding significant correlations between posttreatment family environment indices (cohesion, support, conflict, expressiveness) and outcome measures of relapse, depression, social and occupational functions (Bromet & Moos, 1977; Cronkite & Moos, 1980; Finney, Moos & Mewborn, 1980; Moos & Moos, 1984).

Melahn and O'Donnel's behavioral consultation model, derived from norm-based assessment of the natural setting, is perhaps the furthest possible extension of behavioral tools for environmental description. Norm-based consulting, carried out in schools, for example, initially entails assessing the local norms for potentially important pupil behaviors to determine immediately which behaviors distinguish referred children from their peers in that particular setting. The consultant next informs teachers if a problem behavior in fact exists, when to intervene (if at all), whether the behavior is specific to a time and place, and whether it will improve without intervention.

Behavioral formulations of posttreatment environments can rightfully claim a range of applicability, particularly as reliable tools for pinpointing patterns of immediate antecedent and consequent events determining the path of some dyadic interchanges. However, we sharply question the power of these concepts—generally applied to microlevel processes—to produce satisfying and comprehensive analyses of social environments complicated by the influence of numerous, interdependent, and manifold actors. Clinicians require a broader vision and alternative measures to adequately conceptualize the client's larger social ecology (Price, 1979) and the social system which ultimately governs the survival of treatment changes. Genuine commitment to a social ecology view of posttreatment environments, however, leads to radical reformulation of the generalization dilemma. Leading this departure from the current generalization paradigm, O'Donnell assserts that our current construction of the issue prevents its resolution because we are asking the wrong question (O'Donnell, 1977). The question should not be why behavior isn't maintained over time and generalized to other settings—an unreasonable expectation regarding intervention effects. Rather, by assuming behavior is a component of the setting in which it is assessed, the question becomes; "why has the natural setting not developed or supported the desired behavior, and why are our procedures not readily adopted in natural settings" (O'Donnell, 1984, p. 500)? Since everyday social interactions are largely responsible for behavior acquisition and maintenance, interventions affecting this natural system would not require generalization. Rather than simply being maintained, behavior affected by such interaction would continue to develop as a function of the social system of which it was a part (O'Donnell & Tharp, 1982). Maintenance of behavior over time is determined by a) changes in the type of settings in which people participate, and b) the behavioral norms occurring within each setting in transaction with the individual's abilities as a setting participant (O'Donnell, 1981).

In conclusion, assessing natural settings extends beyond referred individuals and their managers to "extend to other behaviors, all individuals, the social networks of the setting participants, the social relations among people, the influence of the physical design on behavior, the roles available for people, the number of people available for each role, the tasks performed in each role, the skills required for each task, etc." (O'Donnell, 1984, pp. 501–502). Fortunately, the daunting task of building empirical knowledge on how natural settings are organized structurally through interpersonal ties, and how these interlinkages function to promote and constrain social action and mediate personal adjustment, has already begun. It is contained within the work of anthropologists, sociologists, and some psychologists and psychiatrists employing social network analysis. The remainder of this chapter lays a foundation for the use of social network analysis as a clinical method for the assessment of posttreatment environments' capacities to support behavior change. Also presented are social psychological strategies, which can be used to train clients to develop behavior change-enhancing networks of their own.

NETWORK ANALYSIS AS A CLINICAL METHOD FOR ASSESSING POSTTREATMENT ENVIRONMENTS

The Theoretical Promise

Clinicians wishing to comprehend their client's extratherapy social reality have discovered allies among European anthropologists laboring to shed the abstract and static social view of structural-functionism. Both groups value the promise of network analysis: to accurately map configurations of inter-linked and interdependent persons, and in so doing provide an efficient and productive way of penetrating to the heart of various formal and ephemeral social structures (Whitten & Wolfe, 1974). First, warns the anthropologist Boissevain, network analysis is not a theory but an *analytic method*, viewing informants' perceptions of circles of relatives or friends, coalitions, groups, and even nations as scatterings of *points* connected by *lines* that form *networks*. "Network analysis asks questions about who is linked to whom, the content of those linkages, the patterns they form, the relationships between patterns and behavior, and the relationship between those patterns and other social factors" (Boissevain, 1979, p. 392). Through these questions it provides a single framework, accounting for both the actual exchanges between individuals and the structural nets that underlie their repeated occurrence among a number of individuals across time (Pilisuk & Parks, 1981). The clinical power of network analysis accrues when its descriptions of observable human interaction are combined with social exchange and transaction theory to predict which patterns of posttreatment interpersonal arrangements stifle behavior change and, conversely, which networks can be used or created to strengthen therapeutic gains. Before arriving at such predictions, clinicians must first comprehend the theoretical relationships between networks and the types of social transactions they constrain.

Several important assumptions can be distilled from preliminary theorizing regarding the link between network structure and social exchange (Pilisuk & Parks, 1981; Van Poucke, 1980; Whitten & Wolfe, 1974). First, Fischer et al.'s (1977) choice-constraint model posits that people act as rational decision-makers, *choosing* to construct personal relationships with selected individuals whom they encounter in various social contexts. However, an individual's opportunities for forming relationships, as well as the resources available with which to pursue these ties, is constrained by their position within the social structure as determined by family- and life-cycle position, gender, education, social class and geographic mobility (Allan, 1979). What an individual values, expects and needs from exchanges are of course also determined by these constraints. For example, access to and participation in various social contexts is slowly eroded among the elderly, while for the young, education provides cohorts of classmates and sharpened social skills. Similarly, marriage isolates women but not men from non-kin ties, while higher income provides people with the resources to explore diverse social settings and keep in touch with friends and relatives (Fischer & Phillips, 1979). Borrowing the core assumption in Thibaut and Kelley's (1959) theory of interpersonal interdependence, the choice constraint model stresses active evaluation of social exchanges during friendship formation. Personal bonds, derived from available contexts, develop and dissolve over time depending on the rewards and costs they bring to the individuals involved.

Second, Van Poucke (1979) extends our critical awareness of network processes by recognizing that relationships are characterized by the aims participants seek during exchanges—whether they be goods, services, emotional support, power, or other social commodities. Significantly, knowing the particular aims governing the ties among individuals in a network enable predictions about the structure of the resulting network, the type of social control exerted, and the type of exchanges taking place within the network. Specifically, Van Poucke (1979) identifies three network prototypes. "Sentiment" networks arise when the action goal maintains that the relationship is an end in itself. Because durability is valued, sentiment network structure tends to be permanent and fixed; actions are strongly norm- and tradition-oriented, to preserve this stability over time and create a close-knit web of interrelationships among network members. The price of collective solidarity is subdued self-interest and the flourishing of reciprocal exchanges. Longstanding sentiment-based relationships, valued in their own right, are cemented through reciprocal obligations, and foster strongly shared values among a tight clique of associates. Subsequently, strong social control is exerted over members' actions.

In contrast, "interest" networks are comprised of relationships activated as means to achieve an end, and are dissolved once concrete goals are attained. Interest network structure, in order to give members flexibility for strategic action and for recruiting and coopting additional actors as required, is momentary and fluid. The predominating action logic centers on evaluating each interaction in terms of goal-rational implications, without necessarily taking account of individual members' concerns. The social control processes enforcing the network's norms and rules are general, even indifferent toward particularities of the actors. "Power" networks, the third Van Poucke prototype, arise when goals whose attainment requires collective action are made permanent. Long-term interest relations are transformed into power relations when they establish goal-directedness on a continual basis and acquire central coordination to achieve intended results. Redistributive exchange characterizes power networks; individuals make contributions to some central agency and these efforts are converted into the goal striving of the organization.

Network theory's tenets sensitize clinicians to critical processes operating in posttreatment settings. Clients assume an active role in selecting personal network members, and make subjective judgments regarding the desirability of these ties based on a cost/benefit rationale. These choices are biased by personal needs, values, and social skills; in addition, limited opportunities, imposed by the client's location within the social structure, help to determine which social contexts are available. Relationships are formed to achieve various goals and evolve different network types congruent with each goal orientation. The situation logic of one type of network directs social action in harmony with that type of relationship context (e.g., durability requirements of sentiment networks dictate social conformity).

Additionally, contexts available to clients differ in relative constraint upon freedom of choice and interaction. More constrained contexts, such as work settings and kinfolk, produce close-knit networks and low social similarity; while more voluntary contexts, such as childhood ties and clubs, allow loose-knit networks and high social similarity (Fischer et al., 1977). Finally, each network is held together by an appropriate type of social exchange. Clients joining sentiment networks, for example, require competencies in fulfilling reciprocal obligations to successfully maintain their membership. Our objective is to mine these critical network processes—relationship evaluation, network type and structure, reciprocal exchange, network constrained social action, and contextual determinants of network membership—for research hypotheses which focus on the clinician's need to predict the behavior change potential of client networks. Prior to precise specification of clinical research hypotheses, however, we must undertake a momentary diversion, to develop a uniform nomenclature of network terms to efficiently guide us through complex phenomena.

Network Dimensions

Network phenomena are typically described as coalescing along two dimensions. Network structural or morphological qualities describe diverse shapes networks can assume, while functional and interactional criteria refer to the actual exchanges (content and quality) that define ties between people (Marsella & Snyder, 1981; Mitchell, 1969; Pilisuk & Parks, 1981). Clinical research employing network analysis is better served by a more refined typology tailored to concern for the client's sentiment network. Hence, we construe network phenomena according to three dimensions shown in Table 7.1: network capacity, network resource exchange style, and network intensity.

Before proceeding, two methodological cautions should be aired. First, although these dimensions are now clearly conceptualized, researchers still struggle to achieve a uniform operationalization with standardized, reliable, and accepted instruments for network mapping (see Donald & Ware, 1982; House & Kahn, 1985; Wood, 1984). Second, there is strong evidence suggesting that informants' accuracy when self-reporting their network contacts markedly diverges from behavioral observations of those same contacts (Bernard, Killworth & Sailer, 1979/1980). It may well be, as Bernard warns, that there are distinct cognitive and behavioral networks. Who people *think* they talk to and who people *really* talk to constitute different networks, and should be treated as such. Similarly, Heller and Swindle (1983) warn researchers to clearly distinguish between two relatively independent constructs: the individual's *observed* social support network (i.e., behaviors the social environment provides) as against the subjective appraisal of that behavior by the individual. Methodological dilemmas of informant inaccuracy, perceived versus observed networks, and lack of consensually validated instruments, however, do not outweigh the power of network analysis as a fruitful domain for clinical research.

Table 7.1 Typology of Network Analysis Concepts Describing Client Sentiment Networks*

TYPE	TERM	DEFINITION OF FUNCTION
Network Capacity	*Personal Delivery System* Infrastructure:	
	Size	Number of client's associates providing supportive resources
	Density	Extent to which links or interconnections are formed among the client's network of supportive associates
	Cluster	Degree to which members of the client's support network form cliques or high density subgroups
	Assessibility or Reachability	Ease with which any member of the supportive unit can be reached for the supportive function of an individual or overall for the group
	Structural Stability	Degree to which network infrastructure changes over a period of time
	Composition:	
	Source Type	Categories of individuals comprising the client's support network (e.g., kin, friends, neighbors, co-workers, professionals, etc.)
	Intimacy	Social distance zones: distinguished by closeness, importance, and basis of the relationship (e.g., high intimacy of nuclear family; low intimacy of neighbors)
	Homogeneity	Demographic uniformity or mixture of network members; their racial, income, sex and age diversity
	Resource Content	
	Availability	Categories of key social support resources exchanged through network ties (e.g., material aid, emotional support, recreation, etc.)
	Quality	Client perceived satisfaction with each support resource category in relation to felt need
Resource Exchange Style (Interactional Factors)	Frequency	Number of supportive transactions occurring per tie
	Duration	Degree to which supportive interaction changes or remains the same over time
	Mode	Means or channels of transaction; for example, face-to-face exchange, telephone conversation or letters

Table 7.1 Continued

TYPE	TERM	DEFINITION OF FUNCTION
Resource Exchange Style (Interactional Factors)	Multiplexity	The number of different support resource categories exchanged across an individual linkage
	Directionality	Extent to which exchanges are symmetrical, involving reciprocity and mutual participation, or asymmetric, where support resources flow in one direction only
	Interactional Stability	The loss or reestablishment of contacts and of the expectations that they will continue to be of functional value
Network Intensity	Intensity	Degree to which client is compelled to honor obligations arising from network ties; i.e., network capacity, through strength of interpersonal commitments —intimacy, source type, multiplexity, and density—to exert conformity pressure

*(Adapted from Pilisuk & Parks, 1981)

Table 7.1, adapted from Pilisuk and Parks (1981), summarizes network analysis concepts we shall be referring to later in assessing the capacity of client sentiment networks to extinguish or extend therapeutic behavior change. Network terms are clustered along three dimensions related to a) the client's structural opportunities for receiving personally sustaining exchanges (social support), the nature of resources received and from who; b) how resources are delivered; and c) the overall strength of the client's sentiment network to dictate appropriate behavior. More specifically, the client's *network capacity* for securing personally sustaining resources is determined by both the variety of support resources available *and* the personal delivery system constructed to acquire such resources. Analogous to a community's system of human service delivery, a client creates and operates a personal system, distinguished by its infrastructure and membership composition, along which interpersonal aid is delivered (e.g., Hayes & Oxley, 1986). Infrastructure refers to the delivery system's shape: the number of network members (size), the extent to which they know one another and form interconnections (density), and whether a dense cluster of network member links is found constituting a clique within the overall group. Infrastructure reachability denotes the ease of making a direct connection within the network and is dampened by physical distance and number of intermediaries separating those desiring to get together. Membership losses and gains by reason of change in residence, employment, or death naturally alter the network's structural stability. Vital to understanding the delivery system's support capacity is identification of the providers' characteristics or *composition*. Support quality, perceived satisfaction, availability, and influence covary with source type—whether friend, kin, co-worker or professional—and with the intimacy level associated with provider. Moreover, nonhomogeneous networks, containing members from various racial, income, sex, and age groups, link the clients across broader social strata and potentially draw upon more diverse resources.

Resource content, the second attribute of network capacity, identifies supportive exchanges available to the client and their perceived quality (e.g., Shumaker & Brownell, 1984; Wills, 1985). Barrera's social support taxonomy is well researched. It provides a satisfying range of resource exchanges, which are both behaviorally defined and subjectively evaluated using criteria of perceived satisfaction and need (Barrera, 1981; Barrera & Ainlay, 1983). Briefly, Barrera's taxonomy encompasses material aid; help with physical tasks; the sharing of private feelings; guidance or advice; feedback about one's ideas or performance; and recreation.

Interaction between client and network providers and among network members achieves a distinctive style of resource exchange. Significant communication attributes comprising exchange style include *frequency* of supportive transactions, communication *channels* used (face to face, third party, etc.), and *duration* of resource exchange. Clients with multi-stranded (multiplex) links with a provider receive several categories of social support, and are likely to interact with that person across many different contexts. Most importantly, though, the resource exchange style can be symmetrical, with aid flowing reciprocally in both directions across network links, or asymmetrical; with aid flowing in one direction only. Asymmetric or unbalanced exchanges promote power differentials, patron-client dependency, and the possibility of exploitation (Fischer et al., 1977). Additionally, client network interaction patterns have measurable stability based on a composite index of changes in exchange variables and the client's expectation of the functional value of provider interactions.

The final network analysis concept, *intensity*, recognizes that structural and exchange style variables can sometimes combine to create exceedingly strong personal ties and commitments that then constrain social action, as per Van Poucke's (1979) theory. High-intensity links may compel the client to honor obligations and conform to norms stabilizing group solidarity. Intensity is a byproduct of high density networks or clusters, often comprised largely of kin and deeply intimate friends, and multiplex bonds which are much more difficult to withdraw completely from than social links involving only single support strands (Mitchell, 1969). Clusters often form through selection procedures whereby friends of existing intimates meet and form ties. Hence, people like or dislike those who their partners like or dislike and tend to engage in interaction with these second-hand contacts (Van Poucke, 1979). Operating through dense interconnections, intense networks encourage values that promote continuity of a stable clique over time, provide feedback regarding conformity or violation of subgroup norms, and demand adherence to existing roles (Moos & Mitchell, 1982). Consequently, a disagreement or conflict in one relationship could have repercussions on others and potentially disrupt many areas of social life.

NETWORK TYPOLOGIES OF POSTTREATMENT ENVIRONMENTS AND PREDICTED BEHAVIORAL OUTCOMES

Forearmed with an appreciation of network analysis concepts and theory, we can now comb the field's empirical findings to construct hypotheses linking social network configurations with predicted treatment generalization outcomes. Given the multivariate complexity of network phenomena, hypothesis construction is guided foremost by the desire to achieve prediction specificity. We hope to pinpoint different network effects on generalization outcome depending upon: network configuration, the client's traits, the client's personal life-development transition, and type and source of support (e.g., Moos & Mitchell, 1982). Specifically, we aim to identify those types of posttreatment client networks which are potentially counter-therapeutic because they are stressful or help maintain deviant behavior. Discussed are network types which serve therapy goals by providing a social environment allowing or even promoting behavior change. Considered first are stress-producing networks. They extinguish new responses, either because they lack the infrastructure to support behavior change or, equally undermining, are highly aversive. Second, deviance maintenance networks are described, relying heavily on the concept of intensity and extreme social pressure accruing through dense, multiplex social links. Finally, the massive literature depicting social support networks is examined for evidence of network typologies which *enhance* behavior change by allowing individuals to build skills, express competence, assume new role opportunities, and manage personal stress. The section concludes with a distillation of network attributes and processes essential for maximizing behavior change. Creating behavior change oriented networks through social cognitive strategies—setting selection and interpersonal interdependence—become the chapter's final foci.

Stress Producing Networks

Deficit networks

Low network capacity. The next set of hypotheses predict negligible transfer of therapy gains for clients whose networks are so stress producing that newly developed self-management behaviors are overwhelmed and inconsequential. Generalization is undermined by both deficient networks (those with low capacity, inadequate interactional stability or asymmetry) and networks characterized by interpersonal conflict and delivery of aversive or nonsupportive events.

Social learning principles underlying deficient and aversive networks' inhospitability as treatment transfer environments can be surmised from our discussion of Wahler and Sanders' studies. These include: a) pervasive paucity of social reinforcement; b) incapacity to deliver available rewards contingently; c) presence of powerful stimulus conditions which pull highly defensive or stereotypic behaviors, diminishing opportunities to implement self-control strategies; and d) predominance of punishing contingencies and "coercion traps" rendering ineffective behaviors acquired in treatment. By juxtaposing these learning conditions with deficient network structures, we formulate hypothesis 7.2.

Hypothesis 7.2
Client network capacity characterized by weak delivery system infrastructure, i.e., small size, only one or two dense clusters, low reachability, and structural instability, will fail to provide social exchange resources capable of sustaining behavior change.

Accumulated evidence supporting this hypotheses arises from studies linking network infrastructure variables with life distress indices (Barrera, 1981; Berkman, 1985, 1986; Liem & Liem, 1978; Lin, Dean & Insel, 1986; Pilisuk & Froland, 1978). Pilisuk, in his summary of the converging findings from epidemiological and laboratory research, convincingly argues that "persons who are socially marginal, or those who have experienced a recent dislocation in their supportive networks (whether through mobility, bereavement, divorce or changes in life cycle status), appear to be of higher risk for tuberculosis, psychiatric admission, schizophrenia, traffic accidents, alcoholism, hypertension, stroke, suicide, clinical depression, disorders of pregnancy, school problems, deterioration of certain cancers, and medical absenteeism" (Pilisuk, Chandler & D'Onofrio, 1983, p. 45).

These data reveal that persons least immune to stressful life circumstances, and most prone to psychological and physiological dysfunction, operate within networks which are: small, fragile, and low in overall density; easily collapsed when one key figure departs; and disproportionately comprised of family members or helping professionals. Deficient networks are marked by a few overdependent links with these family members on a higher or lower generational level, with few clusters and connections between friends and kin, and are arranged so that the client occupies a peripheral network position, with information flow mediated by another person (Baker & Singer, 1980; Cohen & Sokolovsky, 1978; Fischer & Phillips, 1979; Froland, Brodsky, Olson & Stewart, 1979; Garrison, 1978; Hammer, Makiesky-Barrow & Gutwirth, 1978; Henderson, 1980; Mueller, 1980; Sokolovsky, Cohen, Berger & Geiger, 1978; Tolsdorf, 1976; Wahler, 1980a).

The classic account of ex-mental patients' networks in a Manhattan rooming house by Sokolovsky et al. (1978) remains the clearest portrayal of the association between symptom expression and number of personal connections. Non-psychotic residents developed networks twice as large as their discharged schizophrenic neighbors, while those expressing residual symptoms formed the fewest social links and were likely to fall into a cycle of re-hospitalization when their network size dropped below five or key contacts moved away.

E. M. Pattison's larger survey, employing the Psychosocial Kinship Inventory, also identified distinctive network size and configurations associated with levels of impairment (Pattison et al., 1975; Pattison, Llamas & Hurd, 1979). Non-impaired urban samples maintained five clusters, each containing five or six persons with over half of these knowing each other. The neurotic subgroup's network contained half as many members (10–12), including negative relationships and significant others far away. They were arranged in a low density pattern placing the neurotic person at the hub of a wheel, with individual relations like spokes that have no interconnections. Psychotics, in contrast, appeared bound in a tiny (4–5) dense matrix made up almost exclusively of family members. This finding was replicated in a sample of 35 "baa" (spirit possession) cases drawn from 27 rural Lao villages who would be expected to belong to large extended kin groups (Westermeyer & Pattison, 1981). Extreme dependence by impaired persons on their intimate kin cluster may temper distress levels and reduce hospital admissions. Yet, accessibility to wider social resources and productive roles is sacrificed, perpetuating community isolation and minimum growth in skills for coping with day to day life stressors (Baker & Singer, 1980; Froland, Brodsky, Olson & Stewart, 1979; Mitchell, 1981). The following hypothesis concerns deficiencies associated with networks maintaining unbalanced composition.

Hypothesis 7.2a
Clients maintaining personal delivery systems with homogeneous or unbalanced compositions (e.g., containing only kin or professionals), will lack the dispersion of social exchange resources necessary to support behavior generalization.

Network capacity for moderating life stress and creating opportunities for therapeutic behavior maintenance is greatly diminished when the network composition is dominated by one category of individual. This restricts exchanges to the supportive transactions and roles associated with that one category. Wahler's (1980a, 1980b) documentation of the relationship between insular mothers' extrafamily social contacts and continued compliance with treatment instructions concurs with this hypothesis. Insular mothers were those whose networks contained a lopsided proportion of kin and helping agency personnel, who frequently offered unsolicited and unappreciated critical advice. Marked improvements in mother–child problem exchanges during treatment did not continue into the follow-up phase, *except* during days when mothers enjoyed a high proportion of contact with their friends. Wahler's example, developing the connection between category of network member (friend), social exchange type (non-judgmental emotional support), and behavioral outcomes (reductions in aversive and abusive child interactions) is documented in other studies. Depending upon ethnicity and educational status, family ties, especially parent–child, are the most supportive, intimate, and regular sources of personal consultation, reliable alliance, and material aid (Cutrona, 1986; Fischer, 1977). Friends' emotional support can equal, and sometimes outweigh, that from family, as well as offering social companionship, advice and physical assistance. Extended kin are perceived as close, but not especially supportive, while neighbors and work mates are valued for social enjoyment and instrumental exchanges (Fischer, 1977).

Problems emerge, however, when a resource type specifically required to ameliorate a stressful circumstance or recurring need is outside the network capacity (see Cohen & McKay, 1984; Cohen & Wills, 1985). For example, the very few friends and relatives in touch with "schizophrenics" may be inadequate conveyors of the social feedback which Hammer and colleagues (1978) see as vital to the development and maintenance of culturally appropriate behavior. More precisely, their diminished networks afford few redundant communication channels, so missing or misleading messages have little chance of being corrected and intensify with time (Hammer et al., 1978). Moreover, when a support type is too closely associated with one network subgroup, its availability becomes tenuous. Keefe, Padilla and Carlos (1979) noted that while Anglo Californians were likely to seek emotional help from diverse network components—friends, neighbors, co-workers, and groups—Mexican Americans relied heavily on their extended kin ties. Using familial bonds as the only informal emotional resource means that those without local kin are not likely to have substitute sources of help in stress times, and would experience more distress than Anglos in similar circumstances. Other population segments, especially the older generation and mobile career families, must also reach beyond kinship to find adequate sources of support, given the interruption in their customary access to blood relatives in the community (Pilisuk & Parks, 1986).

However, the narrowest range of social exchange potential is afforded to networks containing heavy components of agency professionals. Relationships are delimited by power differences, lack of reciprocity, limited opportunities and settings for contact, and clearly defined boundaries of conversation. In addition, dominant-subordinant relationships will show high structural instability, given the ability of professionals to refer clients elsewhere or detach themselves from clients in a variety of ways. In brief, networks offering balanced clusters of friends, kin, workmates, neighbors and so forth, which Pattison, Llamas and Hurd (1979) describe as "normal, intimate psychosocial networks," maximize the range of supportive transactions required to adequately resolve life transition hardships.

Asymmetric exchanges. We postulate that a balanced dispersion of essential social resources will maximize network capacity. We must also recognize that overall network configuration and composition is the evolutionary byproduct of former, present and anticipated interactions with specific persons. It is through interactions that supportive transactions unfold. It is the resource exchange style manifested during these events— their frequency, duration, mode, directionality, etc.—which determine the quality of support delivery and, more significantly, the probability that the network structure will remain intact to occasion future resource transactions. Our final hypothesis concerning network deficiencies highlights exchange styles likely to diminish network capacity.

Hypothesis 7.3
Client networks manifesting a resource exchange style dominated by non-reciprocal interactions and lacking multiplex ties decrease social support capacity over time while increasing dependency and powerlessness. Such conditions are devoid of opportunities for clients to initiate self-control procedures or receive social reinforcement for clinical behavior change.

Researchers investigating clinical populations, especially those experiencing more severe dysfunction, uniformly observe exchange styles marked by: a) the absence of reciprocity, in that the patient receives but does not give aid; and b) the primacy of unstable, single-stranded links having only one category of support involved per relationship (Erickson, 1975; Froland et al., 1979; Mitchell & Trickett, 1980; O'Donnell & Tharp, 1982; Pattison et al. 1975; Sokolovsky et al., 1978; Tolsdorf, 1976; Westermeyer & Pattison, 1981). Network theorists widely assume that reciprocal obligations or quid pro quo helping exchange is the social glue binding dyads together into long-term associations. Persons unable or unwilling to reciprocate the help others offer eliminate a major source of satisfaction strengthening relationships and feelings of mutuality. They gradually alienate themselves from all save family caretakers and the few but functionally more powerful people in the network—helping professionals (Froland et al., 1979; Tolsdorf, 1976; Westermeyer & Pattison, 1981). While the Sokolovsky et al. (1978) and Pattison (1975) studies confirmed this association between unidirectional dependency upon others and diminished networks, Westermeyer and Pattison (1981) gained additional insight into the process by observing that those Laotian villagers with episodic spirit possession who were able to maintain reciprocal ties with family and friends during lucid intervals kept their networks intact during phases of incapacitation. It was as though these villagers had been able to build up a reserve of social capital prior to their disorder, through productive work and socializing, which they could draw upon when unable to carry out normal obligations.

Tolsdorf's (1976) extensive network interviews, conducted with ten Veterans' Administration medical patients and ten psychiatric first admissions in the same facility, suggest that the client maintains a "network orientation" or "set of beliefs, attitudes, and expectations concerning the potential usefulness of his network members in helping him cope with life problems" (p. 413). Presumably, network orientation influences willingness to hold the network together through reciprocal efforts. Patients holding negative network orientations dismiss the value of disclosing problems to associates and the efficacy of their advice. From Procidano and Heller's (1983) preliminary investigations linking perceived social support and support-seeking actions, we may infer that a patient's negative network orientation derives from a three step appraisal process. That is, the person a) recognizes a "threat" or harm in a situation, b) decides that more information/assistance is needed, and c) perceives that it is *unlikely* to be available within her or his support network, so that support seeking in that sphere is futile (see Heller & Swindle, 1983, p. 97).

Irrespective of which personal factors interact with setting constraints to produce an asymmetric exchange style, the resulting power difference places the client in a dependent position, open to exploitation. Furthermore, powerlessness will reduce opportunities that allow the client to implement self-control strategies, acquire a sense of self-efficacy, or assume responsibility for his or her own actions. On the contrary, the high resentment potential of non-equitable ties may create psychological reactance—opposing other's suggestions in order to restore personal freedom—or engender the coercion trap situation found among Wahler's insular mothers. That is, the mothers would accept the advice of authority figures to terminate their nagging but fail to follow suggestions once authorities depart. Dependency relationships make clients vulnerable to unsolicited instructions and also force the weaker party to both self-initiate desired help (as opposed to receiving proactive support), and self-disclose troublesome circumstances—actions tending to exacerbate symptoms (Baker & Singer, 1980; see also Cohen & Wills, 1985, p. 350; Rook & Dooley, 1985).

Lastly, the hypothesis draws attention to network deficiencies brought on by a high preponderance of uniplex and single-stranded resource transactions (Marsella & Snyder, 1981; Sokolovsky et al., 1978). Without multiplexity, relationship intimacy is precluded and the range of tangible assistance needed to handle stressors is constricted. Also, attachments are more readily broken since little of one's lifestyle and social investment will be lost. A disadvantage of uniplex links was evident in Hirsch's (1981) network intervention with hospital nursing staff aimed at reducing acute levels of job stress. The primacy of unidimensional relationships among nurses, revolving exclusively around hospital tasks, reduced the workmate network's ability to deal with the occupation's emotional traumas and the need for empowerment vis-à-vis other medical professionals. Hirsch surmised that hospital policy aimed at blocking "alien" interpersonal modes from entering hospital routine was a key factor governing the predominance of uniplex relationships in that setting, although at the cost of a 70 percent turnover rate.

Aversive networks

The final network type presumed to produce stress derives its aversive qualities from the network's intensity and commensurate capacity to deliver inescapable social sanctions, especially criticism, serving the interest of group conformity.

Hypothesis 7.4
Client networks developing high intensity (i.e., coalescence of high density, intimacy and multiplexity) become potent sources of judgmental feedback. Because persons are unable to avoid or detach themselves from these intimate sources of conflict, intense networks may be acutely aversive and discordant with posttreatment adjustment.

Intense networks have unbridled power to bring social pressure to bear on the actions of individual members. The combination of high network density, multiplexity, intimacy, and preponderence of kinship, catches the person in a web of relentless feedback. Such feedback insured adherence to norms and role expectations; it may also turn into critical comment or the threat of more severe sanctions when those expectations are violated. Clients in conflict with intimate network members are at maximum risk of experiencing a reversal in treatment gains because their sources of stress are immediate, penetrating, and inescapable. Yet the complete severance of these ties entails loss of whatever support resources they also represent.

Supporting this prediction are studies correlating inescapable group and family criticism with poor adjustment and high relapse among former psychiatric patients. Brown, Birley and Wing's (1972) classic investigation in Britain of 100 discharged schizophrenic patients' household climates noted that relatives showing a high degree of "Emotional Expression (EE)," that is, critical comments, hostility, dissatisfaction, and little warmth, were more likely to provoke a relapse of symptoms, independent of the dysfunction's duration and previous severity. Significantly, patients most in danger of relapse had the highest exposure to their EE relatives, spending more than 35 hours per week at home in face-to-face contact, and were unable to protect themselves through social withdrawal and drug use (see Vaughn & Leff's [1976] replication of this finding using depressive patients). Moreover, as Wahler (1980a) re-discovered with his observations of insular mothers, relatives producing the highest levels of aversive emotional responses were those living alone with the patient, or only with their spouse, and who had low rates of contacts with their wider network of friends and kin.

Brown et al. (1977) subsequently extended this general hypothesis in a community survey of women's psychiatric status in urban and rural British regions. Women deeply enmeshed in their Scottish island community, through birth, economic production and religious bonds, were buffered against the depression common in their London counterparts, but prone to higher rates of anxiety and obsessional conditions. Again, Brown et al.'s interpretation suggests that while the close-knit rural setting affords women ample support and a meaningful, albeit "traditional," place in life, it simultaneously promotes a "susceptibility to anxiety by the oppressive and even persecutory nature of that very closeness" (p. 374). Zautra's interviews with middle-aged women in Arizona reveal network oppression processes strikingly similar to the British studies. The most frequent response of these women to negative life events was to blame their network for its lack of fairness, while those women not finding fault with their networks reported no stress (Zautra, 1983). Graves and Graves (1985) add that Samoan migrants to New Zealand living in tightly knit communities also endure pressure from relatives and coethnics to maintain traditional practices of obligation and reciprocity. Such pressure is both costly (in food, services and hospitality) and is linked with greater health problems.

Wilcox's (1981) network analysis of women's adjustment during the course of marital disruption further strengthens our argument. The group experiencing the greatest mood disturbance following separation was that comprised of women forced to retreat primarily to the support resources of close kin when friends shared in common with their husbands were lost during the divorce. The successfully adjusting group did not experience the 41 percent turnover in network membership which occurred to the distressed women, could rely on a balanced composition of kin and non-kin for support, and were not subjected to the intensity of judgmental comments delivered by family members refusing to accept that the marriage was over. Wilcox's conclusions, taken together with Hirsch's descriptions of coping difficulties experienced by recent widows and mature women returning to college (Hirsch, 1980), lead us to speculate that the aversive potential inherent in intense networks is triggered when individuals struggle to redefine their roles or pursue novel interests which reverberate through the network as an impetus to radical relationship reformulation.

Barrera (1980, 1981) and Sandler (1980; Sandler & Barrera, 1984) have teased out the relationship between conflicted network size, the number of intimates regularly associated with upsetting interactions, and symptom expression. Correlational data from 86 first-pregnancy teenagers in Arizona revealed that size of conflicted network, although small in absolute sense, related positively to depression and anxiety dimensions of the Brief Symptom Inventory. Also, overall network size demonstrated the life stress-buffering effect only when those intimates who were also sources of unpleasant social interaction were removed from the analysis. In a subsequent study of university students, Sandler and Barrera (1984) sharpened our understanding of how conflicted ties influence the capacity of networks to render support. They found paradoxically that total network size was related to a "negative" stress-buffering effect: a *stronger* correlation between stress and somatic symptoms occurred for students with larger social networks. Sandler and Barrera unravelled this paradox by again separating out the effects of network conflict. The unexpected finding was due to the fact that those with large *conflicted* networks were expressing somatic complaints in the face of stress. In contrast, the size of their unconflicted network was not associated directly with symptom expression nor did it contribute to the negative stress buffering effect.

Finally, Glidewell's study of 36 urban Chicago citizens seeking help for stressful life events refines our perceptions that primary social support is not conflict-free. His interviews uncovered conflict between need for support and value placed on personal autonomy, which led to a reduction in the positiveness of emotional exchange between client and helper. Conversely, satisfaction with help received varied directly with the positiveness of emotional and idea exchange and with one's need for support (Glidewell, 1981).

In review, these studies penetrate the myth that social networks and social support, with its "warm and fuzzy connotations" (Kelly, 1981), are identical phenomena. As conduits, network channels reverberate with aversive as well as psychologically sustaining messages. Network bonds can trap and hold people back or offer them the stimulation and security to acquire competency and power. These findings alert clinicians to the necessity for compiling "maps" which display the client's network configurations of social ties. Network maps allow diagnosis of both deficiencies in the client's personal delivery system of social resources and pinpoint the sources of emotional stress thay may need to be removed, resolved or otherwise compensated for (see Rook & Dooley, 1985).

Deviance Maintenance Networks

On several occasions we have referred to the omnipotent social control mechanisms developing within high intensity networks as the price of maintaining an enduring, reliable, and close-knit web of interrelationships. While noted earlier for their capacity to mobilize punishing sanctions, these control mechanisms also conspire to contravene therapist influence by: a) demanding and rewarding role behavior endemic to that subgroup; b) disallowing actions corresponding to individual change at the expense of collective stability; and c) insulating the person from wider social resources which could be marshalled to disentangle him or her from expected roles, group maintenance obligations, or an abusive spouse (Mitchell & Hodson, 1985). Consequently, intense network insularity helps maintain specific norms serving subgroup interests, which may diverge dramatically from behavioral outcomes deemed desirable by clinicians. Of course, the power of network intensity can conceivably be wielded therapeutically, as when clinician and subgroup hold converging expectations of client behavior change. At this point, though, we shall only consider the negative case. Hence, our next hypothesis identifies network conditions likely to maintain behavior at its baseline level despite intervention counterinfluence.

Hypothesis 7.5
Clients personally committed to high intensity networks (or lacking alternatives) will invariably fail to generalize any treatment response which threatens to destabilize the balance of exchange obligations underpinning network members' sense of solidarity.

In essence, this hypothesis predicts that therapeutic actions that undermine processes holding a client's network together are contextually invalid and at risk of being extinguished. This occurs when the client is unwilling to dismantle his or her personal network, and thus forego its resources, in favor of securing any gains expected from following the therapeutic regimen. The key insight for clinicians is that they must first assess which behavior classes function to keep the network together and which relationships cannot be altered without disadvantageous repercussions throughout the network infrastructure. It is not the case that treatment-inspired changes encounter resistance simply because they are novel, violate "odd" customs, or are "personally threatening" to isolated significant others. Rather, failure to honor expectations governing one relationship connection embedded in an intense network carries repercussions possibly damaging to all other links the individual has in that dense array.

Allan (1979), distilling the anthropological literature on density and conjugal role relationships, invokes the familiar social exchange theory rationale to explain this process. Because each person invests energy, time, service, and so forth in her or his relationships, for which equivalent returns are expected, relationships become systems of exchange in which obligations are continually being created and discharged. Hence, should one individual in a common cluster fail to discharge relationship obligations to another member, that violation will be obvious to others commonly connected to the two parties, who "may expect an increased risk of failing to receive a return on their investment in their relationships with the individul concerned" (Kapferer, 1972, cited in Allan, 1979, p.132). High intensity networks are refractory to individual members' efforts to alter their exchange basis. They achieve near-omnipotence in their ability to constrain and dominate the individual, even to the point of reducing his or her ability to develop new relationships (creating insularity), since any newcomer needs to prove acceptable to the network as a whole (Allan, 1979).

Network social selection processes also create insularity. Careful scrutiny by other network members of each person's new relationships prevents opportunities for someone to develop a new set of friends and operate outside network constraints. Consequently, the homogeneity of background characteristics of network members increases. Understandably, these processes are self-sustaining. From Price's (1979) analysis of social ecology, we can infer that homogeneity ultimately reinforces network intensity by recruiting only members similar in background and attitudes. Homogeneity of attitudes shapes behavior and attitudes of those in the network in the direction of prevailing norms. Those at substantial variance are more likely to leave the setting due to lack of fit between their own background characteristics and those of other network participants (Price, 1979). Besides dampening individual action for society's marginal people, the greatest disadvantage associated with intensely closely-knit groups is their presumed denial of access to large-scale sociopolitical and economic systems. This prevents members from becoming more powerful actors in response to group needs and social change (Burt, Lieban & Fisher, 1980; Granovetter, 1973; Mitchell, Barbarin & Hurley, 1981; Raymond & Rhoads, 1980). Ironically, network intensity binding together a community's interorganizational leaders (i.e., those holding positions of authority in several key institutions simultaneously) is the very process which gives these members of the elite their sociopolitical power base, and thus their capacity to determine the outcome of community issues (Perrucci & Pilisuk, 1970).

The constraining and dominating omnipotence of intense networks has come to light in recent studies. Hirsch (1980) and Jones (1980), in separate investigations, both discovered the intrusive nature of network density among those making life transitions. For the 20 recent widows and 14 mature women taking university courses whom Hirsch interviewed, membership in high density networks had debilitating effects on their capacity to handle the strains of lifestyle reorganization and to secure reinforcement for new social roles. Jones notices that of the three network types found among newcomers to Canberra, Australia, the one in which married couples highly valued sharing most aspects of their lives together produced two constraints. First, the content of the relationships were limited to whatever all members could share together. Secondly, opportunities for individuals to develop and find support for new self-concepts were denied, since one's spouse and cluster of long-term ties continued to perpetuate the original self-definition and associated roles. Similarly, Birkel and Reppucci (1983) found that among 31 high risk women referred to a prevention-oriented parent group, those with denser networks and higher monthly contact with kin attended fewer parent discussion sessions.

Graves and Graves (1980) observed among Polynesian migrants to New Zealand that the reliance upon kin or peer networks as resource centers is an adaptive strategy which carries with it heavy investments of time and energy that dominate one's lifestyle. For example, the migrant wishing to draw upon his or her kin resource base must in turn be counted on to attend family functions, support family members in conflicts with outsiders, feed and house visiting relatives, and give deference and respect to elders when family decisions are made, all in order to maintain a good name in the family. Unfortunately, activities keeping the network in good repair and maintaining one's secure position within it can lead to the resilience of behavior deemed dysfunctional or antisocial by the wider community. Graves and Graves (1980) noted that male New Zealanders adopting a peer-reliant adaptive strategy were required to spend long hours socializing in the local pub in order to stay in touch; this network pressure contravened treatment regimes aimed at preventing or altering alcohol abuse (Brownelli et al., 1986). Similarly, O'Donnell (1984) has characterized adolescent drug use and delinquent acts as behaviors strongly related to interactions with peer networks and participation in peer settings. Drug use by youth, even the particular type of substance taken, is associated with perceptions of whether friends use and approve of the use of drugs (O'Donnell, 1984; see also Flay, 1985).

Even more insidiously, professional agencies become entwined in perpetuating deviant subcultural systems. Hobfoll et al.'s (1981) account of Anchorage, Alaska Skid Row networks reveals how clinics, in order to perpetuate their own existence and as a result of exploitation by client populations, provide assistance that ultimately allows the return to heavy drinking and a sustained presence on Skid Row. Moreover, O'Donnell, Lydgate and Fo (1979), reexamining the long-term effects of their behaviorally based prevention and remediation project for delinquent boys in Hawaii, were surprised to discover that youngsters participating in the Buddy System had a significantly higher arrest rate (22.55 percent) than did those in the control condition (16.4 percent). O'Donnell is convinced that this outcome was the result of friendships established in the project between those with and without offenses in the previous year. He cautions against uniting persons in a self-help group who are at high risk of antisocial behavior. To do so, he warns, risks the possibility of members acquiring information, skills, support and roles (through network dynamics) which may increase the likelihood of antisocial behavior (O'Donnell, 1984).

Change Enhancing Networks

The previous section marshalled evidence enabling us to theorize how stressful and high intensity networks diminish generalization. However, our primary objective is to discover what constitutes a behavior change *enhancing* network, and what conditions originate under such networks to allow new responses to flourist? Our implicit working model postulates that network variables impinge indirectly on generalization by creating the social environment opportunities that allow or support desired behavior change. For example, a client wishing to alter some aspect of his or her lifestyle will benefit by social surroundings permitting the introduction and accurate implementation of procedures for behavioral self-management. The facilitative network can be mobilized to support new responses, by providing the social resources directly needed to practice and acquire competency in the new repertoire and gain positive feedback or success experience in its deployment. Client appraisal of network reliability and utility as a resource base (network orientation) determines when and how it will be mobilized in response to life transition circumstances, such as therapeutic change. These judgments of network supportiveness also determine whether clients evolve a psychological sense of "empowerment" (Kieffer, 1981), enabling them to

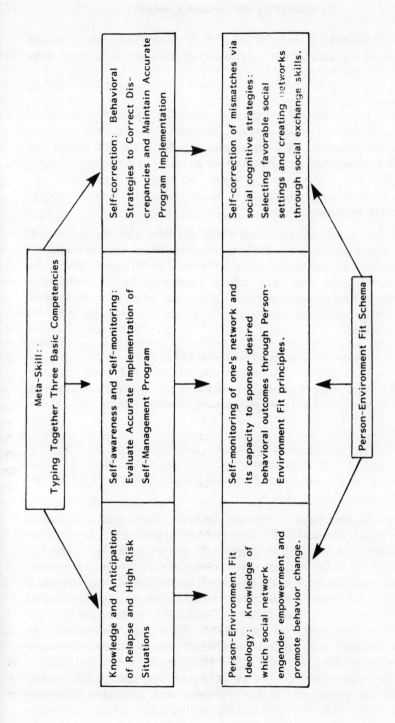

Figure 7.2 Person–Environment Fit schema as a meta-skill competency for programming generalization

The boxes in the figure contain:

Meta-Skill:
Typing Together Three Basic Competencies

Self-awareness and Self-monitoring: Evaluate Accurate Implementation of Self-Management Program

Knowledge and Anticipation of Relapse and High Risk Situations

Self-correction: Behavioral Strategies to Correct Discrepancies and Maintain Accurate Program Implementation

Self-monitoring of one's network and its capacity to sponsor desired behavioral outcomes through Person-Environment Fit principles.

Person-Environment Fit Ideology: Knowledge of which social network engender empowerment and promote behavior change.

Self-correction of mismatches via social cognitive strategies: Selecting favorable social settings and creating networks through social exchange skills.

Person-Environment Fit Schema

continue to energetically confront stressful life events. This tentative model of how networks account for response generalization is formalized in Hypothesis 7.6 and Figure 7.1.

Hypothesis 7.6
Client networks maintaining high network reliability, equitable interpersonal exchange, and freedom of social action, engender "psychological empowerment": a) the perception that one is able to alter one's environment and behavior to achieve satisfying life transitions; and, b) the knowledge that this is accomplished by drawing upon network resources to implement self-management strategies, assume new social roles, or remove aversive environmental constraints.

Figure 7.1 posits direct relationships between the three network dimensions and specific contextual opportunities promoting psychological empowerment. Life transition events are shown as "triggers" prompting network mobilization, but in a fashion determined by the individual's psychological sense of empowerment—given that empowerment involves one's knowledge, skill, and confidence in using network elements to handle such circumstances.

Network Capacity and Perceived Network Reliability
Relationship A in Figure 7.1 denotes the connection between network capacity variables and opportunities to construe one's network as satisfying and reliable. More specifically we propose the following hypothesis.

Hypothesis 7.7
Client network capacity characterized by effective delivery system infrastructure, balanced composition, and support resources specific to transition needs will strengthen the sense of network reliability and satisfaction and contribute to psychological empowerment.

Our previous discussion of deficient networks illuminated attributes of network capacity associated with positive adjustment. Briefly, the infrastructure most likely to be effective in delivering needed support is comprised of 20–30 intimate associates, clustered into several 5–6 member cliques, involving family, friends, neighbors, work or social contacts, with a moderate overall density (50–60 percent knowing one another) and which also has relative ease of accessibility and stability over time. The multiple cluster configuration permits access to dense cliques. These become valuable when, for example, kin support must be quickly mobilized to offset a psychiatric crisis (Baker & Singer, 1980; Erickson, 1975; Mueller, 1980) or when a freshman enters the university dormitories and desires intense intellectual and emotional sharing associated with friendship formation (Hayes & Oxley, 1986; Perl, 1981). Independent social spheres also thrive within the multiple cluster pattern, allowing development of novel roles, alternative self-definitions, even new health practices, by virtue of the fact that they are segregated from action constraints imposed elsewhere in the network (Hirsch, 1980; Jones, 1980; Langlie, 1977; Wilcox, 1981; cf. Stokes, 1983b).

Balanced or nonhomogeneous network composition promotes the maximum range of potentially supportive transactions, given that each relationship type (kin, friend, neighbor, etc.) maintains a predominant support exchange category (Fischer, 1981; Root & Sue, 1981). Spouse and/or close kin are vital sources of positive feedback and emotional nurturance among Chicanos, Blacks, and American Indians (Keefe, Padilla & Carlos, 1979; Manson, 1980; Raymond & Rhoads, 1980). Among Anglos and other white subgroups, they are heavily relied upon initially for mental health consultation (D'Augelli & Ehrlich, 1982; Fandetti & Gelfand, 1978; Fischer & Phillips, 1979) and their presence tends to moderate the full impact of stressful events (Burke & Weir, 1977; La Rocco, House & French, 1980; Pilisuk & Parks 1986; Sandler, 1980). Peers and intimate friends, in contrast, are highly valued suppliers of non-judgmental companionship and tolerance of one's particular personality (Graves & Graves, 1980, Wahler, 1980a & b), while neighbors, co-workers and lay helpers provide physical assistance, social contact, and sympathetic understanding or referral to professionals, respectively (D'Augelli & Ehrlich, 1982; Fischer, 1977). Persons able to draw upon a wide array of sources have the best opportunity to resolve needs and thus evaluate their networks as reliable.

We suspect, therefore, that the accurate matching of life transition needs with a specific supportive resource vital to its remediation is the most cogent determinant of a strong sense of network reliability and satisfaction. For example, the spontaneous offer of likely companionship or a "sympathetic ear" from a neighbor, when one is feeling downhearted by a loved one's prolonged absence, would probably strengthen a positive appraisal of network supportiveness. Essentially, perceptions of milieu reliability arise from knowledge that one is a valued contributor to a set of mutually interdependent persons and the continuing object of their concern (Pilisuk, 1982). It arises from the expectation that when needed, they can be trusted to offer the right kind of aid. Network satisfaction grows from the subjective judgment that support received is both the kind and level appropriate to felt needs. This hypothesis is probed indirectly in studies underscoring the specificity of relationships between network resource content, perceived content, perceived satisfaction, and adaptation (Cohen & Wills, 1985; Moos & Mitchell, 1982).

Barrera sought to develop and refine instruments assessing network support (Barrera, 1980, 1981; Sandler & Barrera, 1984). He found that subjective evaluations of satisfaction with support received were good predictors of symptomatology among pregnant adolescents and university students. Moreover, it is neither the total quantity of helping behavior received nor the number of helpers in the support network which appears to be critical to the stress buffering effect. What appears important is the person's perception that he or she is receiving an appropriate and satisfying level of aid (Sandler & Barrera, 1984; see also Cohen & McKay, 1984, and Procidano & Heller, 1983).

Rhoads, Gonzales, and Raymond (1980) carried out a longitudinal survey of 49 recently discharged clients from a heroin detoxification program. They observed that the amount of social support which the female and male drug user perceived as available appeared causally related to depression and anxiety respectively, over one-month and two-month time lags. When support was seen as available, the women in particular were less likely to experience depression in the following months or to turn to drug use as a coping mechanism. Perceived support acts as an asset, enabling a person to persist at a challenging and frustrating task (Sarason, Levine, Basham & Sarason, 1983).

Additional studies explore the connection between specific resources, stressful life events, and adjustment outcome. La Rocco, House and French (1980) re-analyzed occupation stress data gathered from 636 men. They conclude that co-worker supports produce twice as many buffering effects as supervisor or home supports. In particular, co-worker support dampens the impact of job related stress and strain on depression and somatic complaints. The authors explain the differential health effects of divergent support sources by stating that focused stressors (such as those found only on the job) are most amenable to helping processes directly linked to the context in which the stressor is located (such as one's co-workers). Hence, it is not surprising that those in Hirsch's (1980) group of mid-life women returning to college who were *most* satisfied with the cognitive guidance (advice, explanation, information), experienced fewer symptoms and mood disturbance. Similarly, Higginbotham's sample of Overseas Chinese students and native New Zealanders reported the best adjustment to university pressure when they were most satisfied with physical assistance (help with homework, given a hand when looking for a part-time job, etc.) (Tan, 1983; see also Kasl & Wells, 1985).

A comparable relationship was brought out in Heller and Rasmussen's (1981) investigation of perceived strain in long-term residents of a neighborhood recently undergoing steady invasion by students seeking accommodation from a nearby university. The elderly women interviewed appeared immune to the changing demography of their neighborhood and fairly satisfied with it as long as there remained a best friend nearby and/or spouse available for close companionship. While these and other studies suggest that discrete resource categories, including material aid and other tangible assistance beyond emotional sustenance, are tailored to specific problem contexts (e.g., Schaefer, Coyne & Lazarus, 1981), Moos' (1981) review of his recent series of alcoholism studies noted some occasions when salient features of work and family environments do influence each other. Interpreting these findings (Billings & Moos, 1982; Moos & Moos, 1984), he reasoned that "by reducing the adaptive energy necessary to effectively manage conflicts and maintain a cohesive and supportive family, stress in the workplace may adversely affect spouse and family functioning" (Moos, 1981, p. 13).

Resource Exchange Style and Social Self-Awareness

Relationship B in Figure 7.1 addresses the question of how exchange style variables create opportunities for acquiring knowledge of self and social relations and the competency to undertake interpersonal influence attributes central to psychological empowerment. Hypothesis 7.7a more fully expresses this relationship.

Hypothesis 7.7a
Client networks which manifest a resource style emphasizing reciprocal, equitable, and multiplex type interactions generate more frequent opportunities for learning how to successfully influence others and developing awareness of oneself as an active agent in the social arena.

This hypothesis is inferred from studies previously reviewed, concerning problem behaviors associated with networks lacking reciprocal and multiplex exchanges. We argued then that reciprocal obligation is the key to relationship building, continuity, and power equity, while multiplexity is a significant precursor of intimacy in social links. We extend this argument now by reasoning that it is primarily under these conditions that individuals refine their awareness of how social systems operate and can be operated on. At the same time, individuals can initiate—and build confidence in using— strategies of interpersonal influence or self-management. Although speculative, portions of this hypothesis receive encouraging support from two studies. Mitchell (1982) interviewed 35 psychiatric outpatients and their families, to determine how client personal attributes (interpersonal problem-solving) and family environment contribute to network size and perceived social support. Pertinent to our argument, Mitchell reported that supportive family environments, encouraging independence among family members, were associated with higher levels of interpersonally oriented, cognitive problem-solving skills and peer support attained by the client. An autonomous family environment, encouraging self-sufficiency, assertiveness, and one's own decision-making, could be expected to be highly responsive to client-initiated problem-solving efforts. Mitchell found this social skill central to the ability to build up a larger circle of intimates and mobilize peer support (see also Mitchell & Moos, 1984).

Mitchell's concern with how personal capacities actively interplay with environmental constraints is echoed in Perls' (1981) correlational study of social exploration preference, network formation, and residence hall satisfaction among a sample of university freshmen. Students preferring an active exploratory role in adapting to their new environment, as opposed to more "passive explorers," formed more reciprocal and multidimensional relationships and perceived their hall climate as fostering higher social exploration. Significantly, active explorers showed a greater awareness for campus social activities, belonged to more clubs, and evidenced more willingness to mobilize campus support resources if needed. Perl's results help substantiate our inference that under conditions of reciprocity and multiplexity—where there is encouragement of diverse interpersonal roles, personal flexibility, and intimate sharing and trust (Perl, 1981)— opportunities arise for active learning about how the social system is formed and operates. At the same time, one's initial preference for active social exploration is reinforced.

Networks Allowing Empowerment

Concluding our discussion of Figure 7.1, we posit that networks generating a low overall intensity (apart from independent clusters) accrue minimum leverage to deliver inescapable aversive sanctions when sub-group norms and role expectations are violated. Hence, individual social action within these networks operates in a climate of relatively greater freedom of choice, as shown in Relationship C (see also discussion of Hypothesis 7.4). Moreover, the cognitive and behavioral opportunities resulting from these specific network characteristics combine, as indicated by Relationship D, to produce a heightened sense of psychological empowerment. Empowerment, therefore, is the long-term outcome of network-sponsored events, during which persons come to understand how their networks can be relied upon as dependable assets acrosss diverse life difficulties and transitions.

Empowered individuals develop self-esteem and self-efficacy in three ways. First, intimate others give feedback congruent with one's positive self-image (Pilisuk, 1982). Second, awareness arises of interpersonal competency acquired through equitable and multidimensional relationships. Third, mastery experiences occur, involving skillful mobilization of network resources to resolve important adjustment problems or successful negotiation with persons holding institutional authority.

Finally, Relationship E infers that when life transition events, such as divorce, birth of first child, or job loss, escalate to a "trigger" level, available social resources needed to meet such challenges are activated (Barrera, 1980;

La Rocco, House & French, 1980; Schulz & Rau, 1985). However, the course of the network mobilization response is guided by one's sense of empowerment. For example, a "high" empowered parent wishing to implement non-coercive child management procedures, following Sanders and Glynn's (1981) parent training model, would have the acumen and confidence to identify and successfully coopt the assistance of influential relatives, friends, and teachers also in contact with the child. The empowered parent mobilizes material aid, physical assistance, and socialization resources (i.e., car borrowing, babysitters, recreation with friends who have children of similar ages) as needed to adopt a lifestyle routine congruent with treatment principles. Furthermore, that parent possesses the self-efficacy feelings required to persist when inevitable snags to accurate implementation arise, such as disapproval from close kin. These times require the parent to turn to an independent cluster of friends with ideologies similar to the parent's new child-rearing philosophy.

This scenario contrasts with that of the parent with low empowerment and a negative network orientation. The latter parent risks having his or her morale destroyed by recognizing that he or she cannot accomplish his or her own program goals; does not have needed resources or access to knowledge and people who might be helpful; cannot experience the rejuvenation associated with new ideas and new relationships; and is stagnating alone with his or her problems (Sarason et al., 1977, p. 24). The final section alerts clinicians to a promising social cognitive strategy which individual clients can adopt to transform a negative network orientation into a heightened sense of empowerment.

SOCIAL COGNITIVE STRATEGIES FOR CLIENT PRODUCED AND MAINTAINED BEHAVIOR CHANGE ENHANCING NETWORKS

Self-Schemata Incorporating Person–Environment Fit Ideology

Clinical research, sensitized by the foregoing analysis, is now in a position to conceptualize and validate therapeutic goals directly derived from propositions relating social network processes and desired behavior change. One promising tack entails specifying core competencies, at the perceptual and interpersonal behavior levels, which clients could develop through structured training, enabling them to create, maintain, and optimally participate in their own behavior change networks. In essence, the client him or herself requires a "meta-skill" consisting of three competencies: a) awareness of how network attributes and opportunities engender empowerment and can conversely prevent it (as per Figure 7.1); b) capacity to self-monitor one's network configuration; and c) behavioral skills, for working toward favorable network characteristics when discrepancies occur or when life transitions are confronted. Our final hypothesis is based on the belief that the most auspicious conditions for therapeutic behavior change involve treatment procedures that produce meta-skill competencies. These skills enable clients to actively engage their social network resources, both to advance personal aspirations and to meet stressful circumstances challenging fulfilment of those aspirations. With this hypothesis we break from the traditional assumption of psychotherapy that once a problem is solved, "continual happiness results" as long as behavior change is maintained. Instead, we advance the view that treatment prepares the person to a lifetime manager of setting resources and a collaborator in resource exchange development.[1]

Hypothesis 7.8
Clients trained to call forth a Person–Environment Fit ideology in response to goal-setting or personal crisis circumstances maximize opportunities to design and mobilize the social network resources mediating those circumstances.

Current research on human cognition denotes "schemata" as: the highest level "chunks" of mental data manipulated through cognitive processes (Howe, 1981). Schemata are sets of related propositions about the world—*a priori* knowledge structures—available in an individual's active memory. Importantly, schemata satisfy Anderson's (1981) two criteria for a cognitive unit, in that when any element of the schema are interassociated, all elements are interlinked (producing all-or-none learning), and secondly, when some of the elements in the schema are retrieved into working memory, all are (producing all-or-none retrieval) (Anderson, 1981). Carried over into the social cognition domain, "self-schemata" refer to cognitive units made up of generalizations about the self, derived from past experience, that organize and guide the processing of the self-related information contained in an individual's social experience (Markus, 1977).

Initial empirical work by Markus (1977), Rogers, Kuiper and Kirker (1977), and Snyder and Cantor (1980) concludes that self-schemata are potent encoding devices. Apparently, self-schemata carry great potential for the rich embellishment of stimulus input, by making available to the person immense amounts of previous experience embodied in the self (i.e., all-or-none retrieval). More specifically, Snyder and Cantor (1980) made clear predictions regarding differences in the self-schemata content of high versus low self-monitoring individuals. In line with their theory, they found that low

---

[1]The authors wish to thank Manual Barrera for pointing out this implication of our proposition.

self-monitoring individuals have richer and more easily accessible self-images in diverse trait domains than high self-monitoring individuals. On the other hand, high self-monitors have richer and more easily accessible images of prototypic persons on the same set of trait dimensions than do low self-monitors. Snyder (1979) postulates that these differences in schemata of "prototypic others," as opposed to "characteristic selves," are eventually involved in the processes by which individuals plan and guide their actions in social situations. For example, the high self-monitoring person, striving deliberately to create an image appropriate to whatever interpersonal and social forces are at play in the setting, cognitively constructs a person-in-situation scenario. By reading the unique character of each situation, he or she identifies a prototype of the ideal person for that setting. The high self-monitor then uses that cognitive scenario to provide the operating guidelines for constructing and enacting patterns of social behavior (Snyder, 1979).

Hypothesis 7.8 parallels Snyder's view of self-monitoring and person-in-situation scenarios. It recommends that clients receive training directed toward articulating a self-schema for the domain of Person–Environment Fit. This self-schema encompasses those experiences regarding how network resources are activated in response to personal goals and challenges. Therapeutically acquired, the Person–Environment Fit schema is a cognitive unit—capable of producing all-or-none retrieval and all-or-none learning. This schema organizes and guides information pertinent to the level of congruence between one's personal strengths and needs, on the one hand, and the environmental demands and resources interacting *with* those personal attributes, on the other. The Person–Environment Fit scenario accompanying this self-schema is an example of a basic meta-skill. It ties together the self-monitoring of one's situation within the setting with a course of action. In this circumstance, the Person–Environment Fit scenario becomes an active meta-skill constructed from four sources. First is knowledge of self, especially of one's valued actions, dispositions, emotional needs and goals. Second is knowledge of environment, particularly regarding the capacity of one's network to deliver specific supportive resources and either constrain or sponsor actions. Third, is knowledge of "Goodness of Fit." This is one's notion of which network configurations match or moderate action plans and problematic circumstances respectively. Fourth is knowledge of network creation and maintenance strategies, especially selection of network-enriching settings and a network-enhancing interpersonal exchange style.

The challenge remains to translate this description of meta-skill cognitions into the reality of clinical casework. Initially, the therapist offers guidance to the client undergoing life transition stress regarding the construction of personalized Person–Environment-Fit scenarios. Life crisis events will subsequently trigger into active memory his or her Person–Environment Fit scenario. The scenario then functions as a template for imagining how a new role behavior (e.g., following therapist instructions for child management) could be successfully enacted with the current support available from one's circle of family, friends and neighbors. A mismatch may occur between what type and level of support is imagined to be essential for new behavior to unfold and what the client is actually able to mobilize for that cause. The scenario then articulates operating guidelines to address this mismatch. For example, one recommendation might be to judiciously select new settings and gather together (through an appropriate exchange style) additional supportive others sympathetic to one's desired behavior change. Contained within the Person–Environment Fit schema for handling life transitions is community psychology's broader ideological stance. Adjustment is less characteristic of an individual than a state of relative balance or imbalance between component parts of one's life span (Holahan & Spearly, 1980; Rappaport, 1977).

Knowledge of Network Creation from Social Ecology

Fortuitously, two expanding domains of social psychological inquiry— social ecology and social exchange theory—offer a wealth of insights into relationship formation, which clients could be trained to incorporate into their cognitive scenarios. These insights can guide clients, helping them to select environments and interpersonal styles which are most likely to produce and sustain personal networks that allow behavior change. Clients who determine, through Person–Environment Fit analysis, that their existing network membership *undersupports* felt needs may wish to acquire a new cluster of associates whose backgrounds or activities could help resolve those needs. Social ecology theorists point toward a constellation of features—environmental design, climate, "suprapersonal" (i.e., aggregate social backgrounds), and manning level—which distinguish those settings offering potent opportunities for network building. Clients could learn to identify these features when selecting auspicious environments to enter in relation to maximizing personal gains (e.g., Insel, 1980; Moos, 1981; Price, 1979).

Several critical processes appear to mediate social bonds in these network enriching environments. First, functional proximity—drawing persons closely together—is an obvious prerequisite of social contact. Physical space arrangements (proxemics) can quite naturally increase social interaction and participation when they allow face-to-face seating and easy access to enclosed communal space—supporting mixed social activities—and are visually and thermally comfortable to linger in. Living quarters enhancing sociability offer choices of both privacy and propinquity to neighbors with whom one shares responsibility for the security of a shared area (O'Donnell, 1981; Wilcox & Holahan, 1978). This is especially true when these settings provide a variety of environmental resources—toys, games, recreation equipment, interesting scenery, shelter from noise—and corresponding activities, such as accidental meetings, group tasks, mutual helping, leisure, or consumer events, attracting people together and making their contact positive (D'Augelli & Ehrlich, 1982; Holahan, 1976; O'Donnell, 1981).

Second, organizational settings that stress "superordinate goals" tend to foster commitment to communal aims while requiring participant cooperation to achieve group ends. Striving to accomplish superordinate goals thus minimizes individual differences which otherwise might widen into friction, competition, or interpersonal conflict (Sherif, 1958).

Third, network promoting settings are those with social climates perceived to be especially high in interpersonal solidarity. Contributing to solidarity feelings is the perception of homogeneous aggregate background characteristics among one's fellow group members. This marks the setting as more deeply understanding of and relevant to one's unique life situation (Price, 1979). Judgment of background similarity among the setting membership corresponds with the clients' evaluation of the network's tendency to promote group cohesion, mutual involvement, and emotional support. These three variables comprise the "Relationship" dimension of Moos' Social Climate Scale (1974). A decade of research across organizational environments by Moos and his colleagues, using the Social Climate Scale, indicates the pivotal role played by cohesive and supportive climates. These climates create an optimal sense of satisfaction with one's surroundings that allows positive personal ties to flourish (Moos, 1981; Perl, 1981).

Finally, settings operating as "undermanned" and containing "underskilled roles" are likely to demand responsible role fulfilment and active participation of each member. Under these two conditions, one's interaction with and value to other setting participants is increased, maximizing relationship building opportunities among setting occupants (O'Donnell, 1984). Manning theorists, following Barker's early observations in a small Midwestern town (1968), state that when the number of participants in a setting falls below the minimum number of persons required for the setting to be maintained (i.e., "undermanning"), then each participant, even those with marginal qualifications, is obliged to accept more positions of responsibility and become integrated into a wider variety of important activities (Price, 1979; Wicker, 1979). Consequently, unless the stress of involvement overwhelms them, people in undermanned settings have a greater opportunity for intensive interpersonal transactions. These include: a) increasing role performance competency; b) experiencing being valued as a contributing member to setting maintenance; and, as such, c) forming attachments and responsibilities to other members involving reciprocal help giving. Ultimately, they evolve a strong sense of obligation to the setting and their co-workers, with whom they are acting interdependently to keep the setting operational (O'Donnell, 1981; O'Donnell & Tharp 1982).

The same processes that coopt participation in, and strengthen obligation, to undermanned settings, also operate when the roles arranged to facilitate functions in a setting require performance standards beyond the competency of the individuals available to fill those roles. O'Donnell (1984) specifies that settings containing "underskilled roles," like those which are undermanned, maximize the meaningful involvement of all participants in setting activities. These environments should be highly attractive to those wishing to build relevant role performance skills and acquire supportive network members.

In summary, the following corollary to Hypothesis 7.8 expresses social ecology's contribution to client awareness regarding environments best suited for expanding supportive social bonds.

Hypothesis 7.8a
Clients trained to incorporate within their Person–Environment Fit ideology a strategy for selecting settings based on social ecology principles–i.e., to choose settings with favorable proxemics and manning levels, and which emphasize superordinate goals as well as social climate solidarity–increase their probability of developing network clusters capable of supporting specified needs and aspirations.

Knowledge of Network Creation from Social Exchange Theory

After selecting and entering a social ecology ripe with opportunities for meeting potential network members, the client's Person–Environment Fit scenario must next produce prototypes of interpersonal exchange behaviors stylistically appropriate to the formation of stable, mutually rewarding, and supportive friendships. Social exchange theory is a lucrative knowledge reservoir, which therapists may draw upon to give clients insights into relationship growth, development, deterioration, and dissolution. Clients could then have available, within their cognitive scenarios, reliable techniques to guide desirable interpersonal transactions. Furthermore, network researchers make frequent reference to social exchange processes in explaining differences in the infrastructure and supportive capabilities of contrasting network types. It is highly pertinent, therefore, that in closing this chapter we take a fine-grained look at how the accumulated wisdom of social psychologists can be applied by persons wishing to create a social environment both responsive to felt needs and encouraging of newly acquired therapeutic behavior.

Imbued with a Skinnerian world view, sociologist G. C. Homans (1961) created the first psychological version of the familiar economic notion of exchange relations, "in which people pass rewards and costs, as well as attitudes, information, and other psychological 'commodities' back and forth" (Pepitone, 1981, p. 981). At least five separate exchange theories operate within this general perspective, sharing similar assumptions and the overarching objective of developing a comprehensive theory of social interaction, if not of society itself (Roloff, 1981; Mitchell, 1978). Our objective is to distill from this theorizing a set of operating rules or assumed "truths" clients can absorb into their Person–Environment Fit schemata to call upon when relationship building concerns are salient.

Proposition 1. Social behavior can be explained in terms of rewards and costs. Rewards are goods and services, tangible or intangible, that satisfy a person's needs or goals. Costs represent the loss or denial of these rewards (Burns, 1973). This proposition effectively transforms social behavior into a commodity, classified both on the basis of its value for the recipient and the disadvantage incurred by the one giving or not receiving the reward. Behavior must be defined in commodity terms before explaining the concept of *social exchange* as: the voluntary transference of goods or services from one person to another in return for other such commodities (Roloff, 1981).

Proposition 2. People join together in social exchange only insofar as they determine it in their mutual interest to do so (Huston & Burgess, 1979). Underlying this rule is the recognition that individuals are generally motivated by self-interest. They seek preferred resources from others in such a way that their own rewards are maximized and losses or punishments minimized. Social exchanges yield positive outcomes for both participants when the reward minus cost ratios calculated for each interactive partner are mutually advantageous. If so, that action will be repeated and relationship development proceed through the repetition of exchanges (Thibaut & Kelley, 1959). Homans cleverly summarizes this rule: "The open secret of human exchange is to give the other [person] behavior that is more valuable to [him/her] than it is costly to you and to get from that person behavior that is more valuable to you than it is costly to [him/her]" (1961, p. 62). The validity of Proposition 2 is also endorsed by Sarason, in his effort to document the factors influencing the creation of resource exchange networks among lay persons, both in a community and between formal institutions. He observed that mutually beneficial networks of this genre are sustained only when those involved in forming the network links perceive the possibility of giving and getting resources which each participant is known to value (Sarason & Lorentz, 1979).

Proposition 3. Rewards are allocated in exchange relations according to the Rule of Distributive Justice. This social norm indicates that fair exchanges prevail when the profit of each partner in a relationship is proportional to that partner's investment in the relationship (Homans, 1961). Equity theory, derived from the Distributive Justice Rule, states that individuals actively engage in a cognitive social comparison process to judge the equity or fairness of their exchange relations. In addition, people feel displeasure when they find that their input-to-outcome ratio is not the same as that of the other participant (Adams, 1963, 1965; Adams & Freedman, 1976). Walster, Walster & Berscheid's (1978) more recent recasting of equity theory emphasizes that peoples' efforts to maintain equity in their interpersonal relationships are due to strong social group sanctions which reward members who treat others equitably. Of course, the "harm-doer", or partner perpetrating inequity, also confronts the fear that the victim may wish to leave the exchange relationship or retaliate through other means (Roloff, 1981). Hence the "harm-doer" is motivated to find some path to restore equity.

Within the context of equity theory, reciprocity can now be better understood as a special case of distributive justice in which one feels a moral obligation to return benefits to those from whom one has received them (Gouldner, 1960). However, the equity principle involves more than the reciprocal return of outcomes. As Chadwick-Jones (1976) cautions, it involves assessing one's own return against those of another. Equity theory thus suggests to persons wishing to add new network links that they a) present themselves as having rewards to offer their partner, and b) express a willingness to reciprocate any rewards, such as self-disclosing communication, which are received (Chaikin & Derlega, 1976; Cohen, Sherrod & Clark, 1986; Huston & Burgess, 1979). In other words, we are attracted to others with whom we expect equitable exchanges can and will take place. As a result, we tend to match ourselves with them along such relational resource dimensions as physical attractiveness, mental health, physical health, intelligence, or education (Berscheid & Walster, 1978).

Proposition 4. When individuals find themselves participating in inequitable relationships, they will become distressed; the more inequitable the relationship the more distress they will feel (Walster 1978). In addition, the victim of an inequity tends to feel more distress than does the harm-doer or one who benefits, and thus relationship stability may suffer. Accumulated evidence from Hatfield (Walster) and her colleagues (Hatfield, Utne & Traupmann, 1979; Walster, Walster & Traupmann, 1978) clearly supports this proposition.

By implication, this equity theory proposition alerts clients wishing to achieve long-term stability in their network ties to the conflict arising when either they or their partner perceive inequity in profit distribution. Moreover, forces operate to create inequity in previously equitable relationships. These include learning new information about one's partner; one person's needs changing differently than the other's; dramatic changes in the relationship caused by significant events like job loss or hospitalization; or one partner simply changing the way his or her outcomes are viewed, which is the aim of feminist consciousness-raising groups (Roloff, 1981, p. 110). Thibaut and Kelley (1959) further refine this analysis by predicting that the most stable and satisfying relations are produced through interdependence. Relationship growth depends on the extent to which each partner's outcomes depend on the outcomes received by the other person. Growth also depends upon the extent to which each one's profits exceed customary profits (termed "Comparison Level") or those likely to be secured in another relationship ("Comparison Level—Alternative").

Proposition 5. Individuals who discover they are in inequitable relations will attempt to eliminate their distress by restoring equity. The greater the inequity and the more the distress, the harder will be their efforts at equity restoration (Walster, Walster & Berscheid, 1978). The tactics people select to restore equity are of great interest to those concerned with retaining stable network links. Essentially, two restoration mechanisms are available (West & Wicklund, 1980). First, profit ratios may actually be brought back into balance through altering one's own inputs or outcomes or those of one's partner. Second, perceived fairness may be reestablished not objectively, but through altering subjective estimates of inputs and outcomes. These include blaming the victim for the situation or getting her or him to blame herself or himself, interpreting her or his suffering as trivial, or apologizing. Predictably, equity theory anticipates that the mode of rebalance is chosen in a manner consistent with self-interest. The client chooses the less costly alternative from among the equity-restoring mechanisms judged as both adequate and available (Walster, Walster & Berscheid, 1978). Typically, this alternative does not upset one's normal habits, interfere with valued rewards or self-esteem, nor run counter to one's commitments (West & Wicklund, 1980).

West and Wicklund (1980) caution that equity theory's current development does not permit an unambiguous prediction of which tactic is the most prominent or accessible route for establishing equity. However, we would generally suspect that tactics which strongly destabilize network relationships—derogating one's partner, choosing another comparison partner, or avoiding relationships in general—will arise under two conditions: first, when either or both partners perceive a lack of free choice in decisions central to their satisfaction with exchanges (i.e., low commitment); second, when there is present another more rewarding (or less costly) alternative partner. Ironically, inequity could result in stable exchange relations in networks when the victim finds the inequitable relation to be more profitable than alternative relations. Equitable ties may be stable only so long as the outcomes of the relationship are better than others which might be available (Burgess & Nielsen, 1977).

Proposition 6. Imposing a long range perspective on social exchanges, by viewing them from the perspective of past and projected future gains, strengthens relational endurance and mutual supportiveness. This occurs because inequity tolerance is increased and perceptions of mutual responsiveness, equality, and solidarity are bolstered. Proposition 6 alerts the network builder to move as swiftly as possible from a preoccupation with immediate equity evaluations to new rules of allocation justice involving long-term, mutually beneficial exchanges between persons. Persons committed to future involvement are more able to tolerate imbalances when they know that they will have ample time to set things right (Hatfield et al., 1979). Laboratory studies of this proposition indicate that the distributive justice rule may *not* be abandoned among friends and intimates. Rather it operates covertly across a larger number of interactions, so that the friend who takes more than an equal share is identified as denying relationship solidarity only if the unequal allocation has persisted over an extended period of time (Morgan & Sawyer, 1979).

In contrast, other researchers argue that equity machinations are replaced altogether in close relations by other norms sponsoring cooperation, intimacy, and deepened concern for meeting the other's needs. The key competitor is the *equality* norm. It commands that persons receive the same outcomes no matter what their inputs. Belief in equality is thought to promote the interpersonal goal of solidarity, by heightening perceived similarity and thus attraction among couples (Deutsch, 1975; Morgan & Sawyer, 1979). Equity processes are seen as anathema to relationship intimacy. They emphasize status differences among participants and undermine the foundation for establishing mutual respect and self-respect (Huston & Burgess, 1979). Consequently, relationship enjoyment is eroded in the competition over setting valuations and the resultant envy or self-devaluation.

Furthermore, Clark and Mills (1979) sharply distinguish equity based exchange relations from communal relations carried out under the "norm of mutual responsiveness" (Pruitt, 1972). As opposed to the equity rule, a benefit received within the communal exchange context does not create a specific debt or obligation to return a comparable benefit in quid pro quo fashion. Instead, the general obligation—that aid is rendered in circumstances of genuine need—persists unchanged. Any indication that benefits were given in response to benefits received would call into question the "needs responsiveness" theme of the relationship and compromise its communal form. Clark and Mills' (1979) prediction was confirmed in several experiments showing that when college students expected a communal exchange, attraction decreased if someone giving aid subsequently requested a benefit.

Nevertheless, we reiterate the caution that equity considerations continue to operate, alongside equality and mutual responsiveness norms, in intimate relationships (White, 1980). At critical times, equity processes feature strongly in the individuals' evaluation of their bonds. Huston and Burgess (1979) resolve the apparent dilemma of equity and equality co-existence. They assert that partners' judgments using such norms are rooted in their overall satisfaction with the relationship, as determined by its reward–cost history and partners' respective alternatives outside the relationship. Persons dissatisfied with the affiliation are likely to view it as inequitable. Those experiencing satisfaction are apt to see it as both equitable and equal, or to be unconcerned with calibrating profit using equity rules.

In conclusion, the therapeutic objective entails teaching these six propositions to clients, presenting them as prominent guidelines for regulating network-building social exchanges which the clients may choose to draw upon from their Person–Environment Fit schemata. The second corollary to Hypothesis 7.8 proposes research validating this theme.

Hypothesis 7.8b
Clients trained to incorporate equity theory propositions within their Person–Environment Fit ideology–i.e., relationships grow through mutual self-interest and deteriorate when partners' reward/cost ration persists unbalanced–increase their probability of developing stable interpersonal relationships within network clusters desired for specified needs and aspirations.

CONCLUSION:
CLINICAL IMPLICATIONS OF META-SKILL COMPETENCY, PERSON–ENVIRONMENT FIT SCHEMA, AND PSYCHOLOGICAL EMPOWERMENT

The thrust of this chapter has been to explore ways in which basic network analysis research can be exploited to help resolve the persistent dilemma of weak treatment generalization effects. Through adopting a network analysis perspective, we were drawn unintentionally away from our original question of how psychotherapists can increase the durability of their treatment outcomes. Instead, a more fundamental issue became prominent: How can individuals actively construct interpersonal resource exchanges as a lifelong endeavor to manage life transitions and secure behavior change aspirations?

We invoked a problem resolution, the clinical potential of which is premised on the client acquiring a "meta-skill" for behavior change maintenance. The particular meta-skill described, termed the Person–Environment Fit schema, bridges the gap between client encounters with "high risk" situations and employment of a self-correction strategy which

PBC—O

creates network resources required for desired behavior change. In this context, "high risk" refers to those occasions when the client anticipates that his or her social support network will fail to sponsor an accurate implementation of the behavior change program taught by the therapist. Figure 7.2 demonstrates how components of the Person–Environment Fit schema derive from our generic concept of meta-skill.

In brief, we strongly advocate that a portion of the therapist's time be allocated toward guiding the client's acquisition of the schema presented in Figure 7.2. Clients derive from their schema individual scenarios in response to specific behavior change aspirations. For example, consider the case of Wahler's "insular mothers." After training the client to accurately implement the child management program, the therapist begins to lay the foundation for a Person–Environment Fit ideology within the client's perception of her life situation. This is initiated by pointing out that the parent needs to regularly receive supportive social exchanges, especially from friends and other nonjudgmental associates sympathetic to her situation, on order for her to continue using the program and not feel discouraged by the failures that may occur. During this discussion the clinician addresses the question of how the social environment may sponsor or discourage her use of new management skills, depending on network characteristics. Additionally, the client is guided in mapping out the structure and quality of her social network resources. Assessment questions identify who is available, when they can be contacted to provide the various categories of assistance, and how satisfying those supportive exchanges typically are.

The aim of this phase is to acquaint the client indirectly with the model found in Figure 7.1 by personalizing for her the knowledge that certain types of networks enhance behavior change by creating opportunities for the person to feel psychologically empowered. Therapists recognize that empowerment is an essential treatment outcome in and of itself, and also indicates successful deployment by the parent of her Person–Environment Fit scenario. It carries this distinction because empowerment represents a constellation of self-perceptions, social awareness, and behavioral competencies which prompt the individual to make a sustained effort to activate network resources to secure goals and resolve stressful life events.

The second phase of meta-skill training involves teaching the insular mother to become aware of and monitor her social support in light of her need to receive encouragement for implementing the child management program. The client is coached to anticipate those network characteristics associated with high risk of "insularity." For example, she is alerted to the disadvantages produced when her most frequent and intimate contacts are with a dense cluster of kinfolk or agency professionals who feel justified in offering critical comments. Moreover, kin expect conformity to family norms,

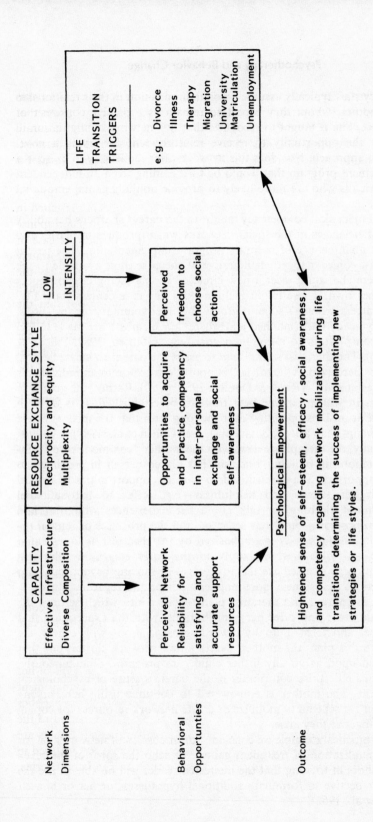

Figure 7.1 Networks enhancing behavior change

while agency staff typically assume a dominant position in their relationship with the mother, whom they expect to remain as a passive consumer of expert advice. She is taught to recognize that this network configuration ill affords her the opportunity to receive reinforcement for trying a novel childrearing approach. Nor does this network offer the leeway to exercise a self-management program that would be forthcoming from an independent cluster of friends who are more likely to provide nonjudgmental emotional support.

The third meta-skill competency taught to the parent sharpens her ability to correct deficiencies in the social networks which produce insularity and prevent the maintenance of accurate program implementation. The parent and therapist consider together the range of social settings available to the mother where she could meet a new circle of people facing circumstances similar to her own. These might include child day care centers staffed by parent volunteers, women's support groups, or other voluntary organizations, which are typically undermanned and where new members are made to feel valued as contributors to a common goal (e.g., Gottlieb, 1982; Pilisuk & Parks, 1980). The therapist's aim is *not* to assist the parent to locate helping relationships perceived as "artificial" support "grafted on to an individual's primary relationships" (Rook & Dooley, 1985, p. 10). Rather, the goal is to find settings in which genuine peer ties can be established. It is through "natural" relationships operating over the long term that the most effective helping exchanges can arise spontaneously (see Cohen et al., 1987).

Additionally, the therapist reviews with the mother "common sense" principles of relationship building, once she has placed herself in proximity to potential supporters. She is sensitized to look for opportunities to reward others with her talents and helpfulness—e.g., offer to babysit, loan unneeded infant clothing, or talk about her experiences with the child management program—and thus set in motion the processes of mutual exchange. Relationship equity is emphasized by the therapist as an essential prerequisite to stable ties, especially in the early stages of relational development. Also stressed are the advantages of moving beyond quid pro quo transactions to assume a more long term perspective regarding the tie.

In short, the parent and therapist plan together into which settings the mother could enter and offer her contributions, with the expectation that she will meet and form mutually rewarding associations with others like herself. With this plan, the mother creates a new network cluster, one that can be relied upon as an ally in her child care program. Simultaneously, success in this enterprise contributes to the parent's sense of psychological empowerment. The mother is empowered to continue using her Person–Environment Fit schema to mobilize or create network resources for coping with life changes as they arise.

With this practical example we conclude our discussion of network analysis and the generalization of treatment gains. We echo the spirit of the text's original authors in trusting that the interested reader will be able to use the network perspective to formulate additional hypotheses for her or himself (Goldstein et al., 1966).

8
Groups and Change

Social scientists have been studying group dynamics for decades. Beginning as early as 1897, when Triplett reported an exploratory study of individual performance in coaction groups, researchers have gradually stockpiled a wealth of information concerning the fundamental dynamics of groups. Building on early studies of such processes as social facilitation (Allport, 1924), group performance (Shaw, 1932), norm formation (Sherif, 1936), and leadership (Lewin, Lippitt & White, 1939), researchers in the 1940s extended their analyses to a wide range of topics, including group formation; intergroup and intragroup conflict; group structure; task performance; intermember influence; conformity; and deviance. By the 1950s, group dynamics emerged as a speciality area within social psychology, and was defined by Cartwright and Zander as "a field of inquiry dedicated to advancing knowledge about the nature of groups, the laws of their development, and their interrelations with individuals, other groups, and larger institutions" (1968, p. 7).

This burgeoning interest in group dynamics paralleled a growing reliance on groups in therapeutic settings. Springing from such divergent sources as Burrow's psychoanalytic "group analysis" (1927), Moreno's psychodrama and sociometry (1978), Freud's *Group Psychology and the Analysis of Ego* (1922), and Lewin's field theory (1936), the period from 1950 to 1970 witnessed the emergence of dozens of different group-oriented approaches to psychotherapy and counseling. Indeed, the fervor and resolve of advocates of group-level interventions prompted Back to label this perspective a "social movement" rather than an emerging field (Back, 1973; Lakin, 1972).

This chapter along with chapter 9 seek to integrate these two distinct, but potentially compatible, fields of inquiry by extrapolating group dynamics theory and research to therapeutic groups. This extrapolation assumes that studies of fundamental group structures and processes can be applied to therapeutic groups in two important ways: First, to increase the accuracy of our basic understanding of these types of groups, and second, to suggest ways to improve their value as change agents. In examining relevant findings, this chapter concentrates on both the individual and the group-level processes and structures that increase the "curative strength" of groups. Following the tradition of Goldstein, Heller and Sechrest (1966), the hypotheses presented here represent only examples of the possible applications of findings obtained in group dynamics research to therapeutic contexts; many other extrapolations are, of course, possible. Both chapters, however, focus on central issues in group psychotherapy. In this chapter, we consider four critical questions: a) Are group approaches effective? b) Does goal- and process-structuring increase the effectiveness of groups? c) How can feedback be used more effectively in groups? and d) What role does cohesiveness play in determining the effectiveness of therapy groups? Chapter 9, examines the impact of the group therapist's leadership behaviors on group therapy.

Before examining the effectiveness of groups as change agents and avenues for improvement, an important limitation should be noted. Although Goldstein, Heller and Sechrest (1966) originally focused on psychotherapy groups, groups are currently used for a variety of purposes (Lakin, 1972; Rudestam, 1982). While some groups may include only hospitalized psychiatric inpatients (traditional psychotherapy groups), other groups are comprised of "normal" individuals who are seeking support from one another (support groups), improved social skills (T-groups) or self-understanding (encounter groups). Similarly, some groups are leader-centered (psychoanalytic or Gestalt groups), while others are group-focused (encounter and T-groups), and the group's activities can range from the highly structured (social skill training groups, such as assertion groups) to the unstructured (encounter groups). In general, and unless otherwise noted, the phrase "group therapy" is used generically to refer to any group-level intervention designed to improve individual's adjustment and/or psychological functioning. However, because of the important differences separating current group techniques, the extrapolations presented here cannot be applied equally across all groups and all group members. Hence, as Goldstein, Heller and Sechrest suggest, applications of group dynamics to therapeutic groups must "be selective and subject to research examination. Extrapolations must be to further formal or clinical research, and not directly to psychotherapeutic practice" (pp. 322–323).

CHANGING PEOPLE IN GROUPS

The most fundamental extrapolation from group dynamics to group therapy is so basic that it is seldom explicitly stated: People are more easily changed when in groups than when they are alone. In one of the earliest studies of this assumption, Lewin contrasted the power of persuasion vs. group-discussion as change mechanisms. This study was conducted during World War II at the request of the Food Habits Committee of the National

Research Council, and aimed at changing homemakers' attitudes about less desirable, but more plentiful, meat products (such as beef hearts or kidneys). One group of volunteer homemakers listened to an "attractive" lecture that stressed the patriotic importance of serving these meats, ways to prepare the foods, and the food's nutritional value. Others, however, discussed these same issues as a group, and were allowed to reach a group consensus concerning the meats. As predicted, only 3 percent of the subjects in the persuasion condition later served the unique meats, while 32 percent of the group members later served the less attractive foods at least once (Lewin, 1943). On the basis of these findings and studies conducted in other contexts, Lewin concluded that "it is easier to change individuals formed into a group than to change any of them separately" (1951, p. 228).

But does Lewin's "law" of change through group participation apply to therapeutic groups? Research suggests that some group-level therapeutic interventions are effective, but the issue is complicated by contradictions in results and inadequacies in methodologies. First, Bednar and Kaul (1978), in their review of hundreds of studies evaluating the effectiveness of group interventions, rejected over 85 percent as so methodologically flawed that they yielded no information whatsoever. Second, of those studies judged as acceptable from a methodological standpoint, most reported changes only on self-report data, rather than behavioral data. For example, several studies of encounter groups have identified changes in such personality characteristics as spontaneity and self-acceptance, but the behavioral implications of these changes are unknown (Budman, Demby, Feldstein & Gold, 1984; Butler, 1977; Ware & Barr, 1977; Ware, Barr & Boone, 1982). Similarly, Lieberman, Yalom and Miles (1973), by using a variety of measurement approaches — self-reports, members' ratings of other members, and ratings of members provided by participants' friends — found that most of the gains produced by the group experience were limited to self-reported changes in the attitude and value realm, rather than actual behavioral changes. And while Miles (1965) found that executives who participated in National Training Laboratories programs received better ratings by their associates than control-group subjects, the participants' self-ratings again revealed much greater change. These and other findings led Bednar and Kaul (1978) to tentatively conclude that "group treatments have been more effective than no treatment, than placebo treatment, or than other accepted forms of psychological treatment" (1979, p. 314), but that changes are more pronounced on self-report measures and less pronounced on behavioral measures. Similarly, Gibb (1970) states that participation in sensitivity groups yields changes in "ability to manage feelings, directionality of motivation, attitudes towards the self, attitudes towards others, and interdependence" (p. 2114), but few changes in behavior.

The consistently greater impact of group therapy on self-percepts than on social behavior suggests that the effectiveness of group interventions could be heightened by strengthening the link between cognitions—self-esteem, self-perceptions, attitudes, values, self-acceptance, and so on—and action. Recent social psychological research indicates that individuals' personal attributes, including their attitudes and personality traits, influence their actions only when certain preconditions are met. Extrapolating to therapeutic settings, these social psychological findings suggest that self-changes brought about by participation in groups will be more likely to influence actions if these preconditions were incorporated in therapeutic settings. This assumption is expressed in the following hypothesis:

Hypothesis 8.1
Behavioral change will be more likely to occur if the group intervention strengthens the link between group members' self-perceptions and their actions.

How can self-behavior links be strengthened? One possible method provides individuals with a script or action structure that directly references their personal preferences and values (Abelson, 1982; Snyder, 1982). As described by Abelson, scripts are cognitive schemata that dictate sequences of actions in specific social settings. In many everyday social situations these scripts are activated by routine events, and thereby generate behavioral consistency over time. However, some scripts include "choice points": points within the sequence where individuals must refer to their own personal attitudes, preferences, and decisions to choose a course of action. If individuals' scripts do not include references to their personal attributes, their actions will remain unchanged even when changes in the self-concept and other self-percepts occur. If, however, the script is modified to include reference to self-perceptions, then self-changes should be reflected in behavior. As Snyder (1982, p. 121) explains, a script that requires reference to self-percepts can be considered a "believing means doing" action structure that "mandates individuals to ask themselves the question 'What course of action do my attitudes suggest that I pursue in this situation?' "

Supporting this viewpoint, Synder and Kendzierski (1982) demonstrated that attitudes are more predictive of behaviors when individuals' scripts include an attitudinal reference point. In this research, individuals who earlier reported a favorable attitude towards participation in psychological experiments were asked to wait with two confederates. During this period, one of the confederates read a notice posted on the wall asking for volunteers for an experiment. When the reader turned to the second confederate and said, "I don't know if I should volunteer or if I shouldn't volunteer. What do you think?" the second confederate either said "Beats me—it's up to you" or "Well, I guess that whether you do or whether you don't is really a question of how worthwhile you think experiments are." This manipulation modeled an attitude-based script which suggested that attitudes toward psychological research should be the guides for action in the situation. Therefore, as predicted, while only 25 percent of the subjects volunteered to participate in the no-script condition, 60 percent volunteered when the confederates' conversation reminded them of the relevance of their attitudes to their actions.

A second method for strengthening the link between group members' self-perceptions and their actions requires increasing the correspondence between the self-change and the behavior-change. This viewpoint, which is advocated by Ajzen and Fishbein (1977), argues that global self-changes do not influence behavior because behaviors are too specific. For example, while socially anxious individuals, through extensive group experiences, may change their self-evaluations so that they think of themselves as "poised," this global self-change may not influence behavior in a specific *place* with a specific *person* at a specific *time*. To achieve such a behavioral change, the intervention should focus on a more specific aspect of the self: self-evaluation of oneself when interacting in such a manner, at such a time with this particular person.

The importance of correspondence was persuasively demonstrated by Weigel, Vernon and Tognacci (1974) in their study of attitude-behavior linkages. These investigators began by assessing subjects' attitudes toward four objects: the environment, conservation, pollution, and an environmentalist organization (the Sierra Club). After five months, the subjects were recontacted and asked to assist the Sierra Club by writing a letter to the local newspaper, joining and paying dues, and so on. As the concept of correspondence suggests, global attitudes concerning the environment, conservation, and pollution served as poor predictors of behavior. However, responses to the more specific attitude measure — attitude toward the Sierra Club itself — were strongly correlated with amount of help given the organization.

Evidence also suggests that changes in self-evaluations and self-concept will be reflected in behavioral changes, provided behavior is not constrained by situational norms (Campbell, 1963). For example, while individuals' increased social sensitivity may surface within the group as they engage in greater self-disclosure and provide others with feedback and emotional support, outside the group these individuals may abandon these behaviors in order to conform to normative expectations. Hence, although many positive self-changes have been achieved within the group, these changes are not reflected in behavior because the group members decide to conform to conventional interaction norms, in order to avoid negative social sanctions. Evidence indicates that if individuals are made aware of the inconsistency between social norms and their personal viewpoint, they are more likely to resist conformity pressures (Hare, 1976).

The hypothesis that behavior change will be more likely to occur if the group intervention strengthens the link between group members' self-perceptions and their actions is also consistent with a number of existing group techniques, including assertiveness training, social skills interventions, and values clarification groups. For example, most social-skills interventions are behaviorally oriented, focusing on discrete skills that are modeled and practiced within the group setting (Bellack & Hersen, 1979; Curran, 1977; Galassi & Galassi, 1979). Although such interventions sometimes include structured analyses of participants' self-perceptions, emotions, and perceptions of others, these self-processes are generally tied to specific, identifiable behaviors. Even behavioral group therapies could be improved, however, by the further strengthening of cognitive-behavioral linkages.

The link between self-percepts and actions is also strengthened when events that occur outside the group are tied to events that occur within the group. As Lieberman, Yalom and Miles (1973) suggest, a "here-and-now" focus gives clients the opportunity to directly observe the social ramifications of their actions. Through feedback from the group leader and other members, clients develop a clearer understanding of their own personal attitudes, values, and characteristics; in Snyder's terms, their self-percepts become more accessible (Snyder, 1982). Going beyond accessibility, however, a here-and-now focus also embeds these self-percepts in clients' behavioral scripts. Once the relevance of a self-percept is recognized, individuals are more likely to "ask themselves the question 'What course of action do my attitudes suggest that I pursue in this situation?' " (Snyder, 1982, p. 121). Thus, the here-and-now focus not only increases self-insight, but also creates new choice points within clients' behavioral scripts. However, to be certain that these new scripts generalize to nontherapy interactions, some therapy time should be used to bring outside events into the group. As Anderson (1985) and Strong and Claiborn (1982) note, group therapy is most effective when a here-and-now focus is occasionally abandoned for an excusion into the "then-and-there."

CREATING CHANGE-ENHANCING GROUP STRUCTURES

Although some approaches to behavior change through groups adamantly argue in favor of unstructured groups, several reviewers have concluded that *some* structure facilitates group development and leads to more positive group outcomes (e.g., Bednar & Kaul, 1978; Bednar & Langenbahn, 1979). In examining this issue, we will concentrate on evidence drawn from industrial and group dynamics studies of goal structures and goal-path structures on group performance.

Goal Clarity, Difficulty, and Performance

Goldstein, Heller and Sechrest (1966), in their discussion of the superiority of group-centered leadership in therapeutic groups, suggested that groups progress more rapidly if they are working towards clearly defined goals. In the years since their suggestion, a number of investigators have examined the relationship between goal clarity and group performance, particularly in organizational settings. In general, these studies indicate that group performance and goal clarity are positively correlated (Zander, 1980). For example, Latham and Kinne (1974), in a study of logging teams, compared groups that were given specific goals to achieve to groups that were simply told to "do their best." As predicted, the crews with specific goals outperformed the no-goal control crews, particularly when their supervisor monitored their performance (Ronan, Latham & Kinne, 1973). Similar findings have been obtained in dozens of other studies (Latham & Yuki, 1975), leading Zander (1980) to conclude:

> When a group's goal is vaguely expressed . . . it is difficult to assess the amount of progress toward that end. The consequence is that members obtain little feedback on the group's performance and have little opportunity to benefit from past experience. It follows that groups with imprecise goals often have poorly developed procedures and operating plans, and because a fuzzily defined objective provides uncertain guidance for actions of members, we expect more discoordination in the functioning of the group and less effectiveness in its work. (p. 229)

Evidence also indicates that groups are more productive when they are working to achieve challenging goals rather than easily attainable ones (Zander, 1971), perhaps because difficult goals enhance motivation and stimulate strategy-based learning (Terborg, 1976). For example, Kolb and Boyatizis (1970) found that positive changes in personality were most pronounced among T-group members who developed personal plans for evaluating their performance in relationship to clearly established goals. Other studies have yielded similar findings (see Locke, Shaw, Saari and Latham, 1981), and can be summarized in the following hypothesis:

Hypothesis 8.2
Challenging, clearly defined group goals enhance the effectiveness of group therapy.

It should be noted, however, that Hypothesis 8.2 has several limitations. First, while goals should be difficult, they should not be so difficult that they cannot be achieved. As will be noted in the analysis of cohesiveness presented later in this chapter, groups that fail repeatedly can experience a number of negative, group-threatening consequences. Second, evidence indicates that the motiving impact of group goals on members is greatest when the members themselves participate in the goal-formation process. As first noted in Coch and French's (1948) classic study of productivity in a garment factory, when group members can participate in the goal-formation phase they display less aggression, hostility, turnover, and dissatisfaction. Third, as noted in the following section, clearly defined goals will not promote positive group outcomes if the path to be taken in reaching these goals is unclear.

Goal-path Clarity

In a 1957 study, Raven and Rietsema demonstrated that both the clarity of group goals and that of the procedures to follow to reach the goals will influence reactions in performance groups. By varying the instructions given to group members, these investigators systematically manipulated subjects' perceptions of the clarity of goals and goal-paths. As predicted, on subsequent measures of cohesiveness, sympathy for group emotions, and interest, high clarity groups outscored the low clarity groups.

To separate the impact of goal-path clarity from the impact of goal clarity, Anderson (1975) performed a subsequent study in which he manipulated the similarity of group members, as well as the clarity of goal-paths. He began by pretesting college females using the Allport–Vernon–Lindzey Study of Values scale, and identifying individuals with similar and dissimilar values. Next, he formed three-person groups of highly similar or dissimilar members, and allowed these individuals to work on a preliminary group discussion task. Then, during a second session, he asked the groups to plan and sketch an ideally-designed dormitory. For half of the triads, the members of the group were all trained to base their plan on the same variable: either recreational facilities, educational facilities, or residential facilities. Each member of the remaining groups, however, was trained to focus on a different variable. Thus, while the groups sought the same clear goal, in some groups the path to that goal was clear to all members (that is, all three members shared the same goal-path), while in other groups the method for reaching the goal was unclear.

Anderson found that the cohesiveness of the group during the preliminary discussion was largely determined by values; groups composed of individuals with highly similar values were more cohesive than groups made up of dissimilar members. However, during the planning session, the impact of similarity was minimal while the clarity of the goal-path was quite influential. Relative to groups with unclear goal-paths, the members of high clarity groups reported greater interpersonal attraction and satisfaction. Furthermore, when the group members were given the chance to terminate their membership, unclear goal-path groups displayed a much higher turnover rate than the clear goal-path groups. Fully 55 percent of the unclear goal-path groups were disrupted by membership terminations, while only 15 percent of the clear goal-path groups included a member who wished to leave the group. This significant impact of goal-path clarity on group satisfaction, cohesion, and turnover is summarized in the following hypothesis.

Hypothesis 8.3
Interventions that clarify the processes used to achieve change in groups enhance the effectiveness of group therapy and decrease premature termination rates.

This hypothesis is consistent with a number of recent attempts to increase the effectiveness of group psychotherapy by pretraining subjects (Jones & Crandall, 1985; Roark & Roark, 1979). Viewing pretraining as a means of increasing goal-path clarity, Anderson's (1975) findings suggest that pretraining should increase group members' levels of satisfaction and commitment to the group while decreasing the number of premature terminations and casualties. Consistent with this prediction, Martin and Shewmaker (1962) found that simply giving patients written instructions concerning group processes led to more positive outcomes. Similarly, when Truax and Carkhuff (1965) and Truax, Shapiro and Wargo (1969) presented clients with tapes of several segments of actual group therapy sessions, they found that this exposure to group processes led to a reduction of schizophrenic symptoms (Truax & Carkhuff, 1965), and positive changes in MMPI scores (Truax et al., 1968). In a similar vein, Strupp and Bloxom (1973) pretrained some group members by exposing them to a film describing the basis for psychotherapy, group members' roles, and the activities to be undertaken during therapy. In clarifying the goal-paths, the film also emphasized a number of specific points, including expression of personal feelings; the value of emotional expression; the responsibilities of the group member; the difference between adaptive and maladaptive behavior; and the potential gains that could be reasonably expected. On measures of improvement, satisfaction with treatment, symptom discomfort, and motivation, clients who saw the film described above responded more positively than clients who saw an irrelevant film.

Studies of the process structuring that occurs later in a group's development also support hypothesis 8.3 (Corazzini, Heppner & Young, 1980; Kivlighan, McGovern & Corazzini, 1984; Warren & Rice, 1972). For example, Kivlighan and his colleagues based their interventions on Tuckman's stage model of group development (Tuckman, 1965; Tuckman & Jensen, 1977). According to this view, most performance and therapeutic groups move through an ordered series of developmental stages. Although the stages receive various labels from various theorists (Bennis & Shepard, 1956; Moreland & Levine, 1982; Pedigo & Singer, 1982; Shambaugh, 1978), the five emphasized by Tuckman include *forming, storming, norming, performing*, and *adjourning*. During the forming stage, individual members are seeking to understand their relationship to the newly formed group, and strive to establish clear inter-member relations. During the storming stage, group members often find themselves in conflict over status and group goals, and in consequence hostility, disruption, and uncertainty dominate group discussions. During the next phase, norming, the group strives to develop a group structure that increases cohesiveness and harmony, while the performing stage is typified by a focus on group productivity and decision-making. Lastly, when the group fulfills its goals, it reaches its final stage of development: adjourning.

Guided by this perspective on group development, Kivlighan et al. predicted that interventions that match the developmental needs of the group will lead to more positive outcomes than interventions that are not appropriate given the "maturity" of the group. Therefore, group members were given written handouts, pertaining to either anger or intimacy in group therapy, prior to either the fourth group session or the ninth group session. The information dealing with anger clarified the value of anger in therapy by providing a justification for anger as a natural part of group participation and suggestions for communicating anger. In contrast, the information dealing with intimacy clarified the value of intimacy in groups, and provided suggestions for the appropriate expression of intimacy toward others. As anticipated, when the interventions were matched to the most appropriate developmental stage—for example, when group members received the anger information during the storming phase (session four) or the intimacy information during the norming phase (session nine)—rather than mismatched, subjects displayed more comfort in dealing with intimacy, more appropriate expressions of intimacy and anger, fewer inappropriate expressions of intimacy, and more congruence between self-ratings and other ratings of interpersonal style.

These and other studies suggest that attempts to clarify the processes used to achieve change in groups by pregroup training, or by providing clarifying information during group therapy, lead to more positive therapeutic outcomes. As Bednar and Kaul (1978) conclude, "ambiguity and lack of clarity tend to be associated with increased anxiety and diminished productivity and learning in a variety of settings," (p. 793) while interventions designed to decrease ambiguity "have been associated with significant and constructive effects" (p. 794).

Although the available data lend strong support to Hypothesis 8.3, additional evidence is needed to examine the long-term impact of group structure on therapeutic change. As Strong and Claiborn (1982) argue, while increasing structure may be effective at the outset of the group, it becomes irrelevant in the long run since change can occur with or without structuring. According to this viewpoint, insight into the dynamics which are responsible for change is not necessary for healthy change to occur. Indeed, in many cases individuals fail to recognize the strength of the social forces which cause them to change their actions, and instead attribute their improvement to personal growth and development. This alternative view of change through indirect social influence will be considered in more detail in chapter 9.

INTERPERSONAL LEARNING AND FEEDBACK

Bednar and Kaul (1978), while documenting the relatively greater impact of groups on self-percepts rather than behavior and the value of increased goal and goal-path structure, also note that very little is known of the processes underlying group-induced change. A relatively small number of studies have contrasted different types of group treatments (e.g., Abramowitz & Jackson, 1974; Beutler, Jobe & Elkins, 1974; Lieberman, Yalom & Miles, 1973; Kivlighan, McGovern & Corazzini, 1984), and fewer still have sought to measure possible mediating processes (e.g., Arbes & Hubbell, 1973; Dies & Sadowsky, 1974; Rugel & Meyer, 1984; Shapiro & Diamond, 1972).

Lieberman, Yalom and Miles' well-known study of encounter groups is, however, a notable exception (Yalom, 1975; Lieberman, Yalom & Miles, 1973; Yalom, Tinklenberg & Gilula, cited in Yalom, 1975). Randomly assigning 206 students enrolled at Stanford University to one of 18 different groups—representing nine theoretical orientations—these investigators assessed adjustment before; during; immediately after; and six months following the participation, using a variety of measurement approaches. Although a number of factors were associated with growth, the trio also found that no one theoretical approach to groups proved more effective than any other. For example, two separate Gestalt groups with different leaders were included in the design, but the members of these two groups evidenced widely discrepant gains. One of the Gestalt groups ranked among the most successful in stimulating participant growth, but the other group yielded fewer benefits than all of the groups.

Going beyond theoretical boundaries, Lieberman and his colleagues sought to identify factors which may have mediated the changes that were observed. Based on the subjects' self-reports and prior clinical experience, Yalom (1975) identified the following "curative factors."

1. Installation of hope.

2. Universality.

3. Guidance.

4. Altruism.

5. Family reenactment.

6. Self-understanding.

7. Identification.

8. Interpersonal learning: Feedback.

9. Interpersonal learning: Relationships with others.

10. Group cohesiveness.

11. Catharsis.

12. Existential factors.

Although some of these factors seem to be more important determinants of therapeutic success than others, Yalom argues that all are necessary conditions for change in groups (Yalom, 1975). However, when group members rate or rank order the curative impact of these factors, they generally emphasize four of these factors: self-understanding, interpersonal learning, cohesiveness, and catharsis (Butler & Fuhriman, 1983; Markovitz & Smith, 1983; Maxmen, 1973, 1978; Rohrbaugh & Bartels, 1975; Rugel & Myer, 1984; Sherry & Hurley, 1976).

Using Yalom's list of curative factors as a foundation, the final extrapolations presented in this chapter focus on ways to increase the effectiveness of therapeutic groups by increasing the magnitude of curative factors. In the tradition of Goldstein, Heller and Sechrest, the extrapolations presented here only exemplify some of the possible applications of group dynamics to therapeutic groups. In this selective sampling of possibilities, we concentrate on two of the most critical curative factors identified by Yalom: interpersonal learning through feedback and cohesion.

Limitations of Interpersonal Feedback

Theorists have repeatedly underscored the value of groups as arenas for interpersonal learning (Lieberman, 1980; Yalom, 1975). Group members not only receive direct, explicit information in the form of therapeutic directives, but also gain, from the group itself, the opportunity to implicity gather data concerning their own interpersonal behavior. Interaction in the group setting is social behavior, and thus has implications for self-definition that go beyond the confines of the temporary group situation. Within the social microcosm of the small group, individuals "become aware of the significant aspects of their interpersonal behavior: their strengths, their limitations, their parataxic distortions, and their maladaptive behavior that elicits unwanted responses from others" (Yalom, 1975, p. 40). Through feedback from the group leader and other group members, as well as self-observations formulated within the group setting, individuals gain an increased understanding of their social selves, and this self-understanding provides the basis for changes in cognitions and actions. The value of interpersonal learning is also recognized by group members themselves, for when rating the most valuable aspect of the group experience, they tend to emphasize feedback and interpersonal processes: "the group's teaching me about the type of impression I make on others;" "Learning how I come across to others;" and "Other members honestly telling me what they think of me" (Yalom, 1975, p. 79).

The emphasis on others' appraisals as a source of self-information is consistent with a number of self-theories. For example, the early symbolic interactionists (Cooley, 1902; Mead, 1934) viewed the self as social in nature since it is built up continually in the course of daily encounters with other people. The symbolic interactionists argued that the self is a dynamic process, is fluid rather than stable, and is based on "reflected" appraisals from others. William James (1890) similarly stressed the social foundations of the self, as did a number of interpersonal theorists, including Rogers (1959), Sullivan (1953), and Haley (1971).

Yet, the logical extrapolation from group dynamics research to therapy groups—group members will modify their behavior and beliefs based on the feedback they receive from the group leader and members—has received only limited empirical support. On the positive side of the feedback debate, evidence generated in laboratory studies in which individuals receive direct feedback about their personality, abilities, skills, or characteristics indicate that subjects usually modify their self-descriptions accordingly (Eagly, 1967; Regan, Gosselink, Hubsch, & Ulsh, 1975; Regan, 1976; Shrauger & Lund, 1975; Snyder & Shenkel, 1976; see Jones, 1973; Shrauger & Schoeneman, 1979, for reviews). Furthermore, studies also suggest that the magnitude of the change is related to a number of theoretically relevant factors, including the credibility of the source of the feedback (Bergin, 1962), the competency of the source person on the relevant evaluative dimension (Webster & Sobieszek, 1974), and the number of individuals providing the feedback (Backman, Secord & Pierce, 1963).

However, a number of studies support an opposing viewpoint, for these negative findings indicate that others' appraisals are rarely internalized. First, in a series of investigations, Swann and his colleagues have shown that individuals process information most effectively when it verifies their original conception of their self (Swann, 1983). For example, when individuals who considered themselves to be likable or dislikable were given written feedback that was either consistent or inconsistent with their self-conception, they spent more time scrutinizing the self-consistent feedback (Swann & Read, 1981). Evidence also indicates that individuals tend to remember self-consistent rather than inconsistent feedback, and also distort inconsistent feedback so that it confirms their original self-conception (Ingram, Smith & Brehm, 1983; Swann & Read, 1981).

Second, individuals tend to be biased in their preference for positive feedback (Greenwald, 1981; Kivlighan, 1985). For example, in a series of investigations Jacobs and his colleagues arranged for subjects to participate in a short-term, highly structured "sensitivity" group (Jacobs, 1974). When subjects rated one another on a series of adjectives, Jacobs found that they consistently accepted positive feedback, but consistently rejected negative feedback. This "credibility gap" occurred despite attempts to vary the source of the information (Jacobs, 1974), the sequencing of the information (Davis & Jacobs, 1985; Jacobs, Jacobs, Gatz & Schaible, 1973; Schaible & Jacobs, 1975), the behavioral and affective focus of the feedback (Jacobs, Jacobs, Cavior & Feldman, 1973), and the anonymity of the appraisals (Jacobs, Jacobs, Cavior & Burke, 1974). Although these findings attest to the potential value of group interventions as self-esteem-enhancing mechanisms, the tendency to accept only positive feedback screens the group members from negative, although potentially therapeutic, social information.

Third, Shrauger and Schoeneman (1979) note that despite the significant impact of interpersonal feedback on self-perceptions in controlled laboratory settings, studies of naturalistic interactions indicate that people's self-perceptions are relatively uninfluenced by others' appraisals. As symbolic interactionism suggests, dozens of studies have confirmed that individuals' self-conception matches their perceptions of others' appraisals. However, these perceptions do not often reflect others' actual appraisals. For example, when Felson (1981) asked football players to describe a) their personal opinion about their athletic ability and b) their estimation of their teammates' ratings of their ability, he discovered that self-appraisals and perceived appraisals correlated at .55. However, when he correlated self-ratings with teammates' actual judgments, the relationship disappeared. These findings have been replicated in a variety of settings with many types of subjects—grade school children, college students, dental students, military personnel, emotionally disturbed children, delinquent males, physically disabled—leading Schrauger and Schoeneman to conclude that "there is little evidence that in their ongoing social interactions people's views of themselves are shaped by the opinions of others" (1979, p. 559).

Feedback and Self-focused Attention

Given the following: a) the tendency to more efficiently process feedback that is consistent with the self-concept; b) the tendency to accept only positive feedback; and c) the weak relationship between perceived appraisals and actual appraisals, what steps can be taken to increase the value of the group setting as an arena for social learning? What can group leaders and members do to minimize the impact of social and psychological mechanisms that impede the impact of the feedback, while increasing the individuals' understanding of their interpersonal behaviors?

Social psychological theories of the self offer one solution. According to several recently developed *attentional* theories, human awareness is limited. If attention is concentrated on objects and events in the surrounding environment, then awareness of one's own self and behavior is necessarily lessened. Conversely, if the individual is self-focused, then he or she can not monitor the external environment as closely (Carver & Scheier, 1981; Duval & Wicklund, 1972). Because of these limits of attention, awareness tends to be dichotomous: individuals vacillate between an environment-focus and a self-focus. In general, any object that reminds the individual of his or her status as an object—the presence of an audience, the sound of his or her voice played on a tape recorder, a mirror, or a videotape camera—increases self- rather than environment-focus.

Both Carver and Scheier (1981) and Wicklund (1975, 1979) have persuasively argued that attentional focus plays a mediating role in determing individuals' compliance with personal behavioral standards. If individuals are self-focused, then they should be more likely to make certain that their actions match their private attitudes and values. If, however, they are environment-focused, their attitudes and actions may be inconsistent. Gibbons (1978), in an attempt to test this hypothesis, first assessed male college students' general opinions concerning erotic books, movies and magazines. One month later, these same males were told to rate the attractiveness of photographs of nude women. Provided subjects made their judgments while seated before a mirror, their ratings were correlated with the attitudes toward erotica. If, however, the self-focusing mirror was removed, then subjects' attitudes did not predict their ratings.

Scheier and Carver (1980) have also shown that when personal standards do not provide guidelines for evaluating the appropriateness or adequacy of the behavior, self-focused individuals tend to seek out feedback about their performance. For example, in one study subjects who were periodically exposed to their mirror image while performing a task were more interested in obtaining data about the quality of their performance than subjects who were not self-focused. In a conceptual replication of this finding, Scheier and Carver also found that high scorers on the Self-Consciousness Scale (Fenigstein, Scheier & Buss, 1975) were also more likely to seek feedback concerning their performance. Carver and Scheier interpret these effects as evidence of a behavioral regulatory system. Self-focus engages a cognitive feedback system, which in turn detects and corrects discrepancies between social and personal standards and behavior. Hence, the Carver–Scheier self-regulation model provides the foundation for the following hypothesis.

Hypothesis 8.4
The impact of feedback from group members will be greater if the individual's focus of attention is shifted to the self.

Support for this hypothesis comes primarily from laboratory studies, although some anecdotal support can also be gathered from clinical settings. Focusing first on the social psychological findings, Fenigstein (1979) conducted two studies in which self-focus was examined as both a personality variable and an experimentally manipulated factor. In the first study, females who were high or low in terms of self-consciousness were either rejected or accepted by two accomplices of the researcher. While supposedly waiting for the actual experiment to begin, the subject was seated in a small room with two confederates. In the rejecting conditions, these confederates treated the subject in a cold, aloof manner; they virtually ignored all of the subject's remarks. In the accepting condition, the confederates welcomed the subject into the conversation, and attended to her comments with enthusiasm and interest. As predicted, self-focused individuals (those high in self-consciousness) showed more extreme reactions to the implicit feedback provided by others. These findings were replicated in a second study, in which self-focus was manipulated by placing a mirror in front of some subjects.

Other researchers have found that a strong self-focus tends to increase individual's ability to take the role, or perspective, of others (e.g., Hass, 1984; Stephenson & Wicklund, 1984). For example, Stephenson and Wicklund manipulated self-focus by asking subjects to work on a problem with a confederate. For half of the subjects, this confederate appeared to be very high in self-focus, while the remaining subjects worked with a low-self-focus partner. As anticipated, through a contagion process, the self-focused state of the confederate triggered a similar reaction in the subject: Those who worked with a self-focused partner became more self-focused themselves. More importantly, however, self-focus was also associated with an increased ability to take the other's perspective into account during the interaction, particularly among subjects who were dispositionally low in self-consciousness. In a more literal illustration of this process, Hass asked subjects to trace an E on their foreheads while seated before a video camera or while facing a blank wall. As expected, 55 percent of the subjects in the self-focus condition drew the E so that it was properly oriented to an observer's perspective; only 18 percent of non-self-focused subjects drew an externally oriented E.

Hypothesis 8.4 also offers an organizing framework that explains the utility of a number of extant therapeutic tools. At the most basic level, audiences tend to generate increases in self-focus, so the group therapy setting should naturally shift clients in the direction of greater receptiveness to feedback. In addition, laboratory studies also indicate that unexpected physical activities—such as jogging in place—can increase self-focus (McDonald, Harris & Maher, 1983; Wegner & Giuliano, 1980). These findings suggest that the effectiveness and popularity of sensation "games" and simulations in encounter groups possibly stems from their self-focusing qualities. Similarly, just as self-focused individuals tend to use personal pronouns more frequently than nonself-focused individuals (Carver & Scheier, 1978), therapists who ask members to express their thoughts and feelings in the first person may be stimulating increased self-focus.

The realities of the therapeutic setting, as well as certain inconsistencies in the empirical findings, also suggest a number of important boundary conditions for the predicted relationship between the impact of feedback and self-focus. First, if individuals feel that they cannot achieve the goals established within the group—and hence must look forward to a constant barrage of corrective feedback concerning their inadequate performance— then they may "disengage" themselves by terminating their membership in the group. Kaplan and his colleagues have found that negative feedback can lead to a number of damaging consequences for "fragile" group members (Kaplan, 1982; Kaplan, Obert & Van Buskirk, 1980), and Carver, Antoni and Scheier (in press) have found that this process becomes more likely when attention is directed towards the self. Second, evidence also suggests that increases in self-focus can be extremely powerful. For example, Reed (1982), in describing a "mirror therapy" program used in substance-abuse groups, warns that "since mirror therapy appears to be so simple—'merely' talking to oneself in a mirror—the dangers and repercussions can often be overlooked" (p. 127). In particular, increased self-focus should be avoided when dealing with depressed clients (Pyszczynski & Greenberg, 1985; Smith, Ingram & Roth, 1983). As is consistent with cognitive theories of depression (e.g., Beck, 1967), depressed individuals tend toward more rather than less self-focus when exposed to negative events, while increasing their environment-focus after positive events. In consequence, self-focus simply serves to exacerbate the depressed individual's negative self-image. Third, the relationship between positive change and self-focused attention may be curvilinear: to be effective, group members must become aware of the impressions they create with others, but this awareness should not be so strong that it engenders social anxiety (Leary, 1983). In a clear demonstration of this third limitation, Ellis and Holmes (1982, p. 70) found that individuals who were so self-focused that they ignored environmental events became insensitive to feedback from others. In a simulated interview setting, some subjects were told to focus their attention on their own thoughts and feelings. The instructions explicitly stated: "A person is often only fleetingly aware of these self-perceptions unless one makes a special attempt to focus on them. For this reason you are being asked to be sensitive to your thoughts and feelings in the interview." Other subjects, in contrast, were told to "pay particular attention to the interviewer," while a third group of subjects were given no attention-focusing instructions. When the interviewer's nonverbal and paralinguistic responses were systematically varied to create a progressive shift from warm to cold or cold to warm, only the other-focused subjects detected this shift and rated themselves accordingly.

COHESION

Cohesion, like interpersonal learning through feedback, was among the list of "curative factors" identified by Yalom, Lieberman and Miles (1973) in their longitudinal study of group processes. According to Yalom (1975), while cohesion may not be a sufficient condition for effective groups, cohesion could be a necessary condition; without cohesion, feedback would not be accepted, norms would never develop, and groups could not retrain their members.

In emphasizing the value of highly cohesive groups, Yalom and his colleagues join a long line of researchers who have reached similar conclusions. As early as 1951, Cartwright suggested that if groups are used as change agents, then the members should have a strong sense of group identity and belonging. Otherwise, the group won't exert sufficient influence over its members. Similarly, Bach (1954, p. 348) noted that the "cotherapeutic influence of peers" in the therapy group requires group cohesion, as did Frank (1957), Truax (1961), and Goldstein, Heller and Sechrest (1966). Indeed, Goldstein et al. devote an entire chapter to the topic, presenting a series of suggestions for increasing cohesiveness by structuring clients' expectancies, promoting intergroup conflict, or planting a deviant within the group.

Yet, in the face of this widespread agreement about the value of cohesiveness, some researchers have noted that cohesion may not always enhance group outcomes. For example, Wolf and Schwartz (1962, p. 224) pointed out that cohesion could create strong pressures for "homogeneity and a denial of the right to deviate" and may therefore inhibit change. More recently, Janis (1972, 1982), after examining a number of historically important decision-making bodies, concluded that in-group pressures caused by cohesiveness were the primary cause of errors in judgment. And Zimbardo (1969), in his cogent analysis of deindividuation, suggests that individuals who become "submerged" in their cohesive groups can become highly agressive. These dissenting theorists suggest that, once again, the most obvious extrapolation—the more cohesive the therapy group, the more effective it will be—may not be the most defensible extrapolation.

In this final section of the chapter, we will examine the relationship between cohesion and group outcomes. After considering some of the positive aspects of cohesion, we will consider some of the potential drawbacks to maintaining high cohesiveness in groups.

The Positive Impact of Cohesiveness

As Donnelly, Carron and Chelladurai (1978) note in their analysis of groups in athletic settings, all groups must be somewhat cohesive in order to exist. If the sum of the forces binding the members to the group are equal to zero

(Festinger, 1950), then the group will exist only momentarily, and may be more accurately labeled an "aggregate of individuals" rather than a "group."

In his review of group dynamics analyses of cohesion, Cartwright (1968) summarizes a number of positive phenomena that occur when cohesiveness increases beyond the minimal level needed to maintain the group. First, cohesive groups retain their members more effectively. Cartwright (1968, p. 91) defines cohesion as "the degree to which the members of the group desire to remain in their group," so cohesive groups are expected to display low turnover and resignation rates. Evidence also indicates, however, that this relationship is strongest when cohesion is based on group members' commitment to the group-as-a-unit rather than their attraction toward each individual member. In studies of cohesion and turnover in industrial settings, when cohesion is defined only as strong liking for one's co-workers it is *not* associated with decreased turnover. Only a strong, group-level relationship, involving a global, positive linkage between the member and the group, decreases turnover (Mobley, Griffeth, Hand & Meglino, 1979).

Second, people are more satisfied when they are members of cohesive rather than noncohesive groups. For example, when workers in industrial settings are aggregated in highly compatible, cohesive subgroups, they report more satisfaction and enjoyment than workers placed in noncohesive subgroups (Hare, 1976). Similarly, in a study of college dormitories, women living in cohesive units reported more satisfaction than women living in noncohesive units (Darley, Gross & Martin, 1951). In a study of classroom groups, Wheeless, Wheeless and Dickson-Markman (1982) found that subjects' perceptions of group solidarity were correlated with ratings of satisfaction with the group and the qualify of the group's interactions (rs = .63 and .68, respectively). Williams and Hacker (1982) found that the cohesiveness of womens' collegiate field hockey teams was significantly correlated with the players' global satisfaction with the team, the coach, quality of play, and relations with teammates. And members of cohesive therapy groups also report more satisfaction than members of noncohesive groups (Drescher, Burlingame & Fuhriman, 1985; Hagen & Burch, 1985; Stokes, 1983a).

Perhaps as a consequence of this increased satisfaction, Deutsch (1968) concludes that people in cohesive groups respond to one another in a more positive fashion than the members of noncohesive groups. As Shaw and Shaw (1962) note in their study of classroom groups, the atmosphere in cohesive groups is cooperative, friendly, and marked by exchanges of praise for accomplishments. In noncohesive groups, hostility and aggression surfaces, along with a tendency to criticize other group members.

Third, communication patterns and rates depend upon cohesiveness. For example, Moran (1966), in a study of Dutch T-groups, identified groups that were high and low in cohesiveness, as well as groups that engaged in high versus low rates of communication. As anticipated, the quantity of communication was much greater in the high cohesion groups as compared to low cohesion groups. Similarly, Lott and Lott (1961) reported a correlation of .43 between communication and cohesion in a study of ongoing student organizations. Furthermore, evidence also indicates that participation is more equally distributed among all members in cohesive groups (Back, 1951), and reaches deeper levels of intimacy (Stokes, 1983b).

Fourth, cohesiveness leads to a number of positive personal consequences for each individual members. Seashore (1954), in a study of industrial settings, found that employees who worked in cohesive groups reported less anxiety and nervousness. Similarly, other evidence (e.g. Myers, 1962) links increased group cohesiveness to heightened self-esteem and reduced anxiety. Pepitone and Reichling (1955) present suggestive evidence that cohesive groups may promote feelings of security.

Fifth, cohesive groups exert a stronger influence on their members than noncohesive groups. As Lewin's field theory of group behavior suggests (Lewin, 1951), people in cohesive groups tend to more readily accept the group's goals, decisions, and norms. Furthermore, conformity pressures are greater in cohesive groups, and individuals' resistance to these pressures is weaker. For example, in an early study of communication patterns in cohesive dyads, cohesiveness was directly manipulated by telling subjects that they would either enjoy being in the group (since care had been taken in assembling highly compatible teams) or that the dyad would not be cohesive since the members were incompatible (Back, 1951). Subsequent analyses revealed that when subjects discovered that they disagreed with their partners' interpretations of three ambiguous stimuli, the members of cohesive groups tried to exert greater influence over their partners than did the members of noncohesive groups. In addition, conformity to the partner's influence attempt was also greater in cohesive dyads. Applied to therapeutic groups, these findings suggest that cohesiveness leads to greater compliance with change-producing norms. For example, Frank (1957) notes that members of cohesive psychotherapy groups tend to "internalize" the group's norms, and to avoid dysfunctional behavior for fear of letting the group down.

The Negative Impact of Cohesiveness

While evidence indicates that cohesive groups a) retain their members longer, b) are more satisfying for members, c) are characterized by better communication relations, d) lead to positive personal consequences for members, and e) exert more influence over members, cohesiveness is a mixed blessing. Although the many positive consequences of increased cohesiveness enhance the value of groups as change agents, the negative consequences of cohesiveness may offset these gains.

Janis' (1963) theory of groupthink underscores the potentially harmful consequences of cohesiveness. Using a case-study approach, Janis identified a number of political groups that made extremely poor decisions. After reviewing historical documents describing the nature of these groups, Janis concluded that they all suffered from groupthink: a distorted style of thinking that renders group members incapable of rational decision-making. Furthermore, in each case the group was extremely cohesive, leading Janis to conclude that groupthink occurs when members of highly cohesive groups strive to agree with their fellow group members at all costs.

Janis suggests that high cohesion fosters the development of a number of dysfunctional group processes that are symptomatic of groupthink. First, pressures to conform become so strong in cohesive groups that members become intolerant of any sort of disagreement, and harsh measures are taken to bring dissenters into line. As Schachter found in his study of reactions to deviants (1951), when groups are highly cohesive, anyone who unwaveringly goes against the group consensus tends to be disliked by the group members and assigned undesirable roles if allowed to remain within the group. Perhaps as a consequence of this low tolerance for disagreement, the members of highly cohesive groups tend to engage in self-censorship when they privately disagree with the group, creating a misleading atmosphere of apparent unanimity.

Second, Janis catalogs a number of illusions and misperceptions that occur in highly cohesive groups. Members tend to become so positive about their group that they forget that they must constantly monitor its progress, and sometimes believe that nothing should be done to improve it. During groupthink, members tend to conclude that the group's perspective on an issue is the only correct perspective, and therefore lose the ability to empathize with people who don't belong to the group. Cohesive groups can also reinforce members' stereotypes, polarize their attitudes and opinions (Lamm & Myers, 1978), promote hostility towards people who don't belong to the group (Pepitone & Reichling, 1955), and encourage collective rationalization.

Third, evidence also suggests that communication within highly cohesive groups can also go awry. For example, in the Schachter study described earlier (1951), when cohesive groups were discussing a topic that was relevant to group goals, group members tended to concentrate nearly all their communicative efforts on dissenters. But when the group members concluded that the dissenter was not going to yield, they psychologically excluded him or her from the group, and the frequency of communications directed to the dissenter dropped dramatically. More recently, Courtwright (1978) found that when the group norms emphasize the value of cooperation and agreement among members, members of highly cohesive groups avoid disagreement more than members of noncohesive groups.

Fourth, evidence indicates that cohesiveness can both increase *and* decrease productivity in groups. Hence, in Courtwright's study the highly cohesive groups with constraining norms performed more poorly than the noncohesive groups, apparently because the lack of dissent interfered with communication. Similarly, studies of work groups indicate that cohesiveness increases productivity only when the group's norms encourage greater productivity. For example, in an experimental study of productivity, half of the subjects were led to believe that they were members of cohesive groups, while the other subjects were convinced that their groups were noncohesive. Next, while they worked on the task, messages were sent from one worker to another to establish performance norms. In some instances the messages called for increased production (positive messages), but in other instances the messages requested a slow-down (negative messages). As expected, the impact of the messages was significantly greater in the cohesive groups. Furthermore, the decreases in productivity brought about by the negative messages were greater than the increases brought about by the positive messages (Schachter, Ellertson, McBride & Gregory, 1951).

Fifth, cohesion can increase negative group processes, including hostility, scapegoating, and rejection. For example, in an early study, French (1941) asked cohesive and noncohesive groups to work on a series of insoluable problems. Although all the groups showed signs of increased hostility, coalitions tended to form in noncohesive groups, while cohesive groups vented their frustrations through interpersonal aggression: overt hostility, joking hostility, scapegoating, and domination of subordinate members. The level of hostility became so intense in one group that observers lost track of how many offensive remarks were made; they estimated that the number surpassed 600 comments during the 45-minute work period.

Lastly, in some cases individuals who have belonged to cohesive groups for an extended period of time become so dependent upon these groups that they cannot adapt to changes in the group's membership. For example, Janis (1963) describes how the formation of strong emotional ties in combat groups can result in maladaptive behavior when the group's composition is altered. Although the cohesiveness of the unit initially provides psychological support for the individual, the loss of comrades during battle causes severe distress. Furthermore, when the unit is reinforced with replacements, the original group members are reluctant to establish emotional ties with the newcomers, partly in fear of the pain produced by separation. Hence, they begin restricting their interactions, and a coalition of old versus new begins to evolve. In time, the group members can become completely detached from the group, and the group's development becomes arrested (Gruner, 1984).

Cohesiveness as an Intensifier of Group Processes

In sum, research indicates that increased group cohesion contributes to both positive and negative group processes. On the positive side, cohesiveness is associated with group stability, satisfaction, effective communication, positive intrapersonal consequences for members, and increased group influence. On the negative side, however, cohesion has also been linked to a variety of pernicious processes: social pressures of such intensity that individual members are overwhelmed, illusions, misperceptions, and faulty communication. Furthermore, given the right (or wrong) combination of circumstances, cohesiveness also decreases the quality of group performance, encourages hostility and interpersonal rejection, and promotes disabling overdependence in long-term members.

A judicious synthesis of these divergent findings suggest that either-or hypotheses concerning the impact of cohesion on therapeutic groups cannot be offered. Clearly, increases in cohesion promote both positive and negative outcomes for both groups and individuals, depending upon the nature of the group situation. However, rather than viewing cohesiveness as either a positive or negative force within a group, the current perspective suggests that cohesiveness works as an "intensifier" of ongoing group processes. If these processes increase the therapeutic value of group participation, then their impact will be heightened in cohesive groups. If, however, these processes inhibit change, then their disruptive effects will be even stronger when cohesiveness is increased. This interpretation of the available evidence is summarized in Hypothesis 8.5

Hypothesis 8.5

Cohesiveness intensifies group processes; if these processes promote positive outcomes for participants, then cohesiveness will enhance the therapeutic effectiveness of the group. If, however, these processes promote negative outcomes for participants, then cohesiveness will exacerbate nontherapeutic effects.

Hypothesis 8.5 can be applied to a range of therapeutic issues. If cohesiveness acts as an intensifier, then therapeutic groups with change-producing norms will be more successful if cohesiveness is high rather than low. Yalom has identified a number of processes needed for positive change in groups—self-disclosure; risk-taking; and here-and-now focus; assumption of responsibility by group members; process observation and analysis; catharsis—and if group members recognize the value of these processes, cohesiveness will increase the occurrence of these dynamics. If, however, group members reject the therapists' attempts to establish change-producing norms, then cohesiveness will only intensify their resistance. For example, if the group accepts the fact that the expression and resolution of hostility and conflict is a legitimate group goal, then cohesiveness will generate even higher levels of conflict and growth. If, however, the group members tend to avoid hostile exchanges, then this tendency will be exacerbated when cohesiveness increases.

Hypothesis 8.5 can also be used to better understand premature terminations and group members' rejection of new members. As a number of studies suggest, some of the most disappointing consequences of group therapy occur among early terminators—individuals who drop out of the group before significant therapeutic changes have been achieved (Bednar & Kaul, 1978; Liberman, Yalom & Miles, 1973, Yalom, 1966). In this early stage of the group's development, individuals are striving to establish the stable relationships necessary for group stability and cohesion. With this gradual increase in cohesion, however, comes a tendency for marginal members to feel more and more excluded by the more central members. In consequence, marginal members become dissatisfied with the group and drop out. According to Hypothesis 8.5, if the growth of cohesiveness was postponed until the marginal member was more firmly embedded in the group's structure, then terminations resulting from exclusion would not occur (although terminations for other reasons might then become more likely).

Applied to the rejection of newcomers who join in-progress, open therapy groups, the "intensification" hypothesis suggests that the magnitude of this rejection will be directly proportional to the level of cohesiveness enjoyed by the group. If the group is tightly knit, new members, despite attempts by the therapist to smooth their entry, experience a rocky reception. If, in contrast, the group is not highly cohesive—if coalitions exist within the group, members are busy challenging the competence of the leader, recent meetings have been boring and unproductive, or several individuals have just left the group—then new members can be added with little problem.

Controlling Cohesiveness

Because cohesion polarizes group processes, the group therapist or leader must be able to moderate the cohesiveness of the group, shifting levels upward and downward depending upon the nature of the group: its developmental level, the members' characteristics, the problems being addressed, the level of hostility, the nature of the group's norms, and so on. Some of the means to effect such shifts in cohesiveness include:

1. Controlling level of self-disclosure. Several studies suggest that level of self-disclosure (or risk-taking) and group cohesiveness are intimately linked (Stokes, 1983b). However, while many researchers assume that cohesiveness causes increases in risk-taking, at least two studies have shown that risk-taking, when manipulated, significantly influences group cohesion (Kirshner, Dies & Brown, 1978; Ribner, 1974). In one approach, the leader could vary

the level of self-disclosure within the group by modeling either high or low risk-taking; as Hurst, Stein, Korchen and Soskin (1978) found, groups led by self-disclosing leaders tend to be more cohesive than groups led by less self-expressive individuals. Alternatively, the leader could control cohesion by shifting the group discussion away from or toward more intimate topics. For example, to increase cohesiveness the leader could ask members to discuss feelings about personal life experiences, their attitudes and feelings toward the group, or their current feelings about the present group experience. In contrast, to decrease cohesiveness, the leader could ask groups to discuss less intimate topics, such as outside activities or relationships between group members and nonmembers (Kavanaugh & Bollet, 1983).

2. Controlling entitativity. Campbell (1958) used the term *entitativity* to describe the extent to which something seems to be an entity; that is, a single, unified object. Applied to groups, Campbell's concept suggests that cohesiveness is greater in groups that are high in entitativity. Drawing on Gestalt principles of perceptual organization, entitativity could be increased by making certain that the group members share a "common fate," possess some similarities, or are seated in close proximity to one another. Entitativity can also be increased if the leader repeatedly emphasizes the unity of the group. In early group dynamics research (e.g., Back, 1951) cohesiveness was manipulated simply by telling group members that they were similar or dissimilar to one another. Evidence also indicates that if the group leader continually refers to the group as a unit, the members will become more cohesive (Zander, Stotland & Wolfe, 1960). Applied to therapy groups, these findings underscore the cohesion-increasing consequences of the global, mass-group process commentary recommended by Bion (1961).

3. Controlling level of deindividuation. Studies of deindividuation suggest that when group members feel submerged in a group, they express strong feelings of liking for the group and believe that the group is very unified (Prentice-Dunn & Rogers, 1980; Rogers & Prentice-Dunn, 1981). Although research is limited, available evidence indicates that deindividuation can be increased by making members feel unidentifiable (e.g., turning down the lights), freeing the group from any observation, and increasing arousal through the use of emotion-elevation games. Conversely, to decrease feelings of cohesiveness, the leader can accentuate the unique qualities of each member, remind the group that it is being observed, and increase members' level of self-awareness (see Forsyth, 1983).

4. Lastly, the group leader can also temporarily manipulate cohesiveness by exposing the group to positive or negative feedback. As a number of studies conducted in a variety of settings suggest, group cohesiveness tends to drop after failure, while after success, cohesiveness increases. For example, Norvell and Forsyth (1984) gave laboratory groups working on a

series of structured experiential tasks feedback which indicated that they had either succeeded or failed. In the success condition, subjects were led to believe that an expert observer rated the group very positively. In contrast, subjects in the failure condition were told that the observer felt the group was unsuccessful, and gave it low rankings on a number of interpersonal dimensions. As expected, cohesiveness dropped in the failure groups.

GROUPS AS CHANGE AGENTS

The five hypotheses presented in this chapter build upon those offered by Goldstein, Heller and Sechrest (1966) in their original extrapolation of group dynamics theory and research to the therapeutic process. Group approaches to treatment are not appropriate for all problems or for all clients, but outcome studies suggest that extant group approaches are relatively effective therapeutic tools. Furthermore, their utility could be enhanced still more if theory and research could be used to guide therapeutic practice. For example, Hypothesis 8.1, which is derived from studies of attitude-behavior linkages, suggest that changes in self-perceptions brought about by group therapy could be extended to the behavioral realm, by creating stronger links between self-percepts and behavior. Hypotheses 8.2 and 8.3 both focus on the question of group structure, and recommend establishing clear goals and clarifying the processes used to achieve these goals. The final two hypotheses presented in the chapter concentrate on the "curative" factors assumed to be necessary for therapeutic growth in groups, and together they argue for caution in the use of interpersonal feedback and cohesion. Hypothesis 8.4, which is predicated on a number of studies that have shown that feedback inconsistent with an individual's self-image is rejected, suggests that feedback will have a greater impact on group members if their attention is self-focused rather than externally focused. Hypothesis 8.5 extends studies of such negative group processes as groupthink and productivity losses to therapy, by predicting that cohesion tends to polarize group processes. Provided the group's processes are effective, cohesion will enhance therapeutic gains. If, however, the group's processes are ineffective, cohesion will inhibit the group's utility as a therapeutic change agent.

9
Leader Therapist Orientation

When "the group" emerged as a topic of study in the social sciences, researchers' attention was inexorably drawn to leadership processes. As early as 1902, Cooley suggested that the leader is the "nucleus" of the group "organism," and that all groups require "such nuclei." By the 1920s theorists had already developed a host of definitions equating leadership with power (Allport, 1924), personality (Bowden, 1926), and persuasion (Schenk, 1928), and researchers fell to the task of identifying effective leaders and the techniques they use to inspire their members. By the 1940s, researchers began exploring leadership using both nonexperimental and experimental methods. For example, Whyte (1943) vividly illustrated the pervasive influence of the leader on each member of the group in his brilliant case study of a street corner gang called the Nortons. At about the same time, Lewin, Lippitt and White (1939; White & Lippitt, 1968) published their remarkable study of democratic, autocratic, and laissez-faire leaders. As the field of group dynamics grew, the concept of leadership became firmly entrenched within this newly founded field.

Practitioners who use group-level interventions as therapeutic instruments have also been preoccupied with leadership processes. Initially, Freud's analyses of the leader as the authority figure in the group dominated therapeutic practices, as therapists fostered the growth of insight through interpretation and the transference process (1922). However, in the late 1940s and 1950s, alternative methods emerged that redefined the role of the leader. For example, in T-groups, the leader was a facilitator who guided the group-centered interactions. In Tavistock groups, leaders remained detached, and thereby forced the members to deal with authority issues. Gestaltists, in contrast, were actively involved in their groups, using role-play methods and emotional stimulation to enhance group members' awareness (Back, 1972).

Although these various approaches to therapeutic change adopted widely divergent perspectives concerning appropriate leader-therapist behaviors, all recognized the pivotal role played by the leader—i.e. the trainer, facilitator, group psychotherapist, or consultant—in facilitating or impeding change. The curative strength of groups arises from a complex of interrelated factors, but these factors can generally be traced to the direct or indirect influence of the leader. Without a qualified group leader, the group may never develop into a therapeutic agent. From Lieberman, Yalom and Miles (1973, p. 264): "how leaders conduct themselves does make a substantive difference in the relative benefit or harm group members experience."

Despite the universal recognition of leadership as a mediator of the effectiveness of group therapy, "the literature does not reflect much empirical interest in the topic" (Bednar & Kaul, 1978, p. 786). Surprisingly, very few studies have systematically examined the relationship between specific leadership attributes and behaviors and therapeutic success. With some exceptions (e.g., Lieberman, Yalom & Miles, 1973), theorists have offered recommendations concerning appropriate leadership qualities and behaviors, but in many cases these recommendations have not been empirically evaluated. To offset this neglect, this chapter applies research conducted in nontherapeutic settings to therapeutic settings in an attempt to increase our understanding of "therapeutic leadership." Results obtained by group dynamicists working in both laboratory and field settings offer a number of insights concerning the process of leadership, and their extrapolation may suggest possible ways to improve existing therapeutic techniques. After advancing an interactional model that defines leadership as a "reciprocal process in which an individual is permitted to influence and motivate others to facilitate the attainment of mutually satisfying group and individual goals" (Forsyth, 1983, p. 209), several hypotheses based on this model are tendered. These hypotheses represent examples of potential applications of group dynamics findings to therapeutic settings, and focus on a) directive versus nondirective leadership styles, b) participatory versus nonparticipatory leadership, and c) task versus relationship-oriented leadership styles.

LEADERSHIP AS RECIPROCAL INTERACTION

Before we translate the findings obtained by group dynamicists into specific suggestions for improving leadership practices in therapeutic groups, we first must perform a theoretical extrapolation. Although several preliminary models of therapeutic leadership have been developed, too often these analyses suffer from one of two basic flaws: either they view leadership as a skill or attribute possessed by a therapist, or they assume that effective leadership involves performing a number of specific behaviors in the group situation. Rejecting both of these assumptions, group dynamicists currently view leadership as a process of mutual influence, linking group members with the group leader. Therefore, before applying empirical findings to therapeutic settings we must *first* apply the interactional theory of leadership to therapy groups.

The Trait View of Therapeutic Leadership

The historian Thomas Carlyle is often credited with the "Great Man Theory" of leadership, which asserts that the historically important political and social leaders possessed certain traits that destined them to be great leaders. To Carlyle, leadership is a quality that exists in some people and not in others (Carlyle, 1841). Russian novelist Leo Tolstoy, in contrast, argued that situational factors shape the course of human affairs. He felt that the Zeitgeist, or spirit of the times, fortuitously propelled certain individuals into positions of prominence. Once in these positions, their own attributes had little impact on their successfulness, for Tolstoy felt that situational factors determined their fate (Tolstoy, 1869).

These two perspectives parallel theorists' attempts to explain therapeutic leadership. Although literally hundreds of leadership theories have been developed, most fall into two categories: Trait theories and situational theories. On the trait side, some theorists, researchers, and practitioners believe that effective group therapists possess certain specific personality traits. Adopting a scaled-down version of Carlyle's great-person theory, advocates of a trait approach feel that the skills and abilities needed in the group setting must be related to measurable personality, intellectual, and physical characteristics. For example, Slavson (1962, 1964) suggested that group therapists should be characterized by poise, maturity, ego-strength, perceptiveness, empathy, intuition, creativity, interest in others, a desire to help people, and a high tolerance for frustration. Parker (1972) emphasized a different set of traits: broad personal experience, self-awareness, open acceptance of others, expressiveness, and personal security. Kellerman's (1979) list is particularly lengthy, and includes: simplicity; honesty; straight-forwardness; an ability to succeed; commitment to diversity; tolerance; authenticity; trust; ability to empathize; warmth; acceptance; understanding; spontaneity; the capacity to maintain distance; experimentation; sense of humor; and flexibility. Bowers, Gauron, and Mines (1984) even offer a procedure that identifies good group psychotherapists by assessing such personality traits as "need for closure," "individualism," "extroversion," and "regression in the service of the ego."

This trait conception of the skilled group therapist parallels a trait theory popular among group dynamicists in the early decades of this century. However, despite the intuitive plausibility of the trait view, empirical evidence offers little support for a strict trait view of leadership. For example, Stogdill, after reviewing 163 studies examining personality and leadership, concluded that leaders are characterized by a "drive for responsibility and task completion," high motivation, creativity, and "readiness to absorb interpersonal stress" (Stogdill, 1948, 1974, as described in Bass, 1981, p. 81). However, he also notes that the correlation between leadership and personality rarely reaches past 0.30, and thus accounts for less than 10 percent of the variation in leadership effectiveness. Furthermore, 65 percent of the traits were identified in only a single study, and the more frequently mentioned "traits" tend to refer to global behavioral qualities, such as interpersonal skills or friendliness. Extrapolating these findings to therapeutic settings suggests that only a small portion of the leader's effectiveness is linked to his or her personality traits.

A Situational View of Group Psychotherapy

In contrast to the trait view, a situational view of therapeutic leadership maintains that the effective leader is one who can "solve the social problems existing in times of stress, change, and adaptation" (Bass, 1981, p. 27). Although this situational perspective is operationalized in many forms, the functional models are the most widely accepted form of situationism. According to these views, therapeutic changes occur if the leader (or group members) fulfill certain critical functions within the group. For example, as early as 1948 Benne and Sheats suggested that an effective leader must be able to meet both task and socioemotional needs. Thus, to be effective the leader must fill such task roles as "initiator contributor," "information seeker," "opinion seeker," and "elaborator," as well as such socioemotional roles as "encourager," "harmonizer," and "group commentator." More recently, Lieberman, Yalom and Miles (1973) have suggested that an effective leader must fulfill four basic functions to be effective: emotional stimulation, caring, meaning-attribution, and executive actions. Similarly, Carkhuff (1969a, 1969b) pinpoints specific behaviors that facilitate positive therapeutic outcomes: empathy, positive regard, concreteness, genuineness, confrontation, and immediacy. Anderson and Robertson (1985) expand Carkhuff's list by adding such specific skills as attending, communicating clearly, modeling, linking, interpreting, regulating, and facilitating closure. Unlike the trait approaches, functional theories tend to equate leadership with specific, adjustment-promoting behaviors.

These functional theories parallel a number of situational theories developed by group dynamicists. Given the need to organize, motivate, and maintain the group, leadership often requires certain behaviors. Indeed, the earliest systematic studies of leadership focused on the actions actually taken by small group leaders (Carter, 1952; Krech & Crutchfield, 1948). For example, the well-known Ohio State University Leadership Studies, which were conducted in the late 1940s, succeeded in identifying four basic categories of leadership actions: consideration, initiating structure, production emphasis, and sensitivity (Halpin & Winer, 1952). Similarly, Bowers and Seashore (1966) suggested that leadership involves supportive and facilitative actions, Likert (1967) emphasized employee-centered versus production-centered leadership actions, and Cartwright and Zander (1968) summarized the bulk of these studies by arguing that leadership involves group maintenance and goal achievement actions.

An Interactional View of Group Psychotherapy

A situational view of leadership avoids some of the pitfalls associated with trait models, but even this approach oversimplifies the leadership process. For example, Bales (1965) persuasively argued that, except in rare circumstances, no single individual can fulfill all the functions required of a leader. Furthermore, fulfilling all these key functions is no guarantee of leadership effectiveness. The effective leader in one group may be ineffective in the next, and the individual who is trained to enact the targeted leadership skills does not necessarily lead any more effectively than an untrained leader (Bass, 1981). In addition, a situational view implies that leadership is a static process, when evidence indicates that leadership involves continual adjustment and change (Hollander, 1978).

In response to the limitations of both the trait and situational views, many group dynamicists currently define leadership as an interactional process. According to this model, the leader's qualities, the nature of the situation, and the group members' characteristics interact to determine leadership effectiveness. Rather than assuming that leaders simply guide their followers, in the interactional model leadership is a mutual social relationship between leader and group members. Although leaders are influenced by the nature of the setting, they can influence the setting or adjust their own behavior accordingly. The model views leadership as a fluid, dynamic process, involving continual adjustments among the three elements (Fisher, 1985; Hollander, 1978, 1985).

Applied to therapeutic settings, an interactional model predicts that therapists' effectiveness cannot be predicted solely on the basis of their traits, or their ability to fulfill certain group functions. Rather, leadership in a psychotherapy setting is a joint function of therapists' qualities (such as leadership style, intelligence, training, adaptability, and age), the group member's characteristics (such as ability, experience, cohesiveness, need for independence), and the situation (such as type of group, physical setting, clarity of goals). This interactional approach is summarized in the following global assumption.

Hypothesis 9.1
The effectiveness of group psychotherapy is a function of the interaction of therapist characteristics and actions, the characteristics and actions of the group members, and the nature of the situation.

The specific hypotheses discussed in the remainder of this chapter are all based on this fundamental assumption. First, this general view is used to describe two alternative pathways to change in therapy groups: direct intervention and indirect intervention. Second, some specific recommendations are offered about leadership participation by considering the nature of the group setting. Last, the "fit" between the leader's task and relationship orientation and the nature of the group is considered.

THE THERAPIST-LEADER AS CHANGE AGENT

Therapeutic groups vary considerably in function. Some are designed to increase interpersonal skills and self-insight by focusing on the "here-and-now"; some are used as arenas for individual psychotherapy; others focus on the acquisition of specific behavioral skills; and some are created to provide members with the social support they need to overcome problems in daily living. Yet, across this wide variety of structure and function, most groups share a basic goal: to help the client adopt more adaptive and psychologically healthier behaviors.

Although most would agree that the therapist-leader strives to stimulate a change in the client's behavior, there is little consensus concerning the methods the leader should use to achieve this goal. As in individual therapy (Strupp, 1986), no one technique has emerged as clearly superior to other techniques. On the one hand, many clinicians advocate the leader-centered approaches typical of psychoanalytic, Gestalt, and behavioral groups. In such groups, the leader is the central figure in the group. He or she controls the course of the interaction, assigns various tasks to the group members, and occupies the center of the centralized communication network. In some instances, the group members may not even communicate with one another but only with the group leader. In contrast, many therapists advocate a nondirective style of leadership in which all group members communicate with one another. These group-oriented approaches, which are typified by encounters or T-groups, encourage the analysis of the group's processes, with the therapist-leader sometimes facilitating process but at other times providing no direction whatsoever.

Research conducted in both therapeutic and nontherapeutic settings does not uniformly support either leadership approach. Overall, group members report greater satisfaction in nondirective, democratic, group-centered groups than in autocratic, leader-centered groups (Stogdill, 1974). However, even this conclusion fails to hold when group members expect an authoritarian leader (Foa, 1957), or when the group is very large (Vroom & Mann, 1960). In addition, when examining productivity or client improvement, neither approach emerges as consistently more effective. In some cases, a leader-centered approach seems to be highly effective

(Cammalleri, Hendrick, Pittman, Blout & Prather, 1973; Hise, 1968; Shaw, 1955); in others, a group-centered approach enhances effectiveness (Day & Hamblin, 1964; Traux, 1961). And in still others, neither approach emerges as clearly more effective (Swartz, 1973).

An interactional approach to leadership suggests that the effectiveness of a leader-centered or group-centered approach depends upon the group, the particular leader, and setting. Both directive and nondirective leaders are powerful change agents within the group, although they take different pathways in seeking this change.

Direct Leadership Influence

Hollander's transactional model of leadership seeks to explain how leaders, through direct influence, create innovation and change among members of the group (Hollander, 1980; Hollander & Julian, 1970). As an interactional theorist, Hollander views leadership as a reciprocal influence process. To achieve change, the leader must be willing to be influenced by the group members, while also providing the valued resources needed for attaining group goals. From Hollander and Julian (1970):

> The leader who fulfills expectations and helps to achieve group goals provides a rewarding resource for others which is exchanged for status, esteem, and greater influence. Thus, he gives something and gets something. And what he gets contributes to his legitimacy insofar as he is "validated" in his role by followers. (p. 35)

Thus, according to Hollander, to remain influential directive leaders must maintain their legitimacy, or status, in the group. This viewpoint provides the basis for the following hypothesis.

Hypothesis 9.2
For directive leadership, influence and status are directly correlated; the greater the leaders' perceived status, the greater his or her influence.

Support for Hollander's transactional view comes from a variety of sources. For example, experimental studies of leadership in small, ad hoc groups have identified dozens of leader, group member, and situational variables that influence the leader's power in the group. For example, when group members believe that their group leader is highly competent on the task at hand, they tend to respond more favorably to a leader's influence attempts (Hollander & Julian, 1970). Michener and Burt (1975) report that compliance with a leader's demands increases when these demands are justified, when the leader can punish noncompliance, and when the leader has been appointed through legitimate means. Initial conformity to the group's norms is also associated with greater status and power to influence (Hollander & Julian, 1970), provided the group members believe that the leader is a) committed to the group and b) is highly competent (Ridgeway, 1981, 1982).

Hypothesis 9.2 has also been supported by a number of social influence studies of counseling and psychotherapy (Strong, 1968). This view, which is best articulated by Strong, assumes that the therapy is a form of persuasive social influence. Clients seek help when they are dissatisfied or frustrated with their current behaviors, but don't feel that they can resolve these problems without assistance. The therapist, therefore, takes the role of the psychological expert who suggests interpretations of the client's experiences and ways to deal with current problems. Interpretations, in the social influence framework, are statements, suggestions, summaries, or questions that offer new ways of viewing the client's problems (Strong & Claiborn, 1982). When conceptualized as a social influence process, the client's acceptance of the therapists' interpretations or recommendations is a direct function of the client's perceptions of the therapist's status.

According to Hypothesis 9.2, effective directive leaders must maintain their status within the group. Otherwise, they will be minimally effective as change agents. Drawing on French and Raven's analysis of power, the directive leader's influence will increase if he or she can control rewards and punishments, is well liked and respected, and is an expert (French & Raven, 1959). However, the bulk of the evidence collected in nontherapeutic settings argues against the use of reward power and coercive power (threats and punishments) to effect social influence. Although rewards and coercion can lead to compliance with the therapist's demands, they do not prompt any private internal acceptance. They can also generate feelings of reactance and rebellions. Such rebellions can take the form of withdrawal from the group, attempts to increase power by forming coalitions or through ingratiation, or by seeking the replacement of the leader (Blau, 1977; Clark, 1971; Fanon, 1963). Direct influence, if viewed as coercive, can also engender anger, dislike, and hostility, as well as continually increasing resistance to subsequent influence (Johnson & Ewens, 1971). Furthermore, rewards and punishments, as extrinsic motivators of behavior, can undermine any intrinsic motivators of the behavior changes (Deci, 1975). If group members are merely complying with the leader's demands, then the clients will more than likely revert back to their original position when not in the group (Kelman, 1961).

In consequence, directive leaders should strive to base their influence on legitimate, referent, and expert power. As a base, legitimate power is particularly potent because it springs from the group structure itself, rather than from the delivery or withholding of valued resources. When individuals follow therapeutic directives because they hope to earn a reward or avoid a punishment, the reason for their behavioral change is transparently obvious. If, however, the therapist is a legitimate authority in the group, members strive to change because they personally accept the norms of the groups. Similarly, when the therapist's status is secured by his or her referent power (also known as attraction power), groups members gain a sense of intrinsic satisfaction from their identification with the leader. Expert power, although not as influential as legitimate or referent power, should also bolster the directive leader's effectiveness.

The value of legitimate, referent, and expert power is evident in a number of studies of social influence in counseling and psychotherapy. Studies of counseling processes have identified three main categories of cues that influence clients' perceptions of their therapists: evidential cues, reputational cues, and behavioral cues (Corrigan, Dell, Lewis & Schmidt, 1980; Heppner & Dixon, 1981). Evidential cues include primarily nonverbal stimuli such as age, physical appearance, style of dress, office location, and decor. Reputational cues pertain to the therapist's level of experience and expertise, and can include degrees, titles, and other professional credentials. Behavioral cues include the verbal and nonverbal actions that clients associate with effective and ineffective interventions.

By manipulating these variables, researchers have consistently confirmed the hypotheses of the social influence model: therapists who possess certain characteristics that enhance their expertness, attractiveness, and legitimacy (or trustworthiness) influence their clients more strongly (Corrigan et al., 1980). These empirical studies also suggest specific techniques that therapists can use to increase the strength of their social influence. Looking first at expertness, evidence indicates that professional-looking facilities, displays of credentials, and even manner of dress influence clients' perceptions, but that reputational and behavioral cues are more powerful than these evidential cues. Applied to group psychotherapy, these findings suggest that directive group therapists will be more influential if they are experienced, possess a doctorate, and are prominent, well-known therapists. Group therapists can also increase their expertness by using appropriate (and abstract) psychological terminology, by asking appropriate, thought-provoking questions, and by adopting "an attentive, confident, and reassuring manner" (Corrigan et al., 1980, p. 434).

Therapists can also increase their attractiveness in a number of ways, although behavioral cues appear to have the most impact on clients. Therapists who appropriately self-disclose, who emphasize their similarity to their clients, and who display "attractive" nonverbal behaviors (for example, eye contact, forward body lean, close proximity, smiling, head nods) are seen as more attractive by their clients.

Strong (1968) offers a number of techniques that therapists can adopt to increase their trustworthiness, including maintaining "a reputation for honesty," adopting a role that is associated with trust (e.g., physician or clergy), emphasizing one's "sincerity and openness," and "lack of motivation for personal gain." Studies of these recommendations have generally found that the therapists, by taking the role of helper, are already viewed as highly trustworthy by their clients. However, recent social psychological findings suggest that therapists could increase their trustworthiness still more by expressing their faith in their client and group, by sticking to agreements and promises, and by behaving in a predictable and positive fashion.

Indirect Leadership Influence

Change can also be achieved through indirect social influence. As client-centered therapists have long advocated, if clients can be permitted to explore their self-conceptions in a positive, unconditionally accepting environment, then they will experience beneficial therapeutic change.

These suggestions are consistent with Moscovici's theory of minority influence. According to Moscovici, direct social influence—which occurs when the authority or majority uses persuasion, rewards, or coercion to change the group member—often leads to public agreement. However, "as soon as social pressure relaxes, if the person is not attracted to the group, public agreement will tend to disappear and private acceptance will not take place" (1980, p. 212). In contrast, indirect social influence—which occurs when the minority consistently takes a novel stance on an issue—eventually results in conversion to the minority viewpoint. From the first, the rejected claims of the minority create conflict within group members. They force individuals to explore their own feelings and beliefs, if only to confirm and validate them. However, this process shifts the group members' attention inward, so that initial viewpoints are reconsidered. As Moscovici explains:

> It would be an overstatement but not a mistake to say that in the face of a discrepant majority all attention is focused on others, while in the face of a discrepant minority, all attention is focused on reality (1980, p. 215).

This conflict produced by the minority must be resolved, and in most cases the easiest, most available path is that of private changes in personal beliefs. Because this change results from indirect, subtle pressures that work at a deeper level than direct social influence, the conversion created by minorities is stronger than the compliance induced by majorities.

To be effective, Moscovici recommends that the indirect leader adopt a consistent behavioral style. In his research, Moscovici examines group members' reactions to a confederate who disagrees with the judgments of the rest of the group members. Care is taken to make certain the subjects don't attribute any special expertise or skill to the minority confederate, and elements in the situation suggest that the minority's responses are not caused by some personal idiosyncrasy. For example, in one study subjects role-played members of a jury in a civil case. Although the facts of the case weighed in favor of a settlement in the $20,000 range, one of the group members (an accomplice of the experimenter) consistently argued for an award of only $3,000. Later, when subjects' recommended awards were assessed privately, they tended to move in the direction advocated by the minority. Furthermore, this shift was strongest when their group was highly cohesive and the minority member could not be ostracized from the group (Wolf, cited in Moscovici, 1980).

Other studies have similarly indicated that a minority of one or two members can sometimes considerably influence the majority. In general, however, the influencer must remain highly consistent over time, the majority must be aware of this consistency, and the majority members must believe the consistency is an indication of the minority's confidence. Applied to a therapeutic group, these stipulations suggest the following hypothesis.

Hypothesis 9.3
For nondirective leadership, influence and consistency are directly correlated; consistent and confident leaders will be more influential than inconsistent leaders.

A Normative Model of Directive-Nondirective Leadership

An interactional model of leadership suggests that change through membership in groups can be achieved through both direct and indirect methods, and Hypotheses 9.2 and 9.3 emphasize the characteristics of the leader-therapist (status and consistency) that are related to effectiveness. However, an interactional model also suggests that effectiveness will also depend upon aspects of the characteristics of the group situation. For example, in very large groups, a directive leadership style may be most appropriate, while a nondirective, group-centered approach may be most effective in intimate, emotionally expressive groups (Vroom & Mann, 1960). Or, if the group will be meeting for only a short period of time, a highly structured intervention may be needed (Friedmann, 1983), while the members of long-term groups may be more satisfied when led by a nondirect leader (Bass, 1981).

Although researchers are continuing to study the factors that mediate the relationship between a leader's participation and the group's effectiveness, Vroom (1973, 1974, 1976) has recently offered a sophisticated model based on studies conducted in industrial settings. According to Vroom, the leader's participation in group activities enhances the satisfaction and effectiveness of the group only in certain situations. His theory is termed a normative model because it offers specific suggestions regarding the maximally effective amount of involvement.

Vroom describes a number of "types" of leadership styles, but those that are most relevant to therapeutic groups include autocratic (leader-centered), consultative, and group-centered. In the autocratic approach, the leader-therapist acquires information from the individual group member, but the leader suggests solutions and evaluates alternatives. Under a consultative style, the leader-therapist shares questions of adjustment with the entire group, but the leader alone makes binding interpretations or recommendations (which may or may not reflect the group members' influences). Lastly, with group-centered leadership, the leader-therapist functions as a facilitator and agenda-setter; he or she helps the members examine problems and generate alternatives, but his or her influence does not necessarily exceed that of any other group member.

Which style is most effective? As an interactional view of leadership suggests, the style must fit the characteristics of the group members and the specific problem facing the group. To again concentrate on therapy-relevant factors, Vroom suggests that different methods will be most effective depending upon the amount of information possessed by the leader, the ambiguity of the problem, the need for acceptance of suggestions by the group members, the likelihood of such acceptance, and group members' acceptance of the group's goals.

Looking first at the autocratic leadership methods, Vroom argues that these methods will be most effective when the group leader possesses sufficient information to make an effective interpretation, the problem is unambiguous (or structured), and the group members will readily accept the therapist's recommendations. Although unstructured groups would very rarely meet these qualifications, some structured group interventions will. For example, behavior therapy, when conducted in groups, is generally strongly structured by the leader. The leader relies on behavioral principles that yield extremely specific recommendations concerning treatment, and the problems themselves are clarified by focusing on discrete behaviors. Provided that the group members respect the therapist and will accept his or her recommendations, Vroom suggests that an authoritative leadership style would be effective in this case. This prediction is summarized in Hypothesis 9.4.

Hypothesis 9.4
Autocratic leadership methods are appropriate when the group faces a clear, unambiguous issue and the high status leader possesses enough information to offer a feasible solution to the problem that the group members will readily accept.

Vroom recommends a consultative style if the group members do not accept the goals of the group. Applied to therapeutic settings, this recommendation is consistent with the general tendency to advocate moderate levels of structure and centralization for individuals with severe psychological problems. As Strong and Claiborn (1982) suggest, individuals who are highly aggressive, pathological, or resistant may be quite unresponsive to the social influences within groups. In consequence, greater structure from the leader is needed to produce beneficial change. Similarly, Grotjahn, Kline and Friedmann (1983) argue that a leader-centered approach is needed with several behavior problems typical of in-patient and crisis groups. For example, Friedmann (1983, p. 75), in describing his work with crisis groups, argues that "passivity on the part of the therapist will be seen by the patient as a sign of disinterest." In consequence, the leader must be both directive and active, to the point of facilitating group processes, prompting self-disclosure, pointing out commonalities among members, and providing interpretation. These recommendations imply the following:

Hypothesis 9.5
Leader-centered, consultative leadership methods are most effective if group members will not accept an autocratic decision, but aren't strongly motivated by the group's goals.

To use a group-centered leadership method, the group members must personally accept the group's interpretations and conclusions, and they must also accept the goals of the group. These conditions are met, in most instances, in support groups and personal growth groups. In these groups, behavioral change is an outgrowth of a number of curative factors—such as universality, information, social learning, and cohesiveness—that do not depend solely upon the efforts of the leader (see chapter 8; Beck & Peters, 1981). In consequence, Hypothesis 9.6 states:

Hypothesis 9.6
Group-centered leadership methods are most effective if behavior change results from group members' acceptance of feedback from others, if clients may not accept an autocratic decision, and if they are motivated by group goals.

Vroom's theory is still in its formative stages, but available evidence seems to support the adequacy of the approach. For example, Vroom and his colleagues have conducted numerous studies in which parrticipants are asked to read a case study of a leadership situation and then make a recommendation about the most appropriate intervention. Although certain participants tend to opt for certain styles of leadership no matter what the situation, others are able to alter their methods depending upon the characteristics of the problem described (Hill & Schmitt, 1977; Jago, 1978; Vroom, 1975).

Issues and Limitations

No one approach to promoting change through influence in groups is most effective. For example, Bray, Johnson and Chilstrom (1982) arranged for groups of college students to discuss three proposed ways of reducing university spending. Four of the group members were actual subjects who were generally opposed to the four proposals, but each group also included one or two confederates who a) first increased their status before advocating a novel suggestion or b) consistently advocated novel suggestions. Bray and his colleagues found that the minority members influenced the majority no matter what approach was taken, although the direct approach was more influential in all-male groups.

Additional research is needed to identify any limitations associated with directive and nondirective approaches to therapeutic leadership. Looking first at directive leadership, Hypothesis 9.2 suggests that leaders who adopt this style must maintain their status in the group if they wish to remain influential change-agents. However, studies conducted in a variety of settings indicate that therapeutic groups often move through a phase or stage in which the leader's competence is challenged. For example, Tuckman notes that after a brief period of mutual support, group members generally enter into a conflict stage, characterized by dissatisfaction with the leader and competition among group members for power (Tuckman, 1965; Tuckman & Jensen, 1977). Similar periods of conflict have been identified by other theorists (Bennis & Shepard, 1956; Hare, 1982; Schutz, 1958) and other researchers (Bell, 1982; Powell, 1982; Stiles, Tupler & Carpenter, 1982). During these conflict phases, leaders should expect a substantial drop in their capacity to facilitate change through direct influence attempts (such as interpretation, process remarks, directives, and structured activities). Members may also withdraw from the group during these phases, or accept direction from one of the other group members rather than the leader.

The members of groups with directive leaders may also become extremely dependent upon the leader. Although this high dependency increases the leader's status within the group, it also shifts the member's personal responsibility for improvement and change to the leader. In consequence, without the leader's guidance and support, the group members make little or no progress (Strong & Claiborn, 1982). Furthermore, directive leaders' centralized position in the group makes them clearer targets for negative affective outbursts. In a clear documentation of this process, Norvell and Forsyth (1984) arranged for college students to work on several "ice-breaker" and experiential-learning tasks. When the group members later learned that their group was characterized by poor communication, they denied responsibility for their performance and instead attributed the outcome to their leader's actions.

Therapists should also realize that the group members' perceptions of their competence will influence their status within the group. Extrapolating from findings obtained in small group research, in many cases group members' reactions to leaders are based on their expectations, or schema, pertaining to typical characteristics of a leader-therapist. If leaders match this schema, then the leaders' position is secure. If, however, leaders do not match the group members' expectations, then they may have difficulty maintaining their status within the group (Calder, 1976; Green & Mitchell, 1979).

In general, directive leaders have little trouble conforming to group members' leadership schemata, since the concept of "leader" generally implies direction and interpretation. However, the therapists' diffuse status characteristics—any quality that group members think is relevant to leadership—may serve to "discredit" the leader. For example, evidence suggests that many people erroneously assume that men make better leaders than women (Jacobson & Effertz, 1974; Rosen & Jerdee, 1978), even though the available evidence indicates that males and females are equal in leadership skill (Brown, 1977). In consequence, female therapists may find themselves avoiding the directive leadership role (Forsyth, Schlenker, Leary & McCown, 1985). Also, female therapists who attempt to use directive leadership methods may face more resistance from group members than would male therapists, particularly if their clients are traditional in their view of role of women in contemporary society (Forsyth & Forsyth, 1984).

This possibility has been documented in several studies of female therapists working with groups (Greene, Morrison & Tischler, 1981; Strauss, 1975; Thune, Manderscheid & Silbergeld, 1981). Greene and his colleagues, for example, examined group members' perceptions of male and female therapists in co-led groups. Although the therapists differed little in terms of skills and qualifications, male co-leaders were perceived as significantly more potent, active, instrumental and insightful than female co-leaders. Similarly, Thune and her colleagues, after examining co-leaders in several psychotherapy groups, discovered that gender was a more important determinant of status than either professional experience or professional affiliation (social worker vs. psychiatric nurse). These findings, which support sociological studies of status-formation processes, suggest that gender stereotypes may cause status problems for women (Berger, Cohen & Zelditch, 1972).

What can women therapists do to overcome these gender-based biases? First, women who wish to use directive methods may have to work harder than men to ensure their status through evidential, reputational, and behavioral cues. Second, because evidence indicates that sex-linked biases are strongest in all-male groups, directive women therapists may be more successful in groups that include both men and women (Yerby, 1975). Third, women therapists could try to restructure clients' expectations through pretherapy interventions and discussions within the group. Fourth, by working with a male co-leader, female therapists can maintain their directive stance while receiving support from their male co-therapist (Paulson, Burroughs & Gelb, 1976; Rutan & Alonso, 1982). Alternatively, women therapists may simply adopt a less directive style, since evidence indicates that conservative males respond more favorably to women who are supportive rather than task-oriented (Forsyth & Forsyth, 1984).

Several limitations associated with indirect leadership approaches can also be identified. First, group members often react negatively to an indirect leadership style, for they initially associate therapy with direct guidance. Furthermore, studies of nontherapeutic groups have consistently found a preference for directive leadership during periods of stress and tension (Hemphill, 1961). In consequence, a nondirective leader will generally be pressured to provide direct interventions during the initial group meetings. If the leader capitulates to these pressures, then he or she will have violated the consistency requirement of Hypothesis 9.3.

Second, indirect leaders must take special precautions to make certain that group members do not associate their lack of direction with a lack of *competence*. One strategy that Moscovici recommends as a solution to this pitfall is co-leadership. When two individuals are included in the group, both of whom accept the appropriateness of an indirect leadership style, group members are more likely to yield to the influencer. This suggestion was supported in the study described above, conducted by Bray, Johnson, and Chilstrom (1982). In all male-groups, a minority consisting of only one individual was less influential than a two-member minority.

LEADERSHIP STYLE AND CHANGE

The question "How much should a leader-therapist participate in the group process?" has been called the "greatest single problem in group psychotherapy" (Gorlow, Hoch & Telschow, 1952, p. 15). From a group dynamics perspective, however, no single answer is possible, for both directive and nondirective leaders are effective change agents. As noted above, studies of social power have repeatedly demonstrated that people frequently change when pressured by direct influence methods. Provided the direct leader is sufficiently powerful (that is, high in legitimate, referent, or expert power), then he or she should succeed in influencing the group members. In contrast, studies of minorities suggest that indirect influence agents can also be successful, provided they are consistent over time.

In addition, Vroom's theory offers specific recommendations concerning the most effective amount of leader involvement in various types of groups: a group-centered leadership style is most appropriate when the members accept the group's goals, while leader-centered methods may be more effective when clients aren't motivated to attain the goals specified by the group. However, in concentrating primarily on the participation issue, Vroom's model offers few behavioral guidelines for leaders in therapeutic groups. For example, even if two leaders adopt a group-centered approach to therapy, they may still differ greatly in their approach to group leadership; one may emphasize clear group norms while the other may prefer unstated goals; one may offer many interpretations, while the other may not; one may provide considerable support and warmth, but the other may remain more neutral. Furthermore, some of these differences in leadership behaviors (or "style") may enhance or detract from the group's effectiveness.

Is one particular leadership tendency or style more effective than another? Despite the obvious relevance to practice, few studies of the link between the leader's behavior and group member change have been undertaken. Therefore, this chapter closes by drawing on studies of work groups to develop a series of hypotheses based on an interactional model of leadership. First, the myriad possible leadership interventions are simplified by concentrating on two general behavioral tendencies that typify leaders in a wide range of settings: task orientation and relationship orientation. Second, two theoretical perspectives that attempt to specify, in precise terms, the link between outcome and leadership are described. Although Bass (1981) reviews many similar theoretical viewpoints, here we apply two perspectives to therapeutic groups: Fiedler's contingency theory (Fiedler, 1978, 1981) and Hersey and Blanchard's developmental model (Hersey & Blanchard, 1976, 1977).

The Duality of Leadership

The tendency for leadership to involve a task component and relationship component is one of the best-replicated findings in the study of leadership. Although leadership requires many different skills and behaviors, investigators have consistently discovered a constellation of task-oriented actions and a constellation of relationship-oriented (or socioemotional) actions. As noted earlier in this chapter, Benne and Sheats, after examining behaviors in T-groups, identified two fundamental functions that leaders fulfill in groups: task and interpersonal (Benne & Sheats, 1948). In the 1950s, studies conducted at Ohio State University found that group members' perceptions of their leaders emphasized these same two dimensions (Halpin & Winer, 1952). During this period, Bales (1958) based his Interaction Process Analysis of groups on this distinction between task and socioemotional behavior. In the 1960s, investigators identified these same two themes in their studies of industrial productivity, referring to them with such labels as "supportive" versus "work-facilitative" (Bowers & Seashore, 1966), "employee-centered" versus "production-centered" (Likert, 1967), and "relations-skilled" versus "administratively skilled" (Mann, 1965). Attributional studies of leadership have also noted a general emphasis on task and relationship activities (Ilgen & Fuji, 1976; Lord, Binning, Rush & Thomas, 1978), and task and relationship behaviors have been identified in several analysis of encounter and experiential groups (Lieberman et al., 1973; Waldie, 1982).

How do these two types of leaders behave? Although the findings vary slightly from study to study, task-oriented leaders generally concentrate on defining problems for the group, establishing communication, providing evaluative feedback, planning, activating task-relevant activity, coordinating members' actions, and facilitating goal attainment by proposing solutions and removing barriers (Lord, 1977). In a therapeutic context, task-oriented leaders may set clear limits and rules for the group, identify specific goals for each session, monitor time spent on issues, and facilitate or redirect communication. They may also rely heavily on structured activities while demonstrating a high level of knowledge and technical expertise. From Lieberman, Yalom and Miles' description of a highly task-oriented leader (1973);

> He seemed to have a preplanned script of exercises he had decided to use in a particular meeting. . . . He did relatively little challenging or confrontation, but he frequently questioned individuals or invited them to participate in the group. In the observers' view, he was a highly managerial, highly structuring leader who made little use of his own person. (p. 59)

In contrast, the relationship-oriented leader focuses on the feelings, attitudes, and satisfactions of the group members. Such leaders strive to make certain the group atmosphere is positive by boosting morale, increasing cohesiveness, and monitoring any interpersonal conflict. In a therapy group, socioemotional leaders strive to establish genuinely positive personal relationships with the group members. They do so by demonstrating an emphatic orientation towards others, providing strong support and acceptance for all group members, and encouraging the expression of emotions and feelings. From Lieberman, Yalom and Miles (1973):

> He often invited questions and confronted members in an effort to "open them up." However, he gave a great deal of support. . . . He offered friendship, as well as protection, to group members. [He] expressed considerable warmth, acceptance, genuineness, and caring for other human beings. (p. 29)

Fiedler's Contingency Approach

Group dynamicists agree that leadership is dualistic, for it involves both task and socioemotional components. Extending this assumption, however, Fiedler (1978) suggests that most leaders lean towards one of these two orientations: some people tend to be task-oriented, while others tend to be socioemotional. Furthermore, this tendency represents a relatively stable aspect of the individual; tantamount to a personality trait. To assess this tendency, he asks people to rate the person they least prefer to work with on a series of adjective pairs such as "pleasant–unpleasant" and "friendly–

unfriendly." People who give relatively low ratings to their least preferred coworker are assumed to be task-oriented in their overall approach to group interaction. In contrast, people who are positive, even when rating their least preferred coworker, tend to be socioemotional.

What type of leader promotes adjustment: The task leader or the socioemotional leader? According to Fiedler, it depends on the leader's *control* in the situation, with control meaning degree of stress or challenge put on the leader. Fiedler argues that control is lowest if the leader is low in status, the group is unstructured, and the leader–member relations are poor. For example, low control may occur in an unstructured training group with a novice leader—if the members don't support their leader, the leader isn't recognized as particularly expert in conducting groups, and the goals of the training require an unstructured format. However, as each one of these factors is improved—the leader has high status, the group is structured, or the leader–member relations become positive—then the group becomes more and more favorable for the leader to control. In the optimal group, leader–member relations are positive, the leader has more power over the members, and the task is clearly structured. Of these three factors, however, leader–member relations is by far the most important. If the leader has the loyalty and support of his or her group members, then structure and status are of little consequence.

Taking both the leader's style and situational control into account, Fiedler predicts that the task-oriented leader will perform most effectively in extremely favorable or unfavorable situations. To supply a clinical example, if a group is composed of volunteers who can leave any time they wish and is led by a novice who the group members distrust and dislike, then the leader will be most effective if he or she is task-oriented. In contrast, the socioemotional leader will be ineffective in this situation; Fiedler suggests that attempts to build positive interpersonal relations in irretrievable situations are inefficient. The socioemotional leader will, however, be most effective in moderately favorable or moderately unfavorable situations. These predictions are summarized in the following hypothesis

Hypothesis 9.7
In extremely favorable or unfavorable group settings, task-oriented leader-therapists will be more effective than socioemotional therapists. In more moderate settings, the reverse relationship will occur.

Fiedler's contingency theory has been supported in many different kinds of groups: navy teams, research groups, shop departments, supermarket personnel, engineering groups, hospitals, government panels, athletic teams, and many others (Fiedler, 1978). Furthermore, although this hypothesis has not been systematically tested in therapeutic groups, Hypothesis 9.7 is consistent with the findings reported by Lieberman, Yalom and Miles (1973) in their study of 17 encounter groups. In most cases, these groups were moderately favorable for their leaders. Most sessions were conducted by prominent therapists, who were well-practiced in their techniques. In consequence, and as these researchers note, the greater these therapists' emphasis on socioemotional concerns, the more effective the groups. If, however, the group leaders were very low in socioemotional support or high in task-orientation, their groups were less effective. The only exception to this general tendency, a Gestalt group characterized by strong emotional content, can also be explained in terms of Hypothesis 9.7. This group may have been one of the few offering a very unfavorable control situation. The leader was quite socioemotional, but he rejected the role of expert, provided little structure, and left group members feeling hostile, confused, and distrustful. Perhaps as a result, the group led to little positive change for members.

Fiedler's hypotheses yield clear recommendations for practitioners. In contrast to leadership theories that recommend increasing task and/or socioemotional behavior as needed in the particular situation, Fiedler believes that individuals strive to engineer the group setting to fit their particular orientation. Citing the failure of previous programs that have emphasized changing leaders to fit situations, Fiedler encourages leaders to become more aware of the nature of the group setting. If, after appraising the group, leaders find that their general leadership style will not be effective, then they should take steps to modify the setting. Thus, the task-oriented leader should make certain that he or she operates in highly favorable settings (or perhaps in unfavorable settings that other group therapists have abandoned). In contrast, the socioemotional leader will work most effectively in moderately favorable settings.

A Developmental Theory of Leadership

A number of theorists, including Fiedler, assume that leaders are either task-oriented or socioemotional. In contrast, some group dynamicists have recently suggested that leaders vary in degree of socioemotionality and degree of task-orientation. For example, Hersey and Blanchard (1976, 1977) assume that leaders can be classified as high or low on the two dimensions. Thus, rather than arguing for two basic types of leaders, Hersey and Blanchard recommend the following four basic leadership styles: a) high task, b) high relationship, c) high relationship/high task and d) low relationship/low task.

Hersey and Blanchard also disagree with Fiedler's suggestions for training group leaders. Rather than recommending a change in the situation to match the leader's personality style, they recommend adapting the leaders' style until it fits the situation. To a large extent, this "fit" between leader and situation is determined by the group members' needs. According to

Hersey and Blanchard, a newly formed group is relatively *immature*: it cannot set its goals, its members are uncertain about their abilities and responsibilities, and they cannot work together efficiently. In consequence, the leader must give the group considerable task-orientation. However, as the group matures and begins working adequately on the task, the leader can increase relationship behavior and adopt a high task/high socioemotional style. Still later in the group's development, the leader can ease off on both types of leadership, starting first with task emphasis. In moderately mature groups the high socioemotional/low task style is most effective, and in fully mature groups a low/low, laissez-faire style is appropriate. As Hypothesis 9.8 states, the most effective leaders are the most flexible leaders; they diagnose the maturity of the group, and then match their actions to fit the group's needs.

Hypothesis 9.8
The relative emphasis on task and socioemotional behavior should follow this developmental sequence: 1) high task/low socioemotional, 2) high task/high socioemotional, 3) low task/high socioemotional, and 4) low task/low socioemotional.

Conclusions

Fiedler's contingency model and the Hersey-Blanchard developmental model offer diverging, but not necessarily incompatible, recommendations for leaders. Fiedler's assumption that task and socioemotional leadership are mutually exclusive highlights the problems leaders face when they try to move the group towards goals *and* maintain positive relations within the group. Eventually—and as is so often the case in therapeutic groups—these somewhat contradictory role requirements may result in high levels of conflict between group members and the leader. To cope with these stresses, the group leader may wish to create a more therapeutic environment by modifying the group situation.

However, Hersey and Blanchard's view of leadership offers an alternative to changing the situation. Although high task/high socioemotional leaders are rare, they have been identified in naturally occuring groups. Furthermore, some researchers believe that the separation of the two dimensions of leadership only occurs during periods of group stress and conflict; when the group is in a high performance phase, then the two functions of the leadership can be combined (Verba, 1961; Wilson, 1970). Indeed, Lieberman and his colleagues found that the most effective leader was very socioemotional, but moderately high in task orientation (Lieberman et al., 1973).

Thus, Hypotheses 9.7 and 9.8 offer two suggestions concerning leadership in therapeutic groups. If group leaders are clearly task or socioemotional in their personal orientation, then they should use these strengths by making certain that their approach matches the needs of the group. In contrast, if leaders wish to adapt their own behavior to meet the needs of the group, they may wish to follow the sequence recommended by Hersey and Blanchard.

In closing, a limitation noted in chapter 7 should be reiterated. Questions about leadership in therapeutic groups have been virtually ignored by researchers, so the value of the hypotheses presented here is not unknown. Furthermore, these issues have been examined in studies conducted in non-therapeutic settings, but researchers have only begun to plumb the complexities of the leadership process. In consequence, the eight hypotheses offered in this chapter must be subjected to further study, in both therapeutic and nontherapeutic settings. Without further research, leadership will remain "one of the most observed and least understood phenomena on earth" (Burns, 1978, p. 2).

10
A Persisting Issue: Cultural Aspects of Clinical Research Design

The clientele served by American and other Western-trained psychotherapists is not homogeneous with respect to culture, let alone with respect to subcultural variables. Even influences such as age, occupation, and geographic location can be associated with important variations in manifestation of distress and with response to ameliorative efforts. Therefore, it behooves us to ask how dependable, generalizable, or widely applicable are any propositions about mental disorder and its treatment. Few psychotherapists work and practice in communities and with clientele that are so homogeneous as to obviate concerns about such variations.

This chapter takes up the problem of generalizing clinical research across cultures by discussing three points. First, a clinically relevant definition of culture is provided. Second, research examples show how culture influences behavior assessment and diagnosis of psychopathology, as well as treatment processes and outcome judgments. Third, we review methods devised by cross-cultural psychologists to test the generalizability of research findings across cultures and discuss the use of these strategies for evaluating the universality of behavior change hypotheses. Despite "good intentions" among clinical and community psychologists, there is a lack of research effort to understand how cultural characteristics interact with intervention strategies in diverse settings (Watts & Steele, 1984). The final section proposes means for overcoming this shortcoming.

A WORKING DEFINITION OF CULTURE FOR RESEARCH CLINICIANS

The clinical perspective requires a concept of culture that refers to the events which clinicians can track through their direct experience with individuals and small groups, including families, client social networks and therapy groups. What makes the most sense is a definition of culture that acknow-

269

ledges its ideational and interactional qualities. This definition locates culture within the realm of human cognition and ideas, as well as the arena of social exchange in which the meaning of ideas is negotiated.

The anthropologist Keesing (1981) identified four attributes that mark an ideational and interactional understanding of culture. When used in this way, culture refers to the "organized system of knowledge and belief whereby a people structure their experience and perceptions, formulate acts, and choose between alternatives." Cultures "comprise systems of shared ideas, systems of concepts and rules and meanings that underlie and are expressed in the ways that humans live" (Keesing, 1981, p. 68).

First, the focus of this definition of culture is not upon what humans do and make, but rather upon what they make of what they do. Of significance is the knowledge learned in face to face contact with other group members; this information provides decision-making standards with which to determine the nature of what is, what can be, how one feels about it, what to do about it, and how to go about doing it (Goodenough, 1961). In essence, culture is an implicit code humans learn, one that both structures our grasp of the social and man-made environment and regulates how we choose to act upon it.

Second, culture consists of *shared* ideas and meanings. Because it is manifest as shared knowledge in the minds of humans, culture cannot be reified as a thing or event that we can directly observe and measure. The comparison of a wink and an involuntary eye twitch clarifies this point. "As physical events they may be identical—measuring them will not distinguish the two. One is a signal in a code of meaning Americans share; the other is not. Only in a universe of shared meaning do physical sounds and events become intelligible and convey information" (Keesing, 1981 p. 70). Cultural codes are in some ways similar to language codes; they do not exist "above and beyond" the people of a community. Rather they are situated in the minds of individuals who draw upon their common knowledge to communicate intelligibly and draw correct inferences from one another's social responses.

Third, individual members of a society will possess partial versions of a cultural tradition. A "culture" can be thought of as a pool of knowledge that is *distributed* unevenly across the various subgroups of a society, according to such factors as the person's gender, age, class position, region, life experience and so forth. Although the vantage points from which persons view their common code are different, they share enough of a common world of meanings to be able to communicate, to live and work together in groups, and to anticipate and accurately interpret one another's behaviors.

This point applies to idiographic clinical research. An ethnographic description of a client's ethnic group may well inform the investigator of the core ideas and values shared within that subgroup. Yet it may not accurately portray the unique slice of cultural knowledge that this particular client has learned based upon his or her position within that society. The negotiation framework suggested in chapters 4 and 5 demonstrates how client and clinician can move from a general comprehension of each other's intentions to a mutual grasp of their respective language and illness codes.

Finally, culture arises from a social process of individual community members sharing meanings publicly in their daily lives. Culture cannot be viewed simply as a set of private conceptions of reality. Rather, common meanings are socially created, negotiated, and sustained, in a process that happens between people. Language is the primary vehicle for the social construction of shared meanings. It is through sets of agreed-upon symbols that culture is created, encodes the meaning of social experience, and is transmitted to others.

CULTURAL KNOWLEDGE INFLUENCING BASIC CLINICAL TASKS

The ideational definition of culture implies that the perceptions, judgments, communications, and planned actions of therapists and researchers originate from the peculiar world of symbolic meanings to which the clinician belongs. Clinical tasks such as defining a "case," identifying "symptoms," choosing a behavior change method, and interpreting outcome effects are culturally derived, both in the standards invoked for decision-making and in the decision-making process itself. Below are examples of how clinical events are grounded in cultural meanings. (See also Marsella & Pedersen, 1981, and Pedersen, Sartorious & Marsella, 1984.)

Cultural Conceptions of Psychopathology

Chapter 5 described the meaning-centered analysis of psychopathology. This orientation argues that it is only through the vehicle of cultural symbols (i.e., language and imagery) that disorder enters human consciousness and can become the object of human actions. Sufferers draw upon medical subcultures, both folk and professional, for the basic language categories they require to reason about illness causality and prognosis. Far from being reducible to the pathology of biochemistry or psychological functioning, the distress experience is encoded as *unit of meaning*. It is comprised of interlinked words, images, and emotions, as well as experiences of personal trauma, culture-specific life stressors, fears about the disorder and its economic impact, and therapy expectations.

White (White & Marsella, 1982; White & Kirkpatrick, 1985) observes from ethnographic evidence that cultural knowledge about mental disorder is tied to the premises that culture members share about the nature of self, personhood, and social behavior. People resort to implicit cultural models of the person (commonsense understandings about physiology, subjective experience, social relations, and the supernatural) in order to identify behavioral abnormalities and interpret such disturbances. For example, Protestant European traditions advance concepts of selfhood emphasizing sharp boundaries that differentiate the self as a distinct social actor in relation to others. American reasoning about social interaction is "egocentric"; the "self" is an autonomous social actor from which behavior eminates. Professional and layperson alike invoke notions of personality, trait, character, attitude, and so forth to describe social behavior. In contrast, the traditions of Asia and Oceania deemphasize the separation of individual and social surroundings. Because of these permeable boundaries, the "sociocentric" person is thought to behave according to "particular self-other *relations* among interdependent social actors" (White & Marsella, 1982, p. 21).

White describes how these contrasting views of selfhood provide their respective culture members with meaningful explanations of the causes of behavioral disturbance. Western explanations attribute the causes of mental disorder to disturbances within the individual's psyche. Non-Western explanatory models "decenter" the locus of causality from within the person, and give greater weight to interdependent somatic processes, supernatural forces, and social relations as causal agents (White & Marsella, 1982, p. 23). Asian and Pacific Island societies are more likely to interpret mental disorder as a consequence of moral transgression, retribution from displeased deities, or strained social relations within the family or village (see also White, 1982).

Cultural conceptions of personhood and social reality underlie psychiatric nosology as well as the actual expression of psychiatric distress in Western societies. Fabrega (1982) draws the connection between the "first rank" symptoms of schizophrenia and Western cultural conventions about the self. The "basic lesion" of schizophrenia is said to be present when the person experiences audible thoughts, insertion into one's mind of other's thoughts, external control of one's feelings and actions, and delusional moods and/or perceptions. It is no coincidence, Fabrega argues, that these "disease" indices are in opposition to our cultural perspective of self as a highly differentiated and autonomous entity which "looks out on an objective, impersonal, and naturalistic world" (Fabrega, 1982, p. 56).

These indices of pathology and normalcy are actually reflections of our assumptions about personal identity. The ethnocentric character of psychiatric classifications is apparent when one becomes familiar with ethnographic accounts of non-Western people who "believe in the constant interconnection between the natural and preternatural, between the 'bodily' and the 'mental' and between the various dimensions and contents of human awareness which are arbitrarily set apart in Western psychology" (Fabrega, 1982, p. 57; see Connor, 1982, for Balinese notions of the "unbounded" self).

Finally, a study by cross-cultural psychologist Marsella argues that cultural conceptions of self shape the actual manifestation of such emotional disturbances as depression. Marsella and his colleagues administered a 60-item symptom checklist composed of items reflecting cognitive, somatic, affective, and interpersonal complaints to college students identified as depressed based upon their scores on the Zung Depression Scale (Marsella, Kinzie & Gordon, 1973). Factor analyses indicated that Japanese-Americans within the sample maintain a strong interpersonal component in their manifestation of depression (e.g., dislike of being around others). In comparison, the Chinese-American students showed a strong somatic component (e.g., stomach pains, weakness), while the Caucasian-Americans expressed the traditional pattern of existential doubt and "psychologization" (e.g., despair, loss of purpose). Marsella's subsequent reviews of cross-national studies of depression reinforces the finding that the psychological aspects of depression (such as depressed mood, guilt, feelings of worthlessness) reported in Western societies are absent in non-Western settings (Marsella, 1980; see also Kleinman & Good, 1985).

Culture and Clinical Assessment

Community members' construction of social reality also encompasses professional judgments made in an effort to evaluate, classify and label mental disorder. Draguns (1973) warned comparative researchers seeking to measure rates of psychopathology that cultural variables penetrate their assessments through various means. First, the cultural biases of psychiatric observers themselves, including professional perspective, determine which symptoms are subsumed under a disorder and the threshold of recognition for its features. For instance, the USA–UK project (Cooper et al., 1972; Gurland & Zubin, 1982) indicated that British psychiatrists diagnose schizophrenia and organic brain syndrome more conservatively and with a narrower range of symptoms than their US counterparts, whereas the opposite is true for depression. Second, differences judged among patients may be associated with: a) differences in cultural values underlying policies and procedures of hospital settings in which patients reside and b) the systematic sociocultural differences governing which patients will end up residing within such institutions.

Draguns also draws attention to cultural influences in the construction and administration of symptom checklists and standardized psychiatric examination schedules. Obviously, the contents of these instruments are tied to symptom patterns emanating from Western psychology (e.g., Higginbotham, 1978; Higginbotham & Marsella, in press). Yet the fixed format method of response is also a deeply ingrained Western practice. Draguns points out that there are cultural variations in the readiness to share subjective experiences and to do so in a standardized, artificial and impersonal manner. While the ability to communicate one's subjective experience may be a universal human quality, the willingness to do so upon the demand of a researcher/stranger, using a fixed-format questionnaire, is culture specific (Draguns, 1982).

Cognitive anthropologists D'Andrade and Shweder have studied empirically the ways that cultural knowledge influences the response patterns given on self-report personality and psychiatric screening inventories (D'Andrade, 1974; Shweder, 1977; Shweder & D'Andrade, 1979, 1980). In order to test their "Systematic Distortion Hypothesis", D'Andrade and Shweder carried out a series of studies involving comparisons of three sets of responses: a) "traits" and "syndromes" derived from memory-based personality ratings by clinicians; b) judgments obtained by asking naive subjects to rate the *similarity of meanings* of the categories used by the clinical raters; and, in some instances, c) interbehavior correlations derived from immediate, on-line scoring by observers of behavioral conduct. Response patterns derived from the Brief Psychiatric Rating Scale, the MMPI, and other rating forms support the researchers' hypothesis "that under difficult memory conditions judges on personality inventories, rating forms, and questionnaire interviews infer what 'must' have happened from their general (i.e., cultural) beliefs about what the world is like and/or find it easier to retrive conceptually related memory items" (Shweder & D'Andrade, 1980, 37–38).

However, cultural beliefs about what the world is like in the area of personality tend to be inaccurate with respect to how behaviors actually covary. Judges confuse "what is like what" (i.e., similarity of meaning) with "what goes with what" (i.e., co-occurrence likelihood). When judges are asked to summarize their experiences about what objects or events frequently occur together, what they report back are cultural conceptions based upon *resemblance* and other conceptual relationships, rather than empirical generalizations. Cultural knowledge provides people with implicit rules specifying what to attend to, how to take cognitive "shortcuts," and how to make "reasonable" inferences in the face of complex, disparate and often contradictory information (White & Marsella, 1982). Thus we end up with such facile generalizations as "friendly people smile a lot," "gentle folks are not managerial", and "leaders have high self-esteem." Judges draw upon such cultural models of individual differences when completing memory-based psychiatric assessments and personality tests (Shweder & D'Andrade, 1980).

Finally, Lopez and Hernandez-Henderson (1986) found that the implicit personality theories guiding clinical assessment are difficult to bring to mind even when "culturally sensitive" clinicians are explicitly asked to do so. These researchers asked 118 therapists in Los Angeles (mostly Anglos) to describe a time when they took culture into account while evaluating and/or diagnosing a culturally diverse patient, and to explain how culture was taken into account. Surprisingly, 61 of the 96 clinicans offering case studies failed completely to reflect upon the way cultural considerations influenced their evaluations and/or diagnoses. Instead, their cases focused on how culture influences some aspect of *treatment*. This finding supports our contention that it is extremely difficult for diagnosticians to step outside of their implicit models of personality and reflect objectively upon how cultural conceptions determine their perceptions, interpretations, and causal reasoning about social behaviour. Apparently, diagnosticians cannot operate without the assumption that mental disorder is the same across cultures. Yet it is relatively easy for them to bring to mind examples of ways that treatments, such as "talk" therapy, are modified to be more effective in relation to client ethnicity, social class, gender, and other culturally derived individual differences.

Cultural Reasoning about Therapy and Outcome

The same causal reasoning that culture members use to interpret mental disorder is implicated in the social construction of means for restoring the desired state of selfhood or group integration and deciding when such means are successful. The symbolic relationships that link treatment forms with cultural premises about personhood do not only influence the clinical encounter. They color the entire sequence of personal and social events that make up the illness experience, including: a) how therapy is conceptualized; b) choice of therapy; c) communication and relationship formation among client and therapist; and d) the subsequent course and perceived outcome of therapy (White & Marsella, 1982). A concise overview of cultural knowledge in relation to behavior change methods helps to integrate the discussions of this topic scattered throughout this volume (see chapters 4–7).

First, folk theories or "explanatory models" of disorder enable persons to organize effective therapeutic strategies (see chapter 5). Treatment decisions — such as selecting from among available remedies and care-providers — follow logically from the illness label, perceived etiology, severity and chronicity, and from reasoning about what must change to permit mental health restoration. Different explanatory models for the disorder sanction their own unique patterns of choice among therapy alternatives and specify whether self-care, family-based, or institutional helping sources will be pursued, and the sequence of their use (e.g., Kleinman, 1978; Higginbotham, 1984).

For example, if a middle-class professional woman in New York City interpreted her recurring dysphoric moods as "depression," she might decide without asking family or friends to consult a "talk therapist" with whom she could delve into this "personal problem." Her choice of an "insight-oriented" therapist conforms with her cultural logic that self-reflection can alter undesirable personality traits. It follows from a Protestant American conception of the person as an independent individual, capable of self-transformation in relative isolation from one's social context (see Gaines, 1982). In contrast, Lock (1982) describes the Japanese notion of an "inner" self which is not easily verbalized, and of a "personality" which is largely unalterable. Hence, the Japanese have little regard for "talk therapy" as a means of behavior change.

Cultural knowledge also informs the client about the constellation of qualities that should be offered by the therapist to enhance a positive outcome. Culture-specific situation–outcome expectancies are especially active during the precontact and initial moments of treatment (chapter 6). These beliefs enable the client to judge the potency of the therapy events in terms of their potential for behavior gains and reduction of distress. Culture knowledge may be quite elaborate with respect to certain treatment domains and rather sparse with regards to others. Consequently, clients may articulate fine discriminations concerning the type of clinic facility, the kind of gender, ethnicity, and training of the therapist. Yet, the person may have no outcome expectancies at all with regard to how treatment goals are set, and whether or not the professional will request demanding homework exercises and lengthy reports of one's behavior outside the clinic. When healer and patient mutually endorse specific situation–outcome expectancies, the therapeutic alliance is enhanced and both are more likely to express hopefulness about behavior gains. The lack of overlap in the participants' culture-specific expectations requires patient socialization by the professional and/or negotiation to decide upon those expectancies to be incorporated into the treatment enterprise.

Third, the participants' evolving relationship is played out through culturally shared conventions of language use and interpersonal communication. Chapter 4 described how therapeutic reality is constructed from this collaborative effort to produce synchronous dialogue and, subsequently, a common conception of the presenting problem (chapter 5). Successful exchanges require a certain degree of shared meaning concerning linguistic and nonverbal symbols. Through such symbols, the partners, negotiate interpretations of disorder in a process of questioning and answering, and decoding and encoding each other's nonverbal information (White &

Marsella, 1982). Discourse synchrony is so critical because it sets up those significant moments of conversation when the therapist attempts to lead the client into a reinterpretation of the basic assumptions about his or her suffering. Effective reinterpretation involves relabeling the problem, setting reachable treatment goals, and choosing logical remedies, all of which transform the sufferer's sense of demoralization and help construct a new, more hopeful, illness reality (Good & Good, 1980, see Friedman et al., 1980).

Finally, cultural knowledge organizes perceptions of therapy outcome, both with respect to definitions of meaningful improvement and how such judgments are performed. Cultural criteria of the positive behavior that therapy should reestablish are extensions of the same theories of personhood used to interpret mental disorder. Cultural models of self and social reality shared by the family, client, and healer draw their attention to the problem —whether it be personality deficits, social skills, morality, somatic functioning, spiritual development, or other issues—and enable them to gauge the client's progress. Measurement of efficacy entails evaluating how closely the client is able to conform in mood, thought, and/or action with cultural standards (see Romanucci-Ross, Moerman & Tancredi, 1983).

Cultural logic is also involved in the choice of means by which efficacy evaluations are made. For example, behavior modification practitioners disvalue self-report methods as unreliable and invalid sources of knowledge regarding behavior change. Oriented toward scientific logic, rationality, and technicism, behavior modifiers select instruments and coding devices that measure rates of observable behavior which represent goal performance. As a system of psychotherapy, Woolfolk and Richardson (1984) argue that behavior therapy is deeply embedded in the ideology of modernity and the values of the modern technological society. The world view of modernity enshrines science as the ultimate source of knowledge and the model for all forms of intellectual activity (Winner, 1977).

In its dedication to rationality, behavior therapy ran counter to three dominant currents of Western thought: a) the Freudian notion that unconcious (irrational) forces motivate behavior; b) the idealized view of self as detached from social context; and c) the distaste for a view of people (even children and institutionalized mental patients) as pawns of environmental control. Consequently, behavior therapists in the early days were met with resistance from parents who interpreted reward contingencies as "bribes," and who failed to keep records of finely discriminated behaviors because it was the child's "attitude" that was bad.

CROSS-CULTURAL GENERALIZATION OF
BEHAVIOR CHANGE HYPOTHESES

Given the pervasive influence of cultural variables, how can the behavior change hypotheses advanced in this volume be tested for their generalizability across cultural boundaries? Indeed, can this set of hypotheses be extended at all beyond the historically and socioculturally situated individuals with whom they were conducted? (See Touhey, 1981.) In order to find out, clinical reseachers must turn to the methods devised by cross-cultural psychologists.

Why Perform Cross-Cultural Research?

The benefits of comparative research are clearly enumerated by cross-cultural psychologists (e.g., Berry, 1980; Brislin, 1983; Lonner, 1979). The foremost advantage is spelled out in the definition of the field: "Cross-cultural psychology includes studies of subjects from two or more cultures, using equivalent methods of measurement, to determine the limits within which general psychological theories hold, and the kinds of modifications of these theories that are needed to make them universal" (Triandis, Malpass and Davidson, 1971, p. 1). Berry (1980) adds that universal statements about causal relationships among variables—the generality of psychological laws—can be asserted *only* on the basis of comparative analysis. Cross-cultural methods sweep into the view of psychological science the total range, the broad variability, and all the possible differences expressed in human behavior. Uniformities and consistencies across humankind can be detected only when all variation is present. Thus, true universals (if any exist) become salient only when all variability is available for analysis (Berry, 1980).

Second, a comparative study of culture groups expands the range of independent variables and conceivable responses to dependent variables, and increases as well the range of values within these variables (see Brislin, 1976, 1980, 1983). Third, variables obtained in a second society may be completely unavailable within those few Western countries where the majority of behavior change research is conducted. Therapeutic alliance among traditional Balinese villagers, for instance, is not determined by conversational synchrony. Rather, it follows from the clients' perceptions of the spirit medium's potency to call down the spiritual presence of a deceased ancestor (Connor, Asch & Asch, 1986).

The fourth advantage is that variables which occur together in one culture, and are thus confounded in any statistical analysis, can be studied separately in other societies. It may be that the relationship between therapeutic alliance and conversation cooperation occurs because the English language masks and reduces social status differences among speakers (Hypothesis 4.1). Thus, achievement of conversational cooperation among American English speakers accurately reflects feelings of harmony. Cultures in which status differences are coded and exaggerated through language use may not show the same relationship between synchronous conversation and strength of interpersonal relationship.

Finally, the personal and professional experience of the comparative method offers the only possibility to culturally decenter psychological science and reduce the discipline's ethnocentrism. A culturally decentered discipline is more capable of developing services for widely differing populations, because it has a framework for assessing and responding sensitively to their special needs (Berry, 1980).

METHOD FOR TESTING CROSS-CULTURAL GENERALITY OF BEHAVIOR CHANGE HYPOTHESES

A behavior change hypothesis tested cross-culturally offers evidence that the theoretical concept a) possesses explanatory power to handle cross-cultural findings (i.e., appears universal); b) requires revisions and/or expansions to be generalized to diverse populations; or c) is monocultural and cannot profitably be applied to behavior change processes in other societies (see Brislin, 1976; Brislin, Lonner & Thorndike, 1973; Lonner & Berry, 1986; Triandis & Berry, 1980). However, to be tested cross-culturally, hypotheses must first clear a set of methodological hurdles. We complete this section with a brief description of these hurdles, because we believe that the research clinician familiar with cross-cultural methods can profitably apply such knowledge to the design of monocultural studies for which subsequent other cultural comparisons could be sought.

The first methodological hurdle involves establishing comparability or equivalence of the two behavior change phenomena being compared across cultures. Valid comparisons are obtained only after the researcher demonstrates that the two phenomena can be placed on a single dimension (i.e., *dimensional identity*) or reflect a common underlying function. For the comparison to be worthwhile, though, surface level variation or differences in the phenomena between cultures should also exist.

Berry (1980) suggests that the dimensional identity of cultural behavior can be demonstrated empirically by establishing equivalence in the data collected from cross-cultural samples. He describes three kinds of equivalence that provide evidence of dimensional identity. *Functional equivalence* exists between the behaviors compared when they have developed in response to a problem shared by the two cultural groups, even though the behavior in one society does not appear to be related to its counterpart in another society (Berry, 1969). *Conceptual equivalence* refers to the discovery of common meaning within the cognitive systems of the people being compared in relation to the research materials or behavior in question (Sears, 1961). Finally, *metric equivalence* is established when the psychometric properties of two (or more) sets of data from two (or more) cultural groups reveal essentially the same coherence or structure. The pattern of statistical relationships among independent and dependent variables, and among the dependent variables, should be similarly patterned for the two or more culture groups before comparisons are allowed (see Hui & Triandis, 1985).

The second methodological hurdle requires the researcher to fashion his or her descriptions of behavior change processes using concepts that are meaningful to members of a particular culture, while at the same time to validly compare such behavior in that culture with behavior in another or all other cultures (Berry, 1980). Cross-cultural psychologists apply the terms *"emic"* and *"etic"* to these two goals of comparative research. An emic approach uses culture-specific descriptions of behavior change: Indigenous concepts alone portray what the people themselves value as important as well as what is familiar to them (Brislin, 1980). Etic analyses draw upon supposedly culture-free or universal dimensions to describe behavior change. The etic approach uses *a priori* definitions and conceptual models of cultural content, imposed by the outside researcher, in order to compare human behavior change among various societies (Sturtevant, 1964). Etic analyses must be used cautiously, however, least the researcher incorrectly assume the presence of universal dimensions in a system (i.e., *imposed* or *pseudo etics*; see Berry, 1969, 1980; Brislin, 1976; Davidson et al., 1976; Malpass, 1977; Triandis et al, 1972). This is apparent when Euro-American emics, measured through personality and intelligence tests, are imposed on behavioral phenomena which occur in other cultural systems (Cole & Scribner, 1974).

The threats to valid measurement that are unique to cross-cultural investigations constitute the third methodological hurdle. Behavior change researchers may not actually be measuring what they think they are measuring in another culture, because of observer bias (Campbell, 1970) due to their own cultural ideologies. When the research designer and subject speak different languages, the investigator cannot be certain that the task that is communicated is the task that is responded to. Campbell (1964) asks: "On what grounds does an experimenter decide whether an unexpected recording (response) is a new phenomenon or an instrumentation error?" (p. 317). Similarly, Triandis argues that psychological methods change their meaning across cultures.

What *appears* to be a cultural difference may be a result of different response sets, differences in familiarity with stimuli, differences in the definition of the testing situation, differential reactions to the experimenter, differences in the motivation to respond to that test, differences in the social desirability of the response, problems of interpretation, [and] differential reactions to anonymity (Triandis, 1980, p. 8).

Observation of any *one* difference through a single measurement is methodologically unsound and uninterpretable (Campbell, 1970; Triandis, 1980). A real difference is more likely if a multimethod measurement (i.e., separate instruments and vantage points, different levels of behavior of a behavior change process leads to consistencies in results (Campbell & Fiske, 1959).

The final hurdle involves selecting appropriate samples. When the researcher's purpose in sampling is to assert the universal generalizability of a hypothesis, sampling must take into account both *range* and *representativeness* of the cultures, individuals, stimuli and behaviors (Berry, 1980). Theoretically, generalizations characterizing the whole world can be established through studies that include culture groups in the sample which represent all known culture groups. The cultures selected should be independent of each other so that each cultural variable is represented in the sample only in its correct proportion to its natural occurrence (see Naroll, Michik & Naroll, 1980). Similarly, the individuals sampled should be representative of their communities and culture as a whole. Since some societies are extremely homogenous and others rather diverse, the standard ratio of sample to population should be modified accordingly.

Evaluation of behavior change frequently involves samples of behavior taken under conditions of standardized testing. The "culture fairness" of tests is essentially a question about the representativeness of the stimuli presented to clients. The test items, interview questions, and performance tasks sampled should represent concepts and demands which already exist in the individual's milieu. Additionally, the responses sampled should fairly represent the population of responses and behaviors that can be detected through emic analyses in a given cultural system. Representativeness means that the cross-cultural researcher is not asking "how well can they do our tricks," but rather, "how well can we measure how *they* do *their* tricks?" (Wober, 1969). Berry (1980) concludes that "only by observing what is actually present can psychologists obtain data which are representative of the behavior and skills of people in a particular culture; continually attempting to sample what is not there is of no value to either party" (p. 17).

References

Abelson, R.P. (1982). Three modes of attitude-behavior consistency. In M.P. Zanna, E.T. Higgins, & C.P. Herman (Eds.), *Consistency in social behavior* (Vol. 2). Hillsdale, NJ: Erlbaum.

Abramowitz, C., & Dokecki, P. (1977). The politics of clinical judgement: Early empirical returns. *Psychological Bulletin, 84,* 460–476.

Abramowitz, S.I. (1983). The social face of clinical psychology. *Journal of Social and Clinical Psychology, 1,* 90–92.

Abramowitz, S.I., & Jackson, C. (1974). Comparative effectiveness of there-and-then versus here-and-now therapist interpretations in group-psychotherapy. *Journal of Counseling Psychology, 21,* 288–293.

Acosta, F.X., Yamamoto, J., & Evans, L.A. (1982). *Effective psychotherapy for low income and minority patients.* New York: Plenum Press, 1982.

Adams, J.S. (1963). Toward an understanding of inequity. *Journal of Abnormal and Social Psychology, 67,* 422–436.

Adams, J.S. (1965). Inequity in social exchange. In L. Berkowitz (Ed.), *Advances in experimental social psychology* (Vol. 2). New York: Academic Press.

Adams, J.S., & Freedman, S. (1976). Equity theory revisited: Comments and annotated bibliography. In L. Berkowitz & E. Walster (Eds.), *Advances in experimental social psychology* (Vol. 9). New York: Academic Press.

Aiken, L.S. (1986). Retrospective self-reports by clients differ from original reports: Implications for the evaluation of drug treatment programs. *International Journal of Addictions, 21,* 767–788.

Aiken, L.S., Sechrest, L.B., West, S.G., & Reno, R. (1987, August). *Survey of PhD granting psychology departments: The current status of graduate training in methodology, statistics, and measurement.* Paper presented at the 95th annual convention of the American Psychological Association, New York.

Aiken, L.S., & West, S.G. (1986). *Internal invalidity of true experiments due to pretest bias.* Unpublished manuscript, Arizona State University, Tempe, AZ.

Ajzen, I., & Fishbein, M. (1977). Attitude-behavior relations: A theoretical analysis and review of empirical research. *Psychological Bulletin, 84,* 888–918.

Algina, J., & Swaminathan, H. (1979). Alternatives to Simonton's analysis of the interrupted and multiple group time series designs. *Psychological Bulletin, 86,* 919–926.

Allan, G.A. (1979). *A sociology of friendship and kinship.* London: George Allen and Unwen.

Alloy, L.B., & Abramson, L.Y. (1979). Judgment of contingency in depressed and nondepressed students: Sadder but wiser? *Journal of Experimental Psychology: General, 108,* 441–485.

Allport, F.H. (1924). *Social psychology.* New York: Houghton Mifflin.

Alwin, D.F. (1974). Approaches to the interpretation of relationships in the multi-trait, multi-method matrix. In H.L. Costner (Ed.), *Sociological Methodology, 1973–1974.* San Francisco: Jossey-Bass.

Anderson, A.B. (1975). Combined effects of interpersonal attraction and goal-path clarity on the cohesiveness of task oriented groups. *Journal of Personality and Social Psychology, 31*, 68–75.

Anderson, J.D. (1985). Working with groups: Little known facts that challenge well-known myths. *Small Group Behavior, 16*, 267–283.

Anderson, J.R. (1981). Concepts, propositions, and schemata: What are the cognitive units? In H.E. Howe (Ed.), *Nebraska Symposium on Motivation, 1980*. Lincoln, NE: University of Nebraska Press.

Anderson, L.F., & Robertson, S.E. (1985). Group facilitation: Functions and skills. *Small Group Behavior, 16*, 139–156.

Anderson, L.R., & Ager, J.W. (1978). Analysis of variance in small group research. *Personality and Social Psychology Bulletin, 4*, 341–345.

Apfelbaum, B. (1958). *Dimensions of transference in psychotherapy*. Berkeley: University of California Press.

Arbes, B.H., & Hubbell, R.N. (1973). Packaged impact: A structured communication skills workshop. *Journal of Counseling Psychology, 20*, 332–337.

Argyle, M., & Cook, M. (1976). *Gaze and mutual gaze*. London: Cambridge University Press.

Argyle, M., & Dean, J. (1965). Eye-contact, distance, and affiliation. *Sociometry, 28*, 289–304.

Aronson, E., Brewer, M.B., & Carlsmith, J.M. (1985). Experimentation in social psychology. In G. Lindzey & E. Aronson (Eds.), *Handbook of social psychology* (3rd Edn.). New York: Random House.

Au, K.H. (1980). Participation structures in a reading lesson with Hawaiian children: Analysis of a culturally appropriate instructional event. *Anthropology and Education Quarterly, 11*, 91–115.

Au, K.H., & Jordan, C. (1981). Teaching reading to Hawaiian children: Finding a culturally appropriate solution. In H.T. Trueba, G.P. Guthrie, & K.H. Au (Eds.), *Culture and the bilingual classroom: Studies in classroom ethnography*. Rowley, MA: Newbury House.

Au, K.H., & Mason, J.M. (1983). Cultural congruence in classroom participation structures: Achieving a balance of rights. *Discourse Processes, 6*(2), 145–167.

Bach, G.R. (1954). *Intensive group psychotherapy*. New York: Ronald Press.

Back, K.W. (1951). Influence through social communication. *Journal of Abnormal and Social Psychology, 46*, 9–23.

Back, K.W. (1973). *Beyond words: The story of sensitivity training and the encounter movement*. Baltimore, MD: Penguin Books.

Backman, D., Secord, P., & Pierce, J. (1963). Resistance to change in the self-concept as a function of consensus among significant others. *Sociometry, 26*, 102–111.

Baer, D., Wolf, M.M., & Risley, T.R. (1968). Some current dimensions of applied behavioral analysis. *Journal of Applied Behavior Analysis, 1*, 91–97.

Baker, L.H., & Singer, V. (1980, May). *Social support and posthospital adjustment: Implications for theory and research*. Paper presented at the Western Psychological Meeting, Honolulu, HI.

Bales, R.F. (1958). Task roles and social roles in problem-solving groups. In E.E. Maccoby, T.M. Newcomb, & E.L. Hartley (Eds.), *Readings in social psychology*. New York: Holt, Rinehart, & Winston.

Bales, R.F. (1965). The equilibrium problem in small groups. In A.P. Hare, E.F. Borgatta, & R.F. Bales (Eds.), *Small groups: Studies in social interaction*. New York: Knopf.

Bandura, A. (1977a). Self-efficacy: Toward a unifying theory of behavior change. *Psychological Review, 84*, 191–215.

Bandura, A. (1977b). *Social learning theory*. Englewood Cliffs, NJ: Prentice Hall.

Bandura, A. (1982). Self-efficacy mechanism in human agency. *American Psychologist, 37*, 122–147.

Bangert-Drowns, R.L. (1986). Review of developments in meta-analytic method. *Psychological Bulletin, 99*, 388–399.

Barker, R.G. (1968). *Ecological psychology: Concepts and methods for studying the environment of human behavior*. Stanford: Stanford University Press.

Barlow, D.H., & Hersen, M. (1984). *Single case experimental designs—Strategies for studying behavior change* (2nd Edn.). New York: Pergamon.

Barnow, B.S. (1973). The effects of Head Start and socioeconomic status on cognitive development of disadvantaged students (Doctoral dissertation, University of Wisconsin). *Dissertation Abstracts International*, 1974, *34*, 6191A.

Barnow, L.S., Cain, G.G., & Goldberger, A.S. (1980). Issues in the analysis of selection bias. In E.S. Stromsdorfer & G. Farkas (Eds.), *Evaluation studies review annual* (Vol. 5). Beverly Hills: Sage.

Baron, R.M., & Kenny, D.A. (1986). The moderator-mediator variable distinction in social psychological research: Conceptual, strategic and statistical considerations. *Journal of Personality and Social Psychology, 51*, 1173–1182.

Barrera, M. (1980). A method for the assessment of social support networks in community survey research. *Connections, 3*, 8–13.

Barrera, M. (1981). Social support in the adjustment of pregnant adolescents: Assessment issues. In B.H. Gottlieb (Ed.), *Social networks and social support*. Beverly Hills, CA: Sage.

Barrera, M., & Ainlay, S.L. (1983). The structure of social support: A conceptual and empirical analysis. *Journal of Community Psychology, 11*, 133–143.

Baskin, D., Bluestone, H., & Nelson, M. (1981). Ethnicity and psychiatric diagnosis. *Journal of Clinical Psychology, 37*, 529–537.

Bass, B.M. (1981). *Stogdill's handbook of leadership*. New York: Free Press.

Bazerman, M.H. (1983). Negotiator judgment: A critical look at the rationality assumption. *American Behavioral Scientist, 27*, 211–228.

Beck, A.P., & Peters, L. (1981). The research evidence for distributed leadership in therapy groups. *International Journal of Group Psychotherapy, 31*, 43–71.

Beck, A.T. (1967). *Depression: Clinical, experimental, and theoretical aspects*. New York: Harper and Row.

Becker, M.H. & Maiman, L.A. (1975). Sociobehavioral determinants of compliance with health and medical care recommendations. *Medical Care, 13*, 10–24.

Bednar, R.L. (1970). Persuasibility and the power of belief. *Personnel and Guidance Journal, 48*, 647–652.

Bednar, R.L., & Kaul, T. (1978). Experiential group research: Current perspectives. In S. Garfield & A. Bergin (Eds.), *Handbook of psychotherapy and behavior change*. New York: Wiley.

Bednar, R.L., & Kaul, T. (1979). Experiential group research: What never happened. *Journal of Applied Behavioral Science, 15*, 311–319.

Bednar, R.L., & Langebahn, D.M. (1979). Structure and ambiguity: Conceptual and applied misconceptions. *Journal of Specialists in Group Work, 9*, 170–176.

Bednar, R.L., & Parker, C.A. (1969). Client susceptibility to persuasion and counseling outcome. *Journal of Counseling Psychology, 16*, 415–420.

Begley, C.E., & Lieberman, L.R. (1970). Patient expectancies of therapists' techniques. *Journal of Clinical Psychology, 26*, 113–116.

Bell, M.A. (1982). Phases in group problem-solving. *Small Group Behavior, 13*, 475–495.

Bellack, A.S., & Hersen, M. (1979). *Research and practice in social skills training.* New York: Plenum.

Benne, K.D., & Sheats, P. (1948). Functional roles of group members. *Journal of Social Issues, 4,* 41–49.

Bennis, W.G., & Shepard, H.A. (1956). A theory of group development. *Human Relations, 9,* 415–437.

Bentler, P.M. (1980). Multivariate analysis with latent variables: Causal modeling. *Annual Review of Psychology, 31,* 419–456.

Bentler, P.M. (1983). Some contributions to efficient statistics in structural models: Specification and estimation of moment structures. *Psychometrica, 48,* 493–517.

Bentler, P.M. (1985). *Theory and implementation of EQS: A structural equations program.* Manual for program version 2.0. Los Angeles: BMDP Statistical Software, Inc.

Bentler, P.M., & Woodward, J.A. (1978). A Head Start re-evaluation: Positive effects are not yet demonstrable. *Evaluation Quarterly, 2,* 493–510.

Berger, J., Cohen, B.P., & Zelditch, M., Jr. (1972). Status characteristics and social interaction. *American Sociological Review, 37,* 241–255.

Bergin, A.E. (1962). The effect of dissonant persuasive communications upon changes in a self-referring attitude. *Journal of Personality, 30,* 423–438.

Berk, R.A. (1983). An introduction to sample selection bias in sociological data. *American Sociological Review, 48,* 386–398.

Berk, R.A., & Rauma, D. (1983). Capitalizing on nonrandom assignment to treatments: A regression–discontinuity evaluation of a crime-control program. *Journal of the American Statistical Association: Applications Section, 78*(381), 21–27.

Berkman, L.F. (1985). The relationship of social networks and social support to morbidity and mortality. In S. Cohen & S.L. Syme (Eds.), *Social support and health.* New York: Academic Press.

Berkman, L.F. (1986). Social networks, support, and health: Taking the next step forward. *American Journal of Epidemiology, 123,* 559–562.

Berman, J.S. (1979, September). *Therapeutic expectancies and treatment outcome: A quantitative review.* Paper presented at the 87th annual convention of the American Psychological Association, New York.

Berman, J.S. (in press). *Social bases of psychotherapy: Expectancy, attraction and the outcome of treatment.* New York: Oxford University Press.

Berman, J.S., & Wenzlaff, R.M. (1983, August). *The impact of therapist expectancies on the outcome of psychotherapy.* Paper presented at the 91st annual convention of the American Psychological Association, Anaheim, CA.

Bernal, M.E., Klinnert, M.D., & Schultz, L.A. (1980). Outcome evaluation of behavior parent training and client-centered parent counseling for children with conduct problems. *Journal of Applied Behavior Analysis, 13,* 677–691.

Bernard, H.R., Killworth, P.D., & Sailer (1979/1980). Informant accuracy in social network data IV: A comparison of clique-level structure in behavioral and cognitive network data. *Social Networks, 2,* 191–218.

Bernstein, B. (1964). Social class, speech systems and psychotherapy. In F. Riessman, J. Cohen, & A. Pearl (Eds.), *Mental health of the poor.* New York: Free Press.

Bernstein, B.L., & Lecomte, C. (1982). Therapist expectancies: Gender, profession, and level of training considerations. *Journal of Clinical Psychology, 38,* 744–754.

Berren, M.R., & Gillis, J.S. (1976). Use of failure models: Application of social comparison theory to changing maladaptive attitudes. *Journal of Contemporary Psychotherapy, 8,* 47–51.

Berry, J.W. (1969). On cross-cultural comparability. *International Journal of Psychology, 4*, 119–128.

Berry, J.W. (1980). Introduction to methodology. In H.C. Triandis & J.W. Berry (Eds.), *Handbook of cross-cultural psychology* (Vol. 2). Boston: Allyn and Bacon.

Berscheid, E., & Walster, E. (1978). *Interpersonal attraction* (2nd edn.). Reading, MA: Addison-Wesley.

Berzins, J.I. (1977). Therapist–patient matching. In A.S. Gurin & A.M. Razin (Eds.), *Effective psychotherapy*. New York: Pergamon.

Berzins, J.I., Friedman, W.H., & Seidman, E. (1969). Relationship of the A–B variable to patient symptomatology and psychotherapy expectancies. *Journal of Abnormal Psychology, 74*, 119–125.

Beutler, L.E., Jobe, A.M., & Elkins, D. (1974). Outcomes in group psychotherapy: Using persuasion theory to increase treatment efficiency. *Journal of Consulting Psychology, 42*, 547–553.

Bion, W.R. (1961). *Experience in groups*. New York: Basic Books.

Billings, A., & Moos, R.H. (1982). Work stress and the stress-buffering roles of work and family resources. *Journal of Occupational Behavior, 3*, 215–232.

Birdwhistell, R.L. (1970). *Kinesics and context*. Philadelphia: University of Pennsylvania Press.

Birkel, R.C., & Reppucci, N.D. (1983). Social networks, information-seeking, and the utilization of services. *American Journal of Community Psychology, 11*, 185–205.

Blau, P.M. (1977). *Inequality and heterogeneity*. New York: Free Press.

Bloch, S., Bond, G., Qualls, B., Yalom, I., & Zimmerman, E. (1976). Patients' expectations of therapeutic improvement and their outcomes. *American Journal of Psychiatry, 133*, 1457–1459.

Blumhagen, D. (1980). Hyper-tension: A folk illness with a medical name. *Culture, Medicine and Psychiatry, 4*, 197–228.

Boissevain, J. (1979). Network analysis: A reappraisal. *Current Anthropology, 20*, 392–394.

Bolles, R.C. (1972). Reinforcement, expectancy and learning. *Psychological Review, 79*, 394–409.

Bootzin, R.R., & Lick, J.R. (1979). Expectancies in therapy research: Interpretive artifact or mediating mechanism. *Journal of Consulting and Clinical Psychology, 47*, 852–855.

Borghi, J. (1968). Premature termination of psychotherapy and patient–therapist expectations. *American Journal of Psychotherapy, 22*, 460–473.

Borin, J. (1974). Patients' pretherapy expectations and their relation to early experience on treatment by beginning psychotherapists. *Dissertation Abstracts International, 31*, 1036B–1037B. (University Microfilms No. 58-09852)

Borkovec, T.D., & Nau, S.D. (1972). Credibility of analogue therapy rationales. *Journal of Behavior Therapy and Experimental Psychiatry, 3*, 257–260.

Boruch, R.F. (1975). On common contentions about randomized field experiments. In R.F. Boruch & H.W. Riecken (Eds.), *Experimental tests of public policy*. Boulder, CO: Westview Press.

Boruch, R.F., McSweeny, A.J., & Soderstrom, E.J. (1978). Randomized field experiments for program planning, development, and evaluation. *Evaluation Quarterly, 2*, 655–695.

Boucher, J.D. (1974). Display rules and facial affective behavior: A theoretical discussion and suggestions for research. *Topics in Culture Learning, 4*, 87–102.

Boulware, D.W., & Holmes, D.S. (1970). Preferences for therapists and related expectancies. *Journal of Consulting and Clinical Psychology, 35*, 269–277.

Bowden, A.O. (1926). A study of the personality of leaders in the United States. *Journal of Abnormal and Social Psychology, 21*, 149–160.

Bowers, D.G., & Seashore, S.E. (1966). Predicting organizational effectiveness with a four-factor theory of leadership. *Administrative Science Quarterly, 11*, 238–263.

Bowers, W.A., Gauron, E.F., & Mines, R.A. (1984). Training of group psychotherapists. *Small Group Behavior, 15*, 125–137.

Bray, R.M., Johnson, D., & Chilstrom, J.T., Jr. (1982). Social influence by group members with minority opinions: A comparison of Hollander and Moscovici. *Journal of Personality and Social Psychology, 43*, 78–88.

Brehm, S.S. (1976). *The application of social psychology to clinical practice.* New York: Halstead Press.

Brehm, S.S. (1980). Social psychology and clinical practice. In R.F. Kidd & M.J. Saks (Eds.), *Advances in applied social psychology* (Vol. 1). Hillsdale, NJ: Erlbaum.

Brehm, S.S., & Brehm, J.W. (1981). *Psychological reactance: A theory of freedom and control.* New York: Academic Press.

Brisbin, R.L. (1981). Relation of therapy outcome to congruence of expected and actual therapy procedures. *Dissertation Abstracts International, 41*, 3171-B. (University Microfilms No. 8102357)

Brislin, R.W. (1976). Comparative research methodology: Cross-cultural studies. *International Journal of Psychology, 11*, 215–229.

Brislin, R.W. (1980). Cross-cultural research methods: Strategies, problems, applications. In I. Altman, A. Rapoport, & J. Wohlwill (Eds.), *Human behavior and environment* (Vol. 4). New York: Plenum.

Brislin, R.W. (1983). Cross-cultural research in psychology. *Annual Review of Psychology, 34*, 363–400.

Brislin, R.W., Lonnor, W.J., & Thorndike, R. (1973). *Cross-cultural research methods.* New York: Wiley.

Bromet, E., & Moos, R. (1977). Environmental resources and the posttreatment functioning of alcoholic patients. *Journal of Health and Social Behavior, 18*, 326–338.

Broverman, I., Vogel, S.R., Broverman, M., Clarkson, F.E., & Rosenkrantz, P.S. (1972). Sex-role stereotypes: A current appraisal. *Journal of Social Issues, 28*, 59–78.

Brown, S.M. (1977). Male versus female leaders: A comparison of empirical studies. *Sex Roles, 5*, 595–611.

Brown, G.W., Birley, J.L.T., & Wing, J.K. (1972). Influence of family life on the course of schizophrenic disorders: A replication. *British Journal of Psychiatry, 121*, 241–258.

Brown, G.W., Davidson, S., Harris, T., MacClean, U., Pollack, S., & Prudo, S. (1977). Psychiatric disorder in London and North Uist. *Social Science and Medicine, 11*, 367.

Brownell, K.D., Marlatt, G.A., Lichtenstein, E., & Wilson, T. (1986). Understanding and preventing relapse. *American Psychologist, 41*, 765–782.

Brucato, L.L. (1980). Therapist and client expectancies: Educated guesses or causal agents. *Dissertation Abstracts International, 41*, 1493B–1494B. (University Microfilms No. 8021209)

Brudner, L.A. (1977). Language creativity and the psychotherapy relationship. In B. Blount & M. Sanches (Eds.), *Sociocultural dimensions of language change.* New York: Academic Press.

Bryk, A.S., Strenio, J.F., & Weisberg, H.I. (1980). A method for estimating treatment effects when individuals are growing. *Journal of Educational Statistics, 5*, 5–34.

Bryk, A.S., & Weisberg, H.I. (1977). Use of the nonequivalent control group design when subjects are growing. *Psychological Bulletin, 85,* 950–962.

Budman, S.H., Demby, A., Feldstein, M., & Gold, M. (1984). The effects of time-limited group psychotherapy: A controlled study. *International Journal of Group Psychotherapy, 34,* 587–603.

Burgess, R., & Nielsen, J. (1977). Distributive justice and the balance of power. In R. Hamblin & J. Kunkel (Eds.), *Behavioral theory in sociology.* New Brunswick, NJ: Transaction Books.

Burke, R.J., & Weir, T. (1977). Marital helping relationships: The moderators between stress and well-being. *Journal of Psychology, 95,* 121–130.

Burns, J.M. (1978). *Leadership.* New York: Harper & Row.

Burns, T. (1973). A structural theory of social exchange. *Acta Sociologica, 16,* 183–203.

Burrows, T. (1927). The group method of analysis. *Psychoanalytic Review, 19,* 268–280.

Burt, R.S., Lieban, K.L., & Fisher, M.G. (1980). Network power structure from informant perceptions. *Human Organization, 39,* 121–133.

Butler, R.R. (1977). Self-actualization: Myth or reality? *Group and Organizational Studies, 2,* 228–233.

Butler, T., & Fuhriman, A. (1983). Curative factors in group psychotherapy. *Small Group Behavior, 14,* 131–142.

Calder, B.J. (1976). An attribution theory of leadership. In B.M. Staw & G.R. Salancik (Eds.), *New directions in organizational behavior.* Chicago: St. Clair Press.

Cammalleri, J.A., Hendrick, H.W., Pittman, W.C., Jr., Blout, H.D., & Prather, D.C. (1973). Effects of different leadership styles on group accuracy. *Journal of Applied Psychology, 57,* 32–37.

Campbell, D.T. (1958). Common fate, similarity, and other indices of the status of aggregates of persons as social entities. *Behavioral Science, 3,* 14–25.

Campbell, D.T. (1963). Social attitudes and other acquired behavioral dispositions. In S. Koch (Ed.), *Psychology: A study of science* (Vol. 6). New York: McGraw-Hill.

Campbell, D.T. (1964). Distinguishing differences of perception from failures of communication in cross-cultural studies. In F.S.C. Northrop & H.H. Livingston (Eds.), *Cross-cultural understanding.* New York: Harper & Row.

Campbell, D.T. (1968). Prospective: Artifact and control. In R. Rosenthal & R. Rosnow (Eds.), *Artifact in behavioral research.* New York: Academic Press.

Campbell, D.T. (1970). Natural selection as an epistemological model. In R. Naroll & R. Cohen (Eds.), *A handbook of methods in cultural anthropology.* New York: Natural History Press.

Campbell, D.T., & Boruch, R.F. (1975). Making the case for randomized assignment to treatments by considering the alternatives: Six ways in which quasi-experimental evaluations tend to underestimate effects. In C.A. Bennett & A.A. Lumsdaine (Eds.), *Evaluation and experience: Some critical issues in assessing social programs.* New York: Academic Press.

Campbell, D.T., & Fiske, D.W. (1959). Convergent and discriminant validation by the multitrait-multimethod matrix. *Psychological Bulletin, 56,* 81–105.

Campbell, D.T., & Stanley, J.C. (1966). *Experimental and quasi-experimental designs for research.* Chicago: Rand-McNally.

Cappella, J.N. (1981). Mutual influence in expressive behavior: Adult–adult and infant–adult dyadic interaction. *Psychological Bulletin, 89,* 101–132.

Carkhuff, R.R. (1969a). *Helping and human relations: Selection and training* (Vol. 1). New York: Holt, Rinehart, & Winston.

Carkhuff, R.R. (1969b). *Helping and human relations: Research and practice* (Vol. 2). New York: Holt, Rinehart, & Winston.

Carlyle, T. (1841). *On heroes, hero-worship, and the heroic.* London: Fraser.

Carter, J.H. (1952). Military leadership. *Military Review, 32,* 14–18.

Cartwright, D. (1951). Achieving change in people: Some applications of group dynamics theory. *Human Relations, 4,* 381–392.

Cartwright, D. (1968). The nature of group cohesiveness. In D. Cartwright & A. Zander (Eds.), *Group dynamics: Research and theory* (3rd edn.). New York: Harper & Row.

Cartwright, D., & Zander, A. (Eds.) (1968). *Group dynamics: Research and theory* (3rd edn.). New York: Harper & Row.

Carver, C.S., Antoni, M., & Scheier, M.F. (in press). Self-consciousness and self-assessment. *Journal of Personality and Social Psychology.*

Carver, C.S., & Scheier, M.F. (1978). Self-focusing effects of dispositional self-consciousness, mirror presence, and audience presence. *Journal of Personality and Social Psychology, 36,* 324–332.

Carver, C.S., & Scheier, M.F. (1981). *Attention and self-regulation: A control-theory approach to human behavior.* New York: Springer-Verlag.

Caspo, M. (1979). The effects of self-recording and social reinforcement components in parent–training programs. *Journal of Experimental Child Psychology, 27,* 479–488.

Chadwick-Jones, J. (1976). *Social exchange theory: Its structure and influence in social psychology.* New York: Academic Press.

Chaikin, A., & Derlega, V. (1976). Self-disclosure. In J. Thibaut, J. Spence, & R. Carson (Eds.), *Contemporary topics in social psychology.* Morristown, NJ: General Learning Press.

Chance, E. (1959). *Families in treatment.* New York: Basic Books.

Charny, E.J. (1966). Psychosomatic manifestations of rapport in psychotherapy. *Psychosomatic Medicine, 28,* 305–315.

Chesler, P. (1971). Patient and patriarch: Women in the psychotherapeutic relationship. In V. Gornick & B. Moran (Eds.), *Woman in sexist society: Studies in power and powerlessness.* New York: Basic Books.

Cialdini, R.B. (1980). Full-cycle social psychology. In L. Bickman (Ed.), *Applied Social Psychology Annual* (Vol. 1), Beverly Hills: Sage.

Cicarelli, V.G., Cooper, W.H., & Granger, R.L. (1969). *The impact of Head Start: An evaluation of the effects of Head Start on children's cognitive and affective development.* Athens, OH: Ohio University and Westinghouse Learning Corporation.

Clark, K.B. (1971). The pathos of power. *American Psychologist, 26,* 1047–1057.

Clark, M.S., & Mills, J. (1979). Interpersonal attraction in exchange and communal relationships. *Journal of Personality and Social Psychology, 37,* 12–24.

Coch, L., & French, J.R.P., Jr. (1948). Overcoming resistance to change. *Human Relations, 1,* 512–532.

Coe, W.C. (1980). Expectations, hypnosis and suggestion in change. In F.H. Kanfer & A.P. Goldstein (Eds.), *Helping people change.* New York: Pergamon.

Cohen, C.I., & Sokolovsky, J. (1978). Schizophrenia and social networks: Expatients in the inner city. *Schizophrenia Bulletin, 4,* 546–560.

Cohen, J. (1962). The statistical power of abnormal-social psychological research: A review. *Journal of Abnormal and Social Psychology, 65,* 145–153.

Cohen, J. (1977). *Statistical power analysis for the behavioral sciences* (Rev. edn.). New York: Academic Press.

Cohen, J., & Cohen, P. (1983). *Applied multiple regression/correlation analysis for the behavioral sciences* (2nd edn.). Hillsdale, NJ: Erlbaum.

Cohen, L.H. (1980). Methodological prerequisites for psychotherapy outcome research: A survey of clinical psychologists. *Knowledge: Creation, Diffusion, Utilization, 2*, 263–272.

Cohen, L.H., Sargent, M.M., & Sechrest, L. (1986). Use of psychotherapy research by professional psychologists. *American Psychologist, 41*, 198–206.

Cohen, S., Mermelstein, R., Baer, J.S., Lichtenstein, E., Kingsolver, K. & Kamarek, T.W. (1987). Social support interventions for smoking cessation. In B.H. Gottlieb (Ed.), *Creating support groups: Formats, processes and effects.* New York: Sage.

Cohen, S., & McKay, G. (1984). Social support, stress, and the buffering hypothesis: An empirical review. In A. Baum, J.E. Singer, & S.E. Taylor (Eds.), *Handbook of psychology and health* (Vol. 4). Hillsdale, NJ: Erlbaum.

Cohen, S., Sherrod, D.R., & Clark, M.S. (1986). Social skills and the stress-protective role of social support. *Journal of Personality and Social Psychology, 50*, 963–973.

Cohen, S., & Wills, T.A. (1985). Stress, social support, and the buffering hypothesis. *Psychological Bulletin, 98*, 310–357.

Cole, M., & Scribner, S. (1974). *Culture and thought: A psychological introduction.* New York: John Wiley.

Condon, W.S., & Ogston, W.D. (1966). Sound film analysis of normal and pathological behavior patterns. *Journal of Nervous and Mental Disease, 143*, 338–347.

Condon, W.S., & Ogston, W.D. (1967). A segmentation of behavior. *Journal of Psychiatric Research, 5*, 221–235.

Cone, J.D., & Hayes, S.C. (1980). *Environmental problems/behavioral solutions.* San Francisco: Brooks/Cole.

Connor, L.H. (1982). The unbounded self: Balinese therapy in theory and practice. In A.J. Marsella & G.M. White (Eds.), *Cultural conceptions of mental health and therapy.* Boston: D. Reidel.

Connor, L.H., Asch, T., & Asch, P. (1986). *Jero Tapakan: Balinese healer.* New York: Cambridge University Press.

Connor, R.F. (1977). Selecting a control group: An analysis of the randomization process in twelve social reform programs. In T.D. Cook, M.L. Del Rosario, K.M. Hennigan, M.M. Mark, & W.M.K. Trochim (Eds.), *Evaluation studies review annual* (Vol. 3). Beverly Hills: Sage.

Conter, K.R., Hatch, C.L., & D'Augelli, A.R.D. (1980). Enhancing the skills of cub scout den leaders: Training, generalization, and maintenance. *Americal Journal of Community Psychology, 8*, 77–85.

Cook, T.D. (1983). Quasi-experimentation: Its ontology, epistemology, and methodology. In G. Morgan (Ed.), *Beyond method: Strategies for social research.* Beverly Hills: Sage.

Cook, T.D. (1985). Postpositivist critical multiplism. In R.L. Shotland & M.M. Mark (Eds.), *Social Science and social policy.* Beverly Hills: Sage.

Cook, T.D., & Campbell, D.T. (1976). The design and conduct of quasi-experiments and true experiments in field settings. In M. Dunnette (Ed.), *Handbook of industrial and organizational psychology.* Chicago: Rand-McNally.

Cook, T.D., & Campbell, D.T. (1979). *Quasi-experimentation: Design and analysis issues for field settings.* Boston: Houghton-Mifflin.

Cook, T.D., Dintzer, L., & Mark, M.M. (1980). The causal analysis of concomitant time series. In L. Bickman (Ed.), *Applied social psychology annual* (Vol. 1). Beverly Hills: Sage.

Cook, T.D., & Fitzgerald, N.M. (1985). *Evaluation design*. Unpublished manuscript, Northwestern University.

Cook, T.D., Leviton, L.C., & Shadish, W.J., Jr. (1985). Program evaluation. In G. Lindzey & E. Aronson (Eds.), *Handbook of social psychology* (3rd edn.). New York: Random House.

Cook, T.D., & Reichardt, C.S. (1976). Statistical analysis of data from the non-equivalent control group design: A guide to some current literature. *Evaluation, 3*, 136–138.

Cooley, C.H. (1902). *Human nature and the social order*. New York: Charles Scribner's Sons.

Cooper, J., & Axsom, D. (1982). Effort justification in psychotherapy. In G. Weary & H.L. Mirels (Eds.), *Integrations of social and clinical psychology*. New York: Oxford University Press.

Cooper, J.E., Kendell, R.E., Gurland, B.J., Sharpe, L., Copeland, J.R.M., & Simon, R. (1972). *Psychiatric diagnosis in New York and London*. Oxford, England: Oxford University Press.

Corazzini, J.G., Heppner, P.P., & Young, M.D. (1980). The effects of cognitive information on termination from group therapy. *Journal of College Student Personnel, 21*, 553–557.

Corrigan, J.B., Dell, D.M., Lewis, K.N., & Schmidt, L.D. (1980). Counseling as a social influence process: A review. *Journal of Counseling Psychology, 27*, 395–441.

Courtwright, J.A. (1978). A laboratory investigation of groupthink. *Communication Monographs, 43*, 229–246.

Crane, J.A. (1976). The power of social intervention experiments to discriminate differences between experimental and control groups. *Social Science Review, 50*, 224–242.

Critelli, J.W., & Neumann, K.F. (1984). The placebo: Conceptual analysis of a construct in transition. *American Psychologist, 39*, 32–39.

Cronbach, L.J. (1982). *Designing evaluations of educational and social programs*. San Francisco: Jossey-Bass.

Cronkite, R.C., & Moos, R.H. (1980). Determinants of the posttreatment functioning of alcoholic patients: A conceptual framework. *Journal of Consulting and Clinical Psychology, 48*, 305–316.

Cundick, B. (1976). The relation of student and counselor expectations to rated counseling satisfaction. *Dissertation Abstracts, 23*, 2983–2984. (University Microfilms No. 63–0044)

Curran, J.P. (1977). Skills training as an approach to the treatment of heterosexual-social anxiety: A review. *Psychological Bulletin, 84*, 140–157.

Cutrona, C.E. (1986). Objective determinants of perceived social support. *Journal of Personality and Social Psychology, 50*, 349–355.

D'Andrade, R.G. (1974). Memory and assessment of behavior. In T. Blalock (Ed.), *Measurement in the social sciences*. Chicago: Aldine and Atherton.

D'Augelli, A.R., & Ehrlich, R.P. (1980). Evaluation of community-based system for training natural helpers. *American Journal of Community Psychology, 10*, 447–456.

Daniel, C., & Wood, F.S. (1980). *Fitting equations to data* (2nd edn.). New York: Wiley.

Darley, J.G., Gross, N., & Martin, W.E. (1951). Studies of group behavior: The stability, change, and interrelations of psychometric and sociometric variables. *Journal of Abnormal and Social Psychology, 46*, 565–576.

Davidson, A., Jaccard, J., Triandis, H.C., Morales, M., & Diaz-Guerrero, R. (1976). Cross-cultural model testing: Toward a solution of the etic–emic dilemma. *International Journal of Psychology, 11*, 1–13.

Davidson, W.S., & Seidman, E. (1974). Behavior modification and juvenile delinquency: A review. *Psychological Bulletin, 81*, 998–1011.

Davidson, W.S., & Wolfred, T.R. (1977). Evaluation of a community-based behavior modification program for prevention of delinquency: The failure of success. *Community Mental Health Journal, 13*, 296–305.

Davis, D., & Jacobs, A. (1985). "Sandwiching" complex interpersonal feedback. *Small Group Behavior, 16*, 387–396.

Davis, M.S. (1968). Variations in patients' compliance with doctors' advice: An empirical analysis of patterns of communication. *American Journal of Public Health, 58*, 274–288.

Davison, G.C. (1969). Appraisal of behavior modification techniques with adults in institutional settings. In C.M. Franks (Ed.), *Behavior therapy: Appraisal and status.* New York: McGraw-Hill.

Day, R.C., & Hamblin, R.L. (1964). Some effects of close and punitive styles of supervision. *American Journal of Sociology, 69*, 499–510.

Deci, E. (1975). *Intrinsic motivation.* New York: Plenum.

DePaulo, B.M., & Rosenthal, R. (1979). Telling lies. *Journal of Personality and Social Psychology, 37*, 1713–1722.

DePaulo, B.M., Rosenthal, R., Eisenstat, R.A., Rogers, P.L., & Finkelstein, S. (1978). Decoding discrepant nonverbal cues. *Journal of Personality and Social Psychology, 36*, 313–323.

DePaulo, B.M., Zuckerman, M., & Rosenthal, R. (1980). Humans as lie detectors. *Journal of Communication, 30*, 129–139.

Derlega, V.J., & Chaikin, A.L. (1975). *Sharing intimacy.* Englewood Cliffs, NJ: Prentice-Hall.

Deutsch, M. (1975). Equity, equality, and need: What determines which value will be used as the basis of distributive justice? *Journal of Social Issues, 31*, 137–150.

Deutsch, M. (1968). Group behavior. In D.L. Sills (Ed.), *International Encyclopedia of the Social Sciences* (Vol. 6). New York: Macmillan.

Dies, R.R., & Sadowsky, R. (1974). A brief encounter group experience and social relations in a dormitory. *Journal of Counseling Psychology, 21*, 112–115.

DiMatteo, M.R. (1979). A social psychological analysis of physician–patient rapport: Toward a science of the art of medicine. *Journal of Social Issues, 35*, 12–32.

DiMatteo, M.R., & DiNicola, D.D. (1982). *Achieving patient compliance: The psychology of the medical practitioner's role.* New York: Pergamon.

DiMatteo, M.R., Taranta, A., Friedman, H.S., & Prince, L.M. (1980). Predicting patient satisfaction from physicians' nonverbal communication skills. *Medical Care, 18*, 376–387.

DiMatteo, M.R., Prince, L.M., & Taranta, A. (1979). Patients' perceptions of physicians' behavior: Determinants of patient commitment to the therapeutic relationship. *Journal of Community Health, 4*, 280–290.

Dirks, J.F., Horton, D.J., Kinsman, R.A., Fross, K.H., & Jones, N. (1978). Patient and physician characteristics influencing medical decisions in asthma. *The Journal of Asthma Research, 15*, 171–178.

Doleys, D.M., Dorster, J., & Cartelli, L.M. (1976). Parent training techniques: Effects of lecture role-playing followed by feedback and self-recording. *Journal of Behavior Therapy and Experimental Psychiatry, 7*, 359–362.

Donald, C.A., & Ware, J.E. (1982). *The quantification of social contacts and resources.* Santa Monica, CA: The Rand Corporation Publication Series.

Donnelly, P., Carron, A.V., & Chelladurai, P. (1978). *Group cohesion and sport.* Ottawa: CAHPER Sociology of Sport Monograph Series.

Doster, J.A., & Nesbitt, J.G. (1979). Psychotherapy and self-disclosure. In G.J. Chelune (Ed.), *Self-disclosure: Origins, patterns and implications of openness in interpersonal relationships.* San Francisco: Jossey-Bass.

Doster, J.A., Surratt, F., & Webster, R. (1975, March). *Interpersonal variables affecting communications of hospitalized psychiatric patients.* Paper presented at the Meeting of the Southeastern Psychological Association, Atlanta.

Drabman, R.S., Hammer, D., & Rosenbaum, M.S. (1979). Assessing generalization in behavior modification with children: The generation map. *Behavior Assessment, 1,* 203–219.

Draguns, J.G. (1973). Comparisons of psychopathology across cultures. *Journal of Cross-Cultural Psychology, 4,* 9–47.

Draguns, J.C. (1982). Methodology in cross-cultural psychopathology. In I. Al-Issa (Ed.), *Culture and psychopathology.* Baltimore, MD: University Park Press.

Drescher, S., Burlingame, G., & Fuhriman, A. (1985). Cohesion: An odyssey in empirical understanding. *Small Group Behavior, 16,* 3–30.

Duckro, P., Beal, D., & George, C. (1979). Research on the effects of disconfirmed client role expectations in psychotherapy: A critical review. *Psychological Bulletin, 86,* 260–275.

Duffin, J.T. (1981). Development of an inventory to measure role expectations about psychotherapy. *Dissertation Abstracts International, 41,* 3175B. (University Microfilm No. 8102364)

Dunbar, J. (1980). Adhering to medical advice: A review. *International Journal of Mental Health, 9,* 70–87.

Duval, S., & Wicklund, R.A. (1972). *A theory of objective self-awareness.* New York: Academic Press.

Dwyer, J.H. (1984). The excluded variable problem in nonrandomized control group designs. *Evaluation Review, 8,* 559–572.

Eagly, A.H. (1967). Involvement as a determinant of responses to favorable and unfavorable information. *Journal of Personality and Social Psychology, 7* (3, Whole No. 643).

Ekman, P. (1972). Universals and cultural differences in facial expressions of emotion. In J. Cole (Ed.), *Nebraska symposium on motivation, 1971.* Lincoln NE: University of Nebraska Press.

Ekman, P., & Friesen, W.V. (1968). Nonverbal behavior in psychotherapy research. In J. Shlien (Ed.), *Research in psychotherapy* (Vol. 3). Washington, D.C.: American Psychological Association.

Ekman, P., & Friesen, W.V. (1969). Nonverbal leakage and cues to deception. *Psychiatry, 32,* 88–106.

Ekman, P., & Friesen, W.V. (1972). Hand movements. *The Journal of Communication, 22,* 353–374.

Ekman, P., & Friesen, W.V. (1974). Detecting deception from the body or face. *Journal of Personality and Social Psychology, 29,* 288–298.

Elkin, I., Parloff, M.B., Hadley, S.W., & Autrey, J.H. (1985). The NIMH Treatment of Depression Collaborative Research Program: Background and research plan. *Archives of General Psychiatry, 42,* 305–316.

Ellis, R.J., & Holmes, J.G. (1982). Focus of attention and self-evaluation in social interaction. *Journal of Personality and Social Psychology, 43,* 67–77.

Ellsworth, P. (1977). From abstract ideas to concrete instances: Some guidelines for choosing natural research settings. *American Psychologist, 32,* 604–616.

Epperson, D.L., Bushway, D.J., & Warman, R.E. (1983). Client self-terminations after one counseling session: Effects of problem recognition, counselor gender, and counselor experience. *Journal of Counseling Psychology, 30,* 307–315.

Epstein, S. (1983). Aggregation and beyond: Some basic issues in the prediction of behavior. *Journal of Personality, 51,* 360–392.

Erickson, F., & Shultz, J. (1982). *The counselor as gatekeeper: Social interaction in interviews.* New York: Academic Press.

Erickson, G. (1975). The concept of personal network in clinical practice. *Family Process, 14*(4), 487–498.

Fabrega, H. (1982). Culture and psychiatric illness: Biomedical and ethnomedical aspects. In A.J. Marsella & G.M. White (Eds.), *Cultural conceptions of mental health and therapy.* Boston: D. Reidel.

Fandetti, D.V., & Gelfand, D.E. (1978). Attitudes toward symptoms and services in the ethnic family and neighborhood. *American Journal of Orthopsychiatry, 48,* 477–486.

Fanon, F. (1963). *The wretched of the earth.* New York: Grove.

Fairbanks, L.A., McGuire, M.T., & Harris, C.J. (1982). Nonverbal interaction of patients and therapists during psychiatric interviews. *Journal of Abnormal Psychology, 91,* 109–119.

Farina, A., Allen, J.G., & Saul, B.B. (1968). The role of the stigmatized person in affecting social relationships. *Journal of Personality, 36,* 169–182.

Feather, N.T. (1961). The relationship of persistence at a task to expectation of success and achievement related motives. *Journal of Abnormal and Social Psychology, 63,* 552–561.

Feather, N.T. (1963). The effect of differential failure on expectation of success, reported anxiety, and response uncertainty. *Journal of Personality, 31,* 289–312.

Feather, N.T. (1965). Performance at a difficult task in relation to initial expectation of success, test anxiety, and need achievement. *Journal of Personality, 33,* 200–217.

Feather, N.T. (1966). Effects of prior success and failure on expectations of success and subsequent performance. *Journal of Personality and Social Psychology, 3,* 287–298.

Feather, N.T. (Ed.) (1982). *Expectations and actions: Expectancy-value models in psychology.* Hillsdale, NJ: Erlbaum.

Feather, N.T., & Saville, M.R. (1967). Effects of amount of prior success and failure on success and subsequent task performance. *Journal of Personality and Social Psychology, 5,* 226–232.

Feldman, R.S., & Theiss, A.J. (1982). The teacher and student as Pygmalions: Joint effects of teacher and student expectations. *Journal of Educational Psychology, 74,* 217–223.

Felson, R.B. (1981). Ambiguity and bias in the self-concept. *Social Psychology Quarterly, 44,* 64–69.

Fenigstein, A. (1979). Self-consciousness, self-attention, and social interaction. *Journal of Personality and Social Psychology, 37,* 75–86.

Fenigstein, A., Scheier, M.F., & Buss, A.H. (1975). Public and private self-consciousness: Assessment and theory. *Journal of Consulting and Clinical Psychology, 43,* 522–527.

Ferber, H., Keeley, S.M., & Shemberg, K.M. (1974). Training parents in behavior modification: Outcome of and problems encountered in a program after Patterson's work. *Behavior Therapy, 5,* 415–419.

Festinger, L. (1950). Informal social communication. *Psychological Review, 57,* 271–282.

Fiedler, F.E. (1978). The contingency model and the dynamics of the leadership process. In L. Berkowitz (Ed.), *Advances in experimental social psychology* (Vol. 12). New York: Academic Press.

Fiedler, F.E. (1981). Leadership effectiveness. *American Behavioral Scientist, 24,* 619–632.

Finney, J.W., Moos, R.H., & Mewborn, C.R. (1980). Posttreatment experiences and treatment outcome of alcoholic parents six months and two years after hospitalization. *Journal of Consulting and Clinical Psychology, 48,* 17–29.

Fischer, C.S. (1981, August). *What do we mean by "friend"? An inductive study.* Working Paper 364, Institute of Urban and Regional Development, University of California, Berkeley.

Fischer, C.S. (1977, November). *The contexts of personal relations: An exploratory network analysis.* University of California, Berkeley, Institute of Urban and Regional Development, Working Paper, No. 281.

Fischer, C.S., Jackson, R.M., Stuve, C.A., Gerson, K., Jones, L.M., & Baldassare, M. (1977). *Networks and places: Social relations in the urban setting.* New York: Free Press.

Fischer, C.S., & Phillips, S.L. (1979, October). *Who is alone? Social characteristics of people with small networks.* Institute of Urban and Regional Development, University of California, Berkeley, Working Paper No. 310.

Fischoff, B., Goitein, B., & Shapira, Z. (1982). The experienced utility of expected utility approaches. In N.T. Feather (Ed.), *Expectations and actions: Expectancy-value models in psychology.* Hillsdale, NJ: Erlbaum.

Fish, J.M. (1973). *Placebo therapy.* San Francisco: Jossey-Bass.

Fisher, B.A. (1985). Leadership as medium: Treating complexity in group communication research. *Small Group Behavior, 16,* 167–196.

Fisher, R. (1983). Negotiating power: Getting and using influence. *American Behavioral Scientist, 27,* 149–166.

Fisher, R., & Ury, W. (1981). *Getting to yes: Negotiating agreement without giving in.* Boston: Houghton-Mifflin.

Fisher, R.A. (1925). *Statistical methods for research workers.* (1st edn.). London: Oliver and Boyd.

Fisher, S., & Todd, A. (Eds.). (1983). *The social organization of doctor–patient communication.* Washington, DC: Center for Applied Linguistics.

Flay, B.R. (1985) What do we know about the social influences approach to smoking prevention?: Review and recommendations. In C. Bell et al. (Eds.), *Prevention research: Deterring drug abuse among children and adolescents.* Health Behavior Research Institute, U.S.C. Washington, DC: NIDA.

Foa, U.G. (1957). Relation of worker's expectation to satisfaction with supervisor. *Personnel Psychology, 10,* 161–168.

Ford, J.D. (1978). Therapeutic relationship in behavior therapy: An empirical analysis. *Journal of Consulting and Clinical Psychology, 46,* 1302–1314.

Forehand, R., & Atkeson, B.M. (1977). Generality of treatment effects with parents as therapists. A review of assessment and implementation procedures. *Behavior Therapy, 8,* 575–593.

Forsyth, D.R. (1983). *An introduction to group dynamics.* Monterey, CA: Brooks/Cole.

Forsyth, D.R., & Forsyth, N.M. (1984, April). *Subordinates' reactions to female leaders.* Paper presented at the Eastern Psychological Association Convention, Baltimore, MD.

Forsyth, D.R., Schlenker, B.R., Leary, M.R., & McCown, N.E. (1985). Self-presentational determinants of sex differences in leadership behavior. *Small Group Behavior, 16,* 197–210.

Forsyth, D.R., & Strong, S.R. (1986). The scientific study of counseling and psychotherapy: A unificationist view. *American Psychologist, 41,* 113–119.

Frank, J.D. (1957). Some determinants, manifestations, and effects of cohesiveness in therapy groups. *International Journal of Group Psychotherapy, 7,* 53–63.

Frank, J.D. (1961). *Persuasion and healing.* Baltimore, MD: Johns Hopkins University Press.

Frank, J.D. (1973). *Persuasion and healing: A comparative study of psychotherapy* (2nd Edn.). Baltimore, M.D: Johns Hopkins University Press.

Frank, J.D., Gliedman, L., Imber, S., Stone, A.R., & Nash, E.H. (1959). Patients' expectancies and relearning as factors determining improvement in psychotherapy. *American Journal of Psychiatry, 115,* 961–968.

Franks, C., & Wilson, G.T. (1978). Generalization and maintenance of treatment produced change. In C. Franks & G.T. Wilson (Eds.), *Annual review of behavior therapy: Theory and practice* (Vol. 6). New York: Brunner/Mazel.

French, J.R.P., Jr. (1941). The disruption and cohesion of groups. *Journal of Abnormal and Social Psychology, 36,* 361–377.

French, J.R.P., Jr., & Raven, B. (1959). The bases of social power. In D. Cartwright (Ed.), *Studies in social power.* Ann Arbor, MI: Institute for Social Research.

Freud, S. (1922). *Group psychology and the analysis of ego.* London: Hogarth.

Friedman, H.J. (1963). Patient-expectancy and symptom reduction. *Archives of General Psychiatry, 8,* 61–67.

Friedman, H.S. (1979). Nonverbal communication between patients and medical practitioners. *Journal of Social Issues, 35,* 82–99.

Friedmann, C.T.H. (1983). Crisis groups. In M. Grotjahn, F.M. Kline, & C.T.H. Friedmann (Eds.), *Handbook of group therapy.* New York: Van Nostrand Reinhold.

Friedmann, C.T.H., Procci, W.R., & Fenn, A. (1980). The role of expectation in treatment for psychotic patients. *American Journal of Psychotherapy, 34,* 188–195.

Froland, C., Brodsky, G., Olson, M., & Stewart, L. (1979). Social support and social adjustment: Implications for mental health professionals. *Community Mental Health Journal, 15*(2), 82–93.

Gaines, A. (1979). Definitions and diagnoses. *Culture, Medicine and Psychiatry, 3,* 381–418.

Gaines, A.D. (1982). Cultural definitions, behavior and the person in American psychiatry. In A.J. Marsella & G.M. White (Eds.), *Cultural conceptions of mental health and therapy.* Boston: D. Reidel.

Galassi, J.P., & Galassi, M.D. (1979). Modification of heterosocial skills deficits. In A.S. Bellack & M. Hersen (Eds.), *Research and practice in social skills training.* New York: Plenum.

Gamst, F.C., & Norbect, E. *Ideas of culture: Sources and uses.* New York: Holt, Rinehart & Winston, 1976.

Garfield, S.L. (1971). Research on client variables in psychotherapy. In A.E. Bergin & S.L. Garfield (Eds.), *Handbook of psychotherapy and behavior change.* New York: Wiley.

Garfield, S.L. (1981). Psychotherapy: A 40-year appraisal. *American Psychologist, 36,* 174–183.

Garfield, S.L., & Bergin, A.E. (Eds.) (1978). *Handbook of psychotherapy and behavior change* (2nd edn.). New York: Wiley.

Garrison, V. (1978). Support systems of schizophrenic and non-schizophrenic Puerto Rican migrant women in New York City. *Schizophrenia Bulletin, 4,* 561–596.

Geertz, C. Ritual and social change: A Javanese example. *American Anthropologist,* 1957, 59, 32–54.

Gelso, C.J. (1979). Research in counseling: Methodological and professional issues. *The Counseling Psychologist, 8,* 7–36.

Gerbert, E.W., & Baer, D.M. (1972). Training parents as behavior modifiers: Self-recording contingent attention. *Journal of Applied Behavior Analysis, 5,* 139–149.

Gerz, H.O. (1966). Experience with logotherapeutic technique of paradoxical intervention in the treatment of phobic and obsessive-compulsive patients. *American Journal of Psychiatry, 123,* 548–553.

Gibb, J.R. (1970). Effects of human relations training. In A.E. Bergin & S.L. Garfield (Eds.), *Handbook of psychotherapy and behavior change*. New York: Wiley.

Gibbons, F.X. (1978). Sexual standards and reactions to pornography: Enhancing behavioral consistency through self-focused attention. *Journal of Personality and Social Psychology, 36*, 976–987.

Gibbons, F.X. (1983). Self-attention and self-report: The "veridicality" hypothesis. *Journal of Personality, 51,* 517–542.

Gilbert, J.P., Light, R.J., & Mosteller, F. (1975). Assessing social innovations: An empirical base for policy. In C.A. Bennett & A.A. Lumsdaine (Eds.), *Evaluation and experiment: Some critical issues in assessing social programs.* New York: Academic Press.

Gilbert, J.P., McPeek, B., & Mosteller, F. (1977). Statistics and ethics in surgery and anesthesia. *Science, 198,* 684–689.

Gladstein, G. (1969). Client expectations, counseling experience, and satisfaction. *Journal of Counseling Psychology, 16,* 476–481.

Glass, D.C. (1977). Stress, behavior patterns and coronary disease. *American Scientist, 65,* 177–186.

Glass, D.C., & Singer, J.E. (1972). *Urban stress: Experiments on noise and social stressors.* New York: Academic Press.

Glass, G.V., McGaw, B., & Smith, M.L. (1981). *Meta-analysis in social research.* Beverly Hills: Sage.

Glass, G.V., Willson, V.L., & Gottman, J.M. (1975). *Design and analysis of time series experiments.* Boulder: Colorado Associated Universities Press.

Glidewell, J.C. (1981, August). *Tensions and preventions in social support systems.* Paper presented at annual meeting of the American Psychological Association, Los Angeles.

Goffman, E. (1962). *Asylums: Essays on the social situation of mental patients and other inmates.* Chicago: Aldine.

Goldberg, C. (1977). *Therapeutic partnership: Ethical concerns in psychotherapy.* New York: Springer.

Goldberger, A.S. (1972, April). *Selection bias in evaluating treatment effects: Some formal illustrations* (Discussion Paper 123-72). Madison: University of Wisconsin, Institute for Research on Poverty.

Goldfried, M.R., & Davison, G.C. (1976). *Clinical behavior therapy.* New York: Holt, Rinehart and Winston.

Goldfried, M.R., & Robins, C. (1982). On facilitation of self-efficacy. *Cognitive Therapy and Research, 6,* 361–380.

Goldstein, A.P. (1960). Therapist and client expectation of personality change in psythotherapy. *Journal of Counseling Psychology, 7,* 180–184.

Goldstein, A.P. (1962). *Therapist–patient expectancies in psychotherapy.* New York: Macmillan.

Goldstein, A.P. (1971). *Psychotherapeutic attraction.* New York: Pergamon.

Goldstein, A.P. (1980). Relationship-enhancement methods. In F.H. Kanfer & A.P. Goldstein (Eds.), *Helping people change.* New York: Pergamon.

Goldstein, A.P. (1981). Evaluating expectancy effects in cross-cultural counseling and psychotherapy. In A.J. Marsella & P.B. Pedersen (Eds.), *Cross-cultural counseling and psychotherapy.* New York: Pergamon.

Goldstein, A.P., & Heller, K. (1960, August). *Role expectations, participant personality characteristics, and the client–counselor relationship.* Unpublished manuscript, Syracuse University.

Goldstein, A.P., Heller, K.H., & Sechrest, L.B. (1966). *Psychotherapy and the psychology of behavior change.* New York: Wiley.

Goldstein, A.P., & Kanfer, H. (1979). *Maximizing treatment gains.* New York: Academic Press.

Goldstein, A.P., Lopez, M., & Greenleaf, D.O. (1979). Introduction. In A.P. Goldstein & F.H. Kanfer (Eds.), *Maximizing treatment gains.* New York: Academic Press.

Goldstein, A.P., & Shipman, W.G. (1961). Patient expectancies, symptom reduction and aspects of the initial psychotherapeutic interview. *Journal of Clinical Psychology, 17,* 129–133.

ds.), *Handbook of psychotherapy and behavior change.* New York: Wiley.

Goldstein, A.P., & Stein, N. (1976). *Prescriptive psychotherapies.* New York: Pergamon.

Gomez-Schwartz, B. (1978). Effective ingredients in psychotherapy: Prediction of outcome from process variables. *Journal of Consulting and Clinical Psychology, 46,* 1023–1035.

Good, B. (1977). The heart of what's the matter: The semantics of illness in Iran. *Culture, Medicine and Psychiatry, 1,* 25–58.

Good, B., & Good, M.J. (1980). The meaning of symptoms: A cultural hermeneutic model for clinical practice. In L. Eisenberg & A. Kleinman (Eds.), *The relevance of social science for medicine.* Boston: D. Reidel.

Good, B., & Good, M.J. (1981). The semantics of medical discourse. In E. Mendelsohn & Y. Elkana (Eds.), *Sciences and cultures: Sociology of the Sciences* (Vol. V), Boston: D. Reidel.

Good, B., & Good, M.J. (1982). Toward a meaning-centered analysis of popular illness categories: "Fright illness" and "heart distress" in Iran. In A.J. Marsella & G. White (Eds.), *Cultural conceptions of mental health and therapy.* Boston: D. Reidel.

Goodenough, W.H. (1961). Comment on cultural evolution. *Daedalus, 90,* 521–528.

Gorlow, L., Hoch, E.L., & Telschow, E.F. (1952). *Nondirective group psychotherapy.* New York: Columbia University Press.

Gottman, J.M. (1981). *Time series analysis for the behavioral sciences.* New York: Cambridge University Press.

Gottlieb, B.H. (1982). Opportunities for collaboration with informal support systems. In S. Cooper & W.F. Hodges (Eds.), *The field of mental health consultation.* New York: Human Sciences Press.

Gouldner, A. (1960). The norm of reciprocity: A preliminary statement. *American Sociological Review, 25,* 161–178.

Granovetter, M.S. (1973). The strength of weak ties. *American Journal of Sociology, 78,* 1360–1380.

Graves, T.D., & Graves, N.B. (1980). Kinship ties and the preferred adaptive strategies of urban migrants. In S. Beckman & L. Cordell (Eds.), *The versatility of kinship.* New York: Academic Press.

Graves, T.D., & Graves, N.B. (1985). Stress and health among Polynesian migrants to New Zealand. *Journal of Behavioral Medicine, 8,* 1–19.

Green, S.G., & Mitchell, T.R. (1979). Attributional processes of leaders in leader-member interactions. *Organizational Behavior and Human Performance, 23,* 429–458.

Greene, L.R., Morrison, T.L., & Tischler, N.G. (1981). Gender and authority: Effects on perceptions of small group co-leaders. *Small Group Behavior, 12,* 401–413.

Greenwald, A.G. (1981). The totalitarian ego: Fabrication and revision of personal history. *American Psychologist, 35,* 603–618.

Greer, F.L. (1980). Prognostic expectations and outcome of brief therapy. *Psychological Reports, 46,* 973–974.

Grier, W., & Cobbs, P. (1968). *Black rage.* New York: Bantam Books.

Grosz, R.D. (1968). Effect of client expectations on the counseling relationship. *Personnel and Guidance Journal, 46,* 797–800.

Grotjahn, M., Kline, F.M., & Friedmann, C.T.H. (1983). *Handbook of group therapy.* New York: Van Nostrand Reinhold.

Gruner, L. (1984). Membership composition of open and closed therapeutic groups: A research note. *Small Group Behavior, 15,* 222–232.

Gulas, I. (1974). Client-therapist congruence in prognostic and role expectations as related to client's improvement in short-term psychotherapy. *Dissertation Abstracts International, 35,* 2430B. (University Microfilms No. 74-23852)

Gulliver, P.H. (1979). *Disputes and negotiations: A cross-cultural perspective.* New York: Academic Press.

Gumprez, J.J. (1982). *Discourse strategies.* New York: Cambridge University Press.

Gurland, B.J., & Zubin, J. (1982). The United States-United Kingdom cross-national project: Issues in cross-cultural psychogeriatric research. In L.L. Adler (Ed.), *Cross-cultural research at issue.* New York: Academic Press.

Gurman, A.S., & Razin, A.M. (1977). *Effective psychotherapy: A handbook of research.* New York: Pergamon.

Hagen, B.J.H., & Burch, G. (1985). Therelationship of group process and group task accomplishment to group member satisfaction. *Small Group Behavior, 16,* 211–234.

Haley, J. (1971). *Changing families.* New York: Grune & Stratton.

Hall, S.M. (1980). Self-management and therapeutic maintenance: Theory and research. In P. Karoly & J.J. Steffen (Eds.), *Improving the long-term effects of psychotherapy: Models of durable outcome.* New York: Gardner Press.

Halpin, A.W., & Winer, B.J. (1952). *The leadership behavior of the airplane commander.* Columbus: Ohio State University Research Foundation.

Hammer, M., Makiesky-Barrow, S., & Gutwirth, L. (1978). Social networks and schizophrenia. *Schizophrenia Bulletin, 4*(4), 522–545.

Hare, A.P. (1976). *Handbook of small group research.* New York: Free Press.

Hare, A.P. (1982). *Creativity in small groups.* Beverly Hills: Sage.

Harper, R.G., Wiens, A.N., & Matarazzo, J.D. (1978). *Nonverbal communication: The state of the art.* New York: Wiley.

Harrison, B. (1972). *Meaning and structure: An essay in the philosophy of language.* New York: Harper & Row.

Hartlage, L.C., & Sperr, E.V. (1980). Patient preferences with regard to ideal therapist characteristics. *Journal of Clinical Psychology, 36,* 288–290.

Harvey, J.H., & Parks, M.M. (Eds.). (1982). *Psychotherapy research and behavior change.* Washington, DC: American Psychological Association.

Harvey, J.H., & Weary, G. (1979). The integration of social and clinical psychology training programs. *Personality and Social Psychology Bulletin, 5,* 511–515.

Harwood, A. (1981). Communicating about disease: Clinical implications of divergent concepts among patients and physicians. In A. Harwood (Ed.), *Ethnicity and medical care.* Cambridge, MA: Harvard University Press.

Haspel, K.C. (1982). Decreasing therapy dropout at a community mental health center: An attempt to change client expectations and to increase therapist motivation. *Dissertation Abstracts International, 43,* 1254–1255. (University Microfilms No. DA8215336)

Hass, R.G. (1984). Perspective taking and self-awareness: Drawing an E on your forehead. *Journal of Personality and Social Psychology, 46,* 788–798.

Hatfield, E., Utne, M.K., & Traupmann, J. (1979). Equity theory and intimate relations. In R.L. Burgess & T.L. Huston (Eds.), *Social exchange in developing relations.* New York: Academic Press.

Hayes, R.B., & Oxley, D. (1986). Social network development and functioning during a life transition. *Journal of Personality and Social Psychology, 50,* 305–313.

Hayes, S.C., Rincover, A., & Solnick, J.V. (1980). The technical drift of applied behavior analysis. *Journal of Applied Behavior Analysis, 13,* 275–285.

Heatherington, E.M., Cox, M., & Cox, R. (1981). Effects of divorce on parents and children. In N. Lamb (Ed.), *Non-Traditional Families*. Hillsdale, NJ: Erlbaum.

Heckhausen, H. (1977). Achievement motivation and its constructs. *Motivation and Emotion, 1*, 283–329.

Heckman, J.J. (1979). Sample selection bias as a specification error. *Econometrica, 47*, 153–161.

Heine, R., & Trosman, H. (1960). Initial expectations of the doctor–patient interaction as a factor in continuance in psychotherapy. *Psychiatry, 23*, 275–278.

Heise, D.R. (1975). *Causal analysis*. New York: Wiley.

Heitler, J. (1976). Preparatory techniques in initiating expressive psychotherapy with lower-class, unsophisticated patients. *Psychological Bulletin, 83*, 339–352.

Heller, K., & Rasmussen, B.R. (1981). The effects of personal and social ties on satisfaction and perceived strain in changing neighborhoods. *Journal of Community Psychology, 9*, 35–44.

Heller, K., & Swindle, R.W. (1983). Social networks, perceived social support, and coping with stress. In R.D. Felner, L.A. Jason, J. Moritsugu, & S.S. Faber (Eds.), *Preventive psychology: Theory, research and practice*. New York: Pergamon.

Hemphill, J.K. (1961). Why people attempt to lead. In L. Petrullo & B.M. Bass (Eds.), *Leadership and interpersonal behavior*. New York: Holt, Rinehart, & Winston.

Henderson, S. (1980). A development of social psychiatry: The systematic study of social bonds. *The Journal of Nervous and Mental Disease, 168*, 63–69.

Hendrick, C. (1983). Clinical social psychology: A birthright reclaimed. *Journal of Social and Clinical Psychology, 1*, 66–78.

Heppner, P.P., & Dixon, D.N. (1981). A review of the interpersonal influence process in counseling. *Personnel and Guidance Journal, 59*, 542–550.

Heppner, P.P., & Heesacker, M. (1983). Perceived counselor characteristics, client expectations, and client satisfaction with counseling. *Journal of Counseling Psychology, 30*, 31–39.

Hepworth, J.T., & West, S.G. (1987). *Media effects in interrupted time-series data: Two empirical examples*. Unpublished manuscript, Arizona State University, Tempe, AZ.

Hepworth, J.T., West, S.G., & Woodfield, T.J. (1987). *Time series analysis in the behavioral sciences: Box-Jenkins ARIMA modeling and beyond*. Unpublished manuscript, Arizona State University, Tempe, AZ.

Hersey, P., & Blanchard, K.H. (1976). Leader effectiveness and adaptability description (LEAD). In J.W. Pfeiffer & J.E. Jones (Eds.), *The 1976 annual handbook for group facilitators* (Vol. 5). La Jolla, CA: University Associates.

Hersey, P., & Blanchard, K.H. (1977). *Management of organizational behavior: Utilizing human resources* (3rd edn.). Englewood Cliffs, NJ: Prentice-Hall.

Hesselbrock, M.M., Hesselbrock, V.M., Tennen, H., Meyer, R.E., & Workman, K. (1983). Methodological considerations in the assessment of depression in alcoholics. *Journal of Consulting and Clinical Psychology, 51*, 399–405.

Hibbs, D.A., Jr. (1974). Problems of statistical estimation and causal inference in time-series regression models. In H.L. Costner (Ed.), *Sociological methodology 1973–1974*. San Francisco: Jossey-Bass.

Higginbotham, H.N. (1977). Culture and the role of client expectancy in psychotherapy. *Topics in Culture Learning, 5*, 107–124.

Higginbotham, H.N. (1978). Cross-cultural anxiety. Edited by C.D. Spielberger & R. Diaz-Guerrero. *Journal of Cross-Cultural Psychology, 9*, 499–501.

Higginbotham, H.N. (1984). *Third World challenge to psychiatry: Culture accommodation and mental health care*. Honolulu: University of Hawaii Press.

Higginbotham, H.N., & Marsella, A.J. (in press). International consultation and the homogenization of psychiatry in Southeast Asia. *Social Science and Medicine*.

Higginbotham, H.N. & Tanaka-Matsumi, J. (1981). Behavioral approaches to counseling across cultures. In P. Pedersen, W. Lonner, J. Draguns, & J. Trimble (Eds.), *Counseling across cultures*. Honolulu: University of Hawaii Press.

Higginbotham, H.N., Yamamoto, K., & Takemoto-Chock, N. (1978). *The client-expectations inventory for cross-cultural research*. Unpublished technical report, Department of Psychology, University of Hawaii, Manoa.

Hill, M.G., & Weary, G. (1983). Perspectives on the *Journal of Abnormal and Social Psychology*: How it began and how it was transformed. *Journal of Social and Clinical Psychology, 1*, 4–14.

Hill, T.E., & Schmitt, N. (1977). Individual differences in leadership decision making. *Organizational Behavior and Human Performance, 19*, 353–367.

Hirsch, B.J. (1980). Natural support systems and coping with major life changes. *American Journal of Community Psychiatry, 8*, 153–166.

Hirsch, B.J. (1981, August). *Social networks and the ecology of preventive intervention*. Paper presented at the American Psychological Association meeting, Los Angeles.

Hise, R.T. (1968). The effect of close supervision on productivity of simulated managerial decision-making groups. *Business Studies, 2*, 96–104.

Hobfoll, S.E., Kelso, D., & Peterson, W.J. (1981, September). *When are support systems support systems?* Paper presented at the International Congress on Drug and Alcohol, Jerusalem, Israel.

Hoffman, S.S. (1982). An investigation of patient and therapist role expectations and preferences related to premature termination in short-term psychotherapy. *Dissertation Abstracts International, 43*, 251B. (University Microfilm No. DA8212702)

Holahan, C.J. (1976). Environmental effects on outdoor social behavior in a low-income urban neighborhood: A naturalistic investigation. *Journal of Applied Social Psychology, 6*, 48–63.

Holahan, C.J., & Spearly, J.L. (1980). Coping and ecology: An integrative model for community psychology. *American Journal of Community Psychology, 8*, 671–685.

Hollander, E.P. (1978). *Leadership dynamics: A practical guide to effective relationships*. New York: Free Press.

Hollander, E.P. (1985). Leadership and power. In G. Lindzey & E. Aronson (Eds.), *Handbook of social psychology* (Vol. 2, 3rd edn.). New York: Random House.

Hollander, E.P., & Julian, J.W. (1970). Studies in leader legitimacy, influence, and innovation. In L. Berkowitz (Ed.), *Advances in experimental social psychology* (Vol. 5). New York: Academic Press.

Homans, G.C. (1961). *Social behavior: Its elementary forms*. New York: Harcourt, Brace.

Horne, G.P., Yang, M.C.K., & Ware, W.B. (1982). Time series analysis for single subject designs. *Psychological Bulletin, 91*, 178–189.

House, J.S., & Kahn, R.L. (1985). Measures and concepts of social support. In S. Cohen & S.L. Syme (Eds.), *Social support and health*. New York: Academic Press.

Howard, G.S. (1981). On validity. *Evaluation Review, 5*, 567–576.

Howe, H.E. (Ed.). (1981). *Nebraska symposium on motivation, 1980*. Lincoln, NE: University of Nebraska Press.

Hoyt, R.H. (1980). Effects of pretherapy role induction interviews upon treatment expectations and outcome in brief psychotherapy. *Dissertation Abstracts International, 40*, 4486B–4487B. (University Microfilm No. 8005610)

Hui, C.H., & Triandis, H.C. (1985). Measurement in cross-cultural psychology: A review and comparison of strategies. *Journal of Cross-Cultural Psychology, 16*, 131–152.

Huitema, B.E. (1980). *The analysis of covariance and alternatives.* New York: Wiley.

Hurst, A.G., Stein, K.B., Korchin, S.J., & Soskin, W.F. (1978). Leadership style determinants of cohesiveness in adolescent groups. *International Journal of Group Psychotherapy, 23,* 263–277.

Huston, T.L., & Burgess, R.L. (1979). Social exchange in developing relationships: An overview. In R.L. Burgess & T.L. Huston (Eds.), *Social exchange in developing relations.* New York: Academic Press.

Ilgen, D.T., & Fuji, D.S. (1976). An investigation of the validity of leader behavior descriptions obtained from subordinates. *Journal of Applied Psychology, 61,* 642–651.

Imber, S.D., Glanz, L.M., Elkin, I., Sotsky, S.M., Boyer, J.L., & Leber, W.R. (1986). Ethical issues in psychotherapy research: Problems in a collaborative clinical trials study. *American Psychologist, 41,* 137–146.

Imber, S.D., Pande, S.K., Frank, J.D., Hoehn-Saric, R., Stone, A.R., & Wargo, D.G. (1970). Time focused role induction: Report of an instructive failure. *Journal of Nervous and Mental Disorder, 150,* 27–30.

Ingram, R.E., Smith, T.W., & Brehm, S.S. (1983). Depression and information processing: Self-schemata and the encoding of self-referent information. *Journal of Personality and Social Psychology, 45,* 412–420.

Insel, P.M. (1980). The social climate of mental health. *Community Mental Health Journal, 16,* 62–78.

Jacobs, A. (1974). The use of feedback in groups. In A. Jacobs & W.W. Spradlin (Eds.), *Group as an agent of change.* New York: Behavioral Publications.

Jacobs, A., Jacobs, M., Cavior, N., & Burke, J. (1974). Anonymous feedback: Credibility and desirability of structured emotional and behavioral feedback delivered in groups. *Journal of Counseling Psychology, 21,* 106–111.

Jacobs, M., Jacobs, A., Cavior, N., & Feldman, A. (1973). Feedback II: The "credibility gap": Delivery of positive and negative emotional and behavioral feedback in groups. *Journal of Consulting and Clinical Psychology, 41,* 215–223.

Jacobs, M., Jacobs, A., Gatz, M., & Schaible, T. (1973). Credibility and desirability of positive and negative structured feedback in groups. *Journal of Consulting and Clinical Psychology, 40,* 244–252.

Jacobson, M.B., & Effertz, J. (1974). Sex roles and leadership perceptions of the leaders and the led. *Organizational Behavior and Human Performance, 12,* 383–396.

Jago, A.G. (1978). Configural cue utilization in implicit models of leader behavior. *Organizational Behavior and Human Performance, 22,* 474–496.

James, W. (1890). *The principles of psychology.* New York: Henry Holt.

Janis, I.L. (1963). Group identification under conditions of external danger. *British Journal of Medical Psychology, 36,* 227–238.

Janis, I.L. (1972). *Victims of groupthink.* Boston: Houghton-Mifflin.

Janis, I.L. (1982). *Groupthink.* Boston: Houghton-Mifflin.

Janoff-Bulman, R., & Brickman, P. (1982). Expectation and what people learn from failure. In N.T. Feather (Ed.), *Expectations and actions: Expectancy-value models in psychology.* Hillsdale, NJ: Erlbaum.

Johnson, C.A. (1980). *Prevention of multi-substance abuse in youth.* Unpublished manuscript, University of Southern California, Los Angeles.

Johnson, D.W. (1980). Group processes: Influences of student-student interaction in school outcomes. In J.H. McMillan (Ed.), *The social psychology of school learning.* New York: Academic Press.

Johnson, M.P., & Ewens, W. (1971). Power relationships and affective style as determinants of confidence in impression formation in a game situation. *Journal of Experimental Social Psychology, 7,* 98–110.

Johnson, S.M., & Christensen, A. (1975). Multiple criteria follow-up of behavior modification with families. *Journal of Abnormal Child Psychology, 3,* 135–154.

Jones, A., & Crandall, R. (1985). Preparing newcomers to enhance assimilation into groups: A group therapy example. *Small Group Behavior, 16,* 31–57.

Jones, E. (1982). Psychotherapists' impression of treatment outcome as a function of race. *Journal of Clinical Psychology, 38,* 722–731.

Jones, R.A. (1977). *Self-fulfilling prophecies: Social, psychological, and physiological effects of expectancies.* Hillsdale, NJ: Erlbaum.

Jones, W.L. (1980). Couple network patterns of newcomers in an Australian city. *Social Networks, 2,* 357–370.

Jöreskog, K.G., & Sörbom, D. (1979). *Advances in factor analysis and structural equation models.* Boston: Abt Associates.

Judd, C.M., Jessor, R., & Donovan, J.E. (1986). Structural equation models and personality research: Stability, discriminant validity, and the prediction of behavior. *Journal of Personality, 53,* 149–198.

Judd, C.M., & Kenny, D.A. (1981a). *Estimating the effects of social interventions.* New York: Cambridge University Press.

Judd, C.M., & Kenny, D.A. (1981b). Process analysis: Estimating mediation in treatment evaluations. *Evaluation Review, 5,* 602–619.

Jurs, S.G., & Glass, G.V. (1971). The effect of experimental mortality on the internal and external validity of the randomized comparative experiment. *Journal of Experimental Education, 40,* 62–66.

Kanfer, F.H. (1979). Self-management: Strategies and tactics. In A.P. Goldstein & F.H. Kanfer (Eds.), *Maximizing treatment gain.* New York: Academic Press.

Kaplan, R.E. (1982). The dynamics of injury in encounter groups: Power, splitting, and the mismanagement of resistance. *International Journal of Group Psychotherapy, 32,* 163–187.

Kaplan, R.E., Obert, S.L., & Van Buskirk, W.R. (1980). The etiology of encounter group casualties: Second facts. *Human Relations, 33,* 131–148.

Kasl, S.V., & Wells, J.A. (1985). Social support and health in the middle years: Work and the family. In S. Cohen & S.L. Syme (Eds.), *Social support and health.* New York: Academic Press.

Katon, W., & Kleinman, A. (1981). Doctor–patient negotiation and other social science strategies in patient care. In L. Eisenberg & A. Kleinman (Eds.), *The relevance of social science for medicine.* Boston: D. Reidel Publishing Co.

Kavanaugh, R.R., Jr., & Bollet, R.M. (1983). Levels of verbal intimacy technique (LOVIT): An initial validation study of the measurement of verbal intimacy in groups. *Small Group Behavior, 14,* 34–49.

Kazdin, A.E. (1975). Recent advances in token economy research. In M. Hersen, R.M. Eisler, & P. Miller (Eds.), *Progress in behavior modification* (Vol. 1). New York: Academic Press.

Kazdin, A.E. (1979). Nonspecific treatment factors in psychotherapy outcome research. *Journal of Consulting and Clinical Psychology, 47,* 846–851.

Kazdin, A.E. (1980). *Research design in clinical psychology.* New York: Harper & Row.

Kazdin, A.E. (1982). *Single-case research designs: Methods for clinical and applied settings.* New York: Oxford University Press.

Kazdin, A.E. (1984). Statistical analyses for single-case experimental designs. In D.H. Barlow & M. Hersen, *Single-case experimental designs: Strategies for studying behavior change* (2nd Edn., pp. 285–324). New York: Pergamon.

Kazdin, A.E., & Wilcoxon, L.A. (1976). Systematic desensitization and nonspecific treatment effects: A methodological evaluation. *Psychological Bulletin, 83,* 729–758.

Keefe, S.E., Padilla, A.M., & Carlos, M.L. (1979). The Mexican-American extended family as an emotional support system. *Human Organization, 38*, 144–152.

Keeley, S.M., Shemberg, K.M., & Carbonell, J. (1976). Operant clinical intervention: Behavior management or beyond? Where are the data? *Behavior Therapy, 7*, 292–305.

Keesing, R.M. (1981). *Cultural anthropology: A contemporary perspective*. New York: Holt, Rinehart, & Winston.

Kellerman, H. (1979). *Group psychotherapy and personality: Intersecting structures*. New York: Grune & Stratton.

Kelly, J.G. (1981, August). Discussant's remarks. *Social support systems, quality of life, and primary prevention symposium*. Paper presented at the annual meeting of the Americal Psychological Association, Los Angeles, CA.

Kelman, H.C. (1961). Processes of opinion change. *Public Opinion Quarterly, 25*, 57–78.

Kemmerling, R.G. (1973). The effect of the intake interview on client expectations: A study utilizing videotape treatments to manipulate client expectations. *Dissertation Abstracts International, 33*, 3387A. (University Microfilms No. 73-644)

Kendon, A. (1970). Movement coordination in social interaction: Some examples described. *Act 9 Psychologica, 32*, 100–125.

Kendon, A. (1972). Review of *Kinesics and context: Essays on body motion* by R.L. Birdwhistell, *American Journal of Psychology, 85*, 441–445.

Kenny, D.A. (1975). A quasi-experimental approach to assessing treatment effects in the nonequivalent control group design. *Psychological Bulletin, 82*, 345–362.

Kenny, D.A. (1979). *Correlation and causality*. New York: Wiley.

Kenny, D.A., & Judd, C.M. (1986). The consequences of violating the independence assusmption in analysis of variance. *Psychological Bulletin, 99*, 422–431.

Kernberg, O.F., Bernstein, C.S., Coyne, R., Appelbaum, D.A., Horwitz, H., & Voth, T.J. (1972). Psychotherapy and psychoanalysis: Final report of the Menninger Foundation's psychotherapy research project. *Bulletin of the Menninger Clinic, 36*, 1–276.

Kessler, R.C., & Greenberg, D.F. (1981). *Linear panel analysis: Models of quantitative change*. New York: Academic Press.

Kieffer, C.H. (1981, August). *Empowerment: An alternative approach to prevention*. Paper presented at the meeting of the American Psychological Association, Los Angeles, CA.

Kimmel, M.J., Pruitt, D.G., Magenau, J.M., & Konard-Goldband, E. (1980). Effects of trust, aspiration, and gender on negotiation tactics. *Journal of Personality and Social Psychology, 38*, 9–22.

Kirshner, B.J., Dies, R.R., & Brown, R.A. (1978). Effects of experimental manipulation of self-disclosure on group cohesiveness. *Journal of Consulting and Clinical Psychology, 46*, 1171–1177.

Kivlighan, D.M., Jr. (1985). Feedback in group psychotherapy: Review and implications. *Small Group Behavior, 16*, 373–386.

Kivlighan, D.M., Jr., McGovern, T.V., & Corazzini, J.G. (1984). Effects of content and timing of structuring interventions on group therapy process and outcome. *Journal of Counseling Psychology, 31*, 363–370.

Kleiner, R., & Parker, S. (1963). Goal striving, social status, and mental disorder: A research review. *American Sociological Review, 28*, 189–203.

Kleinman, A. (1975). Explanatory models in health care relationships. In National Council for International Health, Health of the family. Washington, DC: Author.

Kleinman, A. (1978). International health care planning from an ethnomedical perspective: Critique and recommendations for change. *Medical Anthropology, 1*, 71–96.

Kleinman, A. (1980). *Patients and healers in the context of culture*. Berkeley: CA. University of California Press.

Kleinman, A., & Good, B. (1985). *Culture and depression: Studies in the anthropology and cross-cutural psychiatry of affect and disorder.* Berkeley, CA: University of California Press.

Kleinman, A., Eisenberg, L., & Good, B. (1978). Culture, illness and care: Clinical lessons from anthropologic and cross-cultural research. *Annals of Internal Medicine, 88*, 251-258.

Kleinman, A., & Sung, L.H. (1979). Why do indigenous practitioners successfully heal? *Social Science and Medicine, 13*, 7-26.

Klepac, R. (1970). An experimental analogue of psychotherapy involving "client" behavior as a function of confirmation and disconfirmation of expectations of "therapist" directiveness. *Dissertation Abstracts International, 30*, 5690B-5691B. (University Microfilms No. 70-11348)

Klepac, R., & Page, H. (1974). Discrepant role expectations and interviewee behavior: A reply to Pope, Siegmann, Blass, and Cheek. *Journal of Consulting and Clinical Psychology, 42*, 139-141.

Kmenta, J. (1986). *Elements of econometrics.* New York: Macmillan.

Koegel, R., Glahn, T.J., & Niemann, G.S. (1978). Generalization of parent training results. *Journal of Applied Behavioral Analysis, 11*, 95-109.

Kolb, D.A., & Boyatzis, R.E. (1970). Goal-setting and self-directed behavior change. *Human Relations, 23*, 439-457.

Kopel, S.A. (1982). Commentary: Social psychological processes in the development of maladaptive behaviors. In G. Weary & H.L. Mirels (Eds.), *Integrations of clinical and social psychology.* New York: Oxford University Press.

Korsch, B.M., & Negrete, V.F. (1972). Doctor-patient communication. *Scientific American, 227*, 66-74.

Kratochwill, T.B. (1978). *Single-subject research: Strategies for evaluating change.* New York: Academic Press.

Krause, M.S. (1968). Clarification at intake and motivation for treatment. *Journal of Consulting Psychology, 15*, 576-577.

Krause, M.S., Fitzsimmons, M., & Wolf, N. (1969). Focusing on the client's expectations of treatment. *Psychological Reports, 24*, 973-974.

Krauss, R.M., Geller, V., & Olson, C. (1976, September). *Modalities and cues in the detection of deception.* Paper presented at the meeting of the American Psychological Association, Washington, DC.

Kraut, R. (1980). Humans as lie detectors: Some second thoughts. *Journal of Communication, 30*, 209-216.

Krech, D., & Crutchfield, R.S. (1948). *Theory and problems of social psychology.* New York: McGraw-Hill.

Kriesberg, G.J. (1977). The relationship of the congruence of patient-therapist goal expectancies to psychotherapy outcome and duration of treatment. *Dissertation Abstracts International, 38*, 3890B. (University Microfilms No. 7730997)

LaCrosse, M.B. (1975). Nonverbal behavior and perceived counselor attractiveness and persuasiveness. *Journal of Counseling Psychology, 22*, 563-566.

Lakin, M. (1972). *Experiential groups: The uses of interpersonal encounter, psychotherapy groups, and sensitivity training.* Morristown, NJ: General Learning Press.

Lakoff, G., & Johnson, M. (1980). *Metaphors we live by.* Chicago: University of Chicago Press.

Lambert, R.G. (1982). The effects of role preparation for psychotherapy on immigrant clients seeking mental health services in Hawaii. *Dissertation Abstracts International, 42*, 3305A. (University Microfilms No. 8129929)

Lamm, H., & Myers, D.G. (1978). Group-induced polarization of attitudes and behavior. In L. Berkowitz (Ed.), *Advances in experimental social psychology* (Vol. 11). New York: Academic Press.

Langer, E.J., & Rodin, J. (1976). The effects of choice and enchanced personal responsibility for the aged: A field experiment in an institutional setting. *Journal of Personality and Social Psychology, 34,* 191–198.

Langlie, L. (1977). Social networks, health beliefs, and preventive health behavior. *Journal of Health and Social Behavior, 18,* 244–260.

LaRocco, J.M., House, J.S., & French, J.R. (1980). Social support, occupational stress, and health. *Journal of Health and Social Behavior, 21,* 202–218.

Latham, G.P., & Kinne, S.B., III. (1974). Improving job performance through training in goal setting. *Journal of Applied Psychology, 59,* 187–191.

Latham, G.P., & Yukl, G.A. (1975). A review of research on the application of goal setting in organizations. *Academy of Management Journal, 18,* 824–845.

Lazarus, R. (1966). *Psychological stress and the coping process.* New York: Appleton-Century-Crofts.

Leary, M.R. (1983). *Understanding social anxiety.* Beverly Hills: Sage.

Lee, S., & Temerlin, M. (1970). Social class, diagnosis, and prognosis for psychotherapy. *Psychotherapy: Theory, Research, Practice, 7,* 181–185.

Legge, J.S., & Webb, L. (1982). 'Publicity' as a problem in the internal validity of time series quasi-experiments. *Policy Studies Review, 2,* 293–299.

Leventhal, H. (1980). Toward a comprehensive theory of emotion. In L. Berkowitz (Ed.), *Advances in experimental social psychology* (Vol. 13). New York: Academic Press.

Leventhal, H., Meyer, D., & Nerenz, D. (1980). The common sense representation of illness danger. In S. Rachman (Ed.), *Medical psychology* (Vol. 2). New York: Pergamon.

Leventhal, H., & Nerenz, D. (1983). A model for stress research with some implications for the control of stress disorders. In D. Meichenbaum & M. Jeremko (Eds.), *Stress reduction and prevention.* New York: Plenum.

Leventhal, H., & Nerenz, D.R. (1985). The assessment of illness cognition. In P. Karoly (Ed.), *Measurement strategies in health psychology.* New York: Wiley.

Levine, D.W., & Dunlap, W.P. (1982). Power of the F test with skewed data: Should one transform or not? *Psychological Bulletin, 92,* 272–280.

Levine, D.W., & Dunlap, W.P. (1983). Data transformation, power, and skew: A rejoinder to Games. *Psychological Bulletin, 93,* 596–599.

Lewin, K. (1936). *Principles of topological psychology.* New York: McGraw-Hill.

Lewin, K. (1943). Forces behind food habits and methods of change. *Bulletin of the National Research Council, 108,* 35–65.

Lewin, K. (1951). *Field theory in social science.* New York: Harper.

Lewin, K., Lippitt, R., & White, R. (1939). Patterns of aggressive behavior in experimentally created "social climates." *Journal of Social Psychology, 10,* 271–299.

Lick, J.R., & Bootzin, R.R. (1975). Expectancy factors in the treatment of fear: Methodological and theoretical issues. *Psychological Bulletin, 82,* 917–931.

Lieberman, M.A. (1980). Group methods. In F.H. Kanfer & A.P. Goldstein (Eds.), *Helping people change.* New York: Pergamon.

Lieberman, M., Yalom, I., & Miles, M. (1973). *Encounter groups: First facts.* New York: Basic Books.

Liem, R., & Liem, J. (1978). Social class and mental illness reconsidered: The role of economic stress and social support. *Journal of Health and Social Behavior, 19,* 139–156.

Light, R.J., & Pillimer, D.B. (1984). *Research synthesis.* Cambridge, MA: Harvard University Press.

Likert, R. (1967). *The human organization.* New York: McGraw-Hill.

Lin, N., Dean, A., & Insel, W. (1986). *Social support, life events, and depression.* New York: Academic Press.

Linn, R.L., & Werts, C.E. (1973). Errors of inference due to errors of movement. *Educational and Psychological Measurement, 33*, 531–545.

Lock, M. (1982). Popular conceptions of mental health in Japan. In A.J. Marsella & G.M. White (Eds.), *Cultural conceptions of mental health and therapy.* Boston: D. Reidel.

Locke, E.A., Shaw, K.N., Saari, L.M., & Latham, G.P. (1981). Goal setting and task performance: 1969–1980. *Psychological Bulletin, 90,* 125–152.

Lonnor, W.J., & Berry, J.W. (1986). *Field methods in cross-cultural research.* Beverly Hills, CA: Sage.

Lonnor, W.J. (1979). Issues in cross-cultural psychology, In A.J. Marsella, R.G. Tharp, & T.J. Ciborowski (Eds.), *Perspectives on cross-cultural psychology.* New York: Academic Press.

Lopez, S. (1983). The study of psychotherapy bias: Some conceptual issues and some concluding remarks. In J. Murray & P.R. Abramson (Eds.), *Bias in psychotherapy.* New York: Praeger.

Lopez, S., & Hernandez-Henderson, P. (1986). *The role of culture in the evaluation of mental health patients. Journal of Nervous and Mental Disease, 174,* 598–606.

Lord, R.G. (1977). Functional leadership behavior: Measurement and relation to social power and leadership perceptions. *Administrative Science Quarterly, 22,* 114–133.

Lord, R.G., Binning, J.F., Rush, M.C., & Thomas, J.C. (1978). The effect of performance cues and leader behavior on questionnaire ratings of leadership behavior. *Organizational Behavior and Human Performance, 21,* 27–39.

Lorion, R.P. (1974). Patient and therapist variables in the treatment of low-income patients. *Psychological Bulletin, 81,* 344–354.

Lorr, M. (1965). Client perceptions of therapist: A study of the therapeutic relationship. *Journal of Consulting Psychology, 29,* 146–149.

Lott, A.J., & Lott, B.E. (1961). Group cohesiveness, communication level, and conformity. *Journal of Abnormal and Social Psychology, 62,* 408–412.

Maddux, J.E., Sherer, M., & Rogers, R.W. (1982). Self-efficacy expectancy and outcome expectancy: Their relationship and their effects on behavioral intentions. *Cognitive Therapy and Research, 6,* 207–211.

Madow, W.G. (Ed.). (1983). *Incomplete data in sample surveys* (Vols. 1–3). New York: Academic Press.

Magidson, J. (1977). Toward a causal modeling approach for adjusting for pre-existing differences in the nonequivalent group situation: A general alternative to ANOCOVA. *Evaluation Quarterly, 1,* 399–420.

Magidson, J., & Sörbom, D. (1980, August). *Adjusting for confounding factors in quasi-experiments: Another reanalysis of the Westinghouse Head Start evaluation.* Presented at the American Statistical Association meetings, Houston, TX.

Mahoney, M.J. (1974). *Cognition and behavior modification.* Cambridge: Ballinger.

Malpass, R.S. (1977). Theory and method in cross-cultural psychology. *American Psychologist, 32,* 1069–1080.

Malzer, R.L. (1980). Clients' pretherapy expectations and preferences, and their relationship to early termination of individual psychotherapy. *Dissertation Abstracts International, 41,* 2333B–2334B. (University Microfilms No. 8026864)

Mann, F.C. (1965). Toward an understanding of the leadership role in formal organizations. In R. Dubin, G.C. Homans, F.C. Mann, & D.C. Miller (Eds.), *Leadership and productivity.* San Francisco: Chandler.

Manning, N.M., & Wright, T.L. (1983). Self-efficacy expectancies, outcome expectancies, and the persistence of pain control in childbirth. *Journal of Personality and Social Psychology, 45,* 421–431.

Manson, S. (1980, May). *Problematic life situations: An inquiry into cross-cultural variation of support mobilization among minority elderly.* Paper presented at meeting of the Western Psychological Association, Honolulu, HI.

Marcia, J.E., Rubin, B.M., & Efran, J.S. (1969). Systematic desensitization: Expectancy change or counterconditioning? *Journal of Abnormal Psychology, 74,* 382–387.

Marholin, D., & Siegel, L.J. (1978). Beyond the law of effect: Programming for the maintenance of behavioral change. In D. Marholin (Ed.), *Child behavior therapy.* New York: Gardner.

Marholin, D., Siegel, L.J. & Phillips, D. (1976). Treatment and transfer: A search for procedures. In M. Hersen, R.M. Eisler, & P.M. Miller (Eds.), *Progress in behavioral modification* (Vol. 3). New York: Academic Press.

Marholin, D., & Touchette, P.E. (1979). The role of stimulus control and response consequences. In A.P. Goldstein & F. Kanfer (Eds.), *Maximizing treatment gain.* New York: Academic Press.

Markovitz, R.J., & Smith, J.E. (1983). Patients' perceptions of curative factors in short-term group psychotherapy. *International Journal of Group Psychotherapy, 33,* 21–39.

Markus, H. (1977). Self-schemata and processing information about the self. *Journal of Personality and Social Psychology, 35,* 63–78.

Marlatt, G.A. (1978). Craving for alcohol, loss of control, and relapse. A cognitive-behavioral analysis. In P.E. Nathan, G.A. Marlatt, & T. Loberg (Eds.), *Alcoholism: New directions in behavioral research and treatment.* New York: Plenum.

Marlatt, G.A., & Gordon, J.R. (1985). *Relapse prevention: Maintenance strategies of addictive behavior change.* New York: Guildford.

Marsella, A.J. (1976) Cross-cultural studies of depression: A review of the literature. Paper presented at the Symposium on Cross-Cultural Aspects of Depression. International Association of Cross-Cultural Psychology, Tilburg, Netherlands.

Marsella, A.J. (1980). Depressive experience and disorder across cultures. In H.C. Triandis & J.G. Draguns (Eds.), *Handbook of cross-cultural psychology* (Vol. 6). Boston: Allyn & Bacon.

Marsella, A.J., Kinzie, D., & Gordon, P. (1973). Ethnic variations in the expression of depression. *Journal of Cross-Cultural Psychology, 4,* 435–458.

Marsella, A.J., & Pedersen, P.B. (Eds.). (1981). *Cross-cultural counseling and psychotherapy.* New York: Pergamon.

Marsella, A.J., & Snyder, K.K. (1981). Stress, social supports, and schizophrenia disorders: Toward an interactional model. *Schizophrenia Bulletin, 7,* 152–163.

Marsella, A.J., & White, G.M. (Eds.) (1982). *Cultural conceptions of mental health and therapy.* Boston: D. Reidel.

Martin, H., & Shewmaker, K. (1962). Written instructions in group psychotherapy. *Group Psychotherapy, 15,* 24–29.

Martin, P.J., Moore, J.E., Sterne, A.L., & McNairy, R.M. (1977). Therapists prophesy. *Journal of Clinical Psychology, 33,* 502–510.

Martin, P.J., & Sterne, A.L. (1975). Prognostic expectations and treatment outcome. *Journal of Consulting and Clinical Psychology, 43,* 572–576.

Martin, P.J., Sterne, A.L., Claveaux, R.A., & Acree, N.J. (1976). Significant factors in the expectancy-improvement relationship: A second look at an earlier study. *Research Communications in Psychology, Psychiatry and Behavior, 1,* 367–379.

Martin, P.J., Sterne, A.L., Moore, J.E., & Friedmeyer, M.H. (1976). Patients' and therapists' expectancies and treatment outcome: An elusive relationship re-examined. *Research Communications in Psychology, Psychiatry and Behavior, 2,* 301–314.

Matthews, K.A. (1982). Psychological perspectives on the type A behavior pattern. *Psychological Bulletin, 91,* 293–323.

Maxmen, J. (1973). Group therapy as viewed by hospitalized patients. *Archives of General Psychiatry, 28,* 404–408.

Maxmen, J. (1978). An educative model for in-patient group therapy. *International Journal of Group Psychotherapy, 28,* 321–338.

McCleary, R., & Hay, R.A. (1980). *Applied time series analysis.* Beverly Hills, CA: Sage.

McDonald, P.J., Harris, S.G., & Maher, J.E. (1983). Arousal-induced self-awareness: An artifactual relationship? *Journal of Personality and Social Psychology, 44,* 285–289.

McGlynn, F.D., & Mapp, R.H. (1970). Systematic desensitization of snake-avoidance following three types of suggestion. *Behavior Research and Therapy, 8,* 197–201.

McGlynn, F.D., Mealiea, W.L., & Nawas, M.M. (1969). Systematic desensitization of snake-avoidance under two conditions of suggestion. *Psychological Reports, 25,* 220–222.

McGlynn, F.D., Reynolds, E.J., & Linder, L.H. (1971). Systematic desensitization with pre-treatment and intra-treatment therapeutic instructions. *Behavior Research and Therapy, 9,* 57–63.

McGlynn, F.D., & Williams, C.W. (1970). Systematic desensitization under three conditions of suggestion. *Journal of Behavior Therapy and Experimental Psychiatry, 1,* 97–101.

Mead, G.H. (1934). *Mind, self, and society.* Chicago, IL: University of Chicago Press.

Meichenbaum, D. (1975). Self-instructional methods. In F.H. Kanfer & A.P. Goldstein (Eds.), *Helping people change.* New York: Pergamon.

Meichenbaum, D. (1977). *Cognitive-behavior modification: An integrated approach.* New York: Plenum Press.

Meier, P. (1972). The biggest public health experiment ever: The 1954 field trial of the Salk polio vaccine. In J.M. Tanur et al. (Eds.), *Statistics: A guide to the unknown.* San Francisco: Holden Day.

Melahn, C.L., & O'Donnell, C.R. (1978). Norm-based behavioral consulting. *Behavior Modification, 2,* 309–338.

Mendelsohn, E., & Elkana, Y.E. (Eds.) (1981). *Sciences and cultures: Sociology of the sciences, Volume 5.* Boston: D. Reidel.

Merton, R.K. (1949). *Social theory and social structure.* Glencoe, IL: Free Press.

Miao, L.L. (1977). Gastric freezing: An example of the evaluation of medical therapy by randomized clinical trials. In J.P. Bunker, B.A. Barnes, & F. Mosteller (Eds.), *Costs, risks, and benefits of surgery.* New York: Oxford University Press.

Michener, H.A., & Burt, M.R. (1975). Use of social influence under varying conditions of legitimacy. *Journal of Personality and Social Psychology, 32,* 398–407.

Miles, M.B. (1965). Changes during and following laboratory training: A clinical-experimental study. *Journal of Applied Behavioral Science, 1,* 215–242.

Mischel, W. (1973). Toward a cognitive social learning reconceptualization of personality. *Psychological Review, 80,* 252–283.

Mitchell, J.C. (1969). The concept of use of social networks. In J.C. Mitchell (Ed.), *Social networks in urban situations.* Manchester UK: Manchester University Press.

Mitchell, J.N. (1978). *Social exchange, dramaturgy, and ethnomethodology. Toward a paradigmatic synthesis.* New York: Elsevier.

Mitchell, R.E. (1982). Social networks of psychiatric clients: The personal and environmental context. *American Journal of Community Psychology, 10,* 387–401.

Mitchell, R.E., Barbarin, O.A., & Hurley, D.J. (1981). Problem solving, resource utilization and community involvement in a Black and White community. *American Journal of Community Psychology, 9,* 233–245.

Mitchell, R.E., & Hodson, C.A. (1985). Coping and social support among battered women: An ecological perspective. In S. Hobfoll (Ed.), *Stress, social support and women.* New York: Hemisphere Press.

Mitchell, R.E., & Moos, R.H. (1984). Deficiencies in social support among depressed patients: Antecedents or consequences of stress? *Journal of Health and Social Behavior, 25,* 438–452.

Mitchell, R.E., & Trickett, E.J. (1980). Social networks as mediators of social support: An analysis of the effects and determinants of social networks. *Community Mental Health Journal, 16,* 27–44.

Mobley, W.H., Griffeth, R.W., Hand, H.H., & Meglino, B.M. (1979). Review and conceptual analysis of employee turnover process. *Psychological Bulletin, 86,* 493–522.

Mohr, L.G. (1982). On rescuing the nonequivalent-control-group design: The random-comparison-group approach. *Sociological Methods and Research, 11,* 53–80.

Mook, D.G. (1983). In defense of external invalidity. *American Psychologist, 38,* 379–387.

Moos, R.H. (1974). *The social climate scales: An overview.* Palo Alto, CA: Consulting Psychologist Press.

Moos, R.H. (1981, August). *Creating healthy human contexts: Environmental and individual strategies.* Paper presented at meeting of the American Psychological Association. Los Angeles, CA.

Moos, R.H., & Mitchell, R.E. (1982). Social network resources and adaptation: A conceptual framework. In T.A. Willis (Ed.), *Basic processes in helping relationships.* New York: Academic Press.

Moos, R., & Moos, B.S. (1984). The process of recovery from alcoholism: III. Comparing functioning in families of alcoholics and matched control families. *Journal of Studies on Alcohol, 45*(2), 111–118.

Moran, G. (1966). Dyadic attraction and orientational consensus. *Journal of Personality and Social Psychology, 4,* 94–99.

Moreland, R.L., & Levine, J.M. (1982). Socialization in small groups: Temporal changes in individual–group relations. In L. Berkowitz (Ed.), *Advances in experimental social psychology* (Vol. 15). New York: Academic Press.

Moreno, J.L. (1978). *Who shall survive?: Foundations of sociometry, group psychotherapy, and sociodrama.* Beacon, NY: Beacon House.

Morgan, W.R., & Sawyer, J. (1979). Equality, equity, and procedural justice in social exchange. *Social Psychology Quarterly, 42,* 71–75.

Morrow-Bradley, C., & Elliott, R. (1986). Utilization of psychotherapy research by practicing psychotherapists. *American Psychologist, 41,* 188–197.

Moscovici, S. (1980). Toward a theory of conversion behavior. In L. Berkowitz (Ed.), *Advances in experimental social psychology* (Vol. 13). New York: Academic Press.

Mosteller, F., & Tukey, J.W. (1977). *Data analysis and regression.* Reading, MA: Addison-Wesley.

Mueller, D.P. (1980). Social networks: A promising direction for research on the relationship of the social environment to psychiatric disorder. *Social Science and Medicine, 14,* 147–161.

Murname, R.J., Newstead, S., & Olson, R.J. (1985). Comparing public and private schools: The puzzling role of selectivity bias. *Journal of Business and Economic Statistics, 3,* 23–35.

Murray, J., & Abramson, P.R. (Eds.). (1983). *Bias in psychotherapy.* New York: Praeger.

Muthén, B., & Jöreskog, K.G. (1983). Selectivity problems in quasi-experimental studies. *Evaluation Review, 7,* 139–174.

Myers, A.E. (1962). Team competition, success, and the adjustment of group members. *Journal of Abnormal and Social Psychology, 65*, 325–332.

Myers. D.G. (1983). *Social psychology.* New York: McGraw-Hill.

Naroll, R., Michik, G.L., & Naroll, F. (1980). Holocultural research methods. In H.C. Triandis & J. Berry (Eds.), *Handbook of cross-cutural psychology* (Vol. 2). Boston: Allyn & Bacon.

Nay, W.R. (1979). Parents as real life reinforcers: The enhancement of parent-training effects across conditions other than training. In A.P. Goldstein & F. Kanfer (Eds.), *Maximizing treatment gains.* New York: Academic Press.

Nichter, M. (1981). Idioms of distress: Alternatives in the expression of psychosocial distress, a case study from South India. *Culture, Medicine, and Psychiatry, 5*, 379–408.

Nichter, M., & Trockman, G. (1983). *Toward a psychosociocultural evaluation of the psychiatric patient: Contributions from clinical anthropology.* Unpublished manuscript, Department of Psychiatry, School of Medicine, University of Hawaii, Honolulu.

Nichter, M., Trockman, G., & Grippen, J. (1985). Clinical anthropologist as therapy facilitator: Role development and clinician evaluation in a psychiatric training program. *Human Organization, 44*, 72–80.

Norvell, N., & Forsyth, D.R. (1984). The impact of inhibiting or facilitating causal factors on group members' reactions after success and failure. *Social Psychology Quarterly, 47*, 293–297.

Novaco, R.W., & Monahan, J. (1980). Research in community psychology: An analysis of work published in the first six years of the American Journal of Community Psychology. *American Journal of Community Psychology, 8*, 131–145.

O'Brien, R.G., & Kaiser, M.K. (1985). MANOVA method for analyzing repeated measures designs: An extensive primer. *Psychological Bulletin, 97*, 316–333.

O'Donnell, C. (1977). Behavior modification in community settings. In M. Hersen, R.M. Eisler, & P.M. Miller (Eds.), *Progress in behavior modification* (Vol. 4). New York: Academic Press.

O'Donnell, C.R. (1981). Environmental design and the prevention of psychological problems. In M.P. Feldman & J.F. Ordord (Eds.), *The social psychology of psychological problems.* New York: Wiley.

O'Donnell, C.R. (1984). Behavioral community psychology and the natural environment. In C.M. Franks (Ed.), *New developments in behavior therapy: From research to clinical application.* New York: Haworth.

O'Donnell, C.R., Lydgate, T., & Fo, W.S.O. (1979). The buddy system: Review and follow up. *Child Behavior Therapy, 1*, 161–169.

O'Donnell, C.R., & Tharp, R.G. (1982). Community intervention and the use of multidisciplinary knowledge. In A.S. Bellack, M. Hersen, & A.E. Kazdin (Eds.), *International handbook of behavior modification and therapy.* New York: Plenum.

O'Malley, S.S., Suh, C.S., & Strupp, H.H. (1983). The Vanderbilt Psychotherapy Process Scale: A report on the scale development and a process-outcome study. *Journal of Consulting and Clinical Psychology, 51*, 581–586.

Orlinsky, D.E., & Howard, K.I. (1978). The relation of process to outcome in psychotherapy. In S.L. Garfield & A.E. Bergin (Eds.), *Handbook of psychotherapy and behavior change: An empirical analysis.* New York: Wiley.

Orne, M. (1962). On the social psychology of the psychological experiment. *American Psychologist, 17*, 776–783.

Orne, M.T., & Wender, P.H. (1968). Anticipatory socialization for psychotherapy: Method and rationale. *American Journal of Psychiatry, 124*, 1202–1211.

Overall, B., & Aronson, H. (1963). Expectations of psychotherapy in patients of lower socioeconomic class. *American Journal of Orthopsychiatry, 33*, 421–430.

Paget, M.A. (1983). On the work of talk: Studies in misunderstanding. In S. Fisher & A. Todd (Eds.), *The social organization of doctor–patient communication.* Washington, DC: Center for Applied Linguistics.

Parker, R. (1972). Some personal qualities enhancing group therapist effectiveness. *The Journal of Clinical Issues in Psychology, 4*, 26–28.

Patterson, G.R. (1976). The aggressive child: Victim and architect of a coercive system. In E.J. Mash, L.A. Hammerlynck, & L.C. Hardy (Eds.), *Behavior modification and families.* New York: Brunner/Mazel.

Patterson, G.R., & Moore, D. (1979). Interactive patterns as units of behavior. In M.E. Lamb. S.J. Suomi, & G.R. Stephenson (Eds.), *Social interaction analysis: Methodological issues.* Madison, WI: University of Wisconsin Press.

Patterson, G.R., & Reid, J.B. (1970). Reciprocity and coercion: Two facets of social systems. In C. Neuringer & J.D. Michael (Eds.), *Behavior modification in clinical psychology.* New York: Appleton-Century-Crofts.

Patterson, M.L. (1973). Compensation in nonverbal immediacy behavior: A review. *Sociometry, 36*, 237–252.

Patterson, M.L. (1976). An arousal model of interpersonal intimacy. *Psychological Review, 83*, 235–245.

Patterson, M.L. (1977). Interpersonal distance, affect, and equilibrium theory. *Journal of Social Psychology, 101*, 205–214.

Patterson, M.L. (1982). A sequential functional model of nonverbal exchange. *Psychological Review, 89*, 231–249.

Pattison, E.M., DeFrancisco, D., Wood, P., Frazier, H., & Crowder, J.A. (1985). A psychosocial kinship model for family therapy. *American Journal of Psychiatry, 132*, 1246–1251.

Pattison, E.M., Llamas, R., & Hurd, G. (1979). Social network mediation of anxiety. *Psychiatric Annals, 9*, 56–67.

Paul, G.L. (1966). *Insight vs. desensitization in psychotherapy.* Stanford, CA: Stanford University Press.

Paulson, I., Burroughs, J., & Gelb, C. (1976). Cotherapy: What is the crux of the relationship? *International Journal of Group Psychotherapy, 26*, 213–224.

Pedersen, P.B., Sartorious, N., & Marsella, A.J. (1984). *Mental health services: The cross-cultural context.* Beverly Hills, CA: Sage.

Pedhazur, E.J. (1982). *Multiple regression in behavioral research.* New York: Holt, Rinehart, & Winston.

Pedigo, J.M., & Singer, B. (1982). Group process development: A psychoanalytic view. *Small Group Behavior, 13*, 496–517.

Pedro-Carroll, J., & Cowen, E.L. (1985). The Children of Divorce Intervention Project: An investigation of the efficacy of a school-based prevention program. *Journal of Consulting and Clinical Psychology, 53*, 603–611.

Pennebaker, J.W. (1982). *The psychology of physical symptoms.* New York: Springer-Verlag.

Pennebaker, J.W. (1983). Implicit psychophysiology: Effects of common beliefs and idiosyncratic physiological responses on symptom reporting. *Journal of Personality, 51*, 468–496.

Pepitone, A. (1981). Lessons from the history of social psychology. *American Psychologist, 36*, 972–985.

Pepitone, A., & Reichling, G. (1955). Group cohesiveness and the expression of hostility. *Human Relations, 8*, 327–337.

Perl, H.I. (1981, August). *Social network formation of entering college freshman.* Paper presented at the annual meeting of the American Psychological Association, Los Angeles, CA.

Perrucci, R., & Pilisuk, M. (1970). The interorganizational basis of community power. *American Sociological Review, 35,* 1040–1057.

Pilisuk, M. (1982). Delivery of social support: The social innoculation. *American Journal of Orthopsychiatry, 52,* 20–31.

Pilisuk, M., Chandler, S., & D'Onofrio, C. (1983). Reweaving the social fabric: Antecedents of social support facilitation. *International Quarterly of Community Health Education, 3,* 45–66.

Pilisuk, M., & Froland, C. (1978). Kinship, social networks, social support and health. *Social Science and Medicine, 12,* 273–280.

Pilisuk, M., & Parks, S.H. (1980). Structural dimensions of social support groups. *Journal of Psychology, 106,* 157–177.

Pilisuk, M., & Parks, S.H. (1981). The place of network analysis in the study of supportive social associations. *Basic and Applied Social Psychology, 2,* 121–135.

Pilisuk, M., & Parks, S.H. (1986). *The healing web: Social networks and human survival.* Hanover NH: University Press of New England.

Plaja, A.O., Cohen, L.M., & Samora, J. (1968). Communication between physicians and patients in outpatient clinics. *Milbank Memorial Fund Quarterly, 46,* 161–213.

Posavac, E.L., & Carey, R.G. (1985). *Program evaluation: Methods and case studies* (2nd edn.). Englewood Cliffs, NJ: Prentice-Hall.

Powell, D.R. (1980, September). *Strengthening parents' social networks: An ecological approach to primary prevention.* Paper presented at the American Psychological Association, Montreal, Canada.

Powell. E.R. (1982). Sociometric semantic differential assessment. *Small Group Behavior, 13,* 43–52.

Prentice-Dunn, S., & Rogers, R.W. (1980). Effects of deindividuating situation cues and aggressive models on subjective deindividuation and aggression. *Journal of Personality and Social Psychology, 39,* 104–113.

Price, R.H. (1979). The social ecology of treatment gain. In A.P. Goldstein & F.H. Kanfer (Eds.), *Maximizing treatment gains: Transfer enhancement in psychotherapy.* New York: Academic Press.

Prochaska, J.O. (1979). *Systems of psychotherapy: A transtheoretical analysis.* Homewood, IL: The Dorsey Press.

Procidano, M.E., & Heller, K. (1983). Measures of perceived social support from friends and from family: Three validation studies. *American Journal of Community Psychology, 11,* 1–24.

Pruitt, D.G. (1972). Methods for resolving differences of interest: A theoretical analysis. *Journal of Social Issues, 28,* 133–154.

Pruitt, D.G. (1983). Strategic choice in negotiation. *American Behavioral Scientist, 27,* 167–194.

Pyszczynski, T., & Greenberg, J. (1985). Depression and preference for self-focusing stimuli following success and failure. *Journal of Personality and Social Psychology, 49,* 1066–1075.

Rappaport, J. (1977). *Community psychology: Values, research, and action.* New York: Holt, Rinehart & Winston.

Raskin, D.E., & Klein, Z.E. (1976). Losing a symptom through keeping it. *Archives of General Psychiatry, 33,* 548–555.

Raven, B.H., & Rietsema, J. (1957). The effect of varied clarity of group goal and group path upon the individual and his relation to the group. *Human Relations, 10,* 29–44.

Raven, B.H., & Rubin, J. (1976). *Social psychology: People in groups.* New York: Wiley.

Raymond, J.S., & Rhoads, D.L. (1980). The relative impact of family and social involvement on Chicano mental health. *American Journal of Community Psychology, 8*, 557–569.

Reed, A.C. (1982). Mirror therapy. *Small Group Behavior, 13*, 125–128.

Regan, J.W. (1976). Liking for evaluators: Consistency and self-esteem theories. *Journal of Experimental Social Psychology, 12*, 156–169.

Regan, J.W., Gosselink, H., Hubsch, J., & Ulsh, E. (1975). Do people have inflated views of their own ability? *Journal of Personality and Social Psychology, 31*, 295–301.

Reichardt, C.S. (1979). The statistical analysis of data from nonequivalent control group designs. In T.D. Cook & D.T. Campbell, *Quasi-experimentation.* Boston: Houghton-Mifflin.

Reichardt, C.S., Minton, B.A., & Schellenger, J.D. (1986). *The analysis of covariance (ANCOVA) and the assessment of treatment effects.* Unpublished manuscript, University of Denver.

Reis, H.T. (1980). An introduction to the use of structural equations: Prospects and problems. In L. Wheeler (Ed.), *Review of Personality and Social Psychology* (Vol. 3). Beverly Hills: Sage.

Reynolds, K.D., West, S.G., & Aiken, L.S. (1988, April). *Increasing the use of mammography: A social psychological approach.* Paper presented at the meeting of Western Psychological Association, Burlingame, CA.

Reynolds, K.D., & West, S.G. (1987). A multiplist strategy for strengthening nonequivalent control designs. *Evaluation Review, 11*, 691–714.

Rhoads, D.L., Gonzales, J.R., & Raymond, J.S. (1980, May). *Life change, social support, psychological symptomatology: A search for causal relationships.* Paper presented at the Western Psychological Association, Honolulu, HI.

Ribner, N.G. (1974). Effects of an explicit group contract on self-disclosure and group cohesiveness. *Journal of Counseling Psychology, 21*, 116–120.

Ricoeur, P. (1979). The metaphorical process as cognition, image, and feeling. In S. Sacks (Ed.), *On metaphor.* Chicago, IL: University of Chicago Press.

Ridgeway, C.L. (1981). Nonconformity, competence, and influence in groups: A test of two theories. *American Sociological Review, 46*, 333–347.

Ridgeway, C.L. (1982). Status in groups: The importance of motivation. *American Sociological Review, 47*, 76–88.

Ridley, C.R. (1984). Clinical treatment of the non-disclosing Black client: A therapeutic paradox. *American Psychologist, 39*, 1234–1244.

Riecken, H.W., Boruch, R.F., Campbell, D.T., Coplan, W., Glennan, T.K., Pratt, J., Rees, A., & Williams, W. (1974). *Social experimentation: A method for planning and evaluating social innovations.* New York: Academic Press.

Ringler, K. (1981). *Processes of coping with cancer chemotherapy.* Unpublished doctoral dissertation, University of Wisconsin, Madison.

Roark, A.E., & Roark, A.B. (1979). Group structure: Components and effects. *Journal for Specialists in Group Work, 9*, 187–192.

Robillard, A.B., White, G.M., & Maretzki, T.W. (1983). Between doctor and patient: Informed consent in conversational interaction. In S. Fisher & A. Todd (Eds.), *The social organization of doctor–patient communication.* Washington, DC: Center for Applied Linguistics.

Robinson, V., & Swanton, C. (1980). The generalization of behavioral teacher training. *Review of Educational Research, 50*, 486–498.

Rogers, C.R. (1959). A theory of therapy, personality, and interpersonal relationships, as developed in the client-centered framework. In S. Koch (Ed.), *Psychology: A study of a science.* New York: McGraw-Hill.

Rogers, R.W., & Prentice-Dunn, S. (1981). Deindividuation and anger-mediated interracial aggression: Unmasking regressive racism. *Journal of Personality and Social Psychology, 41*, 63–73.

Rogers, T.B., Kuiper, N.A., & Kirker, W.S. (1977). Self-reference and the encoding of personal information. *Journal of Personality and Social Psychology, 35*, 677–688.

Rogosa, D. (1980). Comparison of some models for analyzing longitudinal panel data. *Journal of Economics and Business, 32*, 136–151.

Rohrbaugh, M., & Bartels, B.D. (1975). Participants' perceptions of "curative factors" in therapy and growth groups. *Small Group Behavior, 6*, 430–456.

Roloff, M.E. (1981). *Interpersonal communication: The social exchange approach.* Beverly Hills: Sage.

Romanucci-Ross, L., Moerman, D.E., & Trancredi, L.R. (1983). *The anthropology of medicine: From culture to method.* Boston: Bergin & Garvey.

Ronan, W.W., Latham, G.P., & Kinne, S.B., III. (1973). Effects of goal setting and supervision on worker behavior in an industrial situation. *Journal of Applied Psychology, 58*, 302–307.

Rook, K.S., & Dooley, D. (1985). Applying social support research: Theoretical problems and future directions. *Journal of Social Issues, 41*, 5–28.

Roos, L.L., Jr., Roos, N.P., & Henteleff, P.D. (1978). Assessing the impact of tonsillectomies. *Medical Care, 16*, 502–518.

Root, M.P., & Sue, S. (1981, August). *The nature and role of social supports in primary prevention.* Paper presented at the American Psychological Association, Los Angeles, CA.

Rosen, A. (1972). The treatment relationship: A conceptualization. *Journal of Consulting and Clinical Psychology, 38*, 329–337.

Rosen, A., & Wish, E. (1980). Therapist content relevance and patient affect in treatment. *Journal of Clinical Psychology, 36*, 242–246.

Rosen, B., & Jerdee, T.H. (1978). Perceived sex differences in managerially relevant characteristics. *Sex Roles, 4*, 837–843.

Rosenberg, M.J. (1969). The conditions and consequences of evaluation apprehension. In R. Rosenthal & R.L. Rosnow (Eds.), *Artifact in behavioral research.* New York: Academic Press.

Rosenthal, R. (1969). Interpersonal expectations: Effects of the experimenter's hypothesis. In R. Rosenthal & R.L. Rosnow (Eds.), *Artifact in behavioral research.* New York: Academic Press.

Rosenthal, R. (1974). *On the social psychology of the self-fulfilling prophesy: Further evidence for Pygmalion effects and their mediating mechanisms* (Module 53). New York: MSS Modular Publications.

Rosenthal, R. (1976). *Experimenter effects in behavioral research.* New York: Irvington.

Rosenthal, R., & DePaulo, B.M. (1979). Sex differences in accommodation in nonverbal communication. In R. Rosenthal (Ed.), *Skill in nonverbal communication: Individual differences.* Cambridge, MA: Oelgeschlager.

Rosenthal, R., & Frank, J.D. (1956). Psychotherapy and the placebo effect. *Psychological Bulletin, 53*, 294–302.

Rosenthal, R., Hall, J.A., DiMatteo, M.R., Rogers, P.L., & Archer, D. (1979). *Sensitivity to nonverbal communication: The PONS Test.* Baltimore: The Johns Hopkins University Press.

Ross, A.O. (1985). To form a more perfect union: It is time to stop standing still. *Behavior Therapy, 16*, 195–204.

Ross, L. (1977). The intuitive psychologist and his shortcomings: Distortions in the attribution process. In L. Berkowitz (Ed.), *Advances in experimental social psychology* (Vol. 10). New York: Academic Press.

Rossi, P.H. (1979). Issues in the evaluation of human services delivery. In L. Sechrest, S.G. West, M.A. Phillips, R. Redner, & W. Yeaton (Eds.), *Evaluation Studies Review Annual, 4*, 68–95.

Rotter, J.B. (1954). *Social learning and clinical psychology.* Englewood Cliffs, NJ: Prentice-Hall.

Rubin, D.B. (1977). Assignment to treatment group on the basis of a covariate. *Journal of Educational Statistics, 2*, 1–26.

Rubin, J.Z., & Brown, B.R. (1975). *The social psychology of bargaining and negotiation.* New York: Academic Press.

Rudestam, K.E. (1982). *Experiential groups in theory and practice.* Monterey, CA: Brooks–Cole.

Ruehlman, L.S., West, S.G., & Pasahow, R.J. (1985). Depression and evaluative schemata. *Journal of Personality, 53*, 46–92.

Rugel, R.P., & Meyer, D.J. (1984). The Tavistock group: Empirical findings and implications for group therapy. *Small Group Behavior, 15*, 361–374.

Ruppel, G., & Kaul, T.J. (1982). Investigation of social influence theory's conception of client resistance. *Journal of Counseling Psychology, 29*, 232–239.

Russell, E.W. (1974). The power of behavior control: A critique of behavior modification methods. *Journal of Clinical Psychology, 30*, 111–135.

Rutan, S., & Alonso, A. (1980). Sequential cotherapy of groups for training and clinical care. *Group, 4*, 40–50.

Sackett, D.L., & Gent, M. (1979). Controversy in counting and attributing events in clinical trials. *New England Journal of Medicine, 301*, 1410–1412.

Sanders, M.R. (1980). The effects of parent self-recording and home feedback in systematic parent training. *The Exceptional Child, 27*, 62–71.

Sanders, M.R. (1982a). The effects of instructions, feedback, and cueing procedures in behavioral parent training. *Australian Journal of Psychology, 34*, 53–70.

Sanders, M.R. (1982b). The generalization of parent responding to community settings: The effects of instructions, plus feedback, and self-management training. *Behavioral Psychotherapy, 10*, 273–287.

Sanders, M.R., & Glynn, T. (1981). Training parents in behavioral self-management: An analysis of generalization and maintenance. *Journal of Applied Behavioral Analysis, 14*, 223–237.

Sanders, M.R., & James, J.E. (1982). Enhancing generalization and maintenance effects in systematic parent training: The role of self-management skills. *Australian Psychologist, 17*, 151–164.

Sanders, M.R., & James, J.E. (1983). The modification of parent behavior: A review of generalization and maintenance. *Behavior Modification, 7*, 3–27.

Sandler, I.N. (1980). Social support resources, stress, and maladjustment of poor children. *American Journal of Community Psychology, 8*, 41–52.

Sandler, I.N., & Barrera, M. (1984). Toward a multi-method approach to assessing the effects of social support. *American Journal of Community Psychology, 12*, 37–56.

Sandler, W. (1975). Patient–therapist dissimilarity of role expectations related to premature termination of psychotherapy with student therapists. *Dissertation Abstracts International, 35*, 6111B–6112B. (University Microfilms No. 75-12691)

Sarason, I.G., Levine, H.M., Basham, R.B., & Sarason, B. (1983). Assessing social support: The social support questionnaire. *Journal of Personality and Social Behavior, 44*, 127–139.

Sarason, S.B., Carroll, C.F., Maton, K., Cohen, S., & Lorentz, E. (1977). *Human services and resource networks: Rationale, possibilities, and public policy.* San Francisco: Jossey-Bass.

Sarason, S., & Lorentz, E. (1979). *The challenge of the resource exchange network.* San Francisco: Jossey-Bass.

Saxe, L., & Fine, M. (1980). Reorienting social psychology toward application: A methodological analysis. In L. Bickman (Ed.), *Applied Social Psychology Annual* (Vol. 1). Beverly Hills: Sage.

Schachter, S. (1951). Deviation, rejection, and communication. *Journal of Abnormal and Social Psychology, 46,* 190–207.

Schachter, S. (1966). The interaction of cognitive and physiological determinants of emotional state. In C. Spielberger (Ed.), *Anxiety and behavior.* New York: Academic Press

Schachter, S. (1971). *Emotion, obesity, and crime.* New York: Academic Press.

Schachter, S., Ellertson, N., McBride, D., & Gregory, D. (1951). An experimental study of cohesiveness and productivity. *Human Relations, 4,* 229–238.

Schaefer, C., Coyne, J.C., & Lazarus, R.S. (1981). The health related functions of social support. *Journal of Behavioral Medicine, 4,* 381–406.

Schaible, T., & Jacobs, A. (1975). Feedback III: Sequence effects: Enhancement of feedback acceptance and group attractiveness by manipulation of the sequence and valence of feedback. *Small Group Behavior, 6,* 151–173.

Scheflen, A.E. (1963). Communication and regulation in psychotherapy. *Psychiatry, 26,* 126–136.

Scheier, M.F., & Carver, C.S. (1980). Private and public self-attention resistance to change, and dissonance reduction. *Journal of Personality and Social Psychology, 39,* 390–405.

Scheier, M.F., Carver, C.S., & Gibbons, F.X. (1979). Self-directed attention, awareness of bodily states, and suggestibility. *Journal of Personality and Social Psychology, 37,* 1576–1588.

Schenk, C. (1928). Leadership. *Infantry Journal, 33,* 111–122.

Scherer, K.R., & Ekman, P. (Eds.) (1982). *Handbook of methods in nonverbal behavior research.* New York: Cambridge University Press.

Schonfield, J., Stone, A., Hoehn-Saric, R., Imber, S., & Pande, S. (1969). Patient-therapist convergence and measures of improvement in short-term psychotherapy. *Psychotherapy: Theory, Research and Practice, 6,* 267–272.

Schulz, R. (1976). Effects of control and predictability on the physical and psychological well-being of the institutionalized aged. *Journal of Personality and Social Psychology, 33,* 563–573.

Schulz, R., & Rau, M.T. (1985). Social support through the life course. In S. Cohen & S.L. Syme (Eds.), *Social support and health.* New York: Academic Press.

Schutz, W.C. (1958). *FIRO: A three-dimensional theory of interpersonal behavior.* New York: Rinehart.

Sears, R.R. (1961). Transcultural variables and conceptual equivalence. In B. Kaplan (Ed.), *Studying personality cross-culturally.* New York: Harper & Row.

Seashore, S.E. (1954). *Group cohesiveness in the industrial work group.* Ann Arbor, MI: Institute for Social Research.

Seaver, W.B., & Quarton, R.J. (1976). Regression discontinuity analysis of dean's list effects. *Journal of Educational Psychology, 68,* 459–465.

Sechrest, L., West, S.G., Phillips, M.A., Redner, R., & Yeaton, W. (1979). Some neglected problems in evaluation research: Strength and integrity of treatments. In L. Sechrest et al. (Eds.), *Evaluation studies review annual* (Vol. 4), Beverly Hills: Sage.

Seligman, M.E.P. (1975). *Helplessness: On depression, development, and death.* San Francisco: Freeman.

Settin, J.M., & Bramel, D. (1981). Interaction of client class and gender in biasing clinical judgment. *American Journal of Orthopsychiatry, 51,* 510–520.

Shambaugh, P.W. (1978). The development of the small group. *Human Relations,* *31*, 283–295.

Shapiro, A.K., & Morris, L.A. (1978). The placebo effect in medical and psychological therapies. In S.L. Garfield & A.E. Bergin (Eds.), *Handbook of psychotherapy and behavior change* (2nd edn.). New York: Wiley.

Shapiro, J.L., & Diamond, M.J. (1972). Increases in hypnotizability as a function of encounter group training: Some confirming evidence. *Journal of Abnormal Psychology, 79*, 112–115.

Shaw, M.E. (1955). A comparison of two types of leadership in various communication nets. *Journal of Abnormal and Social Psychology, 50*, 127–134.

Shaw, M.E., & Shaw, L.M. (1962). Some effects of sociometric grouping upon learning in a second grade classroom. *Journal of Social Psychology, 57*, 453–458.

Shaw, M.R. (1932). A comparison of individuals and small groups in the rational solution of complex problems. *American Journal of Psychology, 44*, 491–504.

Sherif, M. (1936). *The psychology of social norms.* New York: Harper & Row.

Sherif, M. (1958). Superordinate goals in the reduction of intergroup conflict. *The American Journal of Sociology, 63*, 349–356.

Shepherd, G. (1977). Social skills training: The generalization problem. *Behavior Therapy, 8*, 1008–1009.

Shepherd, G. (1980). The treatment of social difficulties in special environments. In P. Feldman & J. Orford (Eds.), *The social psychology of psychological problems.* New York: Wiley.

Sherry, P., & Hurley, J.R. (1976). Curative factors in psychotherapeutic and growth groups. *Journal of Clinical Psychology, 32*, 835–837.

Shiffrin, R.M., & Schneider, W. (1977). Controlled and automatic human information processes: II. Perceptual learning, automatic attending, and a general theory. *Psychological Review, 84*, 127–190.

Shimkunas, A.M. (1972). Demand for intimate self-disclosure and pathological verbalizations in schizophrenia. *Journal of Abnormal Psychology, 80*, 197–205.

Shrauger, J.S., & Lund, A. (1975). Self-evaluation and reactions to evaluations from others. *Journal of Personality, 43*, 94–108.

Shrauger, J.S., & Schoeneman, T.J. (1979). Symbolic interactionist view of self-concept: Through the looking glass darkly. *Psychological Bulletin, 86*, 549–573.

Shumaker, S.A., & Brownell, A. (1984). Toward a theory of social support: Closing conceptual gaps. *Journal of Social Issues, 40*, 11–36.

Shweder, R.A. (1977). Illusory correlation and the MMPI controversy. *Journal of Consulting and Clinical Psychology, 45*, 917–924.

Shweder, R.A., & D'Andrade, R.G. (1979). Accurate reflection or systematic distortion? A reply to Block, Weiss, and Thorne. *Journal of Personality and Social Psychology, 37*, 1075–1084.

Shweder, R.A., & D'Andrade, R.G. (1980). The systematic distortion hypothesis. *New Directions for Methodology of Social and Behavioral Science, 4*, 37–58.

Silverberg, R.T. (1982) Effects of confirmation or disconfirmation of client role expectations on client satisfaction, length of therapy, and outcome ratings of psychotherapy. *Dissertation Abstracts International, 42*, 3442B. (University Microfilms No. 8202170)

Simonson, N.R., & Bahr, S. (1974). Self-disclosure by the professional and paraprofessional therapist. *Journal of Consulting and Clinical Psychology, 42*, 359–363.

Simonton, D.K. (1977). Cross-sectional time-series experiments: Some suggested statistical analyses. *Psychological Bulletin, 84*, 489–502.

Slavson, S.R. (1962). Personal qualifications of a group psychotherapist. *International Journal of Group Psychotherapy, 12*, 411–420.

Slavson, S.R. (1964). *A textbook in analytic group psychotherapy*. New York: International Universities Press.

Sloane, R.B., Cristol, A.H., Pepernik, M., & Staples, F.R. (1970). Role preparation and expectancies of improvement in psychotherapy. *Journal of Nervous and Mental Disease, 150,* 18–26.

Smith, M.L. (1980). Sex bias in counseling and psychotherapy. *Psychological Bulletin, 87,* 392–407.

Smith, M.L., Glass, G.V., & Miller, T.I. (1980). *Benefits of psychotherapy*. Baltimore: Johns Hopkins University Press.

Smith, R.S. (1977). Patients' and therapists' differential expectations of psychotherapy as correlates of patient dropout. *Dissertation Abstracts International, 38,* 380B–381B. (University Microfilms No. 7714910)

Smith, T.W., Ingram, R.E., & Roth, D.L. (1983). *Self-focused attention and depression: Self-evaluation, affect, and life-stress*. Unpublished manuscript, University of Utah, Salt Lake City, UT.

Smith-Hanen, S.S. (1977). Effects of nonverbal behaviors on Judged levels of counselor warmth and empathy. *Journal of Counseling Psychology, 24,* 86–91.

Snyder, C.R., & Shenkel, R.J. (1976). Effects of "favorability," modality, and relevance on acceptance of general personality interpretations prior to and after receiving diagnostic feedback. *Journal of Consulting and Clinical Psychology, 44,* 34–41.

Snyder, M. (1979). Self-monitoring processes. In L. Berkowitz (Ed.), *Advances in experimental social psychology, (Vol. 12,* pp. 85–128). New York: Academic.

Snyder, M. (1982). When believing means doing: Creating links between attitudes and behavior. In M.P. Zanna, E.T. Higgins, & C.P. Herman (Eds.), *Consistency in social behavior* (Vol. 2). Hillsdale, NJ: Erlbaum.

Snyder, M., & Cantor, N. (1980). Thinking about ourselves and others: Self-monitoring and social knowledge. *Journal of Personality and Social Psychology, 30,* 222–234.

Snyder, M., & Kendzierski, D. (1982). Acting on one's attitudes: Procedures for linking attitude and behavior. *Journal of Experimental Social Psychology, 18,* 165–183.

Snyder, M., Tanke, E.D., & Berscheid, E. (1977). Social perception and interpersonal behavior: On the self-fulfilling nature of social stereotypes. *Journal of Personality and Social Psychology, 35,* 656–666.

Sokolovsky, J., & Cohen, C.I. (1981). Toward a resolution of methodological dilemmas in network mapping. *Schizophrenia Bulletin, 7,* 109–116.

Sokolovsky, J., Cohen, C., Berger, D., & Geiger, J. (1978). Personal networks of ex-mental patients in a Manhattan SRO hotel. *Human Organization, 37,* 5–15.

Solyom, I., Garza-Perez, J., Ledwidge, B.L., & Solyom, C. (1972). Paradoxical intention in treatment of obsessive thought: A pilot study. *Comprehensive Psychiatry, 13,* 291–297.

Sörbom, D. (1978). An alternative to the methodology for analysis of covariance. *Psychometrika, 43,* 381–396.

Stack, L.C., Lannon, P.B., & Miley, A.D. (1983). Accuracy of clinicians' expectancies for psychiatric rehospitalization. *American Journal of Community Psychology, 11,* 99–113.

Steffen, J.J., & Karoly, P. (1980). Toward a psychology of therapeutic persistence. In P. Karoly & J.J. Steffen (Eds.), *Improving the long-term effects of psychotherapy: Models of durable outcome*. New York: Gardner Press.

Stein, L.I., & Test, M.A. (1978). An alternative to mental hospital treatment. In L.I. Stein & M.A. Test (Eds.), *Alternatives to mental hospital treatment*. New York: Plenum.

Stephenson, B., & Wicklund, R.A. (1984). The contagion of self-focus within a dyad. *Journal of Personality and Social Psychology, 46,* 163–168.

Stiles, W.B., Tupler, L.A., & Carpenter, J.C. (1982). Participants perceptions of self-analytic group sessions. *Small Group Behavior, 13,* 237–254.

Stogdill, R.M. (1948). Personal factors associated with leadership. *Journal of Psychology, 23,* 35–71.

Stogdill, R.M. (1974). *Handbook of leadership.* New York: Free Press.

Stokes, J.P. (1983a). Components of group cohesion: Intermember attraction, instrumental value, and risk taking. *Small Group Behavior, 14,* 163–173.

Stokes, J.P. (1983b). Predicting satisfaction with social support from social network structure. *American Journal of Community Psychology, 11,* 141–152.

Stokes, J.P. (1983c). Toward an understanding of cohesiveness in psychotherapy change groups. *International Journal of Group Psychotherapy, 33,* 449–467.

Stokes, T.F., & Baer, D.M. (1977). An implicit technology of generalization. *Journal of Applied Behavior Analysis, 10,* 349–367.

Strauss, J.B. (1975). Two face the group: A study of the relationship between cotherapists. In L.R. Wolberg & M. Aronson (Eds.), *Group therapy 1975: An overview.* New York: Stratton Intercontinental.

Strong, S.R. (1968). Counseling: An interpersonal influence process. *Journal of Counseling Psychology, 15,* 215–224.

Strong, S.R. (1978). Social psychological approach to psychotherapy research. In S.L. Garfield & A.E. Bergin (Eds.), *Handbook of psychotherapy and behavior change.* New York: Wiley.

Strong, S.R. (1982). Emerging integrations of clinical and social psychology: A clinician's perspective. In G. Weary & H.L. Mirels (Eds.), *Integrations of clinical and social psychology.* New York: Oxford University Press.

Strong, S.R., & Claiborn, C.D. (1982). *Change through interaction: Social psychological processes of counseling and psythotherapy.* New York: Wiley-Interscience.

Strong, S.R., & Matross, R.P. (1973). Change processes in counseling and psychotherapy. *Journal of Counseling Psychology, 20,* 25–37.

Strupp, H.H. (1986). Psychotherapy research and practice: An overview. In S. Garfield & A. Bergin (Eds.), *Handbook of psychotherapy and behavior change.* (3rd Ed.). New York: Wiley.

Strupp, H.H., & Bloxom, A.L. (1973). Preparing lower-class patients for group psychotherapy: Development and evaluation of a role-induction film. *Journal of Consulting and Clinical Psychology, 41,* 373–384.

Sturtevant, W.C. (1964). Studies in ethnoscience. In A.K. Romney & R. D'Andrade (Eds.), Transcultural studies in cognition. *American Anthropologist, 66,* 99–131 (special issue).

Sullivan, H.S. (1953). *The interpersonal theory of psychiatry.* New York: Norton.

Swaminathan, H., & Algina, J. (1977). Analysis of quasi-experimental time-series designs. *Multivariate Behavior Research, 12,* 111–131.

Swann, W.B., Jr. (1983). Self-verification: Bringing social reality into harmony with the self. In J. Suls & A.G. Greenwald (Eds.), *Psychological perspectives on the self* (Vol. 2). New York: Erlbaum.

Swann, W.B., Jr., & Read, S.J. (1981). Acquiring self-knowledge: The search for feedback that fits. *Journal of Personality and Social Psychology, 41,* 1119–1128.

Swartz, J.L. (1973). *Analysis of leadership styles of college-level head coaches from five midwestern states.* Doctoral dissertation. Greeley: University of Northern Colorado.

Takemoto-Chock, N., & Higginbotham, H.N. (1982). *Psychotherapy expectancy: A cross-cultural examination of New Zealand and Hawaiian University students.* Unpublished manuscript, Department of Psychology, University of Hawaii-Hilo.

Talbot, B.E. (1983). Written preparation for psychotherapy and its effect on patient expectations and premature termination. *Dissertation Abstracts International, 43,* 2718-2719. (University Microfilms No. DA8215997)

Tan, B.H. (1983). *The influence of social support networks on stress and formal helping services: A study of overseas Chinese and Pakeha students.* Unpublished Master's thesis, University of Waikato, Hamilton, New Zealand.

Taylor, S.E., & Fiske, S.T. (1978). Salience, attention, and attribution: Top of the head phenomena. In L. Berkowitz (Ed.), *Advances in experimental social psychology* (Vol. 11). New York: Academic Press.

Terborg, J.R. (1976). The motivational components of goal setting. *Journal of Applied Psychology, 61,* 613-621.

Tharp, R., & Wetzel, R.J. (1969). *Behavior modification in the natural environment.* New York: Academic Press.

Thibaut, J.W., & Kelley, H.H. (1959). *The social psychology of groups.* New York: Wiley.

Thoresen, C.E., & Mahoney, M.J. (1974). *Behavioral self-control.* New York: Holt, Rinehart, & Winston.

Thune, E.S., Manderscheid, R.W., & Silbergeld, S. (1981). Sex, status, and cotherapy. *Small Group Behavior, 12,* 415-442.

Timothy, A.M. (1981). Pretherapy expectations, situational factors, perception of the initial interview and premature termination of outpatient psychotherapy: A multivariate study. *Dissertation Abstracts International, 42,* 1626B. (University Microfilms No. 8119993)

Tinsley, H.E.A., Workman, K.R., & Kass, R.A. (1980). Factor analysis of the domain of client expectancies about counseling. *Journal of Counseling Psychology, 27,* 561-570.

Tolsdorf, C. (1976). Social networks, support, and coping: An exploratory study. *Family Process, 15,* 407-418.

Tolstoy, L. (1869). *War and Peace.* Chicago: Encyclopaedia Britannica.

Torrey, E.F. (1972). *The mind game.* New York: Bantam.

Touhey, J.C. (1981). Replication failures in personality and social psychology: Negative findings or mistaken assumptions. *Personality and Social Psychology Bulletin, 7,* 593-595.

Tracey, T.J., Heck, E.J., & Lichtenberg, J.W. (1981). Role expectations and symmetrical/complementary therapeutic relationships. *Psychotherapy: Theory, Research and Practice, 18,* 338-344.

Triandis, H.C. (1980). Introduction. In H.C. Triandis (Ed.), *Handbook of cross-cultural psychology* (Vol. 1). Boston: Allyn & Bacon.

Triandis, H.C., & Berry, J.W. (Eds.) (1980). *Handbook of cross-cultural psychology* (Vol. 2). Boston: Allyn & Bacon.

Triandis, H.C., Malpass, R.S., & Davidson, A. (1971). Cross-cultural psychology. *Biennial Review of Anthropology,* 1-84.

Triandis, H.C., Vassiliou, V., Vassiliou, G., Tanaka, Y., & Shanmugam, A.V. (1972). *The analysis of subjective culture.* New York: Wiley.

Triplett, N. (1897). The dynamogenic factors in pacemaking and competition. *American Journal of Psychology, 9,* 507-533.

Trochim, W.M.K. (1984). *Research design for program evaluation: The regression discontinuity approach.* Beverly Hills: Sage.

Truax, C.B. (1961). The process of group psychotherapy. *Psychological Monographs, 75,* Whole No. 511.

Truax, C.B., & Carkhuff, R.R. (1965). Personality change in hospitalized mental patients during group psychotherapy as a function of alternate session and vicarious therapy pretraining. *Journal of Clinical Psychology, 21,* 190-201.

Truax, C.B., Shapiro, J.G., & Wargo, D.G. (1968). The effects of alternative sessions and vicarious therapy pre-training on group psychotherapy. *International Journal of Group Psychotherapy, 18,* 186–198.

Tuckman, B.W. (1965). Dvelopmental sequences in small groups. *Psychological Bulletin, 63,* 384–399.

Tuckman, B.W., & Jensen, M.A. (1977). Stages of small-group development revisited. *Group and Organizational Studies, 2,* 419–427.

Tukey, J. (1977). Some thoughts on clinical trials, especially problems of multiplicity. *Science, 198,* 679–684.

Turk, D.C., Meichenbaum, D., & Genest, M. (1983). *Pain and behavioral medicine: A cognitive-behavioral perspective.* New York: Guildford Press.

Ullmann, L.P., & Krasner, L. (1975). *A psychological approach to abnormal behavior* (2nd edn.). Englewood Cliffs, NJ: Prentice-Hall.

Valins, S., & Nisbett, R.E. (1972). Attribution processes in the development and treatment of emotional disorder. In E.E. Jones, D.E. Kanouse, H.H. Kelley, R.E. Nisbett, S. Valins, & B. Weiner (Eds.), *Attribution: Perceiving the causes of behavior.* Morristown, NJ: General Learning Press.

Van Poucke, W. (1980). Network constraints on social action: Preliminaries for a network theory. *Social Networks, 2,* 181–190.

Vaughn, C.E., & Leff, J.P. (1976). The influence of family and social factors on the course of psychiatric illness: A comparison of schizophrenic and depressed neurotic patients. *British Journal of Psychiatry, 129,* 125–137.

Verba, S. (1961). *Small groups and political behavior: A study of leadership.* Princeton: Princeton University Press.

Vontress, C.E. (1971). Racial differences: Impediments to rapport. *Journal of Counseling Psychology, 18,* 7–13.

Vontress, C.E. (1976). Racial and ethnic barriers in counseling. In P. Pedersen, W.J. Lonner, & J.G. Draguns (Eds.), *Counseling across cultures.* Honolulu: University of Hawaii Press.

Vroom, V.H. (1973). A new look at managerial decision making. *Organizational Dynamics, 1,* 66–80.

Vroom, V.H. (1974). Decision making and the leadership process. *Journal of Contemporary Business, 3,* 47–64.

Vroom, V.H. (1976). Leadership. In M.D. Dunnette (Ed.), *Handbook of industrial and organizational psychology.* Chicago: Rand-McNally.

Vroom, V.H., & Mann, F.C. (1960). Leader authoritarianism and employee attitudes. *Personnel Psychology, 13,* 125–140.

Wahler, R.C. (1980a). Parent insularity as a determinant of generalization success in family treatment. In *The ecosystem of the "sick" child.* New York: Academic Press.

Wahler, R.C. (1980b). The insular mother: Her problems in parent–child treatment. *Journal of Applied Behavior Analysis, 13,* 207–219.

Wahler, R.C., Berland, R.M., & Leske, G. (1975). *Environmental boundaries in behavior modification: Problems in residential treatment of children.* Unpublished manuscript, Child Behavior Institute, University of Tennessee.

Wahler, R.C., House, A.E., & Stambaugh, E.E. (1976). *Ecological assessment of child problem behavior.* New York: Pergamon.

Wahler, R.C., Leske, G., & Rogers, E.S. (1979). The insular family: A deviance support system for oppositional children. In L.A. Hamerlynck (Ed.), *Behavioral systems for the developmentally disabled: I. Schools and family environments.* New York: Bruner/Mazel.

Waldie, K.F. (1982). Experiential learning groups: An applications model. *Small Group Behavior, 13,* 75–90.

Walster, E., Walster, G.W., & Berscheid, E. (Eds.). (1978). *Equity: Theory and research*. Boston: Allyn & Bacon.

Walster, E., Walster, G.W., & Traupmann, J. (1978). Equity and premarital sex. *Journal of Personality and Social Psychology, 36*, 82–92.

Ware, R., & Barr, J.E. (1977). Effects of a nine-week structured and unstructured group experience on measures of self-concept and self-actualization. *Small Group Behavior, 8*, 93–100.

Ware, R., Barr, J.E., & Boone, M. (1982). Subjective changes in small group processes: An experimental investigation. *Small Group Behavior, 13*, 395–401.

Warren, N.C., & Rice, L.N. (1972). Structuring and stabilizing of psychotherapy for low-prognosis clients. *Journal of Consulting and Clinical Psychology, 39*, 173–181.

Watts, R.F., & Steele, R.E. (1984). A look at the concept of cultural diversity—past and present. *Division of Community Psychology Newsletter, 27*(2), 3–4.

Weary, G., & Mirels, H.L. (Eds.) (1982). *Integrations of clinical and social psychology*. New York: Oxford University Press.

Weary, G., Mirels, H.L., & Jordan, J.S. (1982). The integration of clinical and social psychology: Current status and future directions. In G. Weary, & H.L. Mirels (Eds.), *Integrations of clinical and social psychology*. New York: Oxford University Press.

Webb, E.T., Campbell, D.T., Schwartz, R.D., & Sechrest, L. (1966). *Unobtrusive measures: Nonreactive research in the social sciences*. Chicago: Rand-McNally.

Webster, M., & Sobieszek, B.I. (1974). *Sources of self-evaluation: A formal theory of significant others and social influence*. New York: Wiley.

Weeks, G.R., & L'Abate, L. (1979). A compilation of paradoxical methods. *American Journal of Family Therapy, 7*, 61–76.

Wegner, D.M., & Giuliano, T. (1980). Arousal-induced attention to self. *Journal of Personality and Social Psychology, 38*, 719–726.

Weigel, R.H., Vernon, D.T.A., & Tognacci, L.N. (1974). Specificity of the attitude as a determinant of attitude–behavior congruence. *Journal of Personality and Social Psychology, 30*, 724–728.

Weissman, M.M. (1984). The psychological treatment of depression: An update of clinical trials. In J.B.W. Williams & R.L. Spitzer (Eds.), *Psychotherapy research: Where are we and where should we go?* New York: Guilford Press.

Wells, K.C., Griest, D.L., & Forehand, R. (1980). The use of self-control package to enhance temporal generality of a parent training program. *Behavior Research and Therapy, 18*, 347–354.

West, S.G., Reich, J.W., Dantchik, A., & McCall, M. (in press). An introduction to applied psychology. In W.L. Gregory & J. Burroughs (Eds.), *An Introduction to applied psychology*. Chicago: Scott Foresman.

West, S.G., & Wicklund, R.A. (1980). *A primer of social psychological theories*. Monterey, CA: Brooks/Cole.

Westermeyer, J., & Pattison, E.M. (1981). Social networks and psychosis in a peasant society. *Schizophrenia Bulletin, 7*, 125–136.

Wheeless, L.R., Wheeless, V.E., & Dickson-Markman, F. (1982). A research note: The relations among social and task perceptions of small groups. *Small Group Behavior, 13*, 373–384.

White, G.L. (1980). Physical attractiveness and courtship progress. *Journal of Personality and Social Psychology, 39*, 660–668.

White, G.M. (1982). The role of cultural explanations in "somatization and psychologization." *Social Science and Medicine, 16*, 1519–1530.

White, G.M., & Kirkpatrick, J. (1985). *Person, self, and experience: Exploring Pacific ethopsychologies,* Berkeley, CA: University of California Press.

White, G.M., & Marsella, A.J. (1982). Introduction: Cultural conceptions in mental health research and practice. In A.J. Marsella & G.M. White (Eds.), *Cultural conceptions of mental health and therapy*. Boston: D. Reidel.

White, G.M., & Robillard, A.B. (1982, August). *Doctor talk and Hawaiian 'Talk Story': The conversational organization of a clinical encounter*. Paper prepared for Interest Group on Doctor-Patient Interaction at the Tenth World Congress of Sociology, Mexico City.

White, R.K., & Lippitt, R. (1968). Leader behavior and member reaction in three "social climates". In D. Cartwright & A. Zander (Eds.), *Group dynamics: Research and theory* (3rd ed.). New York: Harper & Row.

Whitten, N.E., & Wolfe, A.W. (1974). Network analysis. In J. Honigmann (Ed.), *Handbook of social and cultural anthropology*. Chicago: Rand-McNally.

Whyte, W.F. (1943). *Street corner society*. Chicago: University of Chicago Press.

Wicker, A.W. (1973). Undermanning theory and research: Implications for the study of psychological and behavioral effects of excess populations. *Representative Research in Social Psychology, 4*, 185–206.

Wicker, A.W. (1979). *An introduction to ecological psychology*. Monterey: Brooks/Cole.

Wicklund, R.A. (1975). Objective self-awareness. In L. Berkowitz (Ed.), *Advances in experimental social psychology* (Vol. 8). New York: Academic Press.

Wicklund, R.A. (1979). The influence of self-awareness on human behavior. *American Scientist, 67*, 187–193.

Wilcox, B.L. (1981). The role of social support in adjustment to marital disruption: A network analysis. In B.H. Gottlieb (Ed.), *Social networks and social support*. Beverly Hills: Sage.

Wilcox, S.L., & Holohan, C.J. (1978). Social ecology of the megadorm in university student housing. *Journal of Educational Psychology, 68*, 453–458.

Wilkins, W. (1973). Expectancy of therapeutic gain: An empirical and conceptual critique. *Journal of Consulting and Clinical Psychology, 40*, 69–77.

Wilkins, W. (1977). Expectancies in applied settings. In A.S. Gurman & A.M. Razin (Eds.), *Effective psychotherapy*. New York: Pergamon.

Wilkins, W. (1979). Expectancies in therapy research: Discriminating among heterogeneous nonspecifics. *Journal of Consulting and Clinical Psychology, 47*, 837–845.

Williams, J.M., & Hacker, C.M. (1982). Causal relationships among cohesion, satisfaction, and performance in women's intercollegiate field hockey teams. *Journal of Sport Psychology, 4*, 324–337.

Wills, T.A. (1978). Perceptions of clients by professional helpers. *Psychological Bulletin, 85*, 968–1000.

Wills, T.A. (1985). Supportive functions of interpersonal relationships. In S. Cohen & S.L. Syme (Eds.), *Social support and health*. New York: Academic Press.

Wilson, G.T., & Evans, I.M. (1976). Adult behavior therapy and the therapist–client relationship. In C.M. Franks & G.T. Wilson (Eds.), *Annual review of behavior therapy: Theory and practice* (Vol. 4). New York: Brunner/Mazel.

Wilson, G.T., & Evans, I.M. (1977). The therapist–client relationship in behavior therapy. In A.S. Gurman & A.M. Razin (Eds.), *Effective psychotherapy: A handbook of research*. New York: Pergamon Press.

Wilson, G.T., & Franks, C.M. (Eds.). (1982). *Contemporary behavior therapy: Conceptual and empirical foundations*. New York: Guildford.

Wilson, S.R. (1970). Some factors influencing instrumental and expressive ratings in task-oriented groups. *Pacific Sociological Review, 13*, 127–131.

Winer, B.J. (1971). *Statistical principles in experimental design*. New York: McGraw-Hill.

Winner, L. (1977). *Autonomous technology: Technics-out-of-control as a theme in political thought*. Cambridge: MIT Press.

Wober, M. (1969). Distinguishing centri-cultural from cross-cultural tests and research. *Perceptual and Motor Skills, 28,* Wolf, A., & Schwartz, E.K. (1962). *Psychoanalysis in groups*. New York: Grune & Stratton.

Wolf, S. (1977). *Behavioral style of the deviate and group cohesiveness as sources of minority influence*. Unpublished doctoral dissertation, Duke University, Durham, NC.

Wollersheim, J.P., Bordewick, M. Knapp, M., McLellarn, R., & Paul, W. (1982). The influence of therapy rationales upon perceptions of clinical problems. *Cognitive Therapy and Research, 6,* 167–172.

Wollersheim, J.P., & Bugge, I. (1977, May). *The effect of therapy rationale upon the perception of clinical depression*. Paper presented at the Rocky Mountain Psychological Association, Albuquerque.

Wollersheim, J.P., McFall, M.E., Hamilton, S.B., Hickey, C.S., & Bordewick, M.C. (1980). Effects of treatment rationale and problem severity on perceptions of psychological problems and counseling approaches. *Journal of Counseling Psychology, 27,* 225–231.

Wolpe, J. (1981). Behavior therapy versus psychoanalysis: Therapeutic and social implications. *American Psychologist, 36,* 159–164.

Wood, Y.R. (1984). The assessment of social support and social networks. In P. McReynolds & G.J. Chelune (Eds.), *Advances in psychological assessment* (Vol. 6). San Francisco: Jossey-Bass.

Woodall, W.G., & Burgoon, J.K. (1981). The effects of nonverbal synchrony on message comprehension and persuasiveness. *Journal of Nonverbal Behavior, 5,* 207–223.

Woody, E.Z., & Costanzo, P.R. (1981). The socialization of obesity-prone behavior. In S.S. Brehm, S.M. Kassin, & F.X. Gibbons (Eds.), *Developmental social psychology*. New York: Oxford University Press.

Woolfolk, R.L., & Richardson, F.C. (1984). Behavior therapy and the ideology of modernity. *American Psychologist, 39,* 777–786.

Word, C.O., Zanna, M.P., & Cooper, J. (1974). The nonverbal mediation of self-fulfilling prophecies in interracial interaction. *Journal of Experimental Social Psychology, 10,* 109–120.

Wothke, W. (1984). *The estimation of trait and method components in multitrait-multimethod measurement*. Unpublished doctoral dissertation, University of Chicago.

Wright, R.A., & Brehm, S.S. (1982). Reactance as impression management: A critical review. *Journal of Personality and Social Psychology, 42,* 608–618.

Wrightsman, L.S. (1964). Measurement of philosophies of human nature. *Psychological Reports, 14,* 743–751.

Wrightsman, L.S. (1977). *Social psychology* (2nd edn.). Monterey: Brooks/Cole.

Wynne, M.F. (1982). Client and therapist expectations related to the outcome of crisis intervention therapy with Black clients. *Dissertation Abstracts International, 42,* 4220B. (University Microfilms No. DA 8200310)

Yalom, I.D. (1975). *The theory and practice of group psychotherapy* (2nd edn.). New York: Basic Books.

Yalom, I.D., Tinklenberg, J., & Gilula, M. (1975). Curative factors in group therapy. Cited in I.D. Yalom, *The theory and practice of group psychotherapy*. New York: Basic Books.

Yeaton, W.H., & Sechrest, L. (1981). Critical dimensions in the choice and maintenance of successful treatments: Strength, integrity, and effectiveness. *Journal of Consulting and Clinical Psychology, 49*, 156–167.

Yerby, J. (1975). Attitude, task, and sex composition as variables affecting female leadership in small problem-solving groups. *Speech Monographs, 42*, 160–168.

Zander, A. (1971). *Motives and goals in groups*. New York: Academic Press.

Zander, A. (1980). The origins and consequences of group goals. In L. Festinger (Ed.), *Retrospections on social psychology*, New York: Oxford.

Zander, A., Stotland, E., & Wolfe, D. (1960). Unity of group, identification with group, and self-esteem of members. *Journal of Personality, 28*, 463–478.

Zautra, A.J. (1983). Social resources and the quality of life. *American Journal of Community Psychology, 11*, 275–291.

Zedlow, P. (1978). Sex differences in psychiatric evaluation and treatment. *Archives of General Psychiatry, 35*, 89–93.

Ziemelis, A. (1974). Effects of client preference and expectancy upon the initial interview. *Journal of Counseling Psychology, 21*, 23–30.

Zimbardo, P.G. (1969). The human choice: Individuation, reason, and order versus deindividuation, impulse and chaos. In W.J. Arnold & D. Levine (Eds.), *Nebraska Symposium on Motivation*. Lincoln: University of Nebraska Press.

Zuckerman, M., DePaulo, B.M., & Rosenthal, R. (1981). Verbal and nonverbal communication of deception. In L. Berkowitz (Ed.), *Advances in experimental social psychology* (Vol. 14). New York: Academic Press.

Zuckerman, M., Spiegel, N.H., DePaulo, B.M., & Rosenthal, R. (1980). *Nonverbal strategies for decoding deception*. Unpublished manuscript, University of Rochester.

Author Index

327

Subject Index

About the Authors

H. NICK HIGGINBOTHAM received his Ph.D. in clinical-community psychology from the University of Hawai'i in 1979. He directed New Zealand's first community psychology graduate program at Waikato University and has held appointments at the East-West Center and University of Hawai'i-Hilo. Currently he teaches health psychology at the Newcastle College of Advanced Education in New South Wales, Australia, and co-ordinates the social science component of the Centre for Clinical Epidemiology and Biostatistics at the University of Newcastle. This program trains Third World physicians as part of the Rockefeller Foundation's International Clinical Epidemiology Network. In 1984 he authored *Third World Challenge to Psychiatry: Culture and Mental Health Care* (University of Hawai'i Press), based on work in South east Asia, and continues studies of cultural accommodation of clinical services among native Hawaiians and Australian Aboriginals.

STEPHEN G. WEST (Ph.D., University of Texas at Austin) is Professor and Director of the Graduate Training Program in Social Psychology at Arizona State University. He is currently editor of the *Journal of Personality* and is associate editor of *Evaluation Review*. He has research interests in a number of basic and applied issues in personality, social psychology, and research methodology. He is co-author of *A primer of social psychological theories*, co-editor of *Evaluation studies review annual* (Vol. 4), and is editor of special issues of the *Journal of Personality* on "Personality and prediction: Nomothetic and idiographic approaches" and "Methodological developments in personality research."

DONELSON R. FORSYTH (Ph.D., University of Florida) is Associate Professor in the Department of Psychology at Virginia Commonwealth University. His current investigations are concentrated in several related areas of social psychology, but his two major interests are (1) affective and attributional reactions in interpersonal, educational, and clinical settings and (2) individual differences in ethical ideology. He is also the author of *An Introduction to Group Dynamics* (1983) and *Social Psychology* (1987).

Pergamon General Psychology Series

Editors:

Arnold P. Goldstein, Syracuse University
Leonard Krasner, Stanford University & SUNY at Stony Brook

*Out of print in original format. Available in custom reprint edition.